AMERICA AND THE WORLD

From the Truman Doctrine to Vietnam

Published in Collaboration with
The Washington Center of Foreign Policy Research
School of Advanced International Studies
The Johns Hopkins University

AMERICA AND THE WORLD

FROM
THE TRUMAN DOCTRINE
TO VIETNAM

Robert E. Osgood

Robert W. Tucker

Herbert S. Dinerstein

Francis E. Rourke

Isaiah Frank

Laurence W. Martin

George Liska

THE JOHNS HOPKINS PRESS

Baltimore and London

The Johns Hopkins Press, Baltimore, Maryland 21218
The Johns Hopkins Press Ltd., London

Library of Congress Catalog Card Number 72–104780

Standard Book Number 8018–1103–1

FOREWORD

In 1967 the Washington Center of Foreign Policy Research, with the support of a six-year grant from the Ford Foundation, began a project to assess on a continuing basis the state of American foreign policy in the context of major trends in domestic and international politics. A major feature of this project is a volume, to be published during the year after every presidential election, that examines the major issues of American foreign policy, looking forward in the perspective of the past. This is the first volume.

Because this is the first volume and because it appears at a time of more than usual reflection upon the relevance of the past to the future, our assessment of American policy rests on a reappraisal of America's response to its whole Cold War experience. From this foundation we generalize about the elements of continuity and change in American policy that may, or should, govern the nation's response to major domestic and international developments. In this context we deal with the central policy issues facing the United States in the next few years.

In dealing with policy issues we are interested in providing perspective and focus rather than detailed or comprehensive guidance. We are analysts, not pundits. Those who make foreign policy will have to judge whether this study pursues a level of generalization that is relevant to daily decisions. In any case, it is our assumption that this is the level on which scholars with a practical interest in international politics can speak in the most relevant manner to the public that follows foreign affairs closely and at the same time be most useful to those who provide the raw material.

CONTENTS

BIOGRAPHICAL NOTES

HERBERT S. DINERSTEIN is Professor of Soviet Studies at The Johns Hopkins University School of Advanced International Studies and Research Associate of the Washington Center of Foreign Policy Research. Since receiving his doctorate in Russian history at Harvard University in 1943, he has divided his career between teaching, government service, and research. He has published *Communism and the Russian Peasant* (1955), *War and the Soviet Union* (1959), *Intervention Against Communism* (1967), *Fifty Years of Soviet Foreign Policy* (1968), and articles in the professional journals. He is now engaged in a study of Soviet policy in Latin America.

ISAIAH FRANK is William L. Clayton Professor of International Economics at The Johns Hopkins University School of Advanced International Studies. Prior to joining the Hopkins faculty in 1963, Dr. Frank was Deputy Assistant Secretary of State for Economic Affairs. For his distinguished contributions to the development of many aspects of the U.S. government's foreign economic policy, he received the Rockefeller Public Service Award in 1959. A consultant to the World Bank, the U.S. Department of State, the Committee for Economic Development, and other public and private bodies, Dr. Frank is a frequent contributor to professional journals and is the author of *The European Common Market: An Analysis of Commercial Policy*.

GEORGE LISKA, Professor of Political Science at The Johns Hopkins University and its School of Advanced International Studies, is Research Associate of the Washington Center of Foreign Policy Research. Among his publications on international relations, of greatest relevance for his contribution to this volume, are *The New Statecraft: Foreign Aid in American Foreign Policy* (1960), *Nations in Alliance* (1962), *Imperial America* (1967), *Alliances and the Third World* (1968), and

viii

War and Order (1968). Born in Czechoslovakia in 1922, Professor Liska came to this country in 1949, after briefly serving in his native country's Ministry for Foreign Affairs.

LAURENCE W. MARTIN is Director of War Studies at the University of London. He was formerly Wilson Professor in International Politics at the University College of Wales. From 1961–64 he was Research Associate of the Washington Center of Foreign Policy Research and Associate Professor of Political Science at The Johns Hopkins University School of Advanced International Studies. He is author of *Peace Without Victory* (1958), co-author of *The Anglo-American Tradition in Foreign Affairs* (1956), and editor of *Neutralism and Nonalignment: The New States in World Affairs* (1962).

ROBERT E. OSGOOD, Director of the Washington Center of Foreign Policy Research and Professor of American Foreign Policy at The Johns Hopkins University School of Advanced International Studies, is currently on leave to serve on the staff of the National Security Council. He was previously Professor of Political Science at the University of Chicago and, in 1959, NATO Visiting Professor at Manchester University. His books include *Ideals and Self-Interest in America's Foreign Relations* (1953), *Limited War: The Challenge to American Strategy* (1957), *NATO: The Entangling Alliance* (1962), *Force, Order, and Justice* (with Robert W. Tucker, 1967), and *Alliances and American Foreign Policy* (1968).

FRANCIS E. ROURKE is Professor of Political Science at The Johns Hopkins University. His major field of academic interest is administration and public policy. Publications by Professor Rourke which have a special relevance for foreign affairs are *Secrecy and Publicity: Dilemmas of Democracy* (1961), *Bureaucratic Power in National Politics* (1965), and *Bureaucracy, Politics, and Public Policy* (1969).

ROBERT W. TUCKER is Professor of Political Science and Director of International Studies at The Johns Hopkins University. He is also a member of the faculty of the Johns Hopkins University School of Advanced International Studies and a Research Associate of the Washington Center of Foreign Policy Research. His previous publications include *The Just War* (1961), *Force, Order, and Justice* (with Robert E. Osgood, 1967), and *Nation or Empire?* (1968).

AMERICA AND THE WORLD
From the Truman Doctrine to Vietnam

1

INTRODUCTION:
REAPPRAISAL OF AMERICAN POLICY

Robert E. Osgood

1

What are America's vital interests and how should it use its power to support them? This is the fundamental foreign policy question facing the United States after two decades of the Cold War. It is a question that has arisen at other critical periods of America's international involvement—during the war for independence, the acquisition of an empire, in both of the world wars, and as a result of the confrontation of Soviet expansionism after 1945.

The immediate circumstance that brings this recurrent question to the forefront is the war in Vietnam. America's painful, frustrating, morally unsatisfying involvement there would be sufficient in itself to warrant another reappraisal of foreign policy, but this war poses with special poignancy the fundamental question of American interests and power in the world. It does so for three major reasons: (1) because it occurs at a time when the United States has become the most powerful state in the world, with commitments and military preponderance in virtually every major area; (2) because the question is complicated by a diffuse and pervasive development: the erosion of familiar features of the Cold War that have shaped American policy in the last two decades; and (3) because the war in Vietnam coincides with domestic troubles that compete for attention and resources and draw heavily on the moral and political energy of the nation.

The fundamental question of American interests and power is never posed or answered directly or in the abstract. It is posed implicitly in terms of a number of specific immediate issues and decisions; it is answered ambiguously, if at all, by a set of responses that emerge from the unpredictable interaction of external events and domestic politics, of general policies and particular decisions, of underlying premises and pragmatic judgments. Correspondingly, the explicit controversies about U.S. policy, however significant they may be as clues to the national mood, are not necessarily accurate indicators of national policy.

Decisive changes in American policy have usually followed America's wars; but controversies evoked by the issues of intervention, fighting, and peacemaking have seldom indicated the real nature of these changes. Nor has the general emotional reaction to America's wars provided much of a clue to postwar courses of action. The most recent case in point is the Korean War. One could not have foreseen—from the controversy over the proper limits of the war, or from the prevailing postwar sentiment to avoid local wars in the future, or from the determination of the Eisenhower administration to deter such wars at a "bearable cost" by placing more reliance on "a great capacity to retaliate instantly, by means and at places of our choosing"—that the unexpected Korean War would lead to an equally unexpected extension of American commitments in Asia through new alliances, or that these commitments would lead to an even more frustrating local war in South Vietnam.

The war in Vietnam has been even more unpopular than the Korean War. Not only has it been relatively unsuccessful, it has also seemed less crucial to America's security. And it has been fought in behalf of a government that is no more attractive, yet much less effective, than Syngman Rhee's. Although the war has been sustained and directed from the North, as in Korea, its revolutionary aspect has pervaded the decisive battlefield in the South. Accordingly, as a consequence of American artillery and aerial bombing in the South, it has been punctuated by the morally unedifying killing and uprooting of civilians in the very country that the United States is supposed to be defending,[1] and the bombing in the North has been harder to portray as a legitimate defensive action against the aggressor. Moreover, in contrast to the endorsement of the United Nations and the token participation of several allies in the Korean War, the war in Vietnam has been viewed with indifference or antipathy by many of America's most important allies and has been opposed by most other countries. Understandably, therefore, the aversion to the Vietnamese war has been uniquely intense and bitter. But how significant is this aversion beyond its im-

1. By any estimate the number of civilians killed in South Vietnam is far less than the number killed in the Korean War; but in Vietnam the suffering of noncombatants, including the massive refugee movements, outrages moral sentiment far more than in the Korean War because it is the result of violence that many consider unnecessary, ineffective, and even counter productive in a war for stakes that seem less compelling on grounds of national interest or principle.

pact on the war in Vietnam? Does it foretell a basic change in American policy? What can one infer from the alleged lessons of this unpopular war about America's position in other parts of the world or even about the response to other possible local wars in Asia or elsewhere?

The most commonly asserted lesson is simply that there must be "no more Vietnams," that is, no repetition of American involvement in wars like the one in Vietnam. But, if taken literally, this dictum is quite inconclusive, since there is as little—and perhaps less—likelihood of another war like the Vietnamese war as of another Korean War. In its salient characteristics the Vietnam War is almost surely unique: a strong and expansionist local communist government with a large and highly effective army; a weak and fragmented country adjacent to it; nationalist ties with the adjacent country, stemming from the independence movement after World War II; and direction of revolutionary action by the organizing genius of Ho Chi Minh. Consequently, the lessons of Vietnam, whatever they may be, could scarcely have much relevance to the kind of local war that might occur in the Middle East, the Formosan Straits, the Indian border, or Korea. And even in the case of other hypothetical "wars of national liberation" in Asia, the lessons of Vietnam, as stated by opponents of the war, are ambiguous. Do they counsel against any involvement of American forces on the Asian mainland or only against a certain kind and level of involvement under particular circumstances? The more specifically one ponders the policy implications of the no-more-Vietnams sentiment, the less conclusive the sentiment seems to be.

2

If one seeks clues to the impact of the Vietnam War on American policy in the debate the war has aroused, one must examine the criticism that goes beyond the no-more-Vietnams sentiment to question the premises and practices of American policy that underlay American intervention. Here the most significant critics are not the pacifists, xenophobes, or utopians who reject the involvement of the United States in the central stream of power politics. They are "realists" and "internationalists," like the proponents of the policy consensus that has been represented with great continuity over the last two decades by spokesmen of the American government.[2] They criticize the consensus, not for trying to check communist expansion, cultivate bal-

2. The views of the consensus and its critics are examined more thoroughly in Chapter 2.

ances of power, and foster a congenial international environment, but only for pursuing these ends with excessive antiaggression and anticommunist fervor, for lack of discrimination between vital and not-so-vital interests, and for an imprudent commitment of American power to goals that exceed the nation's true interests as well as its effective power and will to use it. They advocate not a radical change in America's basic policy orientation but a more selective use of American power, especially with respect to armed interventions, and a general reduction of the scale, if not the scope, of American commitments that impose demands on military and economic resources.

But what would their view mean in practice, even if it were the prevailing American outlook? The last twenty years of America's foreign relations show that the desire to limit American commitments, to define vital interests and apply American power selectively, and to eschew the role of Pax Americana is not in itself a significant determinant of American policy. From the outset of the Cold War the proponents of the prevailing consensus have avowedly been no less eager than its critics to limit and reduce the involvement of American power in the world. There is no reason to discount the sincerity of President Johnson's and Secretary Rusk's repeated plaintive insistence that "we are not the world's policeman." And yet one unanticipated crisis after another has involved the United States more extensively in commitments and interventions than was imagined beforehand, because at the time there seemed to be no less objectionable alternative consistent with American interests than to resist communist aggression or the threat of aggression.

After World War II the prevailing American hope and expectation was that the Soviet Union could be induced to collaborate with the United States and Britain in making the new world order of the United Nations work. Although Soviet subversion in Iran, Soviet intractability over reaching a settlement of West Germany's position, its brutal assertion of control over the East European countries occupied by its armies, and numerous examples of Stalin's morbid suspicion and hostility concerning the United States dampened these hopes,[3] American

---

3. One of the most revealing examples of Stalin's suspicion and of the American inability to comprehend it except in terms of totalitarian aggressiveness was Stalin's abrupt rejection of Soviet participation in the Marshall Plan, which he and Soviet officials proceeded to excoriate as an American plot to build up Western Europe in order to push back the "socialist area" to its frontiers of 1939. See Adam B. Ulam's account of the Marshall Plan as a watershed in the Cold War. *Expansion and Coexistence: The History of Soviet Foreign Policy, 1917–67* (New York: Frederick A. Praeger, Inc., 1968), pp. 432–40.

leaders still envisaged America's role as that of a disinterested organizer of world order mediating between conflicting Soviet and British interests. In their view, the United States had no special interests in Europe; they abhorred Soviet moves chiefly as violations of the American conception of a new international order rather than as threats to American security. Even when continued Soviet misbehavior convinced the government of the correctness of George F. Kennan's view that the Soviet Union had to be prevented from expanding by the "vigilant application of counterforce at a series of constantly shifting geographical and political points," which would eventually "force upon the Kremlin a far greater degree of moderation and circumspection," there was still no expectation that containment called for the use of American armed force or even military assistance, least of all in Asia.[4]

In 1946 Americans would have been appalled by the thought of taking over Britain's historic role in the Mediterranean area; but the American government, having adopted the rationale of containment, found it impossible to avoid doing just that when Britain announced that it could no longer maintain its commitment to Greek security in the face of communist incursions. Despite the sweeping formulation of the Truman Doctrine, proclaiming that "it must be the policy of the United States to support free peoples who are resisting attempted subjugation by armed minorities or by outside pressures," this pronouncement was no more than the justification of the Greek-Turkish Aid Program. Its authors did not envisage the United States intervening with armed force against revolutions in other parts of the world. Nonetheless, the general objectives embodied in Kennan's exposition of containment and in the Truman Doctrine led the United States to undertake, with remarkable equanimity and general success, unanticipated commitments and interventions in Asia and the Middle East that seemed unthinkable in advance of the specific communist threats and incursions that provoked them.

4. In his *Memoirs: 1925–1950* (Boston: Little, Brown and Company, 1967), Kennan chides himself severely for not having made it clear in his "Mr. X" article (in the July, 1947, issue of *Foreign Affairs*) that when he called for the containment of Soviet power he meant "not the containment by military means of a military threat, but the political containment of a political threat" and that when he advocated confronting the Russians with unalterable counterforce at every point where they show signs of encroaching upon the interests of a peaceful world, he meant to apply this policy only to the United States, the United Kingdom, the Rhine valley and adjacent areas, and Japan—areas "where the sinews of modern military strength could be produced in quantity"—in order to keep them from falling under communist control (pp. 358ff).

When the United States entered into the North Atlantic Treaty in 1949, in the wake of the Berlin blockade, it intended only to guarantee the security of Western European states in order to give them the confidence they needed to proceed with their own defense without jeopardizing their economic revival. Yet, though they fully recovered economically, the United States became the dominant power in Western Europe, heading an international army and stationing its troops on European soil.

American military plans rejected the defense of South Korea as a peripheral point and a military liability, and the American government tried to detach the United States from the Chinese civil war. Yet the United States intervened in the Korean War, fought Communist China, and ended the war as an ally and protector not only of South Korea but also of the Nationalist Chinese on Taiwan. American politicians, diplomats, and military officers regarded the use of American forces to fight Asians on the Asian mainland as anathema,[5] but the United States has twice engaged in large local wars against Asians in Asia in the belief that vital interests were at stake. And the Eisenhower administration's efforts to avoid Korean-type wars and the expense of preparing for them led to deterrent alliances, which created further commitments and, in turn, led to further interventions.

Every president in the Cold War has taken office in the hope of concentrating on domestic welfare (although Kennedy was also determined to improve America's foreign power and prestige). Yet each has presided over a vast extension of American commitments and involvements.

The conflict between professed intentions to limit America's involvements and actual extensions of American involvements strikes some critics as nothing but the well-known hypocrisy of states grown arrogant with power, but the explanation runs deeper than that. It lies in a conflict between wish and reality, in a conception of American purposes and interests that cannot be sustained by the limited, relatively detached role the nation has desired, because unforeseen circumstances keep posing threats—or apparent threats—to those purposes and inter-

---

5. Before the Korean War General MacArthur insisted that America's line of defense in Asia should be defined by an island perimeter avoiding the mainland, since neither American interests nor power could justify a contest between American troops and Asian manpower on Asian territory. As late as October, 1964, President Johnson, referring to Vietnam, declared, "We are not going to send American boys nine or ten thousand miles away to do what Asian boys ought to be doing themselves."

ests that apparently cannot be countered except by the commitment and use of American military power.

3

But is the conception of American purposes and interests held by the critics of the Cold War consensus significantly different? Like the proponents of the consensus, the critics have come to accept a view of American vital interests that goes far beyond the physical security of American territory and identifies American security with balances of power and a modicum of international order against communist expansion in other continents. If there is a significant difference between their orientation toward international politics and that of the consensus—that is, a difference that might have substantial policy consequences—it lies in their assessment of the nature of the communist threat to American security. Such an assessment, whether by critics or proponents of the consensus, has two related aspects: the conception of America's security interests and the perception of the communist threat to these interests. Both may be changing.

The prevailing consensus has shown remarkable continuity in its analysis of the general threat of international communism to American interests. Since the onset of the Cold War most Americans, until recently, have regarded it as axiomatic that the Soviet Union and Communist China are expansionist and that any extension of communist control and influence over noncommunist countries—especially any extension by war, revolution, or subversion—whether undertaken directly by them or by other communist states, would constitute a threat to American security. If this proposition, backed by lessons derived from the chain of fascist aggressions preceding World War II, had not been axiomatic, the United States would not have pursued containment to such lengths. The whole history of America's foreign relations demonstrates that, however strong America's dedication to world order and other missions, the nation does not consistently carry out any policy that has to be executed with military power unless transcendent purposes coincide with a definite perception of security interests.[6]

In the Cold War, America's view of the scope of its security interests has expanded immensely from the period when containment was directed against Soviet pressure on Western Europe to the period in

6. This theme is illustrated extensively in Robert E. Osgood, *Ideals and Self-Interest in America's Foreign Relations* (Chicago: University of Chicago Press, 1953).

which it was applied against communist aggression in Asia. Although the direct, or even indirect, threat to American security of communist incursions against Asian states—with the exception of Japan—is much more problematic than the threat of Soviet or Soviet-supported aggression in Europe,[7] the United States has talked and acted as though such distinctions were of only minor significance. In effect, it has equated communist aggression with a threat to American security and subordinated the precise assessment of the security value of countering any particular aggression to the general requirements of containment. This was natural enough if one assumed—as Americans generally did assume until after the Korean War and the Sino-Soviet split in the late 1950s—that the Cold War was essentially a zero-sum contest between the two superpowers and that an aggression by any small communist state would shift the world balance of power toward the communist bloc. Moreover, there was no need to question this view of American security as long as America's efforts to counter aggression were successful at a tolerable cost.

The critics of the consensus, however, maintain that the communist world has long since ceased to be monolithic and is becoming more pluralistic all the time. This pluralism restrains the Soviet Union in Europe and weakens China—which is already beset with debilitating internal problems—in Asia. It means that revolutions and incursions by other communist states do not necessarily strengthen Russia or China and may actually help containment, since nationalism, whether communist or not, is the strongest antidote to Soviet and Chinese expansion. It means that Soviet competition with the United States for political influence in the nonaligned areas will be accompanied by more and more occasions for Soviet-American cooperation to insulate and pacify local disputes because of parallel interests in keeping the competition within safe limits and blocking Chinese influence. Therefore, where American intervention can accomplish nothing constructive anyway—which is almost always true in civil wars arising from the collapse of political authority—the United States would be better ad-

7. It can be argued that the fate of Berlin or even West Germany is of little more immediate and demonstrable consequence to American territorial security than parts of Asia or the Middle East, given America's immense deterrent power and economic strength. Be that as it may, the experience of being drawn into two world wars by European conflicts, the lessons drawn from the West's failure to check Hitler's bid for hegemony at an early stage, and the special affinity Americans feel for European political culture make the security and independence of Western European democracies an unquestioned vital interest and uniquely valuable among foreign interests.

vised to abstain so as not to deflect indigenous nationalism from its natural resistance to Soviet or Chinese imperialism.

The prevailing view of the communist danger, the critics charge, overestimates the capacity of any communist state or party to acquire or extend its domain by internal war or any other means. The power of North Vietnam, they contend, is unique. Moreover, a communist takeover in one place does not necessarily lead to a communist take-over in another. Dominoes are not likely to fall together unless they are ready to fall separately. The prospect of takeover depends on local conditions, especially on the capacity or incapacity of govern-ments to meet the basic needs of the people. Where the political ele-ments of this capacity are lacking, there is little any outside power can do to bolster a country against revolutionary forces in any case.

In the increasingly pluralistic world, the critics contend, it is foolish for the government to continue to act as though international politics were polarized in a struggle between the communist and the free world. In the real world a gain for one communist country is not neces-sarily a gain for another or a loss for the United States. The free (or noncommunist) world is even more pluralistic than the communist world. Socially and economically, it is agitated by the disruptive im-pact of modern technology and expectations of material progress in backward societies; but politically the impact is much more com-plicated than a struggle between communist and "free" forces. If any single political orientation is dominant in the Third World, it is na-tionalism. Therefore, the critics hold, analogies between communist aggression in the 1960s and fascist aggression in the 1930s are mis-leading myths. Contrary to official rhetoric, peace is eminently divis-ible and is becoming more so every day. By trying to play the world's policeman presiding over a Pax Americana, they charge, the United States is overextending itself in a fruitless and needless effort to im-pose order on an increasingly pluralistic world. The moral they draw is that the United States should revert to a much more selective view of its security interests and adopt a much more limited estimate of the communist threat to them.

This revisionist analysis of threats to American security may not yet prevail, but it could prevail unless international developments were conspicuously to refute it. If this view becomes the core of a new consensus, the war in Vietnam will have acted as a catalyst, which, by showing the excessive costs of containment in a peripheral war, has led the nation to question the vital nature of interests it had virtually taken for granted and, in doing so, has drastically downgraded the nation's view of its security imperatives, at least in Asia.

Undoubtedly, détente with the Soviet Union and the increasing divergencies of interest among communist states and parties are changing the American view of international reality and of the nature and intensity of the communist threat in particular. Thus a gain for China or even North Vietnam is not automatically seen as a gain for the Soviet Union or a loss for the United States, and opportunities for limited cooperation with the Soviet Union occasionally appear attractive. Moreover, notably in Africa, Americans are becoming accustomed to a great deal of disorder and communist meddling, without jumping to the conclusion that the balance of power or American security is jeopardized. To some extent China emerges as a new focus for active containment; but, despite the long strand of American obsession with China, the Chinese do not yet—and may never—have the strength to pose the kind of threat to Asia that the Soviet Union could have posed to Western Europe. Also, Asia is simply not valued as highly on the scale of interests as Western Europe.

On the other hand, another interpretation of the current American orientation to international politics is worth considering: that the very expansion of American commitments and power has transformed America's conception of its vital interests and the meaning of its security. In this view, Americans, without foreseeing and still only dimly realizing the change of role that the determined pursuit of containment has brought about, have come to conceive of their international position in terms more analogous to an imperial (but nonimperialistic) role than to the rationale articulated by either the consensus or its critics. Thus each extension of American power and commitments has enlarged America's conception of the specific national interests it must defend, since its interests tend to become coextensive with the area it has undertaken to protect from hostile incursions. A nation with far-flung commitments naturally wishes to protect them and to conserve its power. It feels that even an intrinsically unimportant incursion may jeopardize the security of many countries who look to it to protect them, and that one successful incursion could cast doubt upon the nation's willingness or ability to withstand other incursions.

So an imperial power's vital interests extend far beyond the protection of the homeland. They embrace all the outlying areas of commitment and compel the continual promotion of an international environment congenial to the protection of these areas. They become equivalent to the preservation of an international order and a distribution of power upon which order must depend. They are viewed with a mixture of resignation, resolution, and pride, as a moral, not only a national, obligation—an obligation seldom appreciated by any but the immediate beneficiaries, if by them. Imperial interests, moreover, create a sense of continual insecurity, since the threats to order are legion, and many are beyond the capacity of the imperial power to foresee or control.

For the United States, the holding of imperial power creates some emotional problems, since, on the one hand, America's equalitarian idealism makes the exercise of hegemony distasteful, yet, on the other hand, this same idealism lends a missionary impetus to armed interventions, which are the cause and consequence of its hegemonial position. If the critics are partly right in asserting that missionary impulses have got the better of America's anti-imperial inhibitions, these impulses are not, however, a sufficient explanation for the persistent extension of American commitments or for the difficulty Americans have found in satisfying their longing to escape the burdens of empire. In reality, not only the insecurity of holding great power but also the objective circumstances that prevent giving up power under hostile pressure with safety and honor make it as difficult for the United States to contract its commitments as it has been for traditional imperial powers to liquidate their empires.

Theoretically, the nation could simply decide, in accordance with the views of Walter Lippmann, that its primary interests—principally its territorial security and welfare—do not warrant the engagement of American forces on foreign soil, except in extreme and quite unlikely circumstances in Western Europe and perhaps to prevent the spread of hostile power in the Caribbean. But having pursued a much more spacious conception of its interests, such a retrenchment could entail a humiliating abdication of power and responsibility, leaving instability and turmoil in its wake, unless the most optimistic assumptions about the international environment should turn out to be true. No American president would want to take responsibility for risking this state of affairs.

So, according to the imperial interpretation of American policy, the sheer inertia—the inner logic, as it were—of America's vast extension of its power and commitments is a great obstacle to any significant deliberate move toward retrenchment. It would follow that the war in Vietnam, far from being a catalyst for establishing a more limited view of American security interests, would find its place in history as America's first imperial war—a war the significance of which was obscured by the familiar rhetoric of containment and the Truman Doctrine, and by the liberal aversion to the rhetoric as applied to Vietnam, but none-theless a war fought for a conception of security that might be called more imperial than national.[8]

It would be a mistake, however, to draw any direct or absolute correlation between the basic conception of America's international position—whether conventional, revisionist, or imperial—and the future of American policy. Whatever the prevailing conception of American vital interests may be or become, its actual impact on American policy will largely depend, as always, on the kinds of events and developments that shape America's international environment. Indeed, the external environment probably shapes the nation's conception of its vital interests more than the other way around. One could not otherwise explain the transformation of America's international outlook since World War II. It follows that the principal clues to the future of American policy lie more in international political trends, both discernible and unforeseeable, than in current reactions to the war in Vietnam. But as always the impact of the international environment will be filtered through the domestic environment of American policy.

4

The principal features of American foreign policy have been shaped by the Cold War. Therefore, one may find intimations of the future by examining international trends in terms of the fundamental continuities and changes in the Cold War.

From the United States' standpoint, the Cold War, though its antecedents lay in Iran and Greece, was at the outset primarily a pattern of international politics dominated by a political and ideological conflict with the Soviet Union in Europe, with the superpowers organizing their power through collective alliances in which they were preponderant both politically and militarily.[9] As this conflict became stabilized in Europe and spread to Asia, the Middle East, Africa, and the Carib-

8. These contrasting interpretations of the larger significance of the Vietnamese war are expounded in George Liska, *War and Order: Reflections on Vietnam and History* (Baltimore: The Johns Hopkins Press, 1968), and Robert W. Tucker, *Nation or Empire? The Debate over American Foreign Policy* (Baltimore: The Johns Hopkins Press, 1968).

9. The Soviet bloc did not become an alliance, nominally, until the creation of the Warsaw Pact. Thereafter, the Warsaw Treaty Organization became less like an empire and more like a contractual alliance; but, consistent with its conception of a "commonwealth of socialist states," the Soviet Union continued to view the Organization as an instrument of internal control as well as external security.

bean, it absorbed the diversified interests and outlooks of a great number and variety of governments and of social and political parties and movements, and was in turn shaped or dissipated by them. States moved by local concerns having little or nothing to do with the political and ideological issues between the United States and the Soviet Union were drawn into the mainstream or at least the eddies of international politics. New patterns of conflict and alignment developed outside the context of American-Soviet relations. The superpowers adapted their competition to the heterogeneous and fluid regional and local patterns of politics emerging out of the destruction of the colonial system, which both the United States and the Soviet Union deliberately hastened for divergent purposes. Thus the spread and diversification of the Cold War greatly complicated the means and substantive forms of this largely bipolar conflict. The emergence, quite apart from Soviet or American initiative, of new centers of political unrest and of independent political activity and conflict, demonstrated the limits of superpower control outside their military alliances.

At the same time, the configurations of interest and power among the superpowers and the second-rank states were changing. The American-Soviet competition was moderated and complicated by the crystallization in the late 1950s of a set of common and parallel interests between the superpowers, derived from their desire to avoid direct military encounters with each other and to prevent additional states from acquiring nuclear weapons. Concomitantly, the emergence of Communist China as a competitor—sometimes verging on an adversary—of the Soviet Union created an incipient tripolar relationship in which each state might seek a limited alignment with another against the third while seeking to prevent the alignment of the other two against its own interests. To these two developments in the relations of the most powerful states was added a third: the growing political independence of Soviet and American allies in Europe, which absorbed a growing proportion of the superpowers' international energy in trying to preserve the cohesion of their alliances.

By the mid-1960s America's conflict with the Soviet Union and its more diffuse conflict with "international communism"—already an unsatisfactory term for the complex reality—no longer encompassed or described the salient features of America's international environment to nearly the same extent as in the mid-1950s. Nevertheless, this dual conflict was still the single most important international factor shaping American policy. If the Vietnam War raised doubts about the value of resisting communist incursions in peripheral areas, the Soviet invasion of Czechoslovakia and the growing Soviet involvement in the

Middle East reminded Americans—though more logically in the second than in the first case—that the central core of the Cold War was far from dead.

In Soviet and Chinese eyes, too, the Cold War has greatly changed in form and means. Yet, although their own rivalry and antagonism and the Soviet Union's problems in Eastern Europe sometimes take precedence over their political and ideological contest with the United States and its major allies, that contest continues to dominate their political and military policies.

For most American or Soviet allies in Europe—the largest exception being the two Germanies—the Cold War slipped into the background of policy concerns some time in the late 1950s, partly because the apparent stability of mutual deterrence in Europe as managed by the superpowers relieved them of immediate security problems. In an atmosphere of détente they became more concerned about their relations with their superpower, their allies, and the allies of the opposing bloc, or they became largely absorbed with domestic affairs. Nonetheless, Soviet-American competition, now complicated by limited Soviet-American cooperation or "collusion," remains the major factor determining the framework within which they can pursue their special interests.

For many nonaligned countries the Cold War was never much more than either an interference with the primary goals of national independence and development or an opportunity to advance these goals by exploiting the competition of the superpowers for their favor. Now some of these countries, having experienced the hardships of independence and the limits of superpower competition, are increasingly preoccupied with local conflicts and alignments and with internal security or survival. Others, like India, grow more conscious of the threat of China to their security but are nevertheless determined not to be absorbed into the contest between China and the United States or between China and the Soviet Union.

Of course, the difference of perspective between the United States and the regional or purely local powers tells as much about the disparity between their power as about changes in international politics. Only a state with the global reach of the United States could formulate its primary interests in terms of a conflict as pervasive and generalized as that between revolutionary communism and a world "safe for diversity." Perhaps the Cold War could remain a dominant concern only in the global perspective of a state with such extensive commitments and vast power that it virtually equates its vital interests with the maintenance of international order in the most dangerous parts of the world. But the persistence of the Cold War in the American perspective also reflects some fundamental continuities in the environment of American policy.

Historically, it is remarkable that, twenty years after a major war causing a decisive redistribution of power, the immediate postwar configurations of power and alignment among the major powers should not have changed more fundamentally. Within twenty years after other such wars in modern times, the structure of power has been upset or radically challenged; the issues of conflict, the pattern of alignments, and the major contestants have changed. Yet amid great international change since the onset of the Cold War, the antagonism and fear between the United States, on the one hand, and the two powerful communist states, on the other, still pervades, if it does not always dominate, America's foreign relations. The principal military and diplomatic issues spring from that contest. It affects almost every major policy problem that engages American attention. None of the particular issues of conflict that aggravated the Cold War—the division of Germany, the status of Berlin, the two Chinas, the international control of arms—has been resolved.

Nor has the distribution of military power changed markedly. The central military balance in the world is still the balance of terror between the United States and the Soviet Union. In most respects the two superpowers remain as powerful, compared to the second-rank states, as at the beginning of the Cold War. And all the advanced states are comparatively richer and stronger than ever in relation to the underdeveloped countries. The capacity of the superpowers to translate their military power into control of the external or internal affairs of either the developed or less developed countries—a capacity that was always quite limited and conditional—may have diminished. But this does not mean that the effect of the superpowers' military preponderance on international relations is negligible. On the contrary, it is immense, as one can readily appreciate simply by noting the pervasive influence of American or Soviet policies in the dominant international issues of the day.

Though the Sino-Soviet rift seems deep and permanent and the independence of Eastern European states from Soviet control seems to be an irreversible organic process, although NATO is stagnant and Western Europe is restive in the shadow of American preponderance, the two major multilateral alliances in Europe, created in the first phase of the Cold War, do remain intact. Soviet-American détente stops far short of entente. Centrifugal tendencies in the American and Soviet alliances stop short of realignment or even nonalignment.

One of the most consequential international changes since World War II is the disappearance of colonial territories and the rise, in their place, of new and relatively impoverished countries to the status of politically active, nationally self-conscious states. Yet the impact of this development on international politics has been anything but clear-cut. Here, too, certain continuities have moderated change and defied radical expectations.

In the mid-1950s it seemed that the so-called Third World, or Afro-Asian bloc, might become the new and decisive arena of the Cold War, as the Soviet Union and China, on the one hand, and the United States, on the other, competed for the allegiance of the new regimes. The Soviet and Chinese switch from reviling nonaligned states not in the communist camp to embracing them as collaborators against the remnants of imperialism (like the United States' earlier program of economic aid and its later endorsement of neutralism) seemed to portend some sort of climactic competition—a competition not only between states but between systems of government and ways of organizing world order. The new regimes themselves capitalized upon the competition to gain status and acquire economic and military assistance. Colorful nationalist leaders—Nehru, Sukarno, Nasser, Nkrumah, and others—stimulated expectations of their decisive importance in world politics by exalting nonalignment as a principle of international order and by touting anticolonialism and economic development as panaceas.

America's preoccupation with the underdeveloped areas increased when the U.S.S.R., China, and communist parties throughout the world appeared to have abandoned the strategy of peaceful coexistence and appeals to bourgeois nationalism, which had failed to pay satisfactory dividends, and adopted a more militant strategy. In 1960 eighty-one communist parties endorsed the strategy of supporting "wars of national liberation," which they considered "inevitable." Though it developed that the Kremlin was staunchly opposed to Peking's active pursuit of this course at the risk of involving the Soviet Union in war, the communists' apparent turn toward a militant revolutionary strategy seemed to confirm American apprehensions that the Third World might be the critical and violent arena of East-West confrontation now that nuclear deterrence had checked the threat of direct military aggression.

The Third World has indeed exerted a great impact on international politics. It has been the area of most intense conflict because it is the most vulnerable to external penetration and most susceptible to anti-Western revolutionary appeals. The contest with the Soviet Union and

China and with other communist states and parties in the underdeveloped areas persists in various forms. Yet the Third World—increasingly an overly abstract concept—has not turned out to be a decisive arena of the Cold War but rather only one important, multifarious area of conflict in an increasingly complicated pattern of international politics.

A number of factors account for this: the inability of the Soviet Union or China to start, control, and capitalize upon revolutionary warfare; the dominance of national and subnational loyalties, the emergence of noncommunist radical groups, and the assertion of moderate, nonromantic, often military, rule in the new states; the superpowers' discovery of the limits of economic aid as an instrument of policy and of the intractable obstacles to economic or political development; the U.S.-U.S.S.R. détente and parallel opposition to Chinese exploitation of local conflicts; Soviet and American discovery of the common danger posed by overly adventurous client states; the intensification and diversification of local animosities among countries in the Third World. In addition there is the devaluation of the mystique of nonalignment, resulting from growing divisions among Afro-Asian states, the pressure of internal and local problems, the discovery by India and others that security against China might require limited alignment with one or preferably both superpowers, and the death or political decline of the charismatic spokesmen of nonalignment (Nehru, Nkrumah, Sukarno, Ben Bella, and even Nasser, to the extent that he has failed to gain prestige as an international leader or status as the undisputed Arab leader). As the Third World has failed to become the decisive arena of the Cold War, so it has also, for many of the same reasons inherent in its diversity and weakness, failed to become the moving agent in a polarization of international politics on a North-South or developed-underdeveloped axis of interests.

So, though changes in international politics during two decades have greatly complicated the environment of American policy, they have not nullified, but only modified, some of its determining political and structural elements. International changes have neither ended the Cold War nor created coherent new patterns of conflict and alignment.

The reasons for such continuity in a period of great and rapid change are varied. In some respects the sheer intractability of the international environment accounts for it. (In the Third World, for example, the failure of great expectations to materialize must be largely attributed simply to the unsusceptibility of local conditions to organization or influence by the superpowers and to the political and material incapacity of underdeveloped states to act on the central stage of world politics.) But two historically unique factors of great importance can be singled out as positive forces for continuity. One is the extent to which the central international conflict and balance of power have been determined by two states because of the disparity between the magnitude and geographical extent of their power and the power of any other state or group of states. The other unique factor is the existence of nuclear weapons.

The American and Soviet possession of large and diversified nuclear arsenals, dependent on vast resources unapproached by other nations, has given them a virtual monopoly in maintaining the central military balance. The second-rank, once-great powers—even when they have acquired their own nuclear forces, as in the case of Britain and France—have apparently been unable to maintain their security or even pursue an independent policy without the protection of a superpower, and they have been unable to gain much if any influence on the superpowers' management of military policies even with respect to their own security. Moreover, the expense of maintaining a first-rank nuclear force, the political and psychological burden of being a completely independent nuclear power, the special stigma attached to nuclear acquisition by the defeated great powers, Germany and Japan, and the political difficulty of equal powers reaching mutually satisfactory terms for joint control of a combined nuclear force, have discouraged the once-great powers from trying to supplant the superpowers as military managers. In another way, too, nuclear weapons have preserved continuities in the Cold War: they have deterred the superpowers from resorting to war or from seeking territorial-political change under the threat of war. Thus a primary instrument for changing the international political status quo in earlier periods of history has been withheld.

On the basis of the history of two decades, one might conclude that, as long as these basic continuities persist, the extent of American involvement in world politics is unlikely to diminish. The imperatives of containment, together with the imperatives of America's imperial position, would override the incentives for retrenchment, regardless of the nation's determination to avoid future Vietnams.

But the continuities in international politics since World War II are not permanent. There are many ways in which they could come to an end. Familiar elements of international politics could change fundamentally or disappear altogether if, for example, the Soviet Union became so conservative in the face of war dangers, fear of German revanchism, and uncontrollable radical revolutionary forces; so preoccupied with the problems of adhesion in Eastern Europe or in the Soviet Union itself; so concerned with the problem of restraining China; and so frustrated by political failures in the Third World as to abandon its search for levers of hegemony or influence beyond its existing regional domain. And one can also imagine a combination of internal problems and external frustrations restricting the United States to little more than a Western Hemispheric role. International politics might be transformed if new active centers of power—for example Japan or a Franco-German coalition—were to exert their weight in regional balances of power; if the superpowers became much more concerned with their parallel interests in checking China, damping down local conflicts in the Third World, and containing nuclear proliferation than with their conflicting political and ideological aims; if China became so powerful that it were not only a regional but a global power, as a major weight against Russian power, seeking limited alignment with the United States or Japan.

There are some kinds of events that might also precipitate basic changes in the Cold War—and rather rapidly: a local armed conflict in the Third World leading to a major war involving Chinese or Soviet forces against American forces; a domestic upheaval or a radical change of regime in the Soviet Union or the United States; a severe economic dislocation in Europe or in one of the superpowers; Soviet attempts to repress forcibly the East European movement toward independence and liberalism; an expansionist or aggressively revisionist regime in West or East Germany.

Few of these developments seem likely. To recognize their possibility simply reminds us of the element of surprise and the limits of foresight in international affairs. But the continuities of the Cold War might also change by erosion. Less spectacular changes in international politics may already be transforming the Cold War to such an extent as to render the chief concepts and strategies of postwar American policy obsolete, even though elements of continuity persist. For we must remember that the familiar outlines of American postwar foreign policy were formed under circumstances in which the containment of communism for the sake of American security served as the great catalyzing motive and simplifying analysis for active participation in world politics. The gradual erosion of this motive and analysis in an increasingly complicated international environment could exert a no less fundamental impact on American policy than would dramatic transformations or sudden critical events. The steady decline of congressional support for foreign aid, with the waning sense of its urgency and efficacy as an instrument of containment, is a case in point.

The expansion, diversification, and dissipation of the Cold War leave us with the uneasy feeling that one distinct era of international politics has ended, but that its remnants linger on, while no coherent new pattern of politics has emerged. As Pierre Hassner has said of the changing international scene in Europe,

> Every period is by definition a time of transition. Some periods, however, tend to give an illusion of permanence, others an expectation of utopia or doom. The peculiar feature of the present time is that it is almost impossible to escape the impression that we are entering a new period of international relations—and almost as difficult to agree on where we go from here. Our feeling of change is based on our witnessing the decay of the old, rather than on any concrete fears or hopes about the emergence of the new.[10]

In this state of transition, the policy designs of the past seem dead or at least drained of hopeful expectations. Regionalism, European unity, Atlantic partnership, economic development of the Third World, nonalignment, Soviet-American duopoly—none of these simplifying concepts and visions is much more promising than the original design for an international order based on the United Nations and the Big Three, a design shattered by the onset of the Cold War. Current official endorsement of the concept of multilateralizing America's commitments and the engagement of its power and resources springs from the forlorn hope that multilateral involvements may be less vulnerable than unilateral involvements to congressional and popular sentiment for retrenchment. It does not represent any realistic analysis of the prospects or consequences of concerting American interests with the interests of other states.

Some Americans, sensing the erosion of incentives for an active foreign policy at the present level of global involvement, and seeking a reduction of America's overseas burdens, yet fearing the consequences of America's retrenchment from its present global position, anxiously look forward to a change in the international environment that would enable the United States to limit its involvement without jeopardizing world order. They find this change in the emergence of major new centers of power that will supplement American power in preserving

10. Pierre Hassner, *Change and Security in Europe. Part I: The Background* (Adelphi Papers, No. 45; London: Institute of Strategic Studies, February, 1966), p. 1.

a modicum of order in the most critical areas of the world.[11] This idea is the latest revival of an old vision of multipolar order. From the beginning of the Cold War, given the objectives of American policy, the absence of other substantial poles of noncommunist power has necessitated the steady extension of America's foreign involvements. Therefore, not only the critics but also the proponents of the prevailing consensus on American foreign policy have looked forward to a world in which power would be diffused rather than concentrated.[12] They have explicitly advocated and hopefully anticipated the devolution of responsibility from the United States to other centers of power, pending the emergence of a universal security organization.

Yet the desire to see new centers of power emerge is strongly qualified by the natural propensity of a great power to keep the security of its realm under its own control so far as possible, and especially to keep control of its nuclear power, upon which that security depends.[13]

11. For example, President Nixon, in an interview in December, 1968, said, "And we must never have another Vietnam. By which I mean that the United States must never find itself in a position of furnishing most of the arms and most of the money and most of the men to help another nation defend itself against Communist aggression. We need a new type of collective security arrangement in which the nations in a particular area of the world would assume primary responsibility in coming to the aid of a neighboring nation rather than have the United States called upon to give direct unilateral assistance every time such an emergency arose.

"It is not just that the United States simply cannot afford to be involved in the old-type Vietnam situation; it is not healthy for the peace of the world for the United States to be involved in situations which may risk direct confrontations with the Soviet Union or Communist China. Getting away from Vietnam, to make my meaning clear, if we are, for example, to protect nations around the perimeter of Communist China against the expansion of that power, we must develop new collective security arrangements in which all the nations in that area, including Japan, will play a role. Much the same goes for Latin America."

(*Washington Post*, December 8, 1968, p. B3. Cf. Nixon's article, "Asia After Vietnam," in *Foreign Affairs*, XLVI, September, 1967, pp. 111–25.)

12. Among the proponents, Walt W. Rostow has been the most articulate predictor and advocate of the diffusion of power. Before joining the Kennedy administration he stated his views on this subject in *The United States in the World Arena* (New York: Harper & Bros., 1960), Book V, Part II. Among the critics, Roger Masters, in *The Nation Is Burdened* (New York: Alfred A. Knopf, Inc., 1967), presents the most thorough case for the diffusion of power.

13. The United States has gone far to consult its NATO allies on nuclear matters and to coordinate nuclear plans and operations. In the aborted MLF plan it even proposed a form of joint decision-making, although with an American veto over the jointly operated seaborne force. Similarly, it has placed

It is also qualified by America's apprehension about the spread of nuclear weapons. And this apprehension is a special manifestation of the more general American fear of a resurgence of national separatism, competitive arming, and other disruptive features accompanying the historic system of power politics.

In concept, Americans have reconciled nationalism with the diffusion of power through the ideal of autonomous but interdependent and harmonious regional "collective security" organizations, which would temper nationalism while aggregating power.[14] The ideal of a united Europe is especially favored in America's postwar visions.[15] Yet the only noncommunist regional organizations that have played a significant role in the distribution of power have been organized under American preponderance. Even in Western Europe, where the material and political conditions of an independent regional organization are far more promising than in any other part of the world, the United States is virtually the exclusive manager of the West's countervailing military power.

Perhaps, as some American and many European critics allege, America's ideal of regionalism sublimates the reality of its hegemony. One wonders whether the proponents of the diffusion of power would prefer the constraints and dangers of full-scale multipolarity to the disadvantages of the existing qualified bipolarity (or, in Asia perhaps, incipient tripolarity) if such a structure of power were in fact to develop. Rather, they seem to assume that the advantages of bipolarity

---

nuclear weapons in Europe under a "double-key" arrangement. Nevertheless, constitutional restrictions as well as popular and congressional sentiment are prohibitive obstacles to handing over control of the use of American or American-manufactured nuclear weapons.

14. See, for example, Walt W. Rostow's address "Regionalism and World Order," June 12, 1967, in the *Department of State Bulletin*, LVII (July 17, 1967), pp. 66–69. "We are finding, then, in regionalism," said Rostow, "a new relationship to the world community somewhere between the overwhelming responsibility we assumed in the early postwar years—as we moved in to fill vacuums of power and to deal with war devastation—and a return to isolationism. From the beginning our objective was not to build an empire of satellites but to strengthen nations and regions so that they could become partners" (p. 69).

15. Former Under Secretary of State Ball has argued that a multipolar international system would be safer and less burdensome for the United States than the existing bipolar confrontation with the Soviet Union. But, aside from welcoming a more active regional role for Japan in Asia, his multipolar model is just a restatement of the vision of a united Europe as "a third superpower lying at the center of power yet sharing the history and culture of the West." George W. Ball, *The Discipline of Power* (Boston: Little, Brown and Company, 1968), p. 349.

can be combined with the advantages of multipolarity to provide the best of both worlds without the disadvantages of either.

Be that as it may, a world of coherent regional organizations, whether as partners or powerful rivals, shows few signs of emerging at this stage of international politics. This is not the result of hegemonial American designs. It is the result of inherent obstacles to the development of autonomous regional poles of power. These obstacles lie in many particular divergencies of interests within every group of interdependent states but also, more generally, in the political problem that roughly equal powers encounter in integrating or even coordinating defense policies, in the special obstacles to an equitable and mutually satisfactory sharing of the control of nuclear weapons (now virtually a prerequisite for creating a major power), in the postwar resurgence of parochial national spirit, and in the domestic opposition to the expenditures necessary to create armed forces independent of the United States.

If any new pole of military power, independent of American preponderance and capable of affecting regional balances of power, arises in the next decade, it will be a single sovereign state that already exists. Japan seems like the only prospect. Yet the emergence of a thoroughly armed Japan, playing a major role in an Asian balance of power and moved by the kind of outward-looking nationalism that would have to be the precondition of such a status, would be no less disturbing than the burdens of American preponderance to the current advocates of multipolarity. Multipolarity may become the new model of international order to capture the fancy of those who seek system and rationality in a congenial international environment. But if a truly multipolar international system emerges, the reality will surely be far more complicated and less satisfying than any of the models. In the meanwhile, the familiar outlines of the old order continue to grow more confusing, like a kaleidoscope that is somewhat out of focus.

What further complicates the effort to foresee, let alone foster, some coherent future design is the present tendency of internal socioeconomic problems to lead toward introversion the states that have the greatest capacity to construct designs. If some of the most advanced industrial states, including the United States and the Soviet Union, are going to be preoccupied with meeting politically mobilized consumer expectations, alleviating urban maladjustments, and accommodating racial or relatively affluent and well-educated minorities who feel alienated from the prevailing establishments and the vast impersonal systems of government, business, and education over which they preside, then international politics will be a much more amorphous phenomenon than in previous transitional periods of the modern state system—except, perhaps, periods of transnational revolution.

It is a question whether this nation, faced with a confusing and patternless international environment and preoccupied with internal problems, will continue to expend the energy it would have to expend just to maintain its existing commitments, let alone foster new systems of order and security. When the containment of communism is no longer a catalyzing purpose and there is no universal ideological adversary against which to mobilize moral sentiments, would a sense of world role and responsibility, or a general feeling that American security and welfare depend on balances of power and a modicum of order in the world, suffice to sustain an active foreign policy? Or would the United States, no longer finding any moral satisfaction in global power politics or feeling the lash of insecurity, liquidate its metaphorical empire and retire to an equally metaphorical fortress? In either case, what difference would it make for America's security or the quality of American life? The alternatives are overstated, but the questions are pertinent.

Part 1

THE PRINCIPALS

2

THE AMERICAN OUTLOOK

Robert W. Tucker

1

That American foreign policy is a matter of debate today is in itself neither unusual nor startling. Throughout the nation's history, and particularly since the close of the nineteenth century, debate over foreign policy has been the norm rather than the exception. During the last thirty years we have had an almost continuous debate—or series of debates. There is no need to examine here the many reasons for the seemingly endemic controversies that attend the diplomacy of what one foreign observer has termed "the most verbose democracy in the world."[1] Suffice it to say that controversy over the substance and conduct of foreign policy is a well-established tradition; it is unlikely to disappear in the foreseeable future.

At the same time, it is true that the intensity of the recurring debates over American foreign policy has varied, and considerably so. On this basis alone the period since 1965 surely merits distinction. For whatever the lasting significance of the present debate there can be little doubt about the passions it has aroused. One must go back to the controversy over intervention in the years prior to 1941 to find a debate comparable in its intensity. The debate attending the Truman Doctrine and the initiation of the policy of containment, significant as it undoubtedly was, neither reached nor sustained a comparable intensity. This is also true of the controversies from the late 1940s to the middle 1960s, with the possible exception of Korea. And even Korea does not provide a close parallel to Vietnam, at least with respect to the scope, depth, and persistence of the dissatisfaction Vietnam has engendered.

The recent debate has not only been distinctive because of its in-

---

This essay is a condensation, much of which is taken verbatim, from my previously published Nation or Empire? The Debate over American Foreign Policy *(Baltimore: The Johns Hopkins Press, 1969).*—R. W. T.

1. Raymond Aron, "Reflections on American Diplomacy," *Daedalus* (Fall, 1962), p. 719.

tensity. It has also been unusual in terms of its participants. Indeed, the intensity must in large measure be explained by the identity of the participants. The debate has not followed party lines and it could scarcely have aroused the passions it has on the basis of party. In the 1968 election the storm center of the debate was to be found within the Democratic Party. By comparison with the conflict that racked the Democratic Party through the period of the primaries and the convention, the subsequent differences between the two major candidates appeared modest.

It is doubtful whether the established party structure any longer affords a basis for serious conflict over foreign policy. It last did so in the years before and during World War II as a result of a growing separation between liberalism and isolationism and the almost exclusive identification of the latter with conservative Republicanism. Korea again appears to be an exception. Yet in 1952, when public confusion and frustration reached proportions that could be effectively exploited by the party in opposition, the exploitation did not consist in rejecting the general policy that had led to the Korean intervention. And once in power the new Republican administration was quite faithful in continuing and building upon the Asian containment policy initiated by its predecessor. What the Korean and more recent examples demonstrate is simply that, in the competition of parties for power, it remains an accepted rule of the game for opponents to capitalize on each other's difficulties and errors, despite the previous support of policies that led to these difficulties and errors. Opportunism is readily tolerated, if not made into a canon of the political game. But, to the extent that recent debates over foreign policy have followed established party lines and have been motivated by normal considerations of political advantage, they have been neither profound nor bitter. It is difficult to see them becoming so.

What has given the recent debate much of its intensity is the fact that the principal participants are former allies who had long been committed to the same causes. It is the mutual sense of betrayal that has done what normal party politics no longer seem able to do. For the most articulate and effective criticism of the Johnson administration and its supporters has come from the ranks of those who have provided the main support for American foreign policy since World War II, the liberal intellectuals and the moderate Republicans. The emergence of the "new left" and of an amorphous peace movement has no doubt contributed considerably to the controversy. But these groups have been comprised for the most part of individuals who have never had a strong sense of identity with American foreign policy. This is clearly the case with the new left and allied groups for whom the war in Vietnam provided an opportunity—a golden opportunity, to be sure—they probably would have sought in any event. It is less true of the peace movement, or of that part of the peace movement distinct from the new left, which comprises many whose interest has largely been limited to the war in Vietnam and who have no apparent desire to confront the establishment on other issues, domestic or foreign. Indeed, many in the peace movement are political moderates on domestic issues and have given varying degrees of support to American foreign policy in the past. At any rate, whatever the long-run influence on foreign policy of a growing radicalization of American politics, its present impact is easily exaggerated. It is not the opposition of those who have never really formed a part of the foreign policy consensus that has been the significant feature of the debate, but the substantial defection of those who have formed a critical part of this consensus for the past generation.

If we consider the character of the opposition, particularly among the intellectuals, which developed in the course of the war, we find that it has comprised at least three quite disparate groups. There have been those who have rather faithfully supported American foreign policy for a generation and then found themselves opposed to the war in Vietnam, though certainly not to the whole of American foreign policy. This group is by no means pacifist in commitment and has not ostensibly opposed the war on moral grounds, though it has not been insensitive to the moral issues raised by the war. (Many among this group endorsed American aims in Vietnam, supported at least some involvement in the conflict, and began to oppose the administration only after the war, and American involvement in the war, went beyond the pre-1965 level.) There are those who have formed a part of the peace movement, who are in varying degree pacifist in commitment and who have opposed the war chiefly on moral grounds. This second group has consisted of many who have not been markedly hostile to American foreign policy in the past, at least when it did not involve the use of force. Finally, there are those who have condemned not only the war in Vietnam but the whole of American foreign policy and who have coupled this condemnation of foreign policy with an equally sweeping condemnation of domestic policy. The former has been found to grow out of, and to reflect, the latter. Both have been seen to need thoroughgoing reform, if not revolution.

There are no reliable studies that show how these three groups have compared in relative strength. But there is no persuasive reason for assuming that the third group has been numerically or otherwise stronger than the first two groups. If anything, the more reasonable assumption is that it has been the smallest of the three. Of the first two groups, there is little evidence to support the contention that they have desired a "significant confrontation with the American establishment."[2] Quite the contrary, many of the first group, when not actually forming a part of the establishment, have been accused of being far too compliant. Whatever the merit of this accusation, it is scarcely reasonable to see in this group a serious challenge to the status quo, whether at home or abroad. The peace groups, by and large, sprang up in response to the expanding American commitment in Vietnam. They do not constitute a cohesive political group, and they have very little to say that is distinctive about American foreign policy beyond Vietnam, save that the nation must stay out of similar—or all—military involvements. Except for that part of the peace movement tied to the new left, they have not taken a distinctive position on domestic issues.

It is another matter to find that the majority of American intellectuals continue to betray in varying degree the residue of an isolationist past.[3] It would be astonishing were this not the case. It is not apparent, however, that this characteristic sets them apart from the rest of society. Nor is it apparent that this characteristic has prevented most of them from accepting the new role that America has played since World War II. The support they have given American foreign policy over the past generation has been marked by misgivings and more than occasional criticism. But this, too, is scarcely cause for surprise. What is surprising is that they have given so little trouble until very recently. Thus it is only in very recent years that opposition to the primacy of foreign over domestic policy has taken an active political form rather than a merely literary expression, and this despite the undoubted domestic orientation of most American intellectuals (again, an orientation they share with the general public).

There are reasons, discussed below, which partly explain this passivity in the face of the reversal of a tradition as deeply rooted as any in American public life. The fact remains that until the Vietnamese war there was no widespread and insistent demand that the government abandon, or even seriously curtail, any of its major security policies in order to give greater attention, let alone a clear priority, to domestic needs. If that demand is insistent and widespread today it may or may not reflect a lingering commitment to, or recrudescence of, the isola-

2. Irving Kristol, "American Intellectuals and Foreign Policy," *Foreign Affairs* (July, 1967), p. 606.

3. *Ibid.*, p. 605.

tionist ideal. The position that it must do so stems from the view that the American commitment in Vietnam throughout its successive phases has been the inescapable response to America's objective security needs and to her unavoidable responsibilities as a world power.

If this view is accepted, the choice that must be made is between acknowledging the imperatives of imperial power, as these imperatives have been broadly defined by the past two administrations, and railing against these imperatives out of a desire somehow to return to an isolationist past. If it is not accepted, it clearly does not follow that one must be an isolationist to protest against an imperial destiny for America, particularly an imperial destiny that results in the kind of war waged in Vietnam. (Indeed, there are many who have accepted an imperial destiny for America—and an imperial rationale for intervention—yet opposed the war in Vietnam in terms of the specific circumstances attending this conflict.) But whether one accepts it or not, the point remains that the intellectual's commitment to an "American way of life," an ideal that is admittedly in some measure inseparable from America's isolationist past, does not distinguish him today from the general society of which he is a part.

2

How are we to account for the debate? What is the significance of the dissent and opposition, particularly on the part of many who have long provided critical support for American foreign policy? The answer cannot be in doubt. It is the war in Vietnam that has given rise to most of the disaffection. It is the war in Vietnam that must explain, above all other considerations, the substantial defection and disaffection of the intellectuals. The best evidence for this is the relative absence of dissatisfaction with American foreign policy in the period immediately prior to the expansion of the war in the winter of 1965. A review of the period from the Cuban missile crisis to the beginning of the aerial bombardment of North Vietnam leads to the conclusion, a striking conclusion in view of what followed, that in terms of domestic dissent over foreign policy it has been one of the more tranquil in recent history. Yet with one exception American foreign policy was then substantially what it is now. And that one exception was already in a far more than embryonic stage. American commitments and policies have not changed. What has happened is that one of our promissory Asian notes has had to be met. If American foreign policy is interventionist now, it was also interventionist then. The

American outlook and style remain the same now as they were then. None of this led to notable unrest or dissatisfaction. It is the war as such, the war taken in isolation from all other considerations, that has provided the principal and immediate cause of the debate. Vietnam raises issues whose significance go well beyond the war. Even so, the debate would not have arisen, and probably could not have arisen, in the absence of the war we have waged in Vietnam.

It is also true that the debate would not have aroused the passions it has were it not for those features which set this war apart from other wars the nation has fought. Although some observers have sought to explain the intensity of dissent over Vietnam in terms of a changed attitude toward war, it seems more plausible to explain the dissent in terms of the features that have marked this particular war. It is by now banal to say that from the very outset the war has seemed confusing, frustrating, and repugnant. Yet it has been all of these things. It has been a confusing war not only in its immediate origins but even in the identity of the adversary. It has been a frustrating war in the elusiveness, if not indefinability, of the objectives for which the war has ostensibly been fought and in the seeming indifference of those we presumably sought to help. It has been a repugnant war not for the reason that it has claimed a larger portion of the noncombatant population than previous wars—indeed, it has not done so—but because the very nature of the war has not permitted a meaningful distinction between combatants and civilians. It has even been a humiliating war, given the disparity in power of the adversaries. The disparity could be glossed over for a time and pride assuaged if only by the device of making North Vietnam the proxy of China. But this device for creating a bigger and more worthy adversary in the end proved unpersuasive. We have been, in fact, at war with a very small state, however much it has been supplied by its major allies, and the only thing more humiliating than being at war with so small a power is to be militarily frustrated by it.

In all these respects, as critics have never tired of pointing out, Vietnam must be distinguished from our previous wars, and particularly the Korean War. Although the contrast with Korea has been frequently overdrawn, it still has enough truth to be effective. In its immediate origins Korea did not raise the doubt and uncertainty, and even the suspicion of duplicity, that Vietnam raised. If both Korea and Vietnam have been civil wars, as they have been, it remains the case that there are civil wars and civil wars, and that the difference between them may be enormous. In Korea the initial objective of the war, to repel the aggressor, was neither elusive nor unobtainable. It was the subsequent and expanded objective of uniting Korea by force that provoked Chinese intervention and was considered, rightly or wrongly, unobtainable without running too great a risk of general war. Even so, the initial objective of the war was realized, and in all likelihood could have been realized much sooner had it not been made to depend on the disputed issue of prisoner-of-war repatriation.

There is little parallel here with Vietnam, just as there is little parallel in the morale and effectiveness of those on whose behalf we intervened in the two instances. Whereas the army of South Korea was an effective fighting force within six months of the outbreak of war, the army of South Vietnam remained ineffective despite years of American effort. In South Korea it was at least possible to distinguish between civilian and enemy combatants, given the absence of a guerrilla movement in the South and the hostility of the South Koreans to their invading northern brothers. In South Vietnam the difficulty of making this distinction could not but prove morally debilitating, not so much because of the actual quantity of death and destruction visited upon the civilian population but because of the circumstances in which this death and destruction occurred. If killing the innocent is an evil whatever the circumstances, there is still a difference between doing so in a war that is broadly supported by the civilian population, which must suffer the incidental if unavoidable consequences of military operations, and doing so in a war that is, at best, borne indifferently by the affected population. This difference is all the more significant where the justification of military intervention is made to depend in large measure on the purpose of enabling a people freely to determine their destiny. Given this purpose, the will of a people to determine their destiny and to preserve their independence justifies, at least in part, the suffering inflicted on those who have taken no direct part in the war. In South Korea there was never much doubt about the quality of this will. In South Vietnam there was never anything but doubt about it.

These considerations point to one side of the dilemma that marked the Johnson administration's persistent attempts to provide a satisfactory rationale for the war in Vietnam. In the main, that rationale followed two principal lines, at times emphasizing the one in preference to the other, more often combining the two with nearly equal emphasis. On the one hand, the American intervention was justified in terms of the freedom and self-determination of the South Vietnamese. "Our objective," President Johnson declared in his first major address following the initiation of aerial bombardment against North Vietnam, "is the independence of South Vietnam, and its freedom from attack.

We want nothing for ourselves, only that the people of South Vietnam be allowed to guide their own country in their own way." On the other hand, the American intervention was justified in terms of America's security interests, whether identified with the integrity and continued independence of the nations of Southeast Asia, or with the containment of China throughout Asia or, more generally still, with the defense of world order. If in the later stages of the conflict the emphasis appeared to shift to America's security interests, they were never really absent from the Johnson administration's rationale for the war.

Thus in the address cited above, the President, far from ignoring the nation's security interests, stated: "We fight because we must fight if we are to live in a world where every country can shape its own destiny. And only in such a world will our own freedom be finally secure." And further: "We are also there to strengthen world order. ... To leave Vietnam to its fate would shake the confidence ... in the value of American commitment, the value of America's word. The result would be increased unrest and instability, and even wider war." Three weary and frustrating years later, in his dramatic announcement that he would neither seek nor accept another term in office, President Johnson declared that "the heart of our involvement in South Vietnam has always been America's security. And the larger purpose of our involvement has always been to help the nations of Southeast Asia become independent, self-sustaining members of the world community, at peace with themselves and with all others."

There is nothing novel in this theme, particularly in the fusion of the interested and disinterested elements which together comprised the American rationale for the war. Essentially the same theme, with the same fusion of arguments, formed the rationale of the policy of containment when it was initiated in 1947. In what is now the historic expression of that policy, the Truman Doctrine, President Truman declared that a willingness "to help free people to maintain their free institutions and their national integrity against aggressive movements that seek to impose upon them totalitarian regimes ... is no more than a frank recognition that totalitarian regimes imposed on free peoples, by direct or indirect aggression, undermine the foundations of international peace and hence the security of the United States." The assistance to Greece and Turkey, which formed the immediate purpose of President Truman's address, was to be understood in these terms, as was the effort to reconstruct and defend Western Europe. The American intervention in the Korean conflict followed along similar lines, as did the subsequent expansion of American commitments in

Asia. In 1960 a high official of the Johnson administration, in reflecting on the manner in which successive American administrations since the turn of the century have conceived of the nation's interests, summarized it in approving terms that might just as well have been later written for Vietnam: "It appears to be a characteristic of American history that this nation cannot be effective in its military and foreign policy unless it believes that both its security interests and its commitment to certain moral principles require the nation to act."[4]

What is novel, then, is clearly not the essential rationale given for the war. Instead, it is the notable lack of success the Johnson administration enjoyed in making this rationale persuasive, at least in making it persuasive to many who had afforded support in the recent past for American foreign policy. The dilemma of the Johnson administration was its apparent inability successfully to represent the war in Vietnam either as a vindication of the principles of freedom and self-determination or as a measure indispensable for American security. Whether such representation could have been successfully made at all, whether the nature of the case permitted it to be made, is not in question here, but only the failure experienced in presenting a persuasive rationale for the war.

It will not do to explain this failure simply in terms of the intrinsic, and perhaps even the unique, difficulties that arose in the course of the Vietnamese war. Nor will it suffice to account for the significance of the ensuing debate simply in terms of these difficulties. Although the debate would not have occurred in the absence of the war, and although the intensity of passion it aroused would not have been as great if the war had been fought in less difficult circumstances, it does not follow that the significance of the debate must be found merely in the fact that we have engaged in a particularly distasteful and difficult war. The meaning of Vietnam, the significance of the debate it has engendered, is not, as some have insisted, simply that we chose a very poor place to wage a war, whatever the reasons for doing so. It is not simply a gigantic piece of bad luck. If the present debate would not have arisen in the absence of the war, if the passions aroused would not have been as great in a war fought in less difficult circumstances, the question persists, why we chose to intervene in circumstances so unpromising. Is the significance of Vietnam that it has revealed, and revealed in the most dramatic manner, the inadequacies of the methods by which the nation conducts its foreign policy, in-

4. Walt W. Rostow, *The United States in the World Arena* (New York: Harper & Bros., 1960), p. 547.

adequacies that reflect not only upon the bureaucracy charged with the conduct of foreign policy but upon the nature of the relations between bureacracy and public? Is the significance of Vietnam that it has revealed the shortcomings of a philosophy of incrementalism when it is taken from its appropriate democratic domestic setting and applied to the far less favorable environment of state relations? Is the significance of Vietnam that it has revealed what can happen as a result of "a long exercise in national inadvertence, of a long series of partial decisions, none of them taken with any clear comprehension of the depths of involvement to which they were bringing us"?[5]

No doubt, this view, which finds in Vietnam a striking failure of the entire foreign policy mechanism, is a signal part of the truth. Yet it is difficult to believe that it is the whole truth or even that it is the most important truth about Vietnam. If Vietnam has a significance that goes beyond the issue of method, if it has an importance that transcends the war itself, it must be seen in the policy—and outlook—that made Vietnam an ever-present possibility. That policy and outlook are not simply the work of the Johnson administration, as some critics appear to believe, just as they are not the work of its immediate predecessor. The essential elements of America's present Asian policy were determined in the course of the war in Korea. In fashioning these elements of policy, the Truman administration applied to Asia a more general policy it had already applied to Europe, a general policy that since its first expression in March, 1947, had become known as the Truman Doctrine. In doing so, the Truman administration was not blind to the obvious differences between Europe and Asia. Nor have succeeding administrations been blind to these differences. Then as now, however, an awareness of the huge disparities between Europe and Asia has not dissuaded four successive administrations from attempting to contain communist power in Asia, whether Soviet, North Korean, Chinese, or North Vietnamese, and to do so, as we have already observed, in terms of the same rationale, the same fusion of interested and altruistic reasons, given today for the war in Vietnam. Then as now American power and leadership were to be employed to create and maintain a stable world order, an order which would enable peoples to work out their own destinies in their own way and, by enabling them to do so, thereby ensure American security. If the recent debate over American foreign policy has a significance that transcends Vietnam, it is because it again has raised the issues of the Truman

5. George F. Kennan, "The Quest for Concept in American Foreign Policy," *Harvard Today* (September, 1967), p. 16.

Doctrine, issues that concern the scope, ideological temper, means, and purposes of American foreign policy. But it has done so in circumstances substantially different from the circumstances of a generation ago. Therein must be found the broader significance of the debate, for the changes that have occurred require us to look at issues that have persisted for a generation in a new light and to invest them with new meaning.

3

It is not the novelty, then, of the arguments marking the debate that ultimately must give it a significance greater than Vietnam, but the novelty of the environment in which the arguments have been made. Indeed, what is striking in the debate has been the remarkable continuity of the arguments with those of a generation ago. This is evidently true of the official rationale given for American foreign policy. There are some variations in theme; it would be astonishing if there were not, given the changes that have occurred in intervening years. If these variations are not without importance, they nevertheless have left unaltered the essential rationale for American policy.

This rationale is based on a vision of world order—a vision that embodies the American purpose—the principal elements of which were set forth in the Truman Doctrine. Reiterated on innumerable occasions, the basic requirements of that order are, to cite a recent expression of them, "that acts of aggression and breaches of the peace have to be suppressed, that disputes ought to be settled by peaceful means, that the basic human rights ought to be sustained, and that governments must cooperate across their frontiers in the great humanitarian purposes of all mankind." In these words of former Secretary of State Dean Rusk, words that formed an almost invariable preface to any of his general pronouncements on the nation's foreign policy or the meaning of the war in Vietnam, critics came to see something intrinsically unserious. But if Secretary Rusk was unserious in his statements, the same must be said of every Secretary of State and President over the past generation. All have insisted that the first and foremost principle of world order is that aggression shall not be resorted to, that states shall not use armed force or the threat of armed force save as a legitimate measure of self- or collective defense. All have insisted upon the right of peoples to choose their own political system free from outside pressures or threats. All have believed that the spread and ultimate triumph of the institutions of freedom would follow upon the observance of these principles.

If the American concept of world order partakes of great general-ities, none of its principal exponents has assumed that these general-ities could provide, in and of themselves, a sufficient guide to action, or that they could be applied without regard to the particular cir-cumstances attending, and invariably limiting, their application. None has assumed that these principles could be sought independently of the existing distribution of power, though few have been willing to acknowledge the scope of potential conflict between requirements of principle and requirements of power. Finally, none has assumed a correspondence between postulated order and political reality, a cor-respondence which would make the pursuit of order superfluous. What has been assumed is both the desirability of these great general-ities as goals and the necessity of seeking them in order to maintain an environment in which freedom in America could and would be assured.

The American concept of world order has not been free of diffi-culties, in part the result of the enduring nature of international so-ciety, which may impose the dilemma of choosing between peace and the preservation of other interests; in part the result of the very inter-ests America has pursued, above all the interest in promoting freedom, which may impose the dilemma of choosing between nonintervention and safeguarding a desirable internal order of states. The difficulties inherent in the American concept of world order have been equally inherent in the principal policy expression of this order—containment. If these difficulties have not prevented the rationalization and even the implementation of policy, it is because they have always been qualified by the conviction that communism—whether monolithic or polycentric—provided the principal and, indeed, the only substantive threat to world order. It is this conviction that gives an apparent con-sistency to what would otherwise appear as inconsistent. It is this con-viction and the actions to which it has led that give concrete meaning to what would otherwise appear as an abstract scheme without tangi-ble relation to the realities of power. And it is the same conviction that permits justifying the neglect and even the occasional open dis-regard of professed principles as not subversive of an order compris-ing those principles.

What is relevant here is not the validity of this conviction but the insistence with which, and the manner in which, successive administra-tions, and particularly the Johnson administration, have identified this concept of world order and American security. Whether projected in immediate or in long-range terms, whether made explicit or merely implicit, whether related directly to traditional purpose or considered separately from purpose, that identification forms the nerve root of efforts to vindicate American foreign policy. Thus the policy of containment in Asia today is seen as the lineal descendant of the policy of containment in Europe, and both are found to serve the same vital interests and to further the same over-all purpose of achieving and maintaining a desirable world order. So, too, the principal instrument of containment (apart, of course, from American power itself), the American alliance system, is still regarded as the vital ligament of world order, the continued integrity of which forms an indispensable condition of American security. In this view, the decisive issues are not whether the circumstances attending a policy of containment in Asia are different from those in Europe, since they obviously are very different, but the reasons for undertaking containment yesterday in Europe and today in Asia. These reasons, it is asserted, remain essentially the same. The threat to world order, hence to American security, may be more subtle and complex today than the threat of twenty years ago, but it is not less real. Failure to oppose, by whatever means necessary, the forcible expansion of Asian communism—whether Chinese, North Korean, or North Vietnamese—will jeopardize the entire structure of world order so painfully constructed over two decades.

The conviction that world order forms an undifferentiated whole, that a challenge by a communist power to one part of this order is a challenge to every part, not only accounts for the corollary conviction that peace is indivisible, it also explains the largely undifferentiated character of interests. To be sure, American foreign policy does not and cannot entirely deny the elementary need to distinguish and to order interests. At the same time, the insistence with which the American conception of world order is seen as an undifferentiated whole, identified with American security, does clearly militate toward such denial. If it is once accepted that all parts are interdependent, then each part is, for all practical purposes, equally important. The consistency with which the "domino effect" has been invoked in every crisis of American foreign policy, from President Truman's request for aid to Greece and Turkey to the war in Vietnam, cannot be attributed simply to the need for exaggeration in order to obtain public support for foreign policy. In large measure, the invocation of that effect must be attributed to the conviction that to pick and choose the circumstances of American opposition to communist aggression, according to some arbitrary scheme of the relative importance of the interests involved, would be to jeopardize the whole fabric of international order upon which American security depends. The insistence on the indivisibility of peace is therefore only another way of insisting on the undifferentiated character of the interests constitutive of world order and American security.

These themes were afforded a striking illustration in the rationale for the American commitment in Vietnam. In its essential form that rationale has had no novel elements distinguishing it from the views set forth by earlier administrations. Despite some variations in emphasis, what is significant has been the element of continuity. For those who have grasped the deeper meaning of American foreign policy over the past generation, Vietnam must be seen as a problem of how the peace of the world is to be organized and maintained. Is that order, and the peace it implies, to be one of consent or one of coercion, one that safeguards the right of self-determination or one that destroys this right, one that provides an environment favorable to the growth of free institutions or one that encourages the spread of arbitrary and irresponsible power? This is the ultimate issue that two administrations have found at stake in Vietnam. It is an issue that is seen to transcend Vietnam and Southeast Asia, however important the immediate interest in preserving the integrity of the region. It is presumably the same fundamental issue that the Truman Doctrine responded to a generation ago in calling for, and in initiating, the historic transformation in American foreign policy.

The continuity that marks the rationale for American foreign policy also marks the criticism presently made of American foreign policy. Thus what is criticized as "globalism" today was also criticized in an earlier period. Globalism is a sin that has many meanings, but none of these meanings was unknown to the critics of a generation ago (some of whom are still the critics of today). The perfect expression of it is, of course, the Truman Doctrine, with its apparently unlimited and consequently indiscriminate commitment—"we must assist free peoples to work out their destinies in their own way"—its sense of universal crisis—"At the present moment in world history every nation must choose between alternative ways of life"—and its messianic hope of redeeming history—"To insure the peaceful development of nations, free from coercion . . . to make possible lasting freedom and independence for all. . . ."

To the critics of yesterday, as to the critics of today, the root of the American crisis in foreign policy is a failure of political intelligence, an incapacity to see the world for what it is rather than what we would like it to be, and, consequently, an unwillingness to accept and to adjust to the "real" world with its never-ending conflict and strife. A mindless, if not quite evil, interventionism was seen to be the almost inevitable consequence of this crusading style marked by its unlimited aspirations and its inability to make those distinctions necessary for a rational and effective foreign policy. The prospect of an overextended America, committed by an indiscriminate anticommunism to intervene anywhere and everywhere in order to maintain the status quo, was raised then as it is raised still more insistently today. And although the great transformation of American foreign policy did not coincide with a domestic crisis, then as now critics predicted that globalism must eventually erode American political institutions and subvert domestic efforts at reform.[6]

If this criticism has an impact today that it did not have before, if it enjoys a degree of acceptance that it did not enjoy a generation ago, the reasons must be found in the circumstances in which it is made. It is not simply that the rhetoric of yesterday has increasingly become the reality of today, that the Truman Doctrine has become policy whereas before it was little more than aspiration. It is that the rhetoric of yesterday has increasingly become the reality of today in circumstances that bear only a limited resemblance to the circumstances of yesterday. Whatever the declared scope and aspiration of the Truman Doctrine, the policy of containment to which it gave rise was primarily a response to what was considered at the time a serious and direct threat to American security resulting from the postwar weakness and instability of Western Europe. The initial measures of containment, the Marshall Plan and the North Atlantic alliance, formally expressed, and thereby made unmistakable, the vital American interest in preserving the security and independence of the nations of Western Europe. In the context of Soviet-American rivalry, they constituted a clear acknowledgment that the domination of Western Europe by the Soviet Union might shift the world balance of power decisively against the United States and thus open the Western Hemisphere to the encroachment of the adversary. At the very least, it was assumed that domination of Western Europe by the Soviet Union would result in a security problem for the United States, the solution of which would severely strain the nation's resources and jeopardize its democratic institutions.

6. These themes formed the substance of Walter Lippmann's critique both of the Truman Doctrine and of the policy of containment as formulated by George F. Kennan in his now famous article "The Sources of Soviet Conduct," *Foreign Affairs* (July, 1947). See Walter Lippmann, *The Cold War* (New York: Harper & Bros., 1947). The charge that containment of the Soviet Union would subvert domestic efforts at reform was central in the break with the Truman administration by Henry Wallace and many of his supporters.

One may ask whether these assumptions were well-founded, whether by the late 1940s the security of the United States was in fact so dependent on the maintenance of a balance of power in Europe. In retrospect, a case can be made that this dependence was exaggerated, that the structure and bases of power had already changed in ways that made the security of America much less dependent upon a European balance of power than only a decade before, and that the prospect had already arisen of a security—at least a physical security— no longer dependent on what transpired outside the Western Hemisphere. It is not surprising, however, that a persuasive case to this effect was not made at the time. If security policies point to the future, as they necessarily must do, the standards they erect are largely anchored in the past. It is men's experience rather than, or more than, their reason that is the decisive influence in the judgments they make on their security. In the case of America in the late 1940s the most relevant experience was, of course, the period preceding and including World War II, an experience that seemed to demonstrate conclusively the intimate dependence of American security on a European balance of power. To be sure, this immediate experience has to be placed against the background of the more general experience of isolationism, that is, the period of well over a century, when American security appeared as unconditioned by events outside the Hemisphere. But it was precisely this more general experience of free and seemingly unconditioned security that accentuated the sense of insecurity when it did finally occur. In view of the nation's experience from the early nineteenth century to the 1930s, the period that followed and that culminated in the early years of the Cold War was bound to provoke a strong, in retrospect perhaps an exaggerated, sense of insecurity.

This emphasis on the security motive in the early policy of containment need not, and should not, be pushed to the point of excluding other considerations. Containment in Europe was not undertaken solely for reasons of security narrowly construed, and no one contended so at the time. Considerations of political and cultural affinity were evidently very important. Moreover, the security motive itself was not clearly separated from other and broader considerations, as, indeed, it has seldom been so separated in American diplomacy. The security of America was not seen as something apart from the broader purpose of America abroad. Then as now the preservation of values and institutions identified with the life of the nation was seen to require an external environment whose characteristics extended beyond the requirements of a balance of power. Then as now the conviction persisted that the preservation of the institutions of freedom in America is dependent upon their preservation—or eventual realization—elsewhere in the world. Then as now security was interpreted as a function both of a balance of power between states and of the internal order maintained by states. Finally, then as now the concern for order formed a general yet important element of policy.

But if it is true that the security motive in the early policy of containment included a broader motive for policy as well, if it is true that American security and the American purpose of preserving and extending freedom were never clearly separated, it is still the case that a narrower and more traditional conception of security—security interpreted as a function of a balance of power—received the greater emphasis. One may say that if containment always implied a concept of world order, which it evidently did, there was still a difference between the two, if only as a matter of emphasis and priority. Whatever the larger implications of the Truman Doctrine, the policy of containment as initially applied to Europe was more or less synonymous with a balance-of-power policy. The security interest of containment overrode all other considerations. And it was the primacy of the security interest, which found its principal expression in America's European policy, that largely neutralized the criticism made against the larger implications of American policy.

These same considerations help to explain the relative absence of dissent to the intervention in Korea as well as to other measures taken in Asia concomitantly with that intervention, measures which laid the basis of American containment policy in Asia. It is ironic that the decision which, more than any other decision, determined America's postwar Asian policy provoked so little controversy at the time it was taken. In some measure, the explanation is to be found in the events immediately marking the outbreak of the Korean conflict and particularly the fortuitous circumstances which permitted the United Nations Security Council to sanction the American action in Korea. Far more significant, however, was the apparent threat to Japanese security held out by the aggression against South Korea, if that aggression were to go unopposed. But the most important consideration, the consideration that seems to have overshadowed all others, was simply the connection drawn, whether rightly or wrongly, between Korea and Western Europe. The attack upon South Korea in June, 1950, followed closely upon the coup in Czechoslovakia, the blockade of Berlin, the first Soviet explosion of an atomic device, and the Chinese communist accession to power. These events were widely interpreted as a mounting communist offensive which was increasingly taking a military form and which, if left unopposed, might well eventuate in an armed attack against Western Europe. During the first year of the Korean War, and even after, the fear that Europe might be attacked was deep and persistent. It was this fear that above all else explains the relative absence of dissent to the Korean intervention and, indeed, to the other measures taken in Asia at the same time. And it was the primacy of the security interest at the time of Korea, an interest centered in Europe, that largely neutralized early criticism of extending American containment policy to Asia.

In the decade following the initiation of containment, Korea stands out as the decisive event in the evolution of American policy. The Korean experience largely determined the form and course that the great transformation in American foreign policy eventually took. At the outbreak of the Korean War, it was uncertain whether America would extend its alliance commitments beyond the Western Hemisphere, the North Atlantic region, and the defensive perimeter in the Pacific running from the Ryukyus to the Philippine Islands. Even within the area of commitment, the means by which America would implement its commitment to Western Europe remained uncertain. Korea put an end to these uncertainties. In Europe, the Korean conflict led to the re-establishment of American forces, the establishment of an integrated command structure, the decision to rearm Germany, and the agreement on a common defense strategy. In Asia, the Korean War led to American intervention in the Chinese civil conflict and prompted the conclusion of a series of bilateral and multilateral alliances that continue today roughly to define the extent of the American commitment in that area.

The wisdom of this sudden extension of containment to Asia, where it was to apply primarily as a barrier to Chinese expansion, did not pass unchallenged. To most critics it appeared, and continues to appear today, as the misapplication of a strategy that was sound only when applied to Europe. In brief the criticism went as follows: Whereas in Europe military containment was undertaken primarily in response to the threat of an overt armed attack, and on behalf of nations only temporarily weak, in Asia military containment would have to be undertaken in response to threats that primarily took the form of civil conflicts, though aided in varying degree from outside, and on behalf of nations that were likely to remain weak and divided for a very long time. Whereas in Europe American alliance policy was directed against a conventional military threat, in Asia it was directed against a threat that fed upon and exploited—though it did not create—genuinely revolutionary conditions. Whereas in Europe American policy had the support of those we sought to protect, in Asia this support was lacking on the whole. Thus even when Chinese expansion assumed a pre-dominantly military character, it would do so in ways (subversion, indirect aggression) that normally could not be countered by a strategy that had been effective in Europe. With few exceptions, alliances with Asian states had no solid foundation, did not express a mutuality of benefits and liabilities, and did not respond to American interests in the area, which are primarily political rather than military. Moreover, given the obvious differences between Europe and Asia, the attempt to carry out a policy of military containment in Asia could not avoid the likelihood of creating highly dependent—that is, imperial—relationships. Finally, in this earlier period as today, it was argued that even where the effort to contain communist expansion through military means might prove relatively effective, it must result in the overexten-sion of American power.

At the root of this criticism over American containment policy in Asia, and more particularly of the means by which this policy was to be implemented, is a persistent and substantial, though frequently ob-scured, disagreement over the nature of American interests in Asia and, indeed, in the world at large. That disagreement, it is true, cannot be usefully considered without regard to the quantity and quality of American power as well as the circumstances in which this power must be employed. To the extent, however, that criticism of American con-tainment policy in Asia is made to turn on the question of American capabilities, it obscures the vital issue of the interests that policy is presumably intended to serve, quite apart from the power available for realizing these interests. Yet the issue of interests is critical if for no other reason than that the insistence on the limits of American power has been as misleading as it has been well founded. In an earlier period, as today, America's Asian policy has not so much exposed the limits of American power—at least, it has not done so in a literal sense—as it has raised the issue of the wisdom and desirability of the interests on behalf of which power is to be employed. No doubt, inter-ests are themselves determined by the price they entail, or the price they are expected to entail. But this truism only serves to emphasize, and particularly in America's case, the central importance of the issue of interests. In this sense, Vietnam is only the latest illustration of a continuing disagreement over the nature of American interests in Asia that is partly obscured by concentration on the limits of American power. Essentially what is at issue is a broad disparity of view over both the conditions, and even the very meaning, of American security and the other interests whose vindication would justify, if necessary, the use of American military power.

If this essential issue was not clearly illuminated in the years following Korea, it was primarily because the circumstances of this period did not put it sharply and clearly to the test. Not only did the nature of the threat seem clear, particularly in its relation to the world balance of power, but also the direct and immediate relevance of the threat to American security went, on the whole, undisputed. Given these circumstances, America's Asian policy was supported for over a decade by what may be termed a negative consensus. Vietnam put this negative consensus to the test and laid bare its fragility. Moreover, the test occurred in circumstances that could not but illuminate the essential issue that has always provoked a disparity of view over America's Asian policy. The central circumstance, the circumstance that comprises, as it were, all other circumstances, is the substantial change in the structure of American security. Whereas in the 1940s it was still entirely possible, if not entirely plausible, to imagine an imbalance of military power that would threaten the physical security of America, today this contingency no longer appears a meaningful possibility. Whereas in the 1940s it was still entirely possible, and altogether plausible, to imagine an imbalance of power resulting in a security problem the solution of which would severely strain the nation's resources and jeopardize its democratic institutions, today this contingency is, at best, very remote.

In part, this change in the structure of American security is the consequence of military-technological developments. Although nuclear-missile weapons have dealt a decisive blow to the territorial "impermeability" of the state, the security effects of these weapons have by no means been consistently negative. On the contrary, short of the extreme situation, they have markedly improved the security problem for their possessors, at least if security is equated with physical security. If in the extreme situation the great nuclear power is indeed absolutely vulnerable vis-à-vis its great adversary, in other than extreme situations these same weapons render a great nuclear power physically secure to a degree that great powers seldom, if ever, enjoyed in the past. For the first time in history the prospect arises of a physical security that need no longer prove dependent on time-honored calculations of a balance of power. For the first time the prospect arises, if it has not already materialized, of a physical security no longer dependent on what transpires outside the North American continent.

In part, this change in the structure of American security is the consequence of economic and technological growth that has steadily widened the margin of power, at least in all forms other than strategic, between America and her nearest competitors, while markedly reducing the nation's economic dependence on the outside world. This growth has not resulted in conferring upon America a new status in the 1960s that was not already enjoyed in the 1940s. What it has done is to consolidate and further strengthen the status of preponderant world power while exorcising the fears (and, for others, the hopes) of America's relative power decline that were widely entertained in the late 1950s and even the early 1960s. So full has the circle of men's expectations turned today that the degree of American preponderance is, if anything, exaggerated. Even so, the margin of power that is currently enjoyed, and the margin of power that is very likely to be enjoyed in the foreseeable future, make it difficult to conjure up the vision of an imbalance of power resulting in a security problem whose solution would severely strain the nation's resources and jeopardize its democratic institutions.

In part, finally, this change in the structure of American security is the consequence of developments by now so apparent that they are mentioned only for the sake of formal completeness. The emergent, though still evolving, political and economic constellation of Western Europe, the fragmentation and increasing state of disarray of the once vaunted communist bloc, the disruption of the Sino-Soviet alliance, the ascendance of Japan to an economic position in Asia and in the world that is bound eventually to find a political and military expression more commensurate with this position—these and yet other developments have resulted in a Eurasia that bears only the faintest resemblance to the Eurasia of the late 1940s. The great fear once entertained by American strategists, a fear which persisted into the postwar period, that a hostile power or combination of powers might succeed in uniting Eurasia and in turning its immense resources against the Western Hemisphere, can no longer be seriously entertained.

The measure of the change that has occurred in the structure of American security is strikingly illustrated in the contrast between the significance of containing the Soviet Union in the 1940s and the significance of containing China today. The early policy of containing the Soviet Union in Europe, as already observed, was more or less synonymous with a policy of the balance of power, and not merely with a regional balance of power but with the world balance. Obviously, if the Soviets had come to dominate Western Europe, they would have destroyed any semblance of a European balance of power. They would also have threatened, if not overturned, the world balance. The equation of containing Soviet expansion in Europe, maintaining a regional and world balance of power, and safeguarding the foundations of American security was reasonably clear and persuasive. A similar equation in the case of China today is neither clear nor persuasive. In Asia, containment has no plausible relation to the world balance of power, because the expansion of China in Asia cannot substantially affect that balance. Even the containment of China and the maintenance of an Asian balance are not identical, unless we are to discount Soviet power to the west and north, dismiss the emergent power of Japan to the east, and neglect the power—if only naval and aerial—of the United States to the east and south. If, however, we take this power into consideration, it is apparent that a balance of power already exists in Asia, that it has existed for some time, and that China does not presently have, and cannot be expected to have in the near future, the power to overturn this balance. It is true that this balance cannot be relied upon to contain Chinese expansion to the south and southeast. But the expansion of China in the south, even if it were to take an overtly military form and to be entirely unimpeded (though neither of these contingencies is plausible), still cannot by itself decisively affect the Asian, let alone the world, balance of power. (The Asian balance would be altered only if China were to dominate Japan, and it is doubtful that even this would affect the world power balance.) The threat that Chinese expansion, or Chinese and North Vietnamese expansion, poses for American security differs not only quantitatively but also qualitatively from the threat posed by Soviet expansion a generation ago.

This conclusion, with its obvious implications for American foreign policy, need not be accepted, especially if security is not limited to the nation's physical security as well as to the integrity of its institutions. And even if security is so limited, it need not be accepted if the safety of the nation's institutions and, more generally, the quality of its domestic life are made dependent on the preservation and the eventual realization of these institutions elsewhere in the world. In turn, the preservation and the eventual realization of these institutions elsewhere in the world may be found to require a congenial world order, the creation and maintenance of which are deemed to be the unavoidable responsibilities of the nation. Through this reasoning a nation's security is made indistinguishable from a purpose that gives to the nation's existence, hence its security, a potentially limitless dimension.

There is nothing new in the insistence upon identifying America's security with her purpose. That insistence is apparent in the Truman Doctrine, which, in turn, reflects a tradition that goes back to the very origins of American diplomacy. What is new are the lengths to which the identification of security and purpose has been carried in recent years. Nor will it do to dismiss expressions of this identification as mere rhetorical hyperbole, for it is the very breadth of the terms in which the American security interest is presently cast that is significant and that requires explanation. Yet there is no mystery in what often appears to critics as an emphasis on security that is almost inversely proportional to the security interests at stake. Whereas in the late 1940s America's purpose was a function of her security, in the late 1960s security has become a function of her purpose. It is because security in its more conventional and limited sense is no longer of paramount concern that its importance is so emphasized. It is because the nation is engaged in the vindication of other than, or more than, traditional security interests that security is so emphasized. This emphasis, then, simply reflects an awareness that security continues to provide the principal, though of course not the only, justification for employing force, that the invocation of security interests remains indispensable in order to sanction the costs of war. However great the emphasis placed on the larger purpose presumably informing American foreign policy, that purpose still cannot alone bear the burden of justifying the sacrifices entailed by the use of force. It can do so only if the nation's purpose is effectively equated with its security.

It is in the apparent failure to make this equation effective that we may find, if not the principal cause of the domestic dissent that emerged in the course of the Vietnamese war, then at least the principal weakness of the Johnson administration in dealing with domestic dissent. It is quite true that the reaction to Vietnam has been in large part a response to those features which have set this war apart from other wars the nation has waged. Moreover, it is well to recall that despite the distinctive characteristics of the war, opposition did not achieve significant proportions until the demands imposed by the war reached a certain level. Even then, it was the inability of the Johnson administration to make a persuasive case for believing military victory was possible, let alone imminent, without a still greater commitment of men and material that proved to be the breaking point. But these considerations could have the effects they ultimately did because the equation of security and purpose was never effectively made. Had that equation been effectively made, the frustration and distaste engendered by the Vietnamese war would in all likelihood never have achieved the proportions they did achieve. Had that equation been effectively made, the purely domestic sources of disaffection over Vietnam would probably never have attained the significance they did attain.

It is the change in the structure of American security that must account for much of the difficulty encountered by the Johnson administration in defending its commitment in Vietnam. For this change has meant that America's present interests and commitments are largely the result of a conception of security that can no longer satisfactorily account for these same interests and commitments. To put the matter somewhat differently, the principal reason for which we acquired our present interests and commitments, particularly in Asia, is no longer the reason for which we hold on to these same interests and commitments. There is a logic to the arguments urged in defense of the war and, more generally, of Asian policy as a whole, but it is not the logic of past arguments.

If the change that has occurred is obscured, this is due in part to the apparent ease with which the American purpose can be reconciled with very disparate policies, including an imperial policy. There has never been either a necessary or a self-evident relationship between commitment to the American purpose and commitment to a given foreign policy. The idea that there is such a relationship, that either a policy of isolationism or one of internationalism (or even one of interventionism) follows from the American purpose, has little basis in American history. The most disparate of policies apparently can be, and historically have been, reconciled with the nation's purpose. It is a commonplace that throughout America's history isolationists have only seldom considered themselves to be truly isolationists. They have not rejected the American purpose or mission of bringing the blessings of freedom to all men, and not only Americans; they have only insisted that this purpose must be achieved in a certain manner, that is, through a policy of nonentanglement. But nonentanglement from the very start encompassed an idea of "national duty," a duty to be served by, and implemented through, the power of moral example. The mission of regenerating the world and the isolationist impulse were seldom seen as contradictory. Instead, both arose from the central conviction of the unique character and absolute significance of our experience.

To say that both isolationist and interventionist impulses are rooted in the American purpose, and that both an isolationist and an interventionist policy may be reconciled with this purpose, is not to deny the obvious and important differences between the two. Although both impulses may have a common spiritual root, and both policies may be encompassed by the same purpose, it is still a matter of enormous importance which impulse and which policy prevail. In less categorical terms, what kind of compromise is reached between these two radical alternatives is enormously important. The nature of that compromise, the manner in which the American purpose is to be sought, has been a critical issue in nearly every great debate over American foreign policy since the beginning of the Republic. It is the larger issue raised by Vietnam, however seldom it is explicitly raised. Not only is it the larger issue raised by the present debate, circumstances have permitted the issue to assume a form it could not assume in the past. Whereas in the past, including even the recent past, America's position in the international system placed relatively narrow limits on the manner in which this issue would—and could—be resolved, America's present position has dramatically broadened the spectrum of possible solutions. At least, this is so if we assume that greater power confers greater freedom.

The point may be put more sharply. The significance of the recurring debate over the means of realizing the American purpose cannot usefully be considered apart from the circumstances surrounding the debate. In an earlier period, the circumstances attending this debate necessarily served to limit its scope and significance. If America was secure throughout the nineteenth century, her power relative to the power of others was still distinctly limited. In the present century, the steady growth of American power relative to the power of others has led to, and even forced, an almost continuing debate over the American purpose and how best to realize it. It is only in the face of a substantial threat to American security, narrowly conceived, that the debate over purpose has diminished in significance. Given the apparent recession of that threat concomitant with the sudden appreciation—perhaps the overappreciation—of America's preponderance, an issue never resolved has once again arisen and in a form it could never before assume. For the first time, circumstances permit the nation to come, as it were, face to face with its purpose, because for the first time circumstances no longer seem to place narrow limits on the means by which this purpose may be pursued.

What is relevant here is not the preferable solution to a traditional problem. It is the recognition that an overweening sense of purpose is one of the distinguishing marks of an imperial power. That this sense of purpose may be expressed, and in an earlier period was expressed, by a policy of isolation indicates its ambivalence for action, in part according to circumstance, not its inherently anti-imperial character. That the principal tenet of this purpose is avowedly and emphatically anti-imperial does not preclude the pursuit of goals

which, again according to the circumstances, may nevertheless result
in imperial relationships. Nor is it sufficient to dismiss the relevance
of the question—nation or empire?—simply by reaffirming that the
American dream remains domestic. If there is necessarily a point—
for America as for all nations—at which foreign policy has primacy
over domestic policy, the all-important issue is the manner in which
the security requirements of the nation are conceived. It may well be
true that so long as security is conceived in a traditional and restricted
manner as a function of the balance of power, the ultimate primacy
of foreign over domestic policy need not detract significantly from the
normal order of things in which domestic happiness and welfare are
primary. This is particularly so for states which, by virtue of relative
power and geography, enjoy a highly favorable measure of security.
Even for such fortunate states, however, the commitment in principle
to the primacy of domestic over foreign policy may mean little in
practice, if security is achieved only when, in the words of former
Secretary of State Rusk, "the total environment is safe." If security is
interpreted as a function both of a favorable balance of power between
states and of the internal order maintained by states, foreign policy
may have primacy over domestic policy in a way that is all-pervasive.

It is the insistence upon defining American security in terms of a
purpose beyond conventional security requirements that reinforces
the significance of that purpose as a national interest which may prove
indistinguishable from an imperial interest. It is the insistence upon
defining American security both in terms of the international relations
of states, though even this definition has been very broad, and in terms
of the internal nature of their politics that may readily transform a national interest into an imperial interest. That transformation need not
be marked by any clear break. The distinction between nation and
empire is one of degree; the imperial state is, as it were, the realization of aspirations already apparent in the less than imperial state.
Thus the identification of the imperial state and of those values presumably represented by it with a potentially universal community is
but a manifestation of a general tendency of states to identify the
collective self with something larger than the self. In turn, the progressive extension of the self must lead to the progressive extension
of perceived threats to that self.

From this viewpoint, the change in emphasis from containment to
world order reflects a progressive change in circumstances rather
than, or as much as, a change in purpose. It reflects, as already noted,
both the success of the initial policy of containment and the steady
expansion, concomitant with that success, of American interests and

the diversity of possible threats to them. At the same time, the change in circumstances that has attended, and in part resulted from, this success and expansion lays bare the principal difficulty of the rationale given for American policy today, a difficulty so clearly illuminated by Vietnam. For it was a narrower and more traditional conception of security that above all led to the transformation of American policy in the late 1940s. The same conception of security can no longer satisfactorily account for American foreign policy in the late 1960s. And it can no longer do so because the defense of American policy is no longer a defense of national security and interests but of imperial security and interests.

If an imperial commitment is nevertheless disavowed, this is scarcely surprising, given the prevailing interpretation of the American tradition and the seriousness with which an egalitarian ethos is taken by most of the world today. Still the question persists: If the measures—political, economic, military—required for the containment of communism in an earlier period elicited broad support, why is it that the measures presumably required for the containment of Asian communism today have failed to do so? In the main,[7] the answer given by defenders of American policy has been that the conditions of security are more difficult to perceive today. And they are more difficult to perceive because they no longer take a familiar form. Containment in Europe was initially undertaken in response to conditions whose meaning for American security was readily apparent, or very nearly so. Containment in Europe was undertaken primarily to prevent an imbalance of power, an imbalance that was seen at the time, and an imbalance that experience had enabled men to see at the time, as threatening American security in the direct and conventional sense. The same perceived threat to Europe and, consequently, to the world balance of power afforded the basis for, and gave support to, the initial extension of containment to Asia. The difficulty of containment in Asia today—apart from the admittedly distasteful and frustrating features that have marked the war in Vietnam—is therefore attributed to conditions of security that are unfamiliar, conditions that experience has not enabled men to perceive clearly, if at all.

The change in the geographical center of gravity of American foreign policy does not account for this failure of perception, though

---

7. We say in the main since there are other factors that are held up to account for this apparent lack of wide-spread support—a general weariness with external concerns, a growing concern with domestic problems, etc. The issue, however, is one of the relative priority or significance of the factors that deprive Asian containment of the broad support enjoyed by its predecessor.

conventional wisdom had decreed that American security could be threatened only by an imbalance of power centered in Europe, not an imbalance in Asia alone. To be sure, an imbalance of power in Asia is held to represent in and of itself a threat to American security. But the principal threat to American security, it is argued, can neither be confined to Asia nor understood simply in conventional balance-of-power terms with its emphasis upon parity or superiority in material power. Instead, it must be found in the temptation afforded adversary states in Asia and elsewhere, consequent upon an American failure to deter communist aggression, to challenge the entire structure of world order that American policy has sought to create and maintain in the post-World War II period, and to do so by means which must ultimately—and inevitably—raise the danger of nuclear war. That this challenge would be decentralized would not diminish the threat to American security. Whether communism is monolithic or pluralistic is not an argument on which all else can be made to depend. For the significance that is so regularly attached by critics to the present division of the major communist powers would prove compelling only if security were still to be understood in traditional, prenuclear terms. As between nuclear powers, however, if we are to speak of a balance of power at all, that balance must be understood not primarily in material terms but in psychological terms, not upon a structure of material power and therefore relative material advantage, but upon a structure of deterrent threat. There is no way to maintain the credibility and integrity of a deterrent threat save by manifesting a willingness to oppose forcible communist expansion, particularly when directed against an ally, and this even though such expansion is directly undertaken—indeed, independently undertaken—by a small communist state. For the deterrence of other and larger potential aggressors, however disunited, is dependent on the deterrence of all aggressors. It is the failure, then, to grasp the changed meaning of security today that must account for the misplaced emphasis critics insist upon attaching to the fact that communism is no longer monolithic.

These considerations also explain the insistence that the American alliance system is still the vital ligament of world order, whose continued integrity forms an indispensable condition of the nation's security. In this view, it is not decisive that the conditions attending the construction of the system no longer obtain. Critics may point out that whereas in the late 1940s an independent Europe, allied to the United States, formed an essential condition of U.S. security, this is no longer clearly the case; that whereas even in the late 1950s the strategic bases provided by allies in Europe and Asia formed an indispensable element of American security, in the late 1960s these bases have become dispensable; and that whereas no marked disparity between motivation and rationale characterized alliance policy in an earlier period, such a disparity is bound to characterize alliance policy today, since the purpose of this policy has changed from one of providing added and needed security to one of providing a manifestation of great power status and a means—though a means not always effective—of ensuring great power control.

The answers to this criticism are that it fails to appreciate the security significance of American alliance policy today and that it partially misinterprets the purpose and significance of this policy in an earlier period. Thus it is argued that even in an earlier period the purpose and significance of American alliance policy were not restricted to security considerations, narrowly and conventionally conceived. To the extent that alliance policy has reflected the more general policy of containment, it has also shared the same interests as containment, which were never narrowly conceived.

If the conditions in which the American alliance system was constructed have changed, the interest in world order this system reflects—and is, indeed, very nearly synonymous with—nevertheless remains. Moreover, that interest in world order cannot be considered today apart from American security. That critics do so is due, once again, to their assumption, however inarticulate and even unconscious, that security must still be seen in the conventional terms of a balance of power. But once this assumption is rejected, as it must be, it will be seen that the alleged changes in purpose and significance of the American alliance system are only apparent. The integrity of this system therefore remains as important today for world order and American security as it has ever been. To fail to defend any one of the component parts of the system is to jeopardize the whole. To jeopardize the whole is inevitably to incur the danger of a nuclear conflict.

This, in brief, has been the case for equating world order and American security. It is, of course, the same equation that has constituted the essential rationale made for the intervention in Vietnam. That equation, it is important to insist, does not depend and has never been made to depend upon the denial of circumstances apparent even to the casual observer. To this extent, critics who belabor the differences between Europe and Asia, and the consequent difficulties attending containment of communism in Asia, are pushing at open doors, since no one denies the differences. (It is another matter to assert that these differences not only render difficult but in fact must preclude the success of a policy of containment, military and otherwise, in Asia;

but this claim is by no means apparent.) The same must be said of the insistence with which critics of Vietnam have called attention to the fact that communism is no longer monolithic.

However slow American policy makers may have been to appreciate the breakdown of communist unity, the fact of this breakdown has not been in dispute during the controversy over Vietnam. What has been very much in dispute is the significance of this breakdown, particularly in the context of Vietnam. For supporters of the war, the fact of communist disunity cannot with safety be relied upon to limit the effect of a communist victory, presumably because the effects of a communist victory in South Vietnam would be limited neither by the independence of Hanoi nor by the breach between Moscow and Peking. A victory for Hanoi must and will be seen as a victory of Hanoi's major allies and supporters. That the allies of North Vietnam are antagonistic to each other, that they differ over the desired outcome in Vietnam, can only mean that the challenge to the present structure of world order consequent upon an American defeat in Vietnam would not be centrally directed. It cannot mean that there would be no challenge. Nor can it be taken to mean that this challenge would be confined to Southeast Asia or even to Asia as a whole.

In sum, then, the central contention has been that failure in Vietnam will place in jeopardy the efforts of twenty years. Even if it were conceded that the commitment in South Vietnam was unwise in the first place, the relevant consideration is that the commitment was made. Having been made, there remains no alternative but to honor it. The failure to do so, as supporters of the war never tire of pointing out, is to undermine faith in the American commitment elsewhere; it is to undermine faith even in the commitment made to those who may express serious doubt and dissatisfaction over American actions in Vietnam. The integrity of the American commitment is therefore at the heart of the problem in Vietnam. Fail on that commitment and all else will once again be placed in doubt. Vindicate that commitment and not only will the so-far desirable outcome of the Cold War be further consolidated, but a substantial step will have been taken toward tempering and moderating a revolution in Asia that as yet refuses to adjust in conduct and aspiration to the style and norms of a more conventional statecraft.

Can it be said that to the degree this argument is true it is a self-fulfilling truth? In part, it is just that. To justify an ever-expanding commitment in Vietnam the commitment had to be seen as vindicating ever-expanding, and vital, interests. To dissuade the adversary from matching that commitment, to persuade him of our seriousness and determination, it was necessary first to persuade ourselves that Vietnam represented vital American interests. For only in this manner could we persuade ourselves, and presumably the adversary as well, that our interests in the outcome of the war were such as to create a disparity of wills favorable to us. Moreover, that favorable disparity of wills, when taken together with our vast material superiority, would not only deter the adversary from continuing the conflict beyond a certain point, it would also deter the adversary's allies from supporting him beyond a certain point. But this by now familiar criticism may be, and frequently has been, pushed too far. The significance Vietnam has come to represent, and came to represent by 1965, was not simply a matter of our creation. In part, that significance was the inevitable outcome of the hegemonial conflict with both the Soviet Union and China, a conflict in which each disputed interest is seen on both or all sides as a symbol of the whole conflict, and in which each confrontation, whether direct or indirect, is looked upon by adversaries as a test case. If Vietnam was regarded as a test case for communist wars of national liberation, however misplaced it may have been so to regard it, no useful purpose is served by insisting that this alleged test case was little more than the invention of American policy makers.

It is, in fact, impossible to deny a certain plausibility to the rationale for the commitment in Vietnam, if only because projections of security ultimately rest on assumptions which have no satisfactory means of validation before the disputed result (after which validation may be superfluous). The lessons of history may be plausibly invoked in support of varying, if not contradictory, assumptions. Then, too, in a period when the bases of security have been largely transformed, it may be argued that the lessons of the past, quite apart from their ambiguity, can have no more than a limited relevance for the present. Indeed, despite the constant emphasis of administration spokesmen in defending Vietnam by invoking the lessons of history, it is not so much the lessons of the past that they have invoked but what are assumed to be the lessons of the present, lessons that are held to result from the transformed nature of the security problem. Finally, and perhaps most significantly, the plausibility of the official position results, ironically enough, precisely from an argument that cannot be openly made, that is, the argument that national security may come to depend upon imperial security, that the protection of conventional, yet vital, national interests may come to depend upon the protection of imperial interests.

This argument has formed the staple of the defense of empire through the ages. That there are scarcely any limits to what it can justify and has justified, once it is accepted, cannot be taken to prove that it is without substance, for it does possess a measure of truth despite its potentiality for abuse. To have achieved an imperial position may have been unwise, if at all avoidable. To hold on to that position may involve danger and certainly sacrifice. Even so, to surrender that position to hostile forces may involve no less, and more likely far greater, danger. As applied to America today, this is not the argument that the world must have order and that such order will be imposed by the powerful. Nor is it the argument that the world must have order and that order presupposes, even necessitates, a guarantor. (The latter argument is, after all, little more than a euphemistic way of stating the former argument, given the nature of international society.) Instead, it is the argument that the world must have order—even more, one of a certain kind—because America's security as a nation is inseparable from the preservation of a certain kind of order.

6

If the defense of American foreign policy rests very largely upon the equation of world order and American security, the criticism of policy has concentrated very largely upon attacking that equation and, of course, the consequences to which it has presumably led.[8] For most critics of American foreign policy, the history of the nation's diplomacy since the immediate post-World War II years is largely a history of decline. It is the history of a diplomacy that has turned almost full circle from clarity of concept, at least at the level of practical action, to obscurantism, and from modesty of action, to what can only be

8. It will be apparent in the pages to follow that little attempt has been made to deal with criticism of American foreign policy emanating either from the old right or the new left. Instead, attention is directed, on the whole, to the "moderate" and "realist" critics who have been in the mainstream of the postwar American approach to foreign policy. (Even this latter group reveals significant differences, for the mainstream is still broad and holds within it quite different fish.) There are, of course, points of correspondence between the critics comprising the new left and the critics who until recently formed a part of the foreign-policy consensus. This apparent agreement, however, may only obscure deeper disagreement. At any rate, the exclusion of critics from the new left is not to be interpreted as a judgment on the intellectual significance—or insignificance—of their position, but as an indication of their largely peripheral political significance in the current debate. We have already noted that it is not the opposition of those who have never really formed a part of the foreign-policy consensus that is the significant feature of the present debate, but the substantial defection of those who have formed a critical part of this consensus for the past generation.

termed a virtual compulsion for the disproportionate act.[9] It is the history of a diplomacy that was once seen by most of the world as the instrument of a progressive nation, and is now seen as the instrument of an increasingly repressive and "counterrevolutionary" imperial America. It is the history of a diplomacy that once responded to the true interests of America but no longer does. Although the world has changed, and changed profoundly, in the course of the past generation, we have not changed with it. "If there is a single indictment of the multiple and self-contradictory forms that American globalism takes," two critics assert, "it is simply that its arguments and rationales are out of date."[10] "To characterize American foreign policy in one sentence," another declares, "one could say that it has lived during the last decade or so on the intellectual capital which was accumulated in the famous fifteen weeks of the spring of 1947 ... and that this capital has now been nearly exhausted."[11] Moreover, what might still prove valid today in earlier policy has long since been eroded, whether through misunderstanding or deliberate rejection. Reviewing the history of American diplomacy since 1947, the author of the first crucial statement of postwar American containment policy concludes: "One by one, its essential elements were abandoned."[12] Thus a policy initially designed to restore and maintain a balance of power has been replaced by one that scorns so modest an objective. A policy once reasonably tolerant of revolutionary change has been succeeded by one intolerant of such change because of an obsessive fear of communism and an equally obsessive identification of revolutionary change with communism. A former reluctance to employ force save on behalf of narrowly construed vital interests has given way to the assertion of a right, and, indeed, an obligation, to take whatever measures are deemed necessary to prevent violent changes in the status quo.[13]

9. If most critics, apart from the revisionists, now see the early years of containment almost as the heroic period of American foreign policy, it is not because of but in spite of the Truman Doctrine. For the early years of containment are presumably marked by the triumph of policy over doctrine.

10. Edmund Stillmann and William Pfaff, *Power and Impotence: The Failure of America's Foreign Policy* (New York: Random House, Inc., 1966), p. 62.

11. Hans J. Morgenthau, "A New Foreign Policy for the United States: Basic Issues," *Bulletin of the Atomic Scientists* (January, 1967), p. 7.

12. George F. Kennan, "The Quest for Concept," *Harvard Today* (September, 1967), p. 16.

13. It is the assertion of this right, and obligation, that is held up as perhaps the essential feature marking America's policy as imperial, and even "imperialistic." Thus one critic writes: "In assuming that we have an obligation to smother violent changes in the status quo by discontented groups within various

This policy is bound to fail if only for the reason that it reflects a view of the world that is profoundly at odds with reality. Although the world is politically and ideologically pluralistic, American foreign policy proceeds from an assumption—or rather a conviction—that denies this pluralism. Instead, the world of the late 1960s is interpreted in essentially the same terms as the world of the late 1940s, as a world, in the words of the Truman Doctrine, dominated by a universal conflict between the forces of freedom and unfreedom. If that interpretation was inadequate even a generation ago, at least it bore some resemblance to reality. Today it no longer does so.

The results of persisting in this interpretation are already clear. A policy that does not and apparently cannot distinguish between vital and less-than-vital interests is bound to result in the overcommitment of the nation's resources. A policy that insists upon the identification of revolutionary change with communism and the latter with the triumph of the forces of unfreedom is bound to be driven into an increasingly futile counterrevolutionary stance which, if anything, succeeds only in promoting communism. And even when that stance does not prove futile or counterproductive, even when it does not overestimate what intervention can accomplish, it runs the danger of betraying the American purpose both abroad and at home. For in a world that is in many respects more diverse than it has ever been, in a world that has as many sources of conflict as it has ever had, the American purpose abroad can be directly pursued only through means which, paradoxically, deny that purpose. The denial of that purpose abroad cannot but eventually mean, as the war in Vietnam has shown, its denial at home as well.

Whether explicitly or implicitly, this criticism of American foreign policy raises four major interrelated questions: What are the vital interests of America? What is the nature of the threat to those interests? What can and should be done to preserve those interests? And, finally, what is America's purpose in today's world and how may that purpose best be realized?

It is scarcely surprising that critics should define the primary ends of American foreign policy in general terms that do not set them apart

---

countries, we are arrogating to ourselves the responsibility for being an international police power. We are doing so without anyone's consent and from no other motive than that we believe that our vision of a proper political order is valid for nations everywhere. This, whether we recognize it or not, is imperialism...." Ronald Steel, *Pax Americana* (New York: The Viking Press, Inc., 1967), p. 325.

from their opponents. For the critics of American policy, as for those who defend that policy, the great ends of policy must be the nation's physical security, the integrity of its institutions, and the well-being of its citizens. There can be little disagreement, then, over the one contingency that would above all others jeopardize the great ends of foreign policy. A major nuclear war—probably any nuclear war involving the great powers—would threaten America's survival as a nation. Accordingly, its prevention must form the foremost objective of policy. And this must be taken to mean that the prevention of any development that might be expected to increase significantly the danger of nuclear war constitutes a vital American interest.

The great ends of American foreign policy are not equated by critics simply with the prevention of nuclear war, however important that objective may be. At the very least, these ends are also equated with, or made dependent upon, the preservation of a balance of power in Europe and Asia. Now, as in the past, the maintenance of a favorable balance of power in Europe and Asia is considered a vital American interest. If anything, the more articulate and influential of the critics have gone out of their way to emphasize the continuity of this interest. Thus America is held to have a vital interest in protecting the nations of Western Europe against armed aggression (which, in present circumstances, can only mean Soviet aggression), just as she has a vital interest in protecting Japan against armed aggression (which, in present circumstances, can only mean Chinese aggression).

Given this definition of America's vital interest in Europe and Asia, *some* kind of policy of containment necessarily follows, so long as the Soviet Union and China are deemed to remain even potentially hostile and expansionist powers. To be sure, there is room for disagreement over the kind of containment policy to pursue, particularly in Asia. There is room for disagreement over what is to be contained and the proper means of containment. But if the assumption of potential hostility and expansion is once granted, it is scarcely consistent to affirm the interest in and to deny the need for some kind of policy of containment. In fact, with very few exceptions, the leading critics of America's Asian policy have insisted that the containment of China is a vital American interest. They have argued over what is to be contained and the proper means of doing so. They have argued over the prospects of Chinese expansion, particularly military expansion. But, at the very least, they have not questioned the need to contain Chinese military expansion, and to do so even when containment and the maintenance of an Asian balance of power are not identical.

This acknowledged continuity of vital interest in Europe and Asia extends as well to the Western Hemisphere. Critics may and do express a variety of views on the definition of, and the means of protecting, this interest. For some, the American hemispheric interest permits, and even requires, armed intervention if necessary to prevent the emergence of communist regimes. Geographical proximity, military security, and tradition (proprietary rights) sanction in Latin America what may not be sanctioned, and should not be undertaken, elsewhere. For others, American interest requires intervention only where a communist regime—or, for that matter, any regime—forms certain kinds of relationships with either the Soviet Union or China. For still others, America's vital interest in this Hemisphere is vindicated merely by the prevention of foreign (extrahemispheric) aggression. This apparently austere view need not prove to be too restrictive in practice, however, if the definition of aggression is sufficiently flexible. Indeed, despite the apparent distinctiveness of these views, they all share one decisive feature. Whatever the definition of America's vital interest in the Western Hemisphere, each assumes the maintenance of an order of power that ensures American hegemony.

The preservation of a favorable balance of power in Europe and Asia and a continued hegemony in the Western Hemisphere do not exhaust for most critics America's vital geographical interests. If these are the hard and undisputed core of those interests, they are not considered to form the whole of the interests that may justify armed intervention. There are other states whose security and well-being constitute a vital interest to America, even though it is not of a military-strategic character. The rationale of this vital interest, like the list of nations selected, may vary from critic to critic. The rationale can be found in a responsibility to nations which share our culture, institutions, and values; or in the broader responsibility and need to preserve serious and creative societies, societies that have something to contribute to the world, societies whose integrity and well-being enrich America. In either case, America has a vital interest in preserving a world in which "open" societies may be permitted to remain open, for it is only in such a world that America can itself realize its full potentiality as an open society.

Finally, there are a large number of critics who consider that the *general evolution* of the underdeveloped nations forms a vital American interest. This interest, in their view, clearly does not commit us to global intervention. Still less does it mean that we should seek to universalize American wants and values. It does mean that we have a vital interest in promoting the stability and development of the underdeveloped areas, principally for the reason that the stability of these areas cannot be separated from world stability. It follows that America is committed not only to resist a course of military conquest in the underdeveloped world, particularly if undertaken by a major communist adversary, but also to prevent a condition of spreading chaos, the consequences of which might jeopardize the security and stability of the advanced states of Western Europe and Japan. This interest in the less developed nations is not denied by opposition to the American involvement in Vietnam. It is the presumably unique character of the war in Vietnam that, if for no other reason, explains why opposition to American involvement may not be equated with indifference to the fate of the underdeveloped nations.

What conclusions may be drawn from this statement of America's vital interests? It is first of all clear that if these interests are considered in their totality they imply a comprehensive concept of order. They assume a favorable distribution of power. They presuppose that America will continue to occupy a favorable, if not a preponderant, position in the international hierarchy. They restrict the manner in which change may be effected and preclude certain types of change altogether. They afford considerable scope for affinities of institutions and values. Moreover, to assert that these interests are vital to America is, in effect, to assert that America has a vital security interest in maintaining a certain kind of world order, that is, a world order of which these interests make up the component parts. To this extent, at least, it is not only the apologists for American foreign policy who insist on equating America's security as a nation with the preservation of a certain kind of order, for the insistence on making this equation is equally characteristic of the critics.

Nor is this all. Whatever the other differences between these two concepts of order, and hence of security, both refuse to limit security to the physical dimension. In the case of the critics, this refusal is apparent, if only in their insistence upon identifying vital interests whose loss would clearly have, in and of themselves, no bearing on America's physical security. Thus no one seriously contends that the continued independence and integrity of an Israel, or an Australia, or even an India is, in and of itself, essential to America's physical security. On the other hand, it is seriously contended that the establishment in this Hemisphere of political and military outposts of the Soviet Union would jeopardize American security. And it is accepted almost as self-evident that the preservation of a balance of power in Europe and Asia is a sine qua non of American security. Yet if security is equated with physical security, these propositions are no longer self-evident. They are self-evident, or very nearly so, only if one falls back on conventional, prenuclear notions of security. They are persuasive if physical security is still to be calculated primarily in terms of geography, spheres of influence, and industrial concentration. Yet it is precisely the adequacy of conventional balance-of-power calculations in the nuclear age that is at issue.

Thus the continuity of America's vital interests should not obscure the changes in the significance of these interests. For it is these changes that have given rise to uncertainty and controversy over the conditions and the very meaning of American security. Yesterday, interests were considered vital in terms of conventional balance-of-power calculations, because, in the first place, their loss could threaten the nation's physical security. Today, the same interests may remain vital, though their loss cannot as such threaten our physical security, since that security is no longer dependent on balance-of-power calculations. It is presumably because their loss may threaten our security in the broader sense that we are willing to risk physical security to preserve them. It is presumably because their loss may threaten the integrity of the nation's institutions and seriously impair the quality of its domestic life that both supporters and critics of American policy are willing to risk physical security to preserve them. The change thereby effected does not mean that interests may no longer be differentiated and graded in order of importance. It does mean that the task of identifying threats to "vital" interests has become increasingly difficult.

These considerations suggest that the critical issue between supporters and most critics of American foreign policy is not so much the issue of what comprises the nation's vital interests as the nature of the threat to them, and, of course, what can and should be done in their defense. It is true that the majority of critics have a more restricted conception of the nation's vital interests, and for this reason alone, though not only for this reason, a more modest conception of the order necessary to American security. Even so, these differences may be and frequently are exaggerated, particularly by undue emphasis on the rhetorical excesses of government officials. If these excesses are discounted, if the emphasis is placed on making a world safe for diversity rather than on a world in which American wants and values are universalized, the gap is substantially narrowed. Moreover, the critics' more restricted view of America's vital interests itself results from a perception of the threat to American security that differs markedly from that of supporters. What is impressive is the extent of the agreement over interests considered intrinsically vital to America and the far-reaching disagreement over the perception of the threat to these interests.

The nature of this disagreement cannot be appreciated, however, by taking at face value the critics' portrayal of American foreign policy and of the consensus on which this policy presumably rests. For that portrayal is one of men, and of a policy, insistently blind to the central political realities of the time. The argument that American policy makers have slept for twenty years and even now refuse to awaken from their dream is overdrawn. So also is the contention that the driving force of American foreign policy is little more than a primitively ideological anticommunism and that this obsession explains the intervention in Vietnam. American policy is not dedicated to exorcising communism from the face of the earth. Where communism represents the status quo, we are not obsessed with its overthrow, certainly not in Europe. Even in Asia, American policy cannot be explained simply as obsessive anticommunism. The containment of China has not been pursued simply because China has a communist government, but because of China's outlook in general and her policy in Asia in particular. It is China's insistence upon changing the Asian status quo, and the methods she has used, that explain American hostility.

This is not to deny that in some sense American foreign policy is anticommunist, since it obviously is. In terms of power realities alone, it could hardly be otherwise. The principal threat to American interests since World War II has stemmed from communist powers. If there remains a substantial threat today to American interests and to an American concept of world order, however defined, it is principally posed by the communist powers. There is room for argument over the intensity of this threat in the past and the extent to which it was the result of communism rather than of more traditional factors. There is room for argument over the nature and scope of the threat to American interests today by the major communist powers. But until some other, and perhaps even greater, threat appears, there is scarcely room for argument over the identity of the one threat, however attenuated it may now be.

There is yet another sense in which American policy is anticommunist, a sense that does border on an ideological anticommunism. It is opposed in principle to the emergence of communist governments quite apart from the ways by which they may be established, the foreign policies they might thereafter pursue, the relationships they might establish with the Soviet Union or China, or the effect their emergence alone might have on Soviet or Chinese behavior. It is so opposed because communism is considered an undesirable political and social form for any people, north or south, developed or under-developed. But this opposition to communism in principle does not and cannot account for opposition to communist expansion in practice, particularly opposition that takes the form of military intervention. What does in part explain this opposition in practice is the fear that in the underdeveloped world communism may otherwise prove to be the wave of the future. It is the threat, in Robert Heilbroner's words, "that the rise of Communism would signal the end of capitalism as the dominant world order, and would force the acknowledgment that America no longer constituted the model on which the future of world civilization would be mainly based."[14] It is the prospect that the American example and purpose might become irrelevant to much of the world that accounts in part for a policy of anticommunism. The prospect of the irrelevance of the American purpose must raise, in turn, the issue of American security. At least it must do so if the proposition is once accepted that the integrity of the nation's institutions and the quality of its domestic life require a congenial international environment.

The critics' response to these considerations is to insist that in either of the above senses a policy of anticommunism is meaningless, if not counterproductive, in view of the diversity of forms "communism" now takes and the subordination by "communist" governments of ideological claims and affinities to national interests. But what follows from the pluralistic or polycentric character of communism today is that the expansion of communism can no longer be equated with the expansion of Soviet power (or of Chinese power). If this is undeniably a very significant development, it remains the case that little else can be deduced from the pluralism of the communist world. Pluralism means that communist regimes, where they are at all able to do so, will act independently and in terms of their own interests. It does not mean that these interests will thereby cease to be inimical to American interests. Moreover, pluralism does not preclude an interdependence of action by communist states in response to irresolution shown toward a minor communist regime, and above all if the latter is allied to one or more major communist powers. The absence of unity of action cannot be taken to imply the absence of interdependence of action. In either case, the deterrence of action may depend on substantially the same policy.

It will not do, then, simply to indict American foreign policy for its blindness to the central political realities of the time and for its naive, though obsessive, anticommunism. What is primarily at issue is not

14. Robert Heilbroner, "Counterrevolutionary America," *Commentary* (April, 1967), p. 37.

these realities but their significance for American interests. What is primarily at issue is not an obsessive anticommunism that has no meaningful relation to American interests, but the continued relevance of the American purpose to most of the world. Critics are right in pointing out that over the course of a generation American policy has been transformed from a policy that was Eurocentric, directed primarily against the expansion of Soviet power and designed to restore a balance of power to a policy that has become increasingly unlimited in geographic scope, motivated in part by fear that communism will prove to be the wave of the future in underdeveloped countries, and designed to preserve the status quo against revolutionary change (which is, in turn, nearly always equated with communism). They are right in insisting that the pluralistic character of communism today— and, indeed, of the world—has not affected the conviction that world order forms an undifferentiated whole, that threats to this order are interconnected, and, consequently, that a challenge by a communist state or movement to one part of this order is likely to result, if unanswered, in challenges to other parts as well. Finally, there is no gainsaying their insistence that the inevitable outcome of this rationale is an imperial policy. Even so, the central issue remains whether this rationale and the policy that it supports respond to, and are necessitated by, the nature of American interests, not only as they are defined by recent administrations and their supporters but in large measure as they are defined by critics as well.

If the question thus posed is answered negatively by the majority of critics, one important reason for so doing is the common conviction that a pluralistic world is a safer world. Pluralism has given rise to a far more complicated world. It is still a safer world in that it must reduce considerably the threat held out to America's interests. Pluralism means that communist expansion, if and when it should occur, no longer carries the threat to American security, whether in the physical or more than physical dimension, that it once carried, for such expansion no longer has the significance it once had. More important, however, pluralism means that the danger that communism will expand at all, whatever the altered significance of such expansion, has markedly and dramatically declined. For the triumph of pluralism is in essence the triumph of nationalism. Where a "communist" movement succeeds, then, as in Vietnam, it does so because it is able to identify more effectively with national aspirations than its competitors. Not only has this identification proven exceedingly rare among the underdeveloped countries, but the indispensable condition for success, as Vietnam again shows, is the assertion and the reality of independence from outside control (not support, but control). And if this condition does not preclude the possibility of communist movements succeeding to power, it must limit the significance of such succession when and where it does occur.

The pluralist thesis does not conclude that there is no need for order, but that there is much less need for order, particularly in the southern hemisphere, than the ideologues of American foreign policy insist upon, and this because there is much less a threat to America's vital interests arising from changes—including violent changes—in the status quo than the official consensus is wont to pretend. It also concludes that what need for order there is can best be fulfilled—indeed, can only be fulfilled—by other and, as it turns out, easier—certainly less painful—means than those presently employed. In sum, American policy both exaggerates the need for order and misconstrues the means for maintaining it. In either case, the end result, indiscriminate intervention, is the same.

Given the nature of American interests, however, these conclusions are less than compelling. They would be compelling, or very nearly so, if pluralism had the significance that critics commonly read into it. But this is precisely what cannot be assumed, for the evidence, such as it is, scarcely proves the reading. If it is absurd to equate interdependence with indivisibility, it is not absurd to insist that interests, though divisible, are interdependent. If it is exaggerated to insist that world order forms an undifferentiated whole, and that a challenge by a communist power to one part of this order is ipso facto a challenge to every part, it is not unreasonable to insist that world order is dependent upon the observance of certain restraints on the manner in which the status quo may be changed, and that a successful breach of these restraints may encourage other, though perhaps dissimilar, breaches. Even if it is true that the war in Vietnam is unique and cannot be regarded as a test case for wars of national liberation, even if it is true that there is no such thing as a typical war of national liberation, it still does not follow that the outcome in Vietnam is without significance for what may—or may not—happen elsewhere. In international as in domestic society, the power of example, whether as a deterrent to disorder or as a challenge to order, does not depend upon the principle of identity.

A pluralistic world does not preclude an interdependent world. In part, this point is acknowledged by critics, though the attempt is made to restrict its significance largely to conventional interstate conflicts. The distinction is commonly drawn between international and internal disorder, between international and domestic violence. In the case of violence that is clearly international, there remains a need today as in the past for the ordering role played by great powers. The matter is otherwise in relation to internal or revolutionary wars. It is here above all that American policy is found to have erred in exaggerating the need for order while misconstruing the means for maintaining it. For pluralism means that, with few exceptions, in the confrontation of communism with nationalism, it is communism that must lose, particularly if we will but refrain from intervening. An eminent critic of the war in Vietnam sets the theme in declaring that "in most of these situations, in the smaller and developing countries, where there seems to be a threat of communism or of forces close to communism taking over, there are usually countervailing forces which, if we keep out, will make themselves felt. If we intervene we paralyze them."[15] The catalogue of American mistakes is by now familiar. Preoccupied with the need to maintain the status quo, and finding communism in every challenge to the status quo, we are driven to equate revolutionary violence with communism. Even where this equation is valid, the question remains in each case whether a communist regime would pose a threat to American interests. In the great majority of cases, however, the equation is not valid, at least not initially. Yet it may and already has increasingly become so through American insistence. By equating revolutionary violence with communism, by a policy of indiscriminate opposition to violent changes in the status quo, we assume the unenviable role of a counterrevolutionary power per se and either allow communist movements to seize the banner of nationalism or force noncommunist revolutionaries into a communist stance.

The principal conclusion drawn from this critique is that intervention in revolutionary wars is with rare exceptions either futile or unnecessary. Where a government is unable to suppress revolutionary forces primarily through its own efforts, intervention is futile. Where a government is able to contain these forces primarily through its own efforts, intervention is unnecessary. But if the immediate accent has been on the futility of intervention in the context of Vietnam, the larger view of critics has stressed the absence of a need to intervene in order to preserve essential American interests—of which, according to most critics, the general evolution of the underdeveloped states is one. If only we have the wisdom to refrain from making the fatal equation of revolution with communism, if we maintain at least a tolerant attitude toward reformist and even revolutionary movements

15. George F. Kennan, *Hearings before the Senate Committee on Foreign Relations*, 89th Cong., 2d Sess., February, 1966, p. 418.

which are noncommunist in character, and, finally, if we distinguish between communist movements and regimes in terms of the compatibility of their policies with American interests, the underlying forces at work in today's pluralist world afford little reason for anxiety. In a way, then, the principal conclusion critics reach manages to have the best of all possible worlds. Intervention in revolutionary conflicts may be futile in most cases and, in any event, beyond America's resources. Yet this need not give rise to despair, for what cannot be done generally need not be done in order to preserve American interests.

7

It is in the effects on the nation's purpose both at home and abroad that critics find perhaps the most serious indictment of American foreign policy. For that policy is considered to have betrayed the nation's purpose. The extent of that betrayal may be measured in the image America now projects to much of the world in contrast with the past. A generation ago America appeared as a self-confident nation whose foreign policy inspired confidence and trust. Today America appears anything but self-confident, and her foreign policy is no longer either wise or benevolent. Once a liberating force in the affairs of men, we are now the "world's self-appointed policeman," a "glorified prison warden"[16] to the world. This denial of the American purpose abroad cannot but have as a consequence the denial of that purpose at home as well. A preoccupation with the exercise of imperial power abroad has inevitably led to the neglect of needed internal reforms. Foreign affairs have thus become a surrogate for fulfillment at home. More generally, the alleged necessities of foreign policy and the awesome "responsibilities" of exercising imperial power ultimately jeopardize our domestic institutions and impair the quality of our domestic life.

These effects, when taken together, form a recognizable theme, one deeply imbedded in the American tradition. Simply stated, that theme emphasizes the dangers inherent in too great a concentration on foreign affairs, a concentration that is considered to reverse the natural order of things. The corrective to these dangers, then, is apparent. The rehabilitation of American prestige abroad is dependent on the performance of America at home. The relevance of the American purpose in the world must come through the relevance and vitality of that purpose in America. Walter Lippmann articulates the view of a legion

16. Steel, *Pax Americana*, p. 325.

of critics in writing: "America can exert its greatest influence in the outer world by demonstrating at home that the largest and most complex modern society can solve the problems of modernity. Then, what all the world is struggling with will be shown to be soluble. Example, and not intervention and firepower, has been the historic instrument of American influence on mankind, and never has it been more necessary and more urgent to realize this truth once more."[17]

There is no need to find in this position a reversion to isolationism, at least not in any historically recognizable sense of that term. It may, and indeed does, reflect a general view toward the significance of foreign policy. In this view, a society fulfills itself mainly by its domestic works; its greatness is measured primarily by its internal achievements. If there nevertheless remains a point at which foreign policy has primacy over domestic policy, it is only because the security and independence of the state are regarded as the indispensable means to the protection and promotion of individual and societal values. To this extent, foreign policy is a "necessity," on the whole a rather burdensome and unwelcome intrusion, the ultimate justification of which must be its contribution to domestic happiness and welfare.

Even so, there is no necessary relationship between this general view of the significance of foreign policy and a policy of isolationism, if only because what is considered indispensable to security in the broader sense may still lead to a policy that is anything but isolationist. Moreover, it is clear that a renewed emphasis on the primacy of domestic policy need not be seen to reflect a skepticism toward, let alone an abandonment of, the American purpose and its continued relevance for the world. The conviction that America may yet regenerate mankind, though now once again by the power of her example, remains an article of faith for many critics. Thus the leader of the opposition to Vietnam in the Senate can decry the arrogance of recent American foreign policy, yet conclude that "at this moment in history at which the human race has become capable of destroying itself, it is not merely desirable but essential that the competitive instinct of nations be brought under control. . . . [America] as the most powerful nation, is the only nation equipped to lead the world in an effort to change the nature of its politics."[18] What separates a Senator Fulbright from those he has so persistently and effectively criticized is not so much

17. Walter Lippmann, "Notes from a Holiday," *International Herald Tribune* (May 11, 1968), p. 4.

18. J. W. Fulbright, *The Arrogance of Power* (New York: Random House, Inc., 1966), p. 256.

a disagreement over the American purpose in the world as it is a disagreement over the manner in which that purpose is to be achieved.[19]

Still the question remains: has America betrayed its purpose, if only by the manner in which it has sought to achieve it? In domestic affairs the question has become meaningful, or, at least, urgent, only in the context of the Vietnamese conflict. For it is only since 1965 that a persuasive case can be made for the debilitating effects of foreign on domestic policy. Vietnam has been deeply devisive, more so perhaps than any issue of the past generation, and has debased the standards of public discourse and behavior. And if the Cold War often acted as a stimulus to domestic change that otherwise would not have been undertaken, Vietnam has reversed this pattern and has either retarded or frustrated social reform both by creating a fierce budgetary competition between foreign and domestic expenditures and by siphoning off mental and spiritual resources. It is no adequate response to point out that the nation can now afford its Vietnams and its great national tasks. It does not wish to pay for both and apparently cannot be induced to do so. Nor is it an adequate response to argue that even with the war government efforts in the fields of health, education, aid to the poor, and aid to urban areas have tripled in less than a decade. What matters is men's definition, which may undergo sudden change, of what constitutes a tolerably just society.

At the same time, if Vietnam has shown that the internal face of reason of state can be malignant, the extent of that malignancy has often been exaggerated. An imperial policy might well lead in time to the derangement of our political institutions, but Vietnam has not had this effect. On the contrary, its principal effect has been to cause the Senate to assert a degree of independence in the area of foreign policy that is perhaps greater than at any time since the pre-World War II period. And if the war has contributed to the debasement of standards of public discourse and behavior, it has not eroded civil liberties. If anything, the war has provided a notable occasion for the exercise of these liberties. Moreover, the recent debasement of public standards is not simply, and perhaps not even primarily, the result of the war. The penchant to attribute to the war almost all that is un-

19. Compare the quoted statement in the text above with these words of President Johnson, taken from his first major address following the initiation of aerial bombardment against North Vietnam: "Our generation has a dream. It is a very old dream. But we have the power and now we have the opportunity to make it come true. For centuries, nations have struggled with each other. But we dream of a world where disputes are settled by law and reason. And we will try to make it so."

settling and alarming in American public life is understandable. It is not for this reason correct. Too much has been made of the argument that the denial of the American purpose at home is the consequence of a preoccupation with the exercise of imperial power abroad. Foreign affairs may have become in part a surrogate for fulfillment at home, but it is also true that failure at home has other and far deeper roots.

These considerations apart, the view that America can exert its greatest influence in the world today through the power of its example at home evidently rests on two assumptions: that influence is primarily a matter of example and that the American example must continue to be relevant to the world. Even if the latter assumption is accepted, and it requires something of an act of faith to accept it, it does not follow that the former assumption is valid. There is no persuasive, or even plausible, reason for believing that the best of examples set at home would somehow resolve the problem of maintaining a world order in which American interests would be preserved. Why should the example that we set at home affect Chinese aspirations in Asia? Why should the example that we set at home affect the prospects of nuclear proliferation? How would a benign example on our part resolve the conflict between the Arab states and Israel? There is something touching in the belief, for which history, including our own, provides little basis, that we can do by example what we cannot do by precept. It reflects, if nothing else, the ironic nature of our present position in the world. When contrasted with our earlier expectations that position, and the policy to which it has given rise, must indeed appear to have little relation to the traditional purpose of America. For that purpose was never seen to imply that we should play the role of policeman to the world. It did imply that the day might come when we would have to free the world, but surely not to police it. One polices the world because men and nations are recalcitrant, because they often have deeply conflicting aspirations, and because they are influenced more by precept than by example—even the best of examples.

8

If the recent debate appears inconclusive, it is not only because its outcome remains in doubt but also because the essential differences separating the principal participants have never been altogether clear. Of course, to the extent the debate has centered on Vietnam, it has been reasonably clear. It is when we go beyond Vietnam that difficulties arise. It is when we go beyond Vietnam that we seem to be left without a clear and salient issue, the resolution of which would indicate the future direction of policy. Thus the general issue Vietnam evidently must raise is the issue of intervention. Yet it would not be accurate to characterize the present debate as one involving the issue of intervention pure and simple. The debate has not raised the issue whether the United States has interests outside this Hemisphere which may require intervention. In this literal sense, it has not been a debate between interventionists and noninterventionists. On the contrary, it is more accurately characterized as one between interventionists and interventionists, for the majority of the more articulate and influential critics are clearly not anti-interventionist in principle. Until very recently most of them generally supported a policy that can scarcely be termed anti-interventionist. There is no reason or justification for equating their defection over Vietnam with anti-interventionism per se, when some of them first supported the war, when others did not oppose the war in its earlier stages, and when still others, although opposing the Vietnamese intervention throughout, have advocated intervention in Asia, if necessary, to meet and contain direct Chinese military expansion.

Moreover, if most critics may be termed qualified anti-interventionists, they are so for different reasons. Some would severely limit the occasions in which intervention is justified because they have a much more restricted view of the nation's vital, and indeed legitimate, interests than has the prevailing view. A very substantial number of critics are qualified anti-interventionists, however, not primarily because they disagree over the interests and purposes of American foreign policy but because they are persuaded that, in many situations, and particularly in predominantly revolutionary conflicts, intervention is an ineffective and even counterproductive means for realizing these interests and purposes. They are the "critics of means," not of the ends or broad interests of policy, and as such they largely share the expansive views of America's world role and security that have marked American policy through four administrations.

These considerations not only place limits on the utility of structuring the debate around the issue of intervention, they also limit the utility of substituting geography for intervention. Clearly, there is much to be said for the view that disaffection with American policy has been roughly proportionate to the degree to which the focus of policy has shifted from Europe to Asia. The foreign policy consensus of the past generation had a geographical center of gravity in Europe. That consensus reflected the unique importance of Europe to America, as well as the initial agreement on the nature of the threat to Europe and the policy of countering it. In contrast, the American interest in

Asia has always been less clear and the nature of the threat subject to constant disagreement. Consequently, at no time in the entire postwar period has there been a measure of agreement over policy in Asia that equalled the agreement obtained in the early years of the Cold War over Europe. To the extent that there has been a kind of consensus over Asian policy, it has been (as noted) a negative consensus. Even so, the consensus over European policy also began to wane by the middle to late 1950s. Since then that policy has been an object of contention almost as much as of consensus. Despite the continued unique importance of Europe, it may therefore be argued that the unusual measure of early agreement on European policy is to be attributed to an equally unusual set of circumstances, which probably cannot be recreated today even in Europe. If European policy does not incur the widespread and intense criticism of Asian policy, it may in part be because European policy no longer seems very consequential, either in the initiatives it appears to compel (or, for that matter, afford) or in the price it entails.[20]

Then, too, the distinctive nature of the war in Vietnam must itself qualify the thesis that recent disaffection with American policy has been the result of its predominantly Asian focus. Even if it is true that disagreement has marked America's Asian policy throughout, and that this policy has never enjoyed more than a negative consensus, it is also true that this negative consensus was put to a test in circumstances which could scarcely have been less fortunate. Unless American policy in Vietnam is to be equated with America's Asian policy as a whole, opposition to the war in Vietnam ought not to be equated with opposition to the foundations on which this broader policy presumably rests. In fact, most critics have not made this equation. While opposing the war in Vietnam, they have not opposed the containment of Chinese power. While criticizing what they consider a misunderstanding of the nature of the Chinese threat, which is held to be political rather than military in character, they have not opposed a policy appropriate to countering this threat. While discounting the prospect of direct Chinese expansion through conventional military methods, they have not opposed meeting such expansion—should it

20. Whether the Soviet armed intervention in Czechoslovakia in August, 1968, has essentially altered this assessment is examined elsewhere. See pp. 302–10. If it has not, then it is not easy to understand current speculation that in the aftermath of Vietnam Europe will once again provide the focus for American foreign policy. Quite apart from the expected persistence of an American interest in the stability and development of the less developed areas, particularly Asia, the scope for policy initiatives in Europe is likely to continue to remain limited.

ever occur—with American military power.[21] The maintenance of a balance of power in Asia is a vital American interest to most critics. Very nearly the same must be said of the interest in Asia's general stability and development.

It is difficult to avoid the conclusion that, in the absence of basic changes in the international environment, American foreign policy will substantially change only to the extent that American interests substantially change. For the nature of American interests, not only as they have been defined by recent administrations and their supporters but also in large measure as they are defined by critics as well, must broadly account for the methods of American policy. The latter cannot be seriously altered without altering the former. Whether the ultimate arbiter of any debate over American foreign policy will eventually insist upon such alteration is at present unclear. It is of course quite clear that the public wants no more Vietnams and cannot be expected to support them. It is equally clear that future administrations will ignore this public disposition only at their peril. But this does not say a great deal about the future course of American foreign policy, given the distinctive characteristics that have marked the conflict in Vietnam. To the extent that the reaction to Vietnam has been a response to those features which have set this war apart from other wars the nation has waged, it may afford little indication of what the public can or cannot be induced to support, or, at least, to tolerate. Moreover, it is well to recall that, despite the distinctive characteristics of the war—the uncertainty over its immediate origins, the dispute over the identity of the aggressor, the elusiveness of the objectives of the war, the seeming indifference of those on whose behalf the war was being fought—the opposition to it did not achieve significant proportions until the demands imposed by the war far exceeded initial expectations, while at the same time affording no imminent prospect of military victory. On the basis of these considerations, we cannot know a great deal about the limits public opinion may impose on the future use of American power. We cannot know, for example, whether the reaction to Vietnam foreshadows a similar reaction to interventions in areas of more traditional interest, particularly if the cost of intervention can be kept relatively modest. That the public cannot be expected

21. Of course, some critics have consistently opposed this. But many clearly have not, and others either have obscured the issue or have simply discounted altogether the prospect. And even Walter Lippmann has opposed only the commitment of American forces to a large land war on the mainland of Asia. He has never opposed the use of any and all forms of American military power. Nor could he do so, agreeing as he does with the proposition that the containment of China is a vital American interest.

to support Vietnams does not mean that it can be expected to tolerate little more than Dominican Republics. If the cost of intervention remains a critical determinant of public tolerance or opposition, the significance of Vietnam for future constraints imposed by public opinion must be read with caution.

To be sure, the opposition to Vietnam must be attributed to other factors as well. Although the cost of vindicating the interests for which intervention was presumably undertaken in Vietnam ultimately proved too high (and in the end this consideration was decisive), it is still true that Vietnam was opposed throughout on other and broader grounds. Indeed, it was these other and broader grounds that in large measure made the cost of the war seem too high. Vietnam could not be effectively represented either as a vindication of the principles of freedom and self-determination or as a measure indispensable to American security. Yet it is difficult to estimate the extent to which these considerations will limit the use of American power in the future. Vietnam and the ensuing debate have shown that there is a broad disparity of view over both the conditions and even the very meaning of American security, as well as over other interests, the vindication of which would justify the use of American military power. But there are no indications that this disparity of view will soon be resolved. Thus the failure to employ effectively the security argument in the case of Vietnam need not be taken to mean that the same argument would fail elsewhere, quite apart from the merits of making it.

In part, speculation on significant and even radical changes in American foreign policy is based on changes in the international and domestic environment that have been long in the making and that Vietnam has dramatically revealed. These changes, it is argued, are so profound and far-reaching as to reverse what has heretofore appeared as something close to a law of history. Whereas in the past power has almost invariably created its own interests, the latter expanding in rough proportion to the former, we are now presumably on the threshold of an era, if, indeed, we have not already entered it, in which this apparently "natural" process will no longer hold true. It will no longer hold true because the external restraints on the use of power (above all, military power) are not only greater than they have ever been in the past but so great as to challenge the traditional meaning of statecraft. At the same time, and largely as a result of these restraints, the stakes of foreign policy seem more elusive and problematic than ever for those states whose physical security can be jeopardized only by a nuclear conflict. Hence the question arises: Is the game any longer worth the candle? Why should the great nuclear powers contend for influence in the underdeveloped areas, when the instruments of power they may bring to bear are increasingly circumscribed, when the competition is costly, and when the stakes of the competition are elusive? And if the Third World disappears as an object of contention, what remains for the great powers to contend over?

Moreover, to the restraints imposed by the international environment must be added the restraints imposed by the domestic environment. With nations, as with individuals, the real revolution of rising expectations is not among the poor but among the affluent. Whether in America, or in Europe, or even in the Soviet Union, the consumer's desire for more continues to increase disproportionately to an ever-expanding economy, while the margin of resources with which governments must conduct foreign policy appears to decrease in proportion to the economy. Nor are the domestic constraints simply a function of the consumer's desire for more. They are also a function of the largely unforseen problems generated by advanced and affluent societies. We have come to discover that the rich too have their problems, and that, even if they are not insoluble, they may be very difficult problems. In America's case, the domestic restraints on foreign policy may be distinguished not only by virtue of a racial crisis that has no parallel elsewhere in the advanced societies but also by the emergence of a generation that does not know, and apparently cannot believe in, the problem of insecurity—at least, in the conventional sense. The depths of this skepticism are revealed not only by the reaction of the younger generation to Vietnam but even more significantly by the approval increasingly shown toward revisionist interpretations of the origins of the Cold War. Contrary to common expectation, this almost radical skepticism of the security claims of the state may prove in the end to have a greater impact on foreign policy than does any other factor.

These tendencies in the international and domestic environment may eventuate in far-reaching changes in American foreign policy. At present, however, they remain tendencies whose consequences are largely indeterminate. Although the restraints on the use of power appear greater today than in the past, they have not changed the traditional meaning of statecraft. It is not necessary to explain Vietnam in terms of these novel restraints, and it may even be misleading to do so. Nor does it follow that once the stakes of foreign policy have become elusive states will thereby give up the game. Physical and economic security apart, the interests over which men and nations have contended in the past have always had an elusive quality. Yet their quality of elusiveness has seldom persuaded men to abandon them. Whether it will do so in the future must remain a matter of conjecture.

3

THE SOVIET OUTLOOK

Herbert S. Dinerstein

1. Introduction

Since its beginnings the Soviet Union has been the object of the close, if not intimate, attention of Western Europe and the United States. Yet our understanding has been limited if the criterion is our ability to predict major political developments in the Soviet Union. The partial liberalization after Stalin's death, the Sino-Soviet split, and the emergence of Eastern European nationalism were unexpected. On the technological level, the early success of the Soviet nuclear-energy program and the development of ballistic missiles surprised foreign observers.

This list of misjudgments could be easily extended, but clearly we have been unable to predict even gross phenomena. The reasons are many. To begin with, Soviet leaders deliberately conceal from their own people, and therefore from the world, how they make decisions. But perhaps the major factor in the distortion of judgment has been the political atmosphere in which Soviet politics have been assessed. The conviction that Soviet gains were irreversible, and the fear of nuclear warfare, resulted in the belief that an error in judgment might have momentous consequences. Judgments therefore of Soviet politics have been more prudential than analytical. Doubts have been generally resolved in the direction of the worst possible outcomes. Such politicization of judgment is understandable and not to be condemned as morally deficient. Such a bias is to be avoided in academic analysis, but how to do so is not immediately obvious. It may be useful, therefore, to assess briefly the approaches to the analysis of Soviet behavior thus far employed by those inside and outside of the universities.

On the highest level of abstraction is the construction of theoretical models of Soviet society. Not only political scientists but statesmen, too, have engaged in model building. Of these models the totalitarian is the most familiar. Its intellectual father was probably George

Orwell, whose novel *1984* (1949) represented the abstraction of the developments then to be observed in the Soviet Union. Years earlier in his novel *We* (1924) Eugene Zamiatin had anticipated Orwell. For the academic elaborations of the totalitarian model we are indebted to Hannah Arendt, Carl J. Friedrich, and Zbigniew K. Brzezinski.[1] In their view Soviet society would inevitably develop further in the direction in which it was already moving. It would become more and more oppressive; its leaders would increasingly lose touch with reality; but the system itself was fated to endure because its very horror endowed it with demonic strength. The very concept of totalitarianism which put nazism, Italian fascism, and Soviet communism into a single category suggested that a totalitarian regime could be dislodged only by war.

For all the brilliance of its exposition, the theory perhaps only conceptualized a transitional phase of Soviet communism. Since Stalin's death events have demonstrated that this theory is of little use as an instrument for the prediction of the proximate future.

Interestingly enough, the contemporary countertheory of Isaac Deutscher has enjoyed a better fate. Deutscher, a former member of the Polish Communist Party, who continued to describe himself as a Marxist, believed that the Soviet system would improve because communism bears within it the seeds of its own redemption. Although Deutscher's optimism probably derived from his faith in the essential goodness of socialism, his projection of the future was closer to the mark than the Brzezinski-Friedrich model. Perhaps Deutscher's model has better stood the test of time because it permitted the assertion of dynamic factors in contrast to the more widely accepted assumption of rigidity.

Others like Harold Lasswell and Alfred Meyer have chosen to consider the Soviet Union and the United States as examples of a single category, the modern industrialized society. Lasswell about twenty years ago predicted that modern industrialized societies and, consequently, both the Soviet Union and the United States were becoming garrison states. Alfred Meyer, however, believes that the modern bureaucratic state is better represented by the American development, and, in his *Soviet Political System*, he projects a Soviet society moving closer to the U.S. model.

To these models must be appended that of John Foster Dulles and

---

1. Hannah Arendt, *The Origins of Totalitarianism* (New York: Harcourt, Brace and Company, 1968). Carl J. Friedrich and Zbigniew K. Brzezinski, *Totalitarian Dictatorship and Autocracy* (Cambridge, Mass.: Harvard University Press, 1956).

Allen Dulles, which, although only a rough sketch, was perhaps more influential than the others. The Dulleses believed that the Soviet system was impermanent because education and industrialization would create a class of technicians who would share the pragmatic outlook of their opposite numbers in the West and also their desire for efficiency. These attitudes would erode the system, which would collapse and then reshape itself to resemble the successful industrial societies of the capitalist countries.

Valuable as these models have been in stimulating empirical research, they are essentially worthless to the political actor because they are of little predictive value, being cast in terms of several generations. Even now, fifteen years after Stalin's death, it is not clear whether the sanguine Dulleses and Deutschers or the saturnine Lasswells and Friedrichs are the better prophets.

Another kind of effort to predict Soviet behavior assumed that the sacred and patristic writings of the Bolsheviks, like any other product of the human psyche, could be forced to reveal the behavioral code of their authors. However, this effort, executed by Nathan Leites[2] with flashing brilliance, fell short of its purpose. The code as finally revealed consisted of unhelpful paradoxes like, "Take advantage of all opportunities," but "Don't fall into any traps." Yet the failure of this effort to attain its most ambitious goals has deflected attention from its genuine accomplishment. By examining the statements of Lenin and Stalin on various political subjects and ordering them into psychological categories, a cogent exposition of Lenin's and Stalin's characters and styles emerged. In an impressionistic way many have formed similar judgments of Stalin's suspiciousness, sometimes bordering on paranoia, his caution, his ruthlessness, and his fanaticism. But we have no other such systematic and refined examination of the character of these two men. Leites' books, however, did not reach policy makers because the psychiatric theory on which they rested was implicit rather than explicit, and only some readers could, and would, draw for themselves the conclusions that lay within the raw material presented. Moreover, just as Stalin differed from Lenin, so Khrushchev differed from both, and Kosygin and Brezhnev differ from all three. Understanding the character of the dictator is essential for a good understanding of Soviet society, but it is not a sufficient guide.

These grand models or approaches, though thought-provoking, do not yield useful generalizations about the assumptions underlying the

2. Nathan Leites, *The Operational Code of the Politburo* (New York: McGraw-Hill, 1951); *A Study of Bolshevism* (Glencoe, Ill.: The Free Press, 1953).

making of Soviet policy. A more limited and traditional approach may better serve to judge the intent and direction of Soviet foreign policy as it unfolds. The perspective of time and improvements in our knowledge make it possible to see some of the major events of the foreign policy of the Soviet Union in a somewhat different light than before. Moreover, liberated from the need for prudential judgment (a burden, it must be said, voluntarily assumed by much of the scholarly community), events can be re-interpreted. Such an exercise yields some modifications of our assumptions about Soviet behavior in the area of foreign policy. It remains for the reader to judge how significant these modifications are. These modified assumptions are now briefly set forth so that the reader may become familiar with the argument of this essay before the supporting material is presented.

1. The changes in the internal organization of Soviet political life have tended to make for fewer rather than more initiatives in foreign policy. The shift from monolithic control to a system more representative of group interests has been associated with a less doctrinaire understanding of the noncommunist world. At the same time the Soviet leadership has been subjected to unanticipated demands from communist countries. In combination the effect of these changes has been to make for a much more differentiated policy toward ideological opponents. Essentially Stalin chose between appeasement, temporizing, or outright hostility because he thought in terms of a Manichean world of capitalism and socialism. Stalin's successors see both the socialist and the nonsocialist world as more complex, and therefore the speculative reconstruction of the assumptions underlying their foreign policy actions must go beyond Stalin's simple categories. The perception of increased complexity has, on the whole, inhibited Soviet initiative.

2. In retrospect it now seems that Soviet foreign policy has been most active (the terms "offensive" and "defensive" are avoided as misleading) when Soviet leaders have been worried about weaknesses in the system of socialist states and within the Soviet Union itself. In this view Tito's defection is seen as more influential than the proclamation of the Truman doctrine; the possibility that Mao's China could establish dominant influence in northeast Asia is seen as more impelling to the invasion of South Korea than the opportunity seemingly offered by Acheson's remarks about Korea being beyond the defense perimeter. And to adduce a more recent example, to be examined in detail, the invasion of Czechoslovakia in August, 1968, owed more to fears of the disintegration of communist party control in Czechoslovakia, Poland, East Germany, and even in the Soviet Union than to

fears of "West German aggression." In reality this "new" outlook on Soviet foreign policy is new only in its application to the Soviet Union. It has long been observed that internal policy usually dominates foreign policy and that great and powerful states can afford to favor domestic over foreign needs more easily than small, weak ones. With the multiplication of socialist states, the socialist self that had to be protected has come to consist of many parts. This circumstance has at once multiplied the Soviet perception of dangerous vulnerabilities and has greatly increased the opportunities for outside observers to note them.

3. Such a re-evaluation requires a fresh look at the political consequences of the strategic military balance between the Soviet Union and the United States. As we review the events of the last twenty years it no longer seems satisfactory to assume that the Soviet Union will take more risks to improve its political position as its military position vis-à-vis the United States improves.

The Berlin crisis of 1948, precipitated by the Soviet blockade of the Western sector of the city, followed a sharp reduction of Soviet and U.S. forces. The question of who was more powerful as a result of these reductions is ambiguous and, perhaps, irrelevant because the Soviet leadership no more foresaw the airlift than U.S. leaders did. Hence they could not foresee such a prolonged crisis over Berlin.

The next important Soviet initiative was the instigation of the attack on South Korea. It will be pointed out subsequently that U.S. unreadiness for nuclear warfare on a substantial scale was a background factor, but one must also assign considerable weight to the Soviet assumptions that the United States had written off the mainland of Asia, and that Mao represented a formidable competitor to Soviet interests in northeast Asia. In any case what turned out to be one of the riskiest and certainly the most costly Soviet initiative in the postwar period is not to be explained simply on the basis of the strategic balance.

The post-1958 Berlin crisis in retrospect seems more explicable by the deterioration of the internal situation in East Germany than by the Soviet conviction that the menace of nuclear war would produce concessions. In any case all during this active phase of Soviet foreign policy the Soviet Union was strategically inferior and realized it fully.

The Soviet initiative in making Cuba a base for strategic nuclear weapons is believed by many to have brought the two major powers closest to a nuclear exchange. Yet this risk was assumed in the expectation that Soviet strategic inferiority would be repaired rather than in the confidence that existing superiority would paralyze U.S. will.

Furthermore, as the U.S.-Soviet strategic ratio has gradually changed in the direction of Soviet equality with the United States, Soviet activism has been confined to maintenance of socialist regimes rather than to probing for opportunities in the opponent's camp. The Soviet intervention in Czechoslovakia falls into this category as does its support of the North Vietnamese after they were subjected to U.S. bombing.

It is never possible to assess precisely the relative weight to be assigned to one of several factors in the policy of a great power. Hence we cannot expect to know with any exactness how much hopes for capitalizing on the opponent's weakness, on the one hand, and fears of the vulnerability of one or more socialist states, on the other, determine Soviet policy. It seems clear, however, that the strategic balance is not the determining factor, and it even seems likely that no direct relationship between Soviet risk-taking propensities and the strategic balance exists.

4. On balance, the extension of socialism to other states has been a source of weakness rather than strength. The imperative to preserve a socialist system, once it exists, is ideological and inescapable, and traditional cost-gain calculations are irrelevant. As a consequence, the Soviet Union was unable to explore the possibility that the new Eastern policy of the Kiesinger government in West Germany could lead to a general Central European settlement and the recognition of East Germany. Fear that such a settlement would remove the raison d'être for the East German and Polish regimes inhibited the Soviet Union from testing the best opportunity it had in the postwar period to reduce dramatically the importance of the United States in European politics.

5. The major purpose of Soviet policy in the underdeveloped world has been first to deny these areas to opponents and then to establish Soviet influence. The establishment of socialist regimes has not been a goal, and it has succeeded in Cuba only by serendipity. Active Soviet interest in Third World areas can be expected to continue out of the momentum already generated and to embroil the Soviets in continual difficulties. The Soviet Union will discover at considerable cost that the role of a world power in the age of client states, as contrasted with the colonial age, is eminently unsatisfactory.

In the pages to follow we shall consider: the Soviet political system, the development of the United States-Soviet strategic relationship, the problem of West Germany and West Berlin, Soviet relations with other socialist states, and the Soviet Union as a global power, i.e. its relations with countries in the Third World.

2. The Soviet Political System

Is the Soviet political system stable or unstable? As we have suggested, one of our assumptions is that Soviet foreign policy and Soviet internal policy are inextricably connected. Hence Soviet views about the stability of their own society are a major factor in the atmosphere in which Soviet foreign policy is formulated.

At the outset it should be said that for extensive periods the Soviet leaders feared that the socialist state was in danger of destruction. Many leaders actually remember World War I and the successful revolution of the communist party. For others, accounts of the birth of their society are thrust upon them from every quarter. As a consequence of the defeats imperial Russia suffered in war, a small conspiratorial group was able to seize power and maintain it. Bolshevik literature stresses the smallness of the communist party before World War I. Hence the Soviet preoccupation with the collapse of great states, their own as well as others. If the momentum of unbroken German victories had continued beyond October, 1941, the continued existence of the Soviet political structure—in the opinion of the Soviet leaders—would have been seriously threatened. Adam B. Ulam in his recent book on Soviet foreign policy[3] has made out a convincing case that Stalin was fearful for the stability of the Soviet political system in the period immediately following World War II. Since the late 1950s, however, the Soviet leaders have believed with increasing conviction that their acquisition of nuclear weapons has much reduced the likelihood of war. (In 1954–55 some of them were much preoccupied with the possibility and the consequences of a surprise attack against them with nuclear weapons.) The actual problem for Soviet leaders is therefore the political health of the Soviet system, not its sheer survival. Even a cursory examination reveals a most unsatisfactory state of affairs from the point of view of the Soviet leadership.

The legitimacy of the Soviet regime and the problem of succession are still unsettled. The Soviet constitution is clear on the procedure for selecting a prime minister and his subordinates. But no established procedure exists for filling a more important post, that of the first or general secretary of the Communist Party of the Soviet Union. This official, who for a long time was the dictator and now is at least *primus inter pares*, seems to be chosen ad hoc. Stalin, who came to his position only after a severe political struggle, did not fully consolidate it until

3. Adam B. Ulam, *Expansion and Coexistence: The History of Soviet Foreign Policy, 1917–1967* (New York: Frederick A. Praeger, 1968.)

he had savagely purged the party and murdered the majority of its upper echelons. We do not know how Malenkov became the first secretary or in what circumstances he relinquished, or was forced to relinquish, that post. Nor do we, or many Soviet citizens, know how Khrushchev in turn was displaced.

Since each new first secretary establishes himself through a struggle and then maintains his position against opponents who make their claims at any, rather than at a fixed, time, he continually searches for constituencies. The manner in which rewards are offered to prospective supporters is peculiarly demoralizing to the society. An incumbent makes his promises to supporters and potential supporters by rejecting particular policies of his predecessor. Thus Khrushchev, in order to convince others that he would not become a Stalin, had to discredit him as a tyrant and even as a madman, though in the process Khrushchev raised many questions about his own association with such a monster. Khrushchev's successors in turn have denigrated him as an ineffective bumbler, and have lately charged him with telling lies about Stalin. The result of this successive assassination of the character of each Soviet leader is demoralization. Soviet school children learn that only one Soviet ruler was free of serious faults, and he is regarded as a saint rather than a man. Since Lenin Soviet rulers have been criminals, fools, or both. It is as if Americans believed that only the Warren Hardings and Andrew Johnsons have succeeded George Washington.

No incumbent can know how long he will retain office. This uncertainty is characteristic of all parliamentary systems, but these are commonly judged as unsuccessful when changes are frequent. In the Soviet Union, although tenures have been comparatively extended, uncertainty is the hallmark of the system. Stalin, who held office for three decades, maintained power by periodic purges of enemies, actual and potential, and by a reign of terror. Malenkov, Khrushchev, and Brezhnev have constantly sought political support. This imparts an air of instability and impermanence to the system, which ill suits the conduct of the business of a state of more than 200 million people.

Like the modern capitalist state, the Soviet state is committed to the provision of creature comforts for its citizens. A comparison with theocratic states is instructive. Poor Moslems and Christians could keep their faith because only spiritual beatitude was promised. But modern societies, including the communist, promise at least a minimum standard of living. The comparatively poor performance of the Soviet Union in providing economic welfare has sapped confidence in the system. The continual juggling of words and statistics, intended to prove that the Soviet Union is soon to surpass capitalist states economically, suggests an appreciation of the political costs of broken promises.

Moreover, the outlook for significant economic progress in the Soviet Union is poor. It is not necessary here to rehearse the familiar deficiencies of an overcentralized command economy, but the political inhibitions on rational economic options may be of interest. The Soviet leadership is a prisoner of its own history. The sacrifices extorted from the population for programs which have produced economically unsatisfactory institutions make it politically impossible to replace the latter. Thus no Soviet leader has ever questioned the correctness of the policy of agricultural collectivization. The memory of the man-produced famine of the early 1930s is still so vivid that the present leadership, many of whom were associated with that policy, simply cannot designate the collective farm system as a mistake of the past and recommend its replacement.

Most of the people, distraught by the political uncertainty, fearful of a return to the repressive measures of Stalinism, and dissatisfied with the halting performance of the economy, perform their assigned duties mechanically and with an air of heavy resignation—hardly the recipe for a forward-looking state which hopes to expand the base of its power. A small but significant element of the population has begun an overt campaign of protest for wider political liberties. The boldness of the critics of the system has mounted as the repressive measures adopted against them have increased. Although from the outside it seems that many years must pass before the intelligentsia can modify the system significantly, from the inside the Soviet leadership may well view these rumblings with apprehension, if not alarm.

To this list of dissatisfactions must be added the re-emergent demands of the non-Russian nationalities of the Soviet Union. Until recently the Soviet regime for minority nationalities, despite some troubles, could have been accounted as moderately successful. Although centralized (that is, Russian control continued to be resented), some nationalities like the Turkic-speaking Moslem groups of central Asia found compensation in being introduced into modern society. Others like the Georgians and Armenians felt that their only real choice was between Turkish and Russian rule, and historical memory permitted only the latter.

The disintegration of the international socialist system, however, has adversely affected the minority nationalities within the Soviet Union. The demands of Chinese, Rumanian, and Czechoslovak allies for Soviet resources, for political autonomy, or for both have stimulated similar demands within the Soviet Union. In many cases national groups, or closely related nationalities, are divided between socialist states. Thus, for example, privileges accorded the Ukrainian minority in Czechoslovakia are noted and envied in the Soviet Ukraine; the Rumanian-speaking population of Bessarabia is aware of the growing independence of Rumania. The problem of nationalities in Eastern Europe has always been religious or cultural rather than racial. Just as in the tsarist system, the acceptance of the Greek Orthodox religion carried with it full political rights, regardless of race, so in the Soviet Union to become a communist or to accept the communist system confers privileges in the first case and equal treatment in the second. (Only the Jews for special reasons are an exception to this generalization.)

Naturally, the minorities have complained that the process of equalization has gone too slowly, but in theory, and very often in practice, political assimilation (along with a command of the Russian language) has been the avenue to economic betterment. The process has been successful in part because the great expansion of the Soviet economy in the 1930s and to a certain extent in the 1940s has opened up many new careers to talent and the non-Russian nationalities have had their share. In the early period of economic growth, sufficient numbers of the newly educated members of minority nationalities received preferment and came to accept the essential fairness of the Soviet multinational state. But now, in a period of economic stagnation, the nationality problem has re-emerged in the Soviet Union, although it is not as serious as it was in the Austro-Hungarian, the Ottoman, or for that matter the Russian empire.

Thus far we have presented a picture of Soviet society as it may appear to Soviet leaders, but we have said nothing about how major political choices are made. To assume that decisions emanate from a single source, or to assume that decisions are reached as a consequence of a clash of interests makes for major differences in the formation of our own policies. If the Soviet Union is a monolithic society, only a few alternative strategies are open to the United States. One can only threaten, damage, or appease such an opponent. One can decide to permit him to have his will, or to deter him by threatening to impose high costs on him, or to seek to destroy him. Thus the opponent's estimate of the cost of his goals is altered. This was the essential rationale of the policy of containment which assumed a single source of power in the Soviet Union.

At the other extreme is the assumption that the opponent is composed of rival political groupings, some of which share a common goal with our whole system or parts of it. Theoretically, once we identify these interest groups and their goals, we can shape our policies to advance those groups with which we have a common interest. In some cases, especially when a developed sense of nationhood is lacking, bribery is sufficient. But in dealing with a cohesive society such as the Soviet Union, bribery only serves trivial ends like intelligence acquisition. A common purpose is the only genuine basis for a coincidence of interest.

In a sense, the general belief that the consequences of nuclear war are unacceptable produces the common goal of avoiding war. Such an agreement on the very largest question underlies whatever community of interest exists between the Soviet Union and the United States; but a greater differentiation of purposes and interest groups in both societies is required to approach all but the overriding questions of survival and destruction. Can the United States and the Soviet Union compete in the Near East, supporting various small states, and make concerted efforts to reach a settlement in Vietnam? Are there groups in the Soviet Union that would welcome a pause in the deployment of ABMs but that are unwilling to achieve that goal if the price is stabilization of the Near East and the concomitant continuation of the U.S. presence in the area? Such questions show that it is not enough to posit that a rival state is composed of various groups that can be played off against one another. The most pertinent question is whether our knowledge of political groupings in the opponent's society is good enough to permit a discriminating approach. This question can perhaps best be approached concretely. We shall begin with the strategic balance between the Soviet Union and the United States.

3. The U.S.-Soviet Strategic Relationship

To be properly understood, the history of the development of the U.S.-Soviet strategic balance must be separated into two parts. The first covers 1945–62, when only the United States could strike directly at the Soviet Union with nuclear weapons, and the second, since 1962, when the capacity for direct nuclear assault was common to both parties.

In the early postwar period, both the United States and the Soviet Union demobilized very extensively. In recent years, the relative strength of Soviet and American forces in the first three or four years after World War II has been reassessed. Though one cannot be precise, both Soviet and American conventional forces were very considerably reduced after the war. American nuclear power was more potential than actual; congressional hearings on the Korean War have revealed that the United States had produced very few atomic weapons by June, 1950. The only American aircraft suitable for the delivery of nuclear weapons were limited in range, so that air bases around the rim of the Soviet Union were necessary—and such bases had been abandoned in the withdrawal of the main American forces from Europe and Asia.

The strategy of both countries was dominated by the experience of World War II, with some new departures. The United States envisaged a rapid massive buildup, the reactivation of bases in Europe and elsewhere, and a damaging nuclear attack against the Soviet Union. In the first stage of the war in Europe the United States would hold where it could and yield where it had to, and then, after remobilization, overwhelm the enemy whose industrial base was so much smaller.

The Soviet Union, for its part, planned a continental war seeking to accomplish what the Germans had failed to do: dominate the continent by making the cost of its conquest prohibitive to the United States. Its large submarine force would have been used to prevent the landing of new American expeditionary forces and perhaps to starve out Great Britain.

Quite clearly Stalin was never tempted to engage in such a war. The terrible devastation of the western regions of the Soviet Union as well as the war weariness and even the disaffection of the population made it uncertain that the Soviet political system could survive another war at that time. For this reason alone a repetition of World War II was an abhorrent idea. If to that prospect was added nuclear bombing, one can understand Stalin's great care in avoiding a war with the United States. But cautious as Stalin thought he had to be, he believed it was safe to test the limits of American toleration. This contrasted with his policy of blanket appeasement of Hitler after the fall of France in the spring of 1940. Paradoxically, the U.S. nuclear monopoly combined with a low level of readiness gave Stalin more leeway. In a Soviet-U.S. crisis, the United States did not have to contemplate striking first in the fear that a Soviet first strike might confer an irreversible advantage. The Soviet Union for its part, could safely estimate that many months, if not a year, would elapse before a campaign of nuclear bombing of the Soviet Union could be inaugurated. Therefore, the Soviet Union could break off a foray, if it seemed to entail too high a risk of war. The possibility of a *prompt*, massive nuclear attack in response to a probe did not have to be entertained.

As for the U.S. disposition to initiate war, the Soviet leaders may have been reassured by the very rapid demobilization of the American forces and their withdrawal from the continents of Europe and Asia. Even those U.S. congressmen most opposed to communism were unwilling to vote the funds for a large military establishment.

Although the actual Soviet and U.S. military dispositions suggested little genuine concern about the likelihood of an armed conflict on the European continent, the rhetoric on both sides was agitated. In his 1946 speech on the Third Five Year Plan Stalin described the United States as a dangerous and aggressive imperialist power. It was probably necessary, in Stalin's view, to reintroduce into Soviet society those tensions which had been dissipated by victory and to dispel hopes for a liberalization of the internal regime. During the war the peasants were encouraged to hope that the kolkhoz system would be abolished after the war. The millions of ordinary people who joined the Communist Party at the front also believed that the fierce oppression of the years immediately preceding World War II would not be revived after victory. Stalin needed a foreign enemy to justify the new sacrifices he demanded of the hard-driven population.

The artificiality of the short-range threat was not inconsistent with a genuine Soviet belief that, sometime in the future, a Soviet-U.S. war could break out. The best means to deter the outbreak of such a war was to improve the quality of Soviet military power. The very successful programs for the fabrication of nuclear weapons and for the development of ballistic missiles were pushed forward vigorously while the forces-in-being were reduced.

A crude parallel is to be found on the American side. Some American leaders had permitted themselves to nourish illusions about a change in the political character of the Soviet Union. The puncturing of illusions produces sharp reactions. It is easier to charge betrayal than to admit self-deception. American reaction to the imposition of communist controls in Eastern Europe mounted sharply, but the response was largely verbal.

A domestic development which intensified this trend was the hunt for and the punishment of subversives. Since the postwar world did not turn out to be eminently satisfactory, a vigorous search for culprits began. Not surprisingly a few Americans were found to have been Soviet espionage agents. Truman's opponents took up the cudgels and put him on the defensive. He therefore found it politically useful to demonstrate his (genuine) anticommunism. As in the Soviet Union, domestic and foreign policy were of a piece.

The loss of Yugoslavia as a satellite made Stalin fear for Soviet control over the other East European satellites. Similarly the Berlin blockade (to be considered in the context of the German question) prepared the way for a more active American military involvement in Europe after the beginning of the Korean War. Between 1950 and 1953 the strategic balance between the Soviet Union and the United States changed radically, with both sides abandoning former views about both the likelihood and the consequences of a war between them.

The very great expansion of the U.S. forces, including the manufacture of many nuclear weapons, during the Korean War meant that by the end of 1953, at the latest, the United States was able to launch a massive nuclear attack upon the Soviet Union on very short notice. The older safety cushion provided by the necessity for U.S. mobilization no longer existed. If the Soviet Union miscalculated the American response (as she had in Berlin and Korea), she might not have the time to withdraw as in the first case or settle for the status quo ante as in the second. Never again did the Soviet Union present the United States with the *fait accompli* of the seizure of a position and the statement in effect that an American attempt to retake it might expand the conflict. Indeed, Mr. Dulles threatened nuclear war as the American response to a repetition of the Korean aggression.

It required several years—at least until the early 1960s—for the Soviet Union to be able to confront the United States with intercontinental nuclear strength. Despite this great military improvement, the Soviet Union had been unable to advance its political goals. In a sense the very magnitude of the expected consequences of a nuclear war has inhibited its outbreak and has therefore made a relative advantage less and less important.

World opinion has been so impressed, and correctly, with the revolutionary nature of nuclear weapons that it has begun to believe incorrectly that a new technological revolution can occur every half decade. Since the appearance of nuclear weapons on the world scene, it has been feared that hydrogen weapons, missile delivery vehicles, and, lately, perfected defense systems could so shift the military balance that whichever power gained a commanding advantage in a technological novelty could initiate and carry through a nuclear war with impunity. But these fears turned out to be groundless. The hydrogen weapon plus the ballistic missile was an important change, but it did not produce the possibility of a meaningful victory; nor will the ABMs (antiballistic missiles) in all probability.

The United States has always enjoyed superiority in the arms race, even when the Soviet Union led in developing ballistic missiles. The reasons for the Soviet failure to convert a technological priority into a military superiority are instructive. Apparently Soviet development of the ballistic missile began in 1945 or 1946 on the basis of the German V-2s, whose experimental models and technicians had been transported to the Soviet Union. A little more than ten years later the Soviet Union launched the first ballistic missile and put into orbit around the earth the first artificial satellite. The ballistic missile in combination with the hydrogen bomb seemed then, and still does to many, an invulnerable weapon. The Soviet Union had stressed the development of ballistic missiles even before it was realized that hydrogen bombs could be developed and that they would weigh enough less than A-bombs to make their combination with missiles of such great military significance. From the late 1940s the United States could extend the range of its aircraft by using intermediate military bases, but the Soviet Union had to wait until the establishment of communism in Cuba to employ overseas bases to extend the reach of its strategic forces. Hence the priority accorded to missiles.

The United States had had some inkling of the progress of this program, and in December, 1954, it inaugurated a crash effort to catch up with the Soviet Union. As it turned out, however, the United States deployed operational ballistic missiles earlier than the Soviet Union. Opinions differ as to when the U.S. ballistic missile was truly operational, but the application of any consistent standard would assign the United States a clear first in time and numbers. It is the much larger and qualitatively superior U.S. technological and economic base which enabled the United States to catch up with and overtake the Soviet Union in this weapons system.

Unfortunately, in the United States this reassuring demonstration of superior American capacity was not appreciated at the time, and President Kennedy "ran scared" instead of moving with the confidence of clear superiority. The Soviet politico-military policy and the election campaign of 1960 combined to mislead him about the true situation.

In the Soviet Union Khrushchev had come around to the conclusion, first enunciated in 1954 by Malenkov, that a nuclear war would destroy civilization. Therefore the proper quantity and balance of forces could not be determined by the traditional calculus of whether they could win a war. The new calculus concerned itself with deterrence of the opponent and the contribution of military strength to Soviet political goals, of which keeping the international communist system intact was a primary one. In his speech in January, 1960, Khrushchev offered an elaboration of the mutual deterrence argument and proposed a reduction of the theater forces in Europe. It was also realized later that the Soviet Union in the same period was unable, or unwilling, to expend the resources necessary to surpass the United States in numbers of ICBMs. Khrushchev's proposal met with opposition from the military leaders and their associates. The struggle lasted for several years, with the military winning out as events demonstrated that the Soviet Union could preserve the integrity of the international communist system only with great difficulty.

The immediate danger was the internal situation in East Germany, which grew continually worse as valuable personnel poured out through Berlin. Khrushchev tried to extract concessions from his foreign opponents by a program of nuclear menace in which he sought to have his opponents draw the erroneous conclusion that the Soviet Union was superior in missile strength. (It was, but in intermediate missiles, not in the ICBMs capable of reaching the United States.) Had Khrushchev succeeded, he would have solved the East German problem in a much more satisfactory fashion than by building a wall, and he would have made out an excellent case to his internal opponents that Soviet military strength was sufficient to prevent Soviet political losses and might even serve as the platform for Soviet political gains. The U-2 incident was the first major setback in Khrushchev's program. The second was the military policy of the Kennedy administration, to which we will now turn.

It was difficult in 1960 for the Democrats to accept at face value Republican reassurances about the military balance. In a closely contested election, it is hard to believe that the opponent's self-serving claims may be true. Thus when Khrushchev returned to the Berlin question soon after the election, as he had warned he would, Kennedy feared that he faced the choice between "holocaust and humiliation." The general expectation in the West was that the Soviet Union, on the model of the Korean attack, would execute a *fait accompli* and leave the United States with the bitter choice of accepting the change or widening the conflict. The situation was judged to be much worse than in Korea, because Soviet troops in preponderant strength were in the contested area and, unlike the situation ten years earlier, *both* sides had nuclear weapons. Given such an appreciation of the situation, Kennedy was naturally very troubled and pursued long- and short-term policies to extricate himself from this painful position. For the short term he continued to insist that he would resist Soviet encroachment on Berlin, and he deliberately implied that he might go to nuclear war. Here was brinkmanship indeed. Kennedy was doubtless greatly relieved (as indeed the West Germans were themselves) that his resolution was never put to the test. The Soviets, who had to take the first step, knew what the military balance really was.

Kennedy and his advisers had anticipated the problem of Soviet pressure on Berlin, and they came prepared with a plan for the expansion of ground forces in Europe, so that they would have more options than instantaneous massive retaliation in response to a Soviet *fait accompli* in West Berlin. This plan was rapidly executed, and the Soviets now had to face not only continued inferiority in intercontinental arms but also a significant alteration of the balance of power in Europe. Until that time the Soviet Union had been generally accorded superiority in Europe, and the United States superiority in strategic bombing forces. In a sense the United States had deterred the Soviet Union from changing the political status quo by force by possessing the capacity to destroy the Soviet Union with strategic air forces. The Soviet Union had deterred the United States by possessing the capacity to conquer Europe, and in the late 1950s and early 1960s to destroy it with nuclear weapons delivered by aircraft and missiles of short and intermediate range. The Soviet generals and Khrushchev's opponents could now convincingly argue that Khrushchev's plan to reduce the forces in the European theater and to be deliberate in the deployment of ICBMs had been a reckless gamble.

When Kennedy realized sometime in the summer of 1961 that he had overestimated Soviet military strength, he hastened to convey this realization to the Soviet Union in order to dissuade Khrushchev from further bluffing and from taking risks. Kennedy's dissuasion succeeded, but only at the price of Khrushchev's trying another expedient to improve the Soviet strategic position and, hardly unimportant to Khrushchev, his own internal political position.

In the fall of 1961 the Soviet Union broke off an unofficial moratorium on nuclear testing, announced plans for making bigger H-bombs (100 megatons), and made greatly exaggerated claims of progress in developing an ABM. Some months later a plan for a quick rectification of the inferior Soviet position was adopted. The idea was obvious. Since 1948 Soviet military planners had dealt with the basic asymmetry of the military balance. The United States could reach the Soviet Union because it could employ bases in Europe and elsewhere to extend the reach, first of its aircraft, and then of its missiles. Now that Cuba had become a communist country, why could not the Soviet Union also enjoy the military advantage of bases close to the opponent?

During the Berlin crisis the agitated discussion of what the United States could and would do to defend the city was in terms of the strategic balance. Whether or not an intellectually satisfying argument could be made on that basis was irrelevant. During the missile crisis Kennedy certainly, and Khrushchev probably, believed that a superior

Soviet capacity to destroy targets in the United States would make it easier for the Soviet Union to make political advances at the expense of the Western alliance. It is now irrelevant to argue that since that time the Soviet Union has altered the strategic balance by gradual augmentation without making political advances in West Berlin or anywhere else in the recognized sphere of the opponent. The beliefs of 1961 were firmly held and influential on decisions.

Khrushchev's political defeat in the missile crisis was assuaged by the partial test ban agreement, which was correctly understood by Khrushchev as an indication that the United States would not try to force concessions from the Soviet Union on the basis of genuine military superiority, as Khrushchev had earlier attempted on the basis of presumed military superiority.

One of the features of informal agreements is that when one party decides that the other has violated the understanding, it is free to take countermeasures without establishing the fact of violation in any tribunal. During the last years of Khrushchev's tenure of office and since then, the advocates of larger Soviet military budgets either believe, or have made out a case for believing, that the United States has violated the stand-off represented by the test ban agreement of 1963. The argument is that the United States pursues a policy of selective co-existence, expecting that the Soviet Union will not intrude into U.S. spheres of influence, but permits itself to attack other socialist countries. The bombing of North Vietnam is the strongest argument for that case. For a time a rough parallel could be drawn between the Soviet situation in Eastern Europe and the U.S. position in Southeast Asia. Both governments justified the dispatch of troops to the territory of an ally on the ground that danger threatened from the other camp. In both cases the danger was much more internal than external. With the bombing of North Vietnam that began in February, 1965, the rough simile becomes unserviceable. The United States had introduced an absolutely new feature into postwar international life. It publicly took the credit, or assumed the onus, for an attack on a socialist state. The Soviet Union had never directly attacked a capitalist state and had consistently maintained that the North Koreans were only responding to an attack from the south. As of this writing, the North Vietnamese do not admit that the troops sent south after the bombing are North Vietnamese regulars.

The open and admitted character of the bombing of North Vietnam has made it possible for the Soviet hard-liners to argue convincingly that the United States permits itself actions it does not permit the Soviet Union simply because it is stronger. After all, the argument may run, only superior strength, not equity, justifies American bases close to the Soviet Union, and denies the same advantage to the Soviet Union. After some hesitation the Soviet Union made an effective response to the bombing of North Vietnam. Its provision of anti-aircraft equipment and of economic aid has eased the situation of the North Vietnamese, who have only to endure to win, as has been remarked more than once. But the basic asymmetry in the Soviet and the American positions remains.

Even if we had access to all the Soviet internal discussion about the strategic balance and the challenge of the American bombing of North Vietnam, we probably would not be able to determine in any precise way just how the Soviet decision was made to increase the offensive missile forces and to go ahead with defensive missile forces. Enough appears in the Soviet press to make it obvious that these large expenditures are continuously debated rather than decided upon by a single center. While it cannot be determined just how much the American bombing or the cessation of bombing, or the U.S. decision to deploy the Safeguard ABM system affects the internal political contest in the Soviet Union, it should be quite clear by now that the strategic systems of both major powers interact both in the rather unreal world of war planning and in the very real world of the struggle over the allocation of scarce resources within each country.

It could perhaps be argued that the successive large increases in military allocations in the Soviet Union and in the United States have brought neither country any benefits in its foreign policy but have only prevented losses. Even though the fear of a loss is often a greater incentive to action than the prospect of gain, it seems likely that on both sides the appetite for continually improving the military balance will become somewhat attenuated. A quarter-century after World War II it seems—and leaders on both sides accept the proposition in varying degrees—that strategic superiority and inferiority are connected with political power only in a very general way, and that the danger of nuclear war is not very high. To the extent that Soviet and American leaders share such an attitude, the political costs of continuing the upward spiral of the arms race will weigh heavier in the balance than the fear of falling behind. While these lines are being written, the future of the Safeguard system is still unresolved. Whether it is funded or not, in the long run the importance of the strategic balance between the United States and the Soviet Union will probably decline. As it is realized that new weapons cannot alter the strategic balance so that the initiation of war becomes an attractive policy, both sides will not search eagerly for technological breakthroughs to gain advantage for themselves or to neutralize the opponent's presumed advantage.

4. The Problem of West Germany and West Berlin

The most enduring of the political problems between the Soviet Union and the United States has been Germany. It has often been remarked that nothing endures like the provisional, and the German settlement after World War II is a case in point. The background of the problem will be reviewed to the extent necessary to examine the present situation.

At the end of World War II Germany was occupied by the troops of the Soviet Union and its nonsocialist allies. Since they quickly recognized that they differed on the future political regime for all Germany, they agreed to administer different parts of Germany separately, leaving open the possibility that in the future Germany could be reunited with suitable provision for the political and security interests of the victorious powers. With the passage of time, however, the basic differences between the powers have seemed to be less rather than more reconcilable.

For the Soviet Union the conceivable objectives for Germany can probably be ranked as follows: first (obviously unattainable in the short run), a unified communist Germany; second, a neutralized, demilitarized Germany that might, under certain assumptions, be an intermediate stage toward the first objective; third, a divided Germany in which the Soviet Union would control one portion and the capitalist powers the other, and in which no Germans would have armed forces; fourth, the present situation; and fifth, and least desirable, a united, remilitarized Germany under Western control. Though at times the more desirable objectives seemed within reach, Stalin and his successors never took any risks to attain them, fearing that if the attempt failed, the net situation would be worse. Some instances will be examined in detail presently.

The Western powers had remarkably similar objectives and apprehensions. They preferred a united, noncommunist Germany, but they feared that to seek only to fail in that most ambitious aim would jeopardize the control of West Germany. Quite naturally, the leaders of each part of Germany shared and reinforced the predispositions of their great-power protectors.

Adenauer, like many charismatic leaders, loved his country but had a rather low opinion of its inhabitants. The comparison with de Gaulle is obvious and explains in part their affinity. Adenauer felt it his mission to purge Germans of their worst qualities and to prepare them for a more worthy destiny. Adenauer also believed and said, not so privately, that the Prussians were the worst of Germans and that Germany could best proceed to her regeneration separated for a term from Prussian influence and leadership. In close association with Western Europe and ultimately integrated with it, Germany would be cleansed of her aggressiveness and would once again occupy an honorable and admired place in a civilized Europe. Adenauer believed further that the communists, Russian and East German, partook of the barbarism and atavism which the Nazis had exploited and inflicted on Germany. For this reason alone they were to be shunned. In addition, Adenauer found negotiations for reunification with the communists distasteful, since by raising what he believed to be illusory hopes, they deflected West Germany from its best course, integration with West Europe. Adenauer was not insincere in his repeated endorsement of reunification as a goal; but he believed that it would be feasible and preferable after West German ties with Western and largely Roman Catholic Europe had become too firm to be easily loosed.

In much the same way, Ulbricht in East Germany considered that the pursuit of the presently unobtainable goal of reunification only raised hopes of an end to communist rule and postponed the readiness of the essentially anticommunist population to come to terms with the regime and make the best of it. Each of the great-power sponsors had, as it were, a stake in the intransigence of its opposite number. This mutual preference for the status quo over new ventures was reinforced by their allies. Moreover, neither in Eastern nor in Western European countries was there much enthusiasm for the reunification of Germany. The memory of the recent war was still vivid.

Although one could justly ascribe a community of policy to the two parts of Germany, their internal situations differed radically. The western part of Germany was not only much larger but it had also been the recipient of extensive allied aid; the eastern part of Germany was smaller and had been ruthlessly exploited by the Soviet Union. As a consequence of this contrast and also of the indifferent success enjoyed by command economies in industrialized countries, Western Germany had become vastly more prosperous by the mid-1950s, and the regime in the east added repression to its other negative features. Consequently many East Germans fled west, generally through West Berlin.

By the supposedly provisional arrangements of 1944, the Western powers retained control of West Berlin with guarantees of free access across land or by air. Once East Germans made the relatively easy passage to West Berlin, travel to West Germany by air was safe and as a rule not subject to East German interference. Consequently there ensued a mass exodus of the most valuable elements of the East German population, many of whom had been trained at the expense of the state. So large was the drain that the very existence of the East German state was in jeopardy. At this point it is appropriate to interrupt the account and to characterize Khrushchev's general purposes in order to demonstrate how much the East German situation hindered their achievement.

Observers of the Soviet scene are coming increasingly to believe that Khrushchev, for all his mercurial alternation between blandishment and threat, was in Soviet terms essentially liberal, or in our terms more flexible. This "liberalism" required reasonably good relations with the West—a goal which untoward developments more than once caused to recede when it was almost within grasp. Khrushchev's freedom of action was limited by his own domestic opposition. When he ousted Malenkov to become himself the main figure in the Soviet Union in February, 1955, Khrushchev had been charging that Malenkov had been reckless with the security of the Soviet Union in trying to reduce allocations to the military sector. Naturally this brought the military leaders and the more conservative elements in the upper echelons of Soviet politics to Khrushchev's side. Once he had grasped power, however, Khrushchev was willing to dispense with the support of some of those who had helped him. During the party crisis of June, 1957, Khrushchev was dexterous enough to align some of the military in the person of General Zhukov against the more conservative elements who sought to replace him. General Zhukov, when he had served his purpose, was dismissed in the fall and returned to obscurity. Once Khrushchev had consolidated his internal position, he was freer than he had been heretofore in his dealings with China. Before he had bested his internal opposition Khrushchev could not afford to answer for poor relations with China. But the continued satisfaction of Chinese demands could only erode the basis of Khrushchev's political position in the Soviet Union. Clearly the Chinese wanted not only Soviet technological assistance but also extensive economic aid, so that, according to the Chinese formula, the Soviet Union and China would reach the stage of consumer abundance at approximately the same time. Obviously the Soviet population, including its ruling elite, was not prepared for such extensive generosity to a fraternal communist state. Once it became clear that the Soviet Union would proffer only very modest technological, economic, and finally even political assistance to China, the Chinese had increasingly less to lose by characterizing the Soviet policy as unworthy of a socialist state, hoping thereby to encourage the anti-Khrushchev forces to dismiss him. If this analysis is accurate, conflict with China was inevitable.

Nor could Khrushchev afford to lose any of the gains of socialism in Eastern Europe. He therefore had to prevent the socialist countries of Eastern Europe from passing out of socialist control. Since Khrushchev's domestic political strategy for besting his internal enemies required him to bring more people into the narrow orbit of decision-making, he supported programs for greater individual prosperity. Consequently he was impelled to keep the arms budget down, and he had to find a way of doing that simultaneously with providing for the security of Eastern Europe. It was not Khrushchev's primary goal to further good relations with the United States, a requirement for moderation in arms expenditure, nor to keep the Chinese in obedient subjection. Both were necessary to secure Khrushchev's internal political position; but he soon found that those goals were contradictory. He had to sharpen conflict with the United States because of the needs of the East Germans. Though in the long run reasonably good relations with the United States were crucial for the accomplishment of Khrushchev's grand design, in the short run a collapse of the regime in East Germany or the necessity for enormous Soviet economic aid could have caused Khrushchev to lose power in the Soviet Union, and it was to that immediate problem that he had to address himself.

To remedy the East German situation, Khrushchev had to stop the westward flow of the best-trained East German personnel. This was a sine qua non. As long as West Berlin was under Western control, he could not expect Western cooperation in stemming the tide. But if West Berlin could be made a free city or (most desirable of all) a part of East Germany, the immediate problem could be solved. In the long range, to have West Berlin as an outpost deep in East German territory, broadcasting by radio and television, represents a constant standard of comparison by no means favorable to East Germany. The building of a wall to keep East Germans in East Germany then achieved the minimal goal of stemming the tide of refugees, but not the wider objective of getting the West out of Berlin. The minimal character of the solution from the communist point of view is indicated at this point in the discussion in order to emphasize the inhibitions that restrained Khrushchev and to offer an explanation of their source. Khrushchev discovered that his efforts to get a better than minimal solution of the German problem aggravated his relations both with the United States and with China. Let us examine the second and less familiar case first.[4]

During the Berlin crisis, which extended from 1958 to 1962, Khrushchev and Ulbricht officially dropped the maximum goal of a unified Germany as unfeasible and damaging to the urgent task of maintaining the East German regime. (This represented less of a change for Ulbricht than for Khrushchev, for the former always realized that in a unified Germany he would play no role.) Khrushchev and Ulbricht were willing to settle for two Germanies or, as they put it, recognition of the consequences of World War II. Once the German problem had been "settled," no major sources of conflict between the Soviet Union and the United States would remain, and the Cold War could be liquidated. Only the "abnormal" situation in West Berlin prevented that devoutly to be wished for consummation, as Khrushchev insisted publicly and privately. While the beneficial consequences of such an agreement for the United States and the Soviet Union were obvious, from Peking's point of view the disadvantages were equally so. China had just started her pressure on the offshore islands and had begun to replace a policy of benevolent neutrality toward India with one of hostility because India was presumed to be slipping into the American camp.

In such a situation of confrontation with the United States, the radical improvement of relations between the United States and the Soviet Union which a settlement of the German question would have represented would have isolated China. Indeed, the much more modest rapprochement represented by the Test Ban Treaty of 1963 accomplished that. As long as the Soviet Union was hoping to improve relations with the United States, China could not hope for Soviet support of her claims to the offshore islands, or to Taiwan, for that matter. Furthermore, a settlement in Europe on the principle of two Germanies was hardly an attractive precedent for the Communist Chinese, who excoriated the idea of two Chinas. In the United States the significance of the Sino-Soviet differences was appreciated only by a few specialists (and rejected by others). Only toward the end of the period did U.S. political leadership realize the importance of the Sino-Soviet break and take it into their calculations.

Khrushchev, in pursuit of the goal of altering the regime in West Berlin and of gaining recognition of the two Germanies, aggravated

4. For the ideas on the Chinese role in the German question I am indebted to Professor Vernon V. Aspaturian, who let me read his manuscript on the subject.

relations with the United States, because he found it necessary to bluster and threaten. The West German political leadership had no overriding reason for yielding on the ultimate goal of a unified Germany. As a matter of fact, giving up on this maximum goal with no visible quid pro quo only threatened to create domestic problems within West Germany. Since the West Germans at that time could see no advantage in a solution calling for two Germanies, the only Soviet recourse seemed to be a program of menace and threat. To make these threats credible, Khrushchev exaggerated his military strength. In a manner frequently described, he led some in the West to believe that his nuclear and missile strength was greater than it was, and he did not spare detail in describing the horrors of nuclear war for Germany, France, and Great Britain, if the situation in Europe were not regularized, that is, if West Germany and the United States did not make concessions on West Berlin. Khrushchev hoped that the combination of bluster and a promise of clear sailing after he had his way would produce such concessions. At times it seemed as if first Eisenhower and then the West Germans might accede, but neither Eisenhower nor his successor, John F. Kennedy, yielded. However, especially when Kennedy was president, the United States greatly increased its military strength, thus adding a new spiral to the arms race. The military build-up during the Kennedy administration leveled off only after the pressure on Berlin ceased. For the sake of achievement of his minimal objective on Berlin, Khrushchev had to give up his cherished project of reducing Soviet forces in Europe, thus freeing resources for his program within the Soviet Union.

If American political leadership had believed at the time that something like the foregoing account of the Berlin crisis represented an accurate appraisal of the situation, could they have behaved very differently? A personal recollection may illustrate the problems of framing policy on the basis of appraisals of an opponent's intentions. In a heated private discussion among specialists on the Soviet Union, one man, who correctly realized that Khrushchev represented flexibility or liberalism in the Soviet context and that he was fighting a running battle with his conservative opposition, urged some U.S. concessions on West Berlin because Khrushchev needed a victory. However, others, though they accepted this general analysis of Soviet internal politics, insisted that Kennedy, particularly after the Bay of Pigs, also needed a victory. The attack on South Korea was still a vivid memory. The Soviet Union had encouraged a proxy to seize South Korea and to confront the West with the alternative of fighting or swallowing a defeat. Now, almost ten years later, the Soviet Union was relatively much stronger, and the general expectation was that the Soviet Union would, through the agency of its East German proxy, execute a *fait accompli* in West Berlin and present the United States with the choice of accepting a defeat or fighting. In fact Khrushchev's and Ulbricht's public statements were framed to suggest just such an outcome, and these statements implied that the United States was offered the more palatable alternative of voluntary surrender.

Khrushchev's foreign opponents did not yet know that he lacked the will to take such a risk. The prudential analysis seemed much more conservative than one based on an interpretation of Soviet internal politics and Khrushchev's position in that constellation. It was widely believed that if the United States agreed to some new arrangements for West Berlin that would make her a partner in suppressing emigration from East Berlin, the political situation in West Germany would deteriorate. There were already signs that the West German posture of defiance would be replaced by a desire to accommodate the power that had demonstrated its superior strength in Central Europe. Even if Khrushchev wanted the political regime in West Berlin changed only in order to stop the refugees, the accomplishment of that goal would create tempting opportunities for his exerting further pressure. After all, during the Korean War the United States had started to repel the North Korean invasion with the limited goal of regaining South Korea, but then for a time it aimed at the reunification of Korea. Nations have often raised their sights as fortune favored their cause. Khrushchev's consistent demeanor of menace supported such a prediction of his reaction to a concession. It seemed that he would have been incited by it rather than appeased.

Does the foregoing necessarily imply that an understanding of the internal politics of the opponent is largely irrelevant because the inevitable uncertainty of such estimates dictates decisions based largely on estimates of one's own vulnerabilities? Such conservatism has informed both Soviet and American action in many crises, but it is hardly an inevitable necessity. Though in retrospect one is inclined to agree with the contemporary judgment that American concessions on West Berlin would have been unwise, this does not exhaust the question. After Ulbricht had built the wall and abandoned the pressure on Berlin, it might have been useful, for example, to have pushed harder on arms control, to have considered slowing down the expansion of ground forces in Europe and even from a position of strength to have seriously considered the solution of two Germanies. If these initiatives had failed, the political cost would probably have been slight; if they had succeeded, Khrushchev and the "liberal cause" in the Soviet

Union would have been strengthened without Khrushchev's being incited to continued pressure. It is safer to make overtures to an opponent who has just suffered a defeat than to one who is celebrating a victory.

Except for a few flurries of activity, the German question lay dormant until 1967–68, when the initiative for a change in the relationship came from West Germany. These developments will be considered in the section on the relationship of the Soviet Union with other socialist states. As will appear, these relationships offer a better vantage point for an analysis of events than does the change in West German policy.

5. Soviet Relations with Other Socialist States

The general theme of this section is that the ideological connection between the Soviet Union and the other socialist countries has become a source of weakness, and that the disintegration of the international socialist system has had deleterious effects on the internal political life of the Soviet Union. A subordinate theme is that Soviet experience with underdeveloped countries (particularly China and Cuba) that became socialist has been so unsatisfactory that the desire to push for revolution in such areas has been much reduced.

During the early 1950s communism and Christianity were often compared. In both systems faith rather than reason justifies men's actions. Like many analogies this comparison illuminates at times and obscures at others. The Soviet ideology, like most, including even the so-called rational systems of the eighteenth century, is essentially based on faith. It was also believed that communism, like Christianity, would endure for centuries. Here a comparison is misleading, since the goals of the respective systems are so different. Christianity promises nothing on this earth. The Christian can only expect that his belief will bring eternal life. On this earth virtue is its own reward. For communists, however, whose God is History, the kingdom of heaven on earth is at hand. The believing communist has been led to expect material goods and creature comforts as recompense for his support of the correct revolutionary program. When these are not forthcoming, as they have not been in any socialist society, disillusionment and apathy follow. Being a secular faith, communism must offer secular rewards.

Christianity also enjoyed the advantage of slow growth. Three hundred years passed before Christianity became the state religion of the Roman empire, and several hundred more before it extended over Europe and across the Atlantic. Christianity by virtue of its slow

growth has sunk very deep roots, and to say that European civilization is Christian is no empty phrase. Communism, however, is shallow-
rooted. Although a case could be made for the proposition that Soviet
Russia is Russian and communist in culture, a common communist
culture cannot be ascribed to Czechoslovakia, China, and Cuba.

Unlike Christianity, communism has always been a state ideology,
burdening the Soviet Union with obligations to other states beyond
the normal obligations of state systems. The caesaro-papism of the
Byzantine empire hardly caused it to treat the Western Christians
with more consideration than it did the pagans and Moslems on its
borders. Church writers frequently deplored the wars fought between
rulers having a common faith, but these were actually a hidden source
of strength, for shifts in the relations between states left the religious
life of subjects untouched. Probably Christianity could not have long
survived the application of the sixteenth century principle *cuius regio
eius religio*, that is, subjects take the ruler's religion. In the communist
system today, however, when a communist heresy is deemed to be in
process of becoming a new ideology, the Soviet Union assumes that
state relations have changed and is ready to take prophylactic military
action. The differences among the socialist states are profound. The
distinctive character of each socialist state has deep historical roots.
In this paper it will perhaps suffice to define briefly the specific character of the socialist revolution in each country.

In Russia in 1917 the old order had been badly shaken by a disastrous war. As has been frequently described, the communist party, as
it came to be known, executed a coup d'état first in the capital city of
Petrograd and then in the major city of Moscow. After a long civil war
and a half-hearted intervention by several other states, the communist
party emerged as the ruler. In contrast to the moment after the seizure
of power, the party had greatly expanded and had organized an army
to fight foreign enemies and a security police to find and punish internal enemies and terrorize the population. The Soviet Union is distinctive in that the communist party and its major instruments of compulsion were essentially forged in the short civil war which ended in
1921.

Some twenty years later the countries of Eastern Europe became
socialist. In Rumania, Bulgaria, Hungary, East Germany, and Poland
socialism was imposed by force or, if one prefers, the presence of the
Red Army served to catalyze a social process that would have occurred anyway somewhat later. In these countries the leadership was
composed largely of party members who had returned from exile in
the van of the Red Armies. Frequently they came from minority na-

tionalities. Richard V. Burks's study demonstrates that in the prewar period East European communist parties recruited heavily from ethnic minorities. The rule of ethnic minorities (often Jews) began to end in 1951–52, when Stalin exported anti-Semitism to the communist parties of Eastern Europe. Stalin commanded the staging of a series of show trials which designated as traitors the very leaders earlier installed by the Soviet Union. Their former contacts with Tito were presented as incontrovertible evidence of guilt, and they were ignominiously done to death.

At present, East Germany excepted, the communist leaders of Eastern Europe represent a second generation of leaders with local roots. Some, like Gomulka, actually spent the war years in their own country, not in the Soviet Union, and represent a group of national communists who have roots in both the party and their own country. Often their political power derives from their ability to defend national against Soviet interests.

The communist countries which had important wartime guerrilla movements represent a second class. Yugoslavia and China, despite their disparate histories, have similar revolutionary origins. In China, as is well known, the communist party after the famous long march settled down in distant Shansi and Shensi. In that refuge the party developed a peasant program and the cadres that were to defeat the Kuomintang, whose structure had been badly damaged in the war. Partial but persuasive evidence suggests that the Chinese communists took power against Soviet advice and without any substantial assistance. Unlike the Russian party, the Chinese communists had been an important political force for twenty years before they assumed power.

In Yugoslavia, as in China, the communist party achieved the reputation of being the most vigorous element in the national resistance to the foreign occupier. But the Yugoslav Communist Party, unlike the Chinese, was insignificant before World War II, and grew up during the war. Here too the Soviet leaders discouraged the attempt to establish a socialist state and pressed Marshal Tito to share political power with King Peter. Like the Chinese, the Yugoslavs ignored Soviet advice and established a socialist state. Irritated by Tito's relative independence, Stalin insisted on the kind of obedience he exacted from leaders he himself had installed. When Tito refused, Stalin ejected him from the socialist camp in the expectation that this official indictment of heresy and treachery would cause Yugoslav communists to overthrow Tito. Once on his own, Tito found it necessary to liberalize his internal regime, economically and politically, in marked contrast to its early character. Yugoslavia's progress from being one of the most rigidly controlled East European states to being the exemplar of the independent path to socialism has marked the beginning of the end of a Soviet led socialist state system.

The communist revolution in Czechoslovakia is sui generis. Since Czechoslovakia is the only industrialized state to become communist, the particular circumstances of its adherence to that system merit close attention, as will its likely differentiation from the system in the future.

Czechoslovakia was born from the ruins of the Austro-Hungarian empire. Its Slovak population and the Ruthenian population of the Transcarpathian region had lived under Hungarian rule for hundreds of years. These areas represented a much lower level of economic and educational development than the Czech lands of Bohemia and Moravia, which had been ruled from Vienna since the early seventeenth century. A large and prosperous German minority populated the westernmost part of the Czech lands and many pockets throughout the country. These four national groups had been imperfectly amalgamated into a single nation by 1938, when Adolf Hitler encouraged the Germans to sue for separation. Czechoslovakia's allies passively, sometimes sorrowfully, contemplated the dismemberment of the country. Slovakia became "independent," and the Czechs, long habituated to foreign rule, reverted to the habit of formal compliance, giving the Germans remarkably little trouble during the war, despite propaganda to convey the opposite impression. The collaboration of the Czech population, especially of its working class, with the German conquerors further demoralized the country and prepared it for a second capitulation. At the end of the war the U.S. armies (though they could have done so) failed to occupy part of the country and its capital, in accordance with a prior agreement with the Soviet Union. For the Czechs this reconfirmed the belief that they had to make the best terms they could with the Soviet Union. To these blows to national confidence another was added. Immediately after the war the German population was expelled from the Sudetenland and its property confiscated. Though most of the German population had unquestionably welcomed the Nazis, their wholesale expulsion was yet another instance of the barbarism that had enveloped Europe. The Czechs who had taken over their properties believed that a communist regime was more likely to protect them against counterclaims in the future than would any other. In this atmosphere the only communist party in Eastern Europe with a solid basis in the working class was able to take power. The unique circumstances in the communization of Czechoslovakia are here emphasized because every other country which became communist was poor. The tsarist regime was called the "prison of the peoples": the socialist system might be called "the prison of the poor."

Cuba is the latest, and, perhaps, the last recruit to the socialist state system. Since Cuba is the only socialist state not contiguous to another, one wonders whether it constitutes a class of one case or of possibly several. Cuba, uniquely, became a socialist state in order to force itself upon the Soviet Union as an ally. Castro's revolution was not socialist, nor was Castro a communist in 1959. Only in the last stages of his revolution did he make some very limited arrangements with the communists of Cuba. At first both the Cuban communists and the Soviet press expressed concern that Castro, like many other Latin American leaders who mouthed radical phrases, would make his peace with the United States and establish a regime much like the one he had replaced. But they underestimated the novelty of the Castro phenomenon. The younger generation of Latin Americans, communist and noncommunist, was more action-oriented and anti-United States than was the older generation. The leadership of the Latin American communist parties believed that their socialist revolutions could take place only in the distant future, presumably after the United States of North America had become a socialist country. The older generation of political leaders in the other parties believed that the United States had to be, and probably would be, a partner in the modernization of Latin America.

The younger generation of Latin Americans believed that any changes, revolutionary or gradual, would be opposed by the United States. Castro, acting on the assumption that the United States would invade, sought an ally in the Soviet Union. (China, although ideologically attractive, was too weak.) To bag the reluctant protector, Castro moved leftwards and announced first that he was a Marxist-Leninist and finally that he was a communist. Since the international socialist system had formally ceased to exist with the abolition of the Comintern in 1943, none could deny Castro's claim that he was now a communist. The Soviet Union finally had to accept his claim, since there was no way of rejecting it. Both Castro and the Soviets understood that acceptance of this claim, even without a formal treaty, imposed an obligation upon the Soviet Union to help Castro survive.

Here was a new phenomenon. A noncommunist had made a successful revolution, created a mass party which absorbed the previous communist party, and then pronounced the whole to be a communist party. In sum, noncommunists could make revolutions which would later become communist when the leader announced his conversion. Johnny-come-lately communists could burden the Soviet Union with the obligation to support these "premature" socialist states. It now seems likely that henceforth the Soviet Union will not unreflectingly encourage any precipitate transition to socialism. The Cuban and Chinese experiences have made it clear that new socialist states bring costs as well as gains to the Soviet Union.

On the whole, the Soviet experience with other socialist states has been disappointing. On the assumption that a new war in Europe would make a defensive glacis advantageous, the new socialist states could be considered as a contribution to Soviet security. Since then, however, the growing nuclearization of Soviet forces has reduced (although not canceled) the military value of Eastern Europe; the Soviet attempt to derive the kind of military advantage from a base in Cuba that the United States derived from its military bases in Europe, North Africa, and the Near East failed. According to the best available estimates, resources on the whole now flow from the Soviet Union to other socialist countries, not vice versa. It would occupy too much space to review the total record of Soviet relations with other socialist states. An account of the 1968 crisis may serve to illustrate the problems other socialist states pose for the Soviet Union.

Despite the persistence of conservatism in the Czechoslovak Communist Party long after the Polish and Hungarian parties had experienced periods of liberalization, communism had not penetrated deeply into Czech life. By contrast, in the Soviet Union even those opposed to communism accept many of its basic tenets as truisms. The evidence is still too fragmentary to permit generalizations about where and under what circumstances the communist value system is internalized, but the persistence of older traditions in Czechoslovakia has been dramatically revealed. Since the Battle of the White Mountain in 1620, when Austrian rule and Catholicism were forced on the Czechs, the Czechs have learned how to maintain inner integrity while outwardly complying with superior force. In a sense the Czechs have been rather superficial Catholics; and their communism too has been only a thin veneer. Despite the extensive political purges and executions that took place between 1949 and 1953, the actual loss of life by comparison with the record of the Soviet Union was limited. In 1968 a large fraction of the population had reached political maturity before World War II, and a yet larger fraction had been formed politically by 1948, so that much of the population had had noncommunist political experience. Moreover, many had also experienced the Austro-Hungarian empire, the Czechoslovak republic, the German protectorate, and the restored republic from 1945 to 1948. Much of this noncommunist experience had been positive. By contrast, very few Soviet citizens can remember a noncommunist regime. Moreover, the very frequency of change in Czechoslovakia since 1918 has established the expectation that political regimes come and go. In the same period only a single system has existed in the Soviet Union, with the concomitant general expectation that change is unlikely. Pre-Soviet and anti-Soviet political literature is virtually unavailable in the Soviet Union. In Czechoslovakia home libraries were not confiscated, and the newest generation could read Masaryk and Beneš. Anyone who has talked with young Czechs and young Russians is struck by the contrast. The Czechs fit easily into the whole Western and Central European political and intellectual tradition; the Russians reveal at every turn their enforced isolation from that tradition. The deep conviction that communism was an imposed system made the Czech population resigned, but inwardly opposed, to communism.

The Slovak population with its more recent exposure to advanced political and intellectual currents, had come to articulate its sense of national identity by opposition to the Czechs, who, they felt, enjoyed unfair privileges. In prewar Czechoslovakia, the Slovaks, because of having long been under Hungarian rule, were what today would be called underdeveloped. The Slovaks demanded compensatory treatment to eliminate their industrial and educational backwardness. These differences should not be exaggerated, however, because by comparison with other East European countries the situation in Czechoslovakia was reasonably good. Nevertheless this uneasy relationship could not survive Hitler's occupation. Hitler set up a puppet regime in Slovakia which gave the Slovaks formal independence. Many Slovak intellectuals joined the German-approved Tiso regime, only later to join the Slovak Communist Party and to find themselves again subordinated to the Czechs. The Slovak nationalist agitation against the Novotny regime coincided with a raging economic crisis.

At the beginning of the 1960s Czechoslovakia was one of the few industrialized countries in the world which had a negative growth rate. The so-called "cadre" policy had been a dismal failure. Managerial and economic posts had been assigned on grounds of political loyalty. A discreditable failure in a traditionally flourishing economy was the consequence. Moreover, Czechoslovak industry had suffered less destruction than had any other in Europe during the war, because Allied bombers could not reach Bohemia and Moravia. The Germans therefore expanded the industrial plant there, thus enabling Czechoslovakia to emerge from the war with an augmented industrial base. Within some twenty years thereafter communist management had ruined the efficiency of a once leading industrial system. To remedy this situation,

Khrushchev had urged Novotny to pay heed to those in Czechoslovakia who wanted to introduce some flexibility and leeway into the economic system. Consequently, in the early 1960s Czech economists were permitted by Novotny, rather grudgingly, to work out plans for reform. But the institutional changes necessary for implementing the reforms were not permitted, because they would have undermined the communist party. In a system in which efficiency rather than party loyalty dictated advancement, the party as then constituted could not survive. Hence, Novotny temporized in instituting the overdue reforms. By the beginning of 1968 the crisis had become so severe that the Novotny-appointed members of the Presidium dismissed him. These Czechoslovak developments fatefully coincided with the changes in West Germany, to which we now turn.

Adenauer's successor, Erhard, continued the Eastern policy largely unchanged, although the conviction was growing that the time for changes in attitudes toward East Germany and Eastern Europe had come. Many developments were contributing to these altered sentiments. For one, the refugees from the Sudetenland, Silesia, and the other Germanic areas of Eastern Europe had become economically well established in West German society, and consequently their interest in the reversion of the lost lands had diminished. But the leaders of this community continued to make irredentist statements which were duly reported in Eastern Europe.

The younger generation, too, played a role in the redirection of policy toward Eastern Europe. The Nuremberg trials had made little impression on the German population as a whole and none on the generation which has just come to political maturity. Little attention was paid to the trials staged by the conquerors, especially the Soviet Union, which bore the onus of the Katyn massacres. The first genuine confrontation of Germans with their past took place when the German courts themselves started to try war criminals a few years ago. Then what had safely reposed between the covers of unread books became a live political issue, causing many younger Germans to examine the past and to pass a harsh judgment on the previous generation for its indifference and passivity in the face of the Nazi atrocities. The new generation knew that few of their fathers had participated directly in the extermination of the Jews, but that did not clear them of the crime of what is called in German, "civil indifference," that is, eschewing personal responsibility for actions carried out by the state. Many understood that such irresponsibility was not peculiarly German, but that knowledge did not diminish the sense of shame and the determination to avoid similar disgraces to the nation. The burning issue of conscience for the West Germans of the early 1960s was East Germany. Adenauer's insistence on unification or nothing was characterized as a policy that ignored the plight of their East German brothers. Improved relations with East Germany, it was said, would stimulate the liberalization of the East German regime, thus relieving the Germans of the charge of being indifferent to the fate of other Germans because they themselves were prosperous.

With the accession to power of the Kiesinger government, representing a coalition of both major parties in Western Germany, a sharp change in West German policy became a distinct possibility. Each of the major parties, as in many other countries, had been reluctant to adopt a stand which might cost a few percentage points in a close election. Despite the growing dissatisfaction with old Cold War policies, most West Germans were not ready to countenance a formal abandonment of the goal of a unified Germany. The coalition government, however, could modify the rigid adherence to a policy of reunification, without challenging it directly, by effectively abandoning the Hallstein doctrine of no recognition of states that recognized East Germany, and by expanding economic relationships. Because of the taboo on giving up the principle of reunification for the foreseeable future, the probable result of the more flexible policy toward the East was not spelled out.

Yet it was obvious that the establishment of state relations with states recognizing East Germany and the acceptance of existing territorial arrangements meant the effective recognition of East Germany. The vagueness of the purpose of the policy permitted its support by groups with diverse goals. Some felt politically embarrassed to oppose it but hoped it would fail; others viewed it as a form of political warfare against communism; still others realized that the settlement of German borders on the basis of the status quo and the recognition of Eastern Germany as a separate state would mean the end of dependence on the United States. Once Germany had made a settlement with the Soviet Union and the Eastern European countries and had effectively abandoned the goal of German reunification, its utter dependence on the United States would no longer be necessary. Once relations with its neighbors to the East had become normal, Germany could pass from a client status to independence.

This analysis somewhat overstates the case, because German political leaders shrunk from stating or even seeing whither the new policy could lead. Different groups had different expectations of the consequences of the policy and feared that to be precise about its consequences would produce a debate which would block the effort to improve relations with the communist states to the east. Thus those who hoped that the new policy would isolate East Germany and cause its collapse found themselves allied to those who hoped that only a policy of reassurance to East Germany would permit the liberalization of the political regime in that country. An outsider cannot judge what the "real" West German purpose was, but the enthusiasm of some of the strongest critics of the Adenauer policy was impressive, as was the recognition in some sections of the Soviet press that the Kiesinger government had struck out in a new direction.

The execution of the West German policy was clumsy, but not abnormally so. It is perhaps unfair to blame West German policies for Soviet responses. Since there were at least two West German policies, the Soviets could have chosen to encourage one over the other. Yet from the very beginning of the Kiesinger initiative, the bulk of the Soviet press excoriated his policies more shrilly than they had Adenauer's. The costs of doing so were great, because it had long been realized what benefits would accrue to the Soviet Union from the recognition of two Germanies. Since December, 1958, Khrushchev had sought the recognition of two Germanies, because he understood that this would remove the chief reason for the United States' presence in Europe and would lead to the radical transformation or the dissolution of NATO. The maximum settlement would have included West Berlin within East Germany, but even the minimal settlement (preserving the status of West Berlin intact) would have completed the legitimization of the East European socialist regimes, since the strongest state in Central Europe now would have formally recognized them. The political recognition of legitimacy might be accompanied by economic aid. When Khrushchev's son-in-law, Adzhubei, visited West Germany in the summer of 1964, he indicated that West German loans to the East were part of the general settlement Khrushchev had in mind. Indirectly, he also held out hopes of liberalization in East Germany by telling interlocutors that it wasn't worth talking about the "Ulbricht problem," since he was mortally ill with cancer. In this scheme the American presence in Europe would diminish, and the West Germans would acquire a stake in the status quo in Eastern Europe.

One of the chief consequences of such a settlement would have been the opportunity to reallocate resources within the Soviet Union. About half the Soviet military budget, as best one can calculate,[5] is devoted

---

5. This was roughly the division between strategic and NATO forces for the United States before the expansion of the Vietnamese war. Strategic forces, especially missile forces, do not require the very large outlays for training and exercising that other forces do.

to forces in the European theater stationed mostly in East Germany. A political settlement in Eastern and Central Europe would have removed the most compelling arguments for the maintenance of large Soviet forces in Eastern Europe. In his speech of January, 1960, Khrushchev advocated just such a reduction, although on more general grounds. Such a change would have reduced the size and the political influence of the military in Soviet decision-making. The great consequences for the political alignment within the Soviet Union made some eager to recognize sincerity in West German initiatives for settlement and others determined to reveal their duplicity.

The Soviet Union, according to the thesis presented above, rejected a genuine chance of achieving long-held goals in Europe. The reasons are to be found in Soviet fears of the vulnerability of the socialist camp to the forces of internal dissolution. The viability of the East German regime was the most immediate problem. Despite the impressive economic improvement that had taken place since the construction of the wall in Berlin and the cessation of emigration, East Germany still felt insecure. It constantly faces another more prosperous and attractive Germany. By law, refugees from East Germany are automatically citizens of West Germany and find positions in the expanding economy of West Germany. The West Berlin radio and television daily present a society more appealing to most East Germans than their own. Good relations with West Germany would be worse than bad because it would offer more opportunities for comparison. As long as West Germany can be pictured as the enemy poised to strike at the accomplishments of socialism in East Germany, the harsh internal regime can find some justification. Would not the West Germans use the economic dependence that would flow from expanded trade and from loans to force changes within East Germany and finally absorb it?

The new West German flexibility also presented problems to the Polish Communist Party, which had signally failed to fulfill the economic and political promise of the semirevolution of October, 1956. The Polish Communist party has only limited popular support, and its greatest strength is the belief that the Soviet Union guarantees to Poland the possession of former German territories. The Silesian territories had been populated by Germans for hundreds of years longer than the Sudetenland, and the Polish tenure depended either on Soviet support or on formal German recognition of the change. Many Poles considered that these western territories were a compensation for the Western Ukrainian territories which had been ceded to the Ukrainian Socialist Republic; but they understood that Germany would not accept that argument, and so felt themselves bound to the Soviet Union. That indeed was one of Stalin's objectives in shifting the Polish frontier westward. Just as West German dependence on American support would be reduced if a Central European settlement were to be reached, so would Polish dependence on the Soviet Union be reduced. But the Polish communists fear the consequences more than any major West German party does.

Significantly, the sharpest crisis with the Catholic Church in Poland was occasioned by a first step toward a re-establishment of relations between German and Polish Catholics. Gomulka, like Ulbricht, finds West German friendly overtures a threat to his position. Unlike Ulbricht, however, Gomulka's opponents within the party openly challenge his authority and his policy. The chief figure in the opposition, General Moczar, obliquely indicated his program of pulling away from the Soviet Union by being relatively silent on West Germany. Such a silence in that context was a challenge to Gomulka and his backers in Moscow. The undisguised and insistent anti-Semitism of the Moczar group was in this Alice-in-Wonderland setting anti-Soviet, because it attacked the remaining Jewish communists who were loyal to Gomulka. Gomulka has been forced to dismiss them, thus weakening his internal position. The threat to the Soviet political position in Poland was never as severe as in Czechoslovakia, but Soviet policy toward the latter is partly explainable by the expected consequences for Poland.

East German, Polish, and Soviet suspicions of the intent, and their fears of the possible consequences of, the new West German initiatives were greatly magnified by the West German recognition of Rumania. By all accounts the initiative in this seems to have come from the Rumanians, the West Germans being more interested in first re-establishing relations with Hungary. The West German recognition of Rumania meant the abandonment of the Hallstein doctrine, according to which the West Germans refused to have any state relations with countries that recognized East Germany, on the ground that East Germany was merely an occupied Soviet zone and that its recognition by others compromised the prospects of reunification. The West German establishment of relations with the Soviet Union was a special case, it was argued. The unstated reason was probably a desire to be able to deal directly with the Soviet Union and dispense with a U.S. go-between. (This initial step in West German self-assertiveness also demonstrated that at some point the Soviet Union might make arrangements with West Germany that were not to East Germany's liking. After all, the Soviet Union did not insist that the United States recognize East Germany simultaneously with Soviet recognition of West

Germany. Such a position would have been consistent with the claim that the two Germanies were equivalent entities. This suggests that the political advantages of a Soviet-West German rapprochement were appreciated quite early by some in the Soviet Union.)

The circumstances of the West German establishment of relations with Rumania were such as to awaken fears of the disintegration of the Soviet position in Eastern Europe. The Rumanians ostentatiously failed to consult their allies, whose objections were well known. The East Germans and the Poles feared that, because neither they nor the Soviet Union would set the pace and fix the point at which each country would be recognized by West Germany, the latter and the stable East European regimes would be in the driver's seat. Obviously, the Rumanians and the Yugoslavs were not deterred by the embarrassment the Poles or East Germans might suffer, and the silence at international communist meetings of the Hungarians and the Czechoslovaks on the West German issue seemed to indicate that they might well follow the Rumanian example. In view of the vulnerability of the Soviet, East German, and Polish governments, even consummate skill and tact in the execution of the West German policy could not have avoided a sharp reaction.

The West Germans, however, were no more skillful or tactful than most. Domestic political necessities made it necessary to stress the political "victories" that West Germany was winning. Thus East Germany and the Soviet Union found abundant evidence for the thesis that West Germany's goal was subversion, not appeasement. A favorite bit of evidence was a book by Zbigniew K. Brzezinski in which he advocated West German settlement with other East European regimes before a settlement with East Germany. This would have the effect of isolating East Germany and forcing her to negotiate on the least favorable basis. One must appreciate the difficult West German position. In effect, the Soviet Union was demanding that the West Germans guarantee the internal regimes of East European countries. This demand is evidence of communist weakness rather than of West German malignity. (In much the same way U.S. plaints that a particular regime is unviable because of Soviet or Chinese subversion suggest that the regime is weak rather than that the Soviet Union or China is politically potent.)

We now return to our starting point: the internal revolt within the Czechoslovak Communist Party in January, 1968. For Czechoslovakia to improve the economic situation, it was necessary to improve the labor productivity of Czech industry, which had declined grievously. Both improved morale and more efficient plants were required. The

West Germans were willing to supply the necessary capital on favorable terms to Novotny's successors as a concomitant to the establishment of state relations. The change in West German policy coincided with the internal changes in Czechoslovakia. Once a liberalized Czechoslovakia could hope for noncommunist economic aid, the Soviet Union had either to acquiesce in the political changes or intervene militarily. The less dramatic option of economic pressure would have been increasingly difficult to exercise. The liberalization of Czechoslovak political life threatened serious political repercussions within the Soviet Union. Novotny's successors had the press censors suspend their activity; the jails began to empty; and the demands of the liberal communists became more and more radical from the Soviet point of view. Not only did free speech bring criticism of the earlier regime but also, by implication, criticism of the Soviet Union. Some of the incumbent Soviet leaders were charged with complicity in the trial and judicial murder of many Czechs. The Soviet security police and Mikoian were linked with the murder of Jan Masaryk, the son of the founder of the Czechoslovak state. The economic reformers realized that the old cadre policy had to go. Economic efficiency was to take precedence over party loyalty. Some even scouted the possibility of a multi-party system.

What kind of communist party would Czechoslovakia have had if events had continued to develop in this way? For the weak Eastern European regimes, immediate problems emerged. For example: though East Germans were not permitted to travel freely to West Germany, they were permitted to go to other East European countries, and very often separated German families from East and West Germany would meet in Prague and Budapest, returning later to their respective homes. In order to prevent these arrangements from being turned into a new flight from East Germany, the border officials prevented East Germans from leaving Czechoslovakia for West Germany. However, with the development of freedom in Czechoslovakia and the extensive relaxation of border controls, it was an open question as to how long the Czechs would continue to serve East Germany in preventing emigration. The ultimate consequence might well have been the prohibition of East German travel in Czechoslovakia. This is only one of the complications which the Czechoslovak events imposed on East Germany.

The feedback was not confined to East European regimes. Soviet citizens have resented the greater liberties and amenities enjoyed by citizens of the countries that the Soviet Union liberated or aided economically. Even with the great stagnation of Czechoslovak economic life, Prague was a much more inviting city than Moscow. When the Czechoslovak population for the first time in twenty years began to criticize the regime, the effect in the Soviet Union was notable. The Soviet repression of the Czechoslovak revolution became another one of the articles of indictment of the Moscow regime leveled by dissidents. Such protest is quite new in the Soviet Union. Now, in contrast to the Stalinist period, political protest and its repression have become a feature of Soviet society. Khrushchev tried to control danger by concessions, such as permission for Yevtushenko to play the role of licensed protestor, but the more conservative elements who have assumed control since Khrushchev's dismissal face sharper challenges to their authority. As the protest becomes bolder, its repression becomes more severe.

But more impressive than the protest of well-placed persons among the intelligentsia is the protest of workers like Marchenko, who was astute enough to understand from the Soviet press that the supression of the Czechoslovak reform movement was likely. Marchenko made the bitter and apt point that the events in China were reported in the press with a certain amount of glee because by comparison with the anarchy of Chinese domestic life, only repression reigned in the Soviet Union. The Soviet Union can more readily accept a harsh communist regime which is destroying the cadres of the communist party and the national economy than a liberalizing regime which may also make economic progress. Since the basic promise of communism is material prosperity, the Soviet Union is embarrassed if younger socialist regimes surpass it. The superior economic performance in capitalist nations does not present as much of a problem, as it can be explained as exploitation of the workers or of foreign dependencies.

The rapid progress toward extensive federal rights for Slovakia was another cause of embarrassment to the Soviet Union. The Czechs at the top of the party who wanted to retire Novotny because of economic failures were not strong enough to do so without the Slovaks, who demanded equal national rights. The Slovaks gained a new federal arrangement in which they enjoyed equality with the Czechs in many major institutions. Whether these constitutional changes would have been reflected in economic equalization, especially in proportional access to favored positions, was uncertain. But no non-Russian republic of the Soviet Union enjoys even a fraction of the federal rights the Slovaks have earned. In recent years nationalist demands in the Soviet Union have again become a feature of Soviet political life. Partial but persuasive evidence suggests that some Ukrainians wanted to emulate the Slovak example.

The Soviet leaders were apparently divided in judging how great a danger the Czechoslovak situation represented and how great the costs of intervention would be. The effect of the East European situation on relations with China was one subject of contention. In Prague during the summer of 1968 well-informed persons believed that Suslov had favored a compromise with Czechoslovakia. Suslov's conciliatory position in this case differs from his generally conservative attitude toward reform within and without the Soviet Union. According to the understanding of some Czechs, Suslov is a member of a group that sees China as a major threat to Soviet interests. It fears Chinese military power in the future; it finds China a present spoiler of international socialist unity. This group believes it necessary to keep things reasonably quiet in Eastern Europe in order to have freedom of action in Asia. But the higher party cadres, as a group, tend to be more relaxed about the Chinese danger. According to a series of articles in *Kommunist*, Mao Tse-tung is destroying the communist party and the economic structure of China. When China recovers her senses and reembarks on a program of modernization, she will again call for Soviet help.

In all probability Czechoslovakia will become a greater drain on Soviet economic resources than it has been. If and when the post-Dubček leadership states that a counterrevolutionary situation existed in Czechoslovakia in July, 1968, and that the Soviet intervention was justified, the Soviet Union will have to ensure the success of this regime. The basic economic problems still remain, and the Soviet Union will have to subsidize the economy extensively if another crisis is to be avoided.

The Soviet leadership probably foresaw some if not all the costs of military intervention. Fear of deterioration within Eastern Europe and the Soviet Union was more compelling than were estimates of the political and economic costs. Fear of damage to the self was the impetus. Such a spur to action is not peculiar to the socialist state system. Most would agree that the events in the Dominican Republic in April, 1965, represented a much smaller threat to the American political system in Latin America and certainly to domestic political stability than the events in Eastern Europe in 1968 represented to the Soviet Union. Yet many Americans then felt (and still do) that the potential danger justified the cost. In propaganda such interventions may be usefully designated as defensive or offensive; but these epithets contribute little to our understanding of the motivation. Fear of one's own vulnerability seems to provoke more and more costly actions than do opportunities to gain at the opponent's expense. Though the two ideological systems seem to share a propensity to act more vigorously from fear of loss rather than from expectation of gain, on the whole the Soviet system is perceived by its leaders to be in a much more dangerous state of disintegration than is the Western system.

The hesitation, the backing and filling, of the Soviet leaders during the crisis reveal their conviction that they were forced to choose between undesirable alternatives. No one in the Politburo was prepared to see counterrevolution succeed in Czechoslovakia—that is, to see the end of socialism in that country. The difficult question at any particular point was whether the situation had deteriorated so badly that it would soon become irreversible. Conflict and shifting opinions on that issue naturally arose. For some the point of no return came when West German loans became a likelihood; for others, it came before the election of a new Slovak Central Committee, which was expected to retire many of the pro-Soviet conservatives; for still others, it came when the censorship was relaxed.

But no Soviet leaders think it a matter of only marginal importance that a socialist regime continue or not. For the Soviet Union it is a matter of vital national interest that the internal regimes in a number of countries remain essentially unaltered. This is a terrible burden, given the political difficulties of many of these regimes. Not to oversimplify, the Soviet Union must either subsidize these regimes to keep them going or intervene to stop them from changing.

The United States has had the task of keeping regimes from "going communist," a much easier one than "keeping them communist." The experience of communism in Cuba, although troublesome for the United States, has perhaps not been without its salutary side. It is now being realized that when a small unimportant country becomes communist the consequences are proportionate to its size and are not absolute. For the Soviet Union this re-emergence of the cost-gain calculus of politics is still not possible, and therefore, to use a non-Marxist expression, the Soviet Union has overextended its commitments.

6. The Soviet Union as a Global Power: Relations with Countries in the Third World

From the preceding sections of this paper it emerges that the focus of Soviet foreign policy (and American for that matter) is in its relations with its allies. For both great powers, for example, the German problem is as much an "alliance" problem as a "confrontation" one. The direct confrontations between the Soviet Union and the United

States have been intermittent and comparatively short in duration, though very tense. The Berlin blockade, the Berlin crises of the late 1950s and early 1960s, and the Cuban missile crisis were resolved on the basis of the status quo ante. Thus a certain rough stability has been achieved between the two powers. The fear that this would eventuate in some sort of condominium or diarchy has proved groundless. The area of coincidence of interest, while important in the extreme, is quite circumscribed. Crises have arisen outside these areas when, as described in the last section, deterioration within a system has been instigated by or attributed to members of the other system. Officials on each side shrink from the term spheres of influence, but it nevertheless describes the situation fairly well.

The undefined area is that of the unaligned powers and to a certain extent the tenuously aligned members of the Western alliances. These two categories, though quite distinct in legal terms, share the characteristics of being poor and inadequately industrialized. Soviet policy in the Third World is concerned with both unaligned and aligned states, but almost without exception these are states whose internal economic and political arrangements are usually regarded as incomplete. The general Soviet goals in the Third World will be discussed next, followed by a detailed exposition of their pursuit in particular regions.

The first Soviet goal has been to deny former colonial areas to the colonial powers. As the colonies became independent after World War II, the Soviet Union used whatever influence it possessed to solidify and consolidate the independence of these new states. In Stalin's judgment, however, the independence that most of the colonies had gained was sham, and he continued to treat them as colonies, except for Israel, which he recognized promptly as a means of reducing the British position in the Eastern Mediterranean. During the Korean War, too, Stalin recognized that India was really not doing the bidding of the United States or Great Britain; but it remained for his successors finally to abandon the two-camp theory and to see the feasibility and utility of denying to the ex-colonial powers any further influence in the area of their former dominion. To this end the Soviet Union has been willing to support the wars of independence of the aspirant nations, but only verbally for the most part. Actually, decolonization has proceeded much more easily than had been expected at the end of World War II. For a considerable time the Soviet Union believed that in many of the former colonies an attempt would be made to reintroduce imperial control in a different guise. Most often neocolonialism, they expected, would employ the instrument of economic domination; sometimes, as in Egypt in 1956, old-fashioned military intervention would be resorted to.

The policy of denial could logically lead to two other goals. It had been generally believed at the end of World War II that the process of decolonization would be protracted and bloody. In this situation the communist parties would first participate in the war of independence together with other groups in the society, then would ultimately proceed to establish political domination. This familiar two-stage revolutionary strategy was hardly tested, since decolonization went off remarkably smoothly. Of all the dozens of states which achieved their independence, only a few had to struggle long for it. In Indochina, Algeria, and Indonesia the struggle for independence was prolonged. Only in Indochina did the communists succeed in establishing a state in part of the country. Though the struggle was prolonged and bitter in Algeria, the communist party's influence in the struggle was limited, because most of its membership was French, and the communist party of France moved to full support of the Algerians only very slowly and gingerly. In Indonesia the Dutch broke off the struggle before the communists had achieved a dominant position. So far only a single national struggle for liberation has yielded a new socialist state.

A third goal more modest than the second but more ambitious than the first is the familiar extension of influence. The Soviet Union would like to have influence in all parts of the world instead of only in adjacent areas. A fourth goal (really a variant of the third) might be called a policy of intrusion. The Soviet Union, by employing the same methods as in poor unaligned countries, tries to gain a measure of influence in such poor countries as are members of the Western diplomatic system. A fifth purpose is specific to China. The first four goals are pursued singly or in combination in the Far East, but the fierce competition with China often determines the thrust of Soviet activity. In some cases the Soviet desire to contain China has made for common purposes with the United States.

We shall examine the question regionally, beginning with the Near East, the scene of the first major Soviet investment of resources in the Third World. Some tentative forays had taken place in Guatemala and Syria in 1954, but the Third World policy really began with aid to Egypt. In 1955 (if we accept the account of Colonel Nasser's intimates) the Egyptians, after approaching the Chinese for military and economic assistance, came to the Soviet Union, which arranged for a large shipment of arms from Czechoslovakia. It is difficult and perhaps unimportant to determine whether the Soviet Union seized an opportunity for which it had previously worked out a general strategy, or whether the theory followed upon moves made simply because opportunity offered. Whatever its origin, the rationale for the new effort was simple enough. First, in the mid-fifties it was not obvious that decolonization would proceed without interruption. The French after their defeat in Indochina were determined to retain Algeria. The invasion of Egypt at the end of 1956 demonstrated that France and Great Britain still hoped to retain something of their former position. Only hindsight permits the judgment that the Soviet concern with neocolonialism was unnecessary, since the impulse in France or Britain to retain parts of their old overseas holdings was very weak. The formation of the Baghdad Pact and the inclusion of Iraq appeared to be an American effort to take over British responsibilities in the Near East and the Eastern Mediterranean. Soviet aid to Egypt was considered as a counterthrust to the new American initiative. The same applies to the inclusion of Pakistan in the CENTO Pact and the inauguration of Soviet aid to India.

The supply of arms to the Egyptians was not inconsistent with Soviet recognition of Israel in 1947. Now that the British had been ejected from their Palestine base, it seemed logical to consolidate Egyptian independence. This effort has earned some Egyptian gratitude and has contributed to the reduction of British and American influence in the area, but it has yielded little more, certainly not a favorable atmosphere for the creation of a new socialist state.

The Soviet attitude toward the transition to socialism in underdeveloped or precapitalist countries is strongly influenced by their own experience. Imperial Russia was less developed than Western Europe, and therefore the success of the first socialist revolution in that country constituted a modification of the expectation that the revolution would come first in the most advanced countries. The Soviet Union developed "socialism in one country," that is, it accumulated capital by saving. This meant a severe limitation of the consumption of the population. Since parts of the Russian empire had been in the premodern stage, it could be said that these areas had skipped the capitalist stage. Since Soviet policies in these areas were used as models for backward countries elsewhere, an appraisal of the relevance of this experience is in order.

Soviet writers have singled out the republics of Central Asia, particularly Uzbekistan, as models for the modernization of backward areas. The Central Asia republics (formerly Turkestan) represented one of the more backward areas of the Moslem world. Literacy was almost nonexistent, the standard of living was low, disease was rampant, and political control was in the hands of reactionary Moslem clerics. The region was backward even compared with the rest of Islam. Now these areas present a totally different picture. Literacy is very high by any standard, public health conditions are excellent, industrialization has come, and the indigenous population is beginning to share political control with the Russians. A small library of studies, many of them written for readers abroad, has presented these developments as proof that the Soviet model for industrialization and modernization is most suited to the needs of the poor countries. Recently, however, some Soviet writers have come to realize, and have obliquely indicated, that the Soviet experience is not relevant to underdeveloped countries elsewhere.

As the Soviet economy became centralized, the poorer areas benefited at the expense of the richer. Thus the absolute Russian and the Ukrainian living standards went down as Central Asian living standards went up. Moreover, Soviet ideological beliefs connected the existence of a native proletariat with effective political control. Hence industry was introduced into areas formerly supplying only raw materials. Soviet personnel in large numbers were dispatched to these areas, not only as security policemen and political controllers but also as teachers, foremen, skilled workers, and the like. Thus within a forty-year period a sparsely populated area benefited from a sizable capital investment both in plants and in skilled personnel. The much larger Slavic populations contributed to the development of the smaller Moslem populations of Central Asia, thus promoting a measure of acquiescence to the sovietization of the area.

This experience was not a model for other nations too distant to enjoy the advantages (together with the disadvantages) of incorporation into the Soviet Union. It was out of the question to make capital and expert personnel available to possible candidates for modernization and socialism in far-away lands. At the outset, however, the Soviet leaders, like others in similar situations, were beguiled by a superficial view of their own historical experience. In aiding Egypt many Soviet leaders were probably exclusively interested in pre-empting the United States; others perhaps cherished the illusion that building the Aswan high dam would put the country on the path to socialism. Soon, however, it was realized that the social composition of the newly liberated countries could not be readily changed; therefore the suppression of the communist parties in Egypt and other Arab countries was accepted. In North Africa particularly, the communist parties drew their membership, as they did in Eastern Europe, from ethnic minorities, who in this case were Europeans. These ethnic minorities could never play a prominent role in the struggle against European states.

At this very time the Soviet leaders unexpectedly found themselves committed in Cuba to extensive economic and political support of a weak country. Consequently, it was easy for them to accept the poor prospects for the transition of anti-European Arab states to socialism. If Algeria, for example, after achieving independence, had become a socialist country, it would no longer have received monetary subsidies from France and would have addressed all its claims to the Soviet Union. Egypt, too, if socialist, would have been deprived of U.S. or West German assistance. The Soviet Union could hardly be eager to add poor and importunate socialist countries to the socialist commonwealth. Cuba, with its comparatively well-developed infrastructure and a more favorable resource-population ratio than Algeria or Egypt, was already a heavy drain. Not surprisingly, Soviet doctrine shifted to an expectation that, unlike the process in Cuba, the national democratic stage (the period between liberation and the adoption of socialism) would be extended. The concept of national democracy envisaged a period in which the communist party would govern together with other parties. Cuba, Indonesia, and sometimes Mali, Ghana, and Guinea were examples. In this transitional period the Soviet Union could hope for a degree of control over the foreign policy of the government in question without assuming the burden of economic support. In the Near East the concept was further watered down into the theory of revolutionary democracy. Reduced to its simplest terms, this meant that, even if communist parties were proscribed or absorbed into state single parties, a positive sobriquet could still be applied, thus qualifying the country for Soviet support.

This sober reappraisal of the prospects for making revolutions in the Near East was probably believed to permit a limitation of Soviet political and economic involvement, but events proved otherwise. The Soviets succeeded to a certain extent in earning the credit for the cessation of the British, French, and Israeli attacks on Egypt, although clearly American pressure on its allies and Israel was determining. But the Soviet Union, in taking the credit for the survival of Colonel Nasser's regime, had to assume the re-equipment and maintenance of the Egyptian armed forces. The Soviet Union also tried to intrude into Turkey, a member of NATO and CENTO, and into Iran, a member of the latter alliance alone. In these countries the irritations of an alliance which had been constructed against a threat now presumed to have receded found overt expression. The Soviet Union was prepared to make modest arrangements for economic and, in the case of Iran, military aid. These arrangements had the double advantage of eroding a U.S. position and establishing a counterweight to Egypt and Syria. The Iranians contested Egyptian pretensions to control of the Persian Gulf. Since 1939 Turkey has possessed the *sanjak* of Alexandretta, an area largely populated by Syrian Christians. According to the principle of divide and rule, supporting Turkey and Iran makes it easier to control Syria and Egypt. The Soviets try, with what success we shall see, to avoid becoming the creatures of their clients.

In the Arab-Israeli conflict the Soviets have never accepted the extreme formulation that Israel must be extinguished as a state. The Soviet position has always been that Israel should relinquish some of the territory occupied at any given time, but never that the state should be made nonexistent. The Soviet position was exemplified in the Soviet effort in 1966 to mediate between the predominantly Arab wing and the predominantly Jewish wing of the communist party of Israel. By rejecting the extreme positions the Soviet Union obliquely offered to support Israel if the latter were willing to make territorial and other concessions. The Soviet Union would like to be the arbiter of a Near Eastern settlement, but as long as the United States furnishes a measure of support to Israel, the latter does not have to settle for the best terms the Soviet Union is willing or able to proffer.

Like others, the Soviet Union accepts as axiomatic the advantages of its enjoying dominant influence in an area rather than its opponent. The Soviet Union has not yet suffered as many disappointments as have the Western countries. Soviet scholars have not yet written books proving that great powers do not really benefit from the extension of their political control.[6] The Soviet leaders still seem to believe that succession to the British position in the Mediterranean will enhance their power. Transposing the values of the nineteenth century to the twentieth is perhaps the source of their error. Once powerful groups in Great Britain derived an important share of their income from India, whether the country as a whole benefited or not. Members of the British upper class benefited directly and many others in trade and manufacturing did so indirectly. Keeping India and protecting communication to it could be justified as being in the national interest. Gains from the colonies justified the costs—at least to large numbers of Englishmen if not to all.

Clients, however, cannot be equated with colonies, since the former

6. Grover Clark, in *The Balance Sheets of Imperialism* (New York: Columbia University Press, 1936), demonstrated before World War II that imperialism did not pay.

continually make claims for economic and military support which can only be met on the ground that they contribute to some higher (and difficult to define) political goal. Surely in the last third of the twentieth century, resources flow to clients, not from them. In Great Britain even the proletariat, according to Lenin, derived immediate economic advantages from imperialism and considerable emotional satisfaction from the assumption of racial superiority implicit in the notion of the "white man's burden." By contrast, in the Soviet Union the population as a whole and, what is more to the point, some with political power oppose Soviet commitments abroad, because it diverts resources from the undertakings in which they play a political role.

One wonders for how many years those who argue that the Soviet Union must behave as a great power even at great cost will be able to prevail over those with domestic constituencies. The disaster of the Arab-Israeli War of June, 1967, highlighted the present costs of involvement. In that year the Soviet Union tried to gain a cheap victory over Israel. The evidence, although incomplete, permits the reconstruction of the main events. In the spring of 1967, as several times earlier, the anti-Western Syrian regime was suffering an internal political crisis, and raiding the Israelis and shelling Galilee from the Golan heights. The Israelis made some reprisals, which shook the Syrian government, and contemplated others.

Clients frequently need to be helped to maintain the governments they head. In order not to "lose," the Soviets had to maintain the internal status quo in Syria, and they tried to do so by restraining the Israelis. They put diplomatic pressure on them (many Jewish hostages were held in the Soviet Union and Eastern Europe), and they urged the Egyptians to threaten the Israelis from the south. Such pressure could reduce the scale of Israeli reprisals or inhibit them altogether. Then the Soviets and the Egyptians could take the credit for preventing an Israeli full-scale attack on Syria—a scheme for which no convincing evidence has thus far been produced.

Accounts differ as to whether the Soviets presented the matter to the Egyptians as a maneuver to prevent Israeli reprisals against Syria or an Israeli war. Whatever the case, events soon got out of Soviet control. Colonel Nasser played his role too zealously and precipitated a war he probably wanted to avoid. According to a credible Israeli account, the Egyptians first put pressure on the Israelis by a partial mobilization which presented no genuine threat to the Israelis but would have permitted the Egyptians to claim later that it had prevented an Israeli attack on Syria. When Nasser raised his sights and sought to earn a symbolic victory by formally closing the Straits of

Tiran (which had been little used by the Israelis), he demanded the withdrawal of some of the U.N. screening forces. When to his surprise all the U.N. forces were withdrawn, he fully mobilized the Egyptian forces. The best evidence is that Nasser did not first consult the Soviet Union. Now the Israelis were no longer confronted with a partial mobilization with only political goals. They now had to cope with choices reminiscent of the 1914 crisis in Europe. Once the Israelis countermobilized, their forces had either to be employed soon or dispersed. Extended mobilization was economically and psychologically insupportable.

The Israeli decision to go to war was not easily reached, and it surprised the Soviet Union. As the Soviet press pointed out in May, when personnel shifts in the Israeli cabinet brought more aggressive figures to the forefront, the Israelis had had to return the territories conquered in 1956, even though they had France and Great Britain as allies. What could they now be contemplating? The Soviet leadership was perhaps more surprised by the outbreak of the war than by its course, since Israeli military superiority was probably appreciated. In a trenchant criticism of the Egyptian armed forces after the war, the Soviet military newspaper *Red Star* put its finger on the source of Egyptian weakness. The Egyptian officer class had changed very little from the pre-Nasser military; they thought more of enriching themselves than of the welfare of their men, and the latter, not surprisingly, fought poorly. In other words, the Soviet newspaper was describing a premodern society. The social transformations needed to make Egypt militarily redoubtable is a matter of many years.

Since the defeat in June, 1967, the Soviet Union has re-equipped the Egyptian armies and has greatly increased the number of Soviet advisors and training personnel. Apparently, despite differences at the highest level, they will continue the pursuit of their objective: to extend Soviet influence in the Near East. What are the natural limits of that influence? Even if we assume that all uncertainties are resolved in favor of the Soviet Union, its position would still be unattractive. If we assume that the United States withdraws its support of Israel and recalls the Sixth Fleet from the Mediterranean, thus forcing Israel to get the best terms it can from the Soviet Union, what will Soviet exclusiveness in the Near East gain them other than a number of importunate and dissatisfied clients? The modernization of the Near East, if and when it comes, will be a painful process. What can the Soviet Union gain from presiding over it? Perhaps some more votes in the United Nations on crucial issues. It seems more likely, however, that just as the proliferation of socialist states since 1945 has weakened the Soviet Union rather than strengthened it, the accumulation of clients will enhance neither Soviet security nor its economic well-being. But to posit that what seems rational to an outsider is, or soon will be, the rationale of Soviet political leaders is almost certainly mistaken. The Soviet political leadership probably believes that more Soviet influence (whatever that might be) is better than less, and it cannot be confidently predicted when and how influence will be seen as fool's gold.

Latin America, except for the period of the missile installation, was an area of secondary importance to the Soviet Union. The exception was the period of the missile crisis, which has been dealt with elsewhere in this paper. Soviet activity in Latin America illustrates their style where the prospects are considered modest and the resources allocated to furthering them are correspondingly small.

The Soviet Union had long held the view that the prospects for revolution in Latin America were poor. The United States, it was believed, was powerful enough not to permit communist revolutions to occur in Latin America. In the 1920s and 1930s, therefore, the Soviet Union concentrated what little attention it devoted to Latin America to the creation of communist parties. The plan was to organize the parties, train cadres, and wait until the right opportunity should come. In all likelihood the Soviet leaders felt that the revolution in Latin America would come after the revolution in the United States itself. During the Great Depression, a communist United States seemed possible to the Soviet Union. Low Soviet expectations of revolution within the colonies and semicolonies were reflected in the bureaucratic organization of the Comintern. The British Communist Party monitored the Indian Communist Party; the French Communist Party, the Algerians and Indochinese, and the affairs of the Latin American communist parties were run first from communist headquarters in Union Square in New York City and later from Mexico.

Many Latin American communist leaders were ex-socialists who had joined the communist party after the Russian Revolution, thus having longer tenure than many of the present Soviet leaders. The very unimportance of these parties has contributed to the stability of the leadership. Elsewhere the turnover in leadership was high, either because leaders could not condone a sharp Soviet shift in policy or because they had to be retired because they were too closely associated with a rejected policy. But in Latin America, where the local communist parties often lived either in a symbiotic relationship with the government which exploited them or else in uneventful exile, they remained from generation to generation.

The events in Cuba rocked these old Latin American parties. A new form of communist revolution had taken place there. The noncommunist revolutionary leader had become a communist, had absorbed the communist party within a new party of his own creation, and had assigned them relatively minor roles, as it turned out. In recent times Castro has gone even further and has imprisoned many of the ex-leaders of the Cuban Communist Party on the ground that they have been guilty of espionage for a foreign power. And in his speeches and commentaries Castro has made it clear that the foreign power meant is the Soviet Union.

In addition to making a revolution and absorbing the old leadership within a new Castroite communist party—a prospect hardly attractive to the old men at the heads of traditional communist parties—Castro has created difficulties for the communist parties in various countries. In order to see what these difficulties are, one must review the nature of guerrilla activity in Latin America.

Castro apparently came to believe the myth he had propagated about the Cuban revolution, that it was an agrarian revolution which had been set into motion by the spark of his uprising in the hills of eastern Cuba. Castro believed that this kind of revolutionary success could be exported to other countries. Soon after taking power, he sent out small bands to Honduras, the Panama Canal, Haiti, and the Dominican Republic to start new revolutions. These attempts all ended in dismal failure, but there is some evidence that between the Bay of Pigs and the Cuban missile crisis, the Soviet Union either encouraged, or did not discourage, such attempts. But after the missile crisis the Soviet Union generally did discourage these attempts, not only out of reluctance to embroil itself with the United States for ventures whose outcome was dubious, but also because these ventures adversely affected the communist parties of Latin America.

Latin America is a continent with much greater political variety than is generally realized. However, one note is common to the politics of the whole continent and also of Central America. Since the end of World War II, particularly since the intervention in Guatemala in 1954, anti-Americanism has grown. Some groups were disappointed that the United States neglected Latin America for Western Europe, because the latter was considered to be much more endangered by communism. After the Guatemalan events, large sections of the youth—not only leftist youth—became convinced that the United States would intervene against Latin American regimes that tried to bring about social reforms. Castro, a representative of this group, demonstrated that they could succeed.

The combination of continuing economic difficulties and rising expectations has made large groups of young Latin Americans critical of the existing regimes. Much of this dissatisfaction has been expressed in guerrilla movements in some countries. These movements have been largely staffed by dissident youth, including young communists restive under the rule of gerontocracy. In Venezuela and Peru, for example, the guerrilla forces were made up of activists, young communists, and youth groups like that of the Acción Democrática in Venezuela or the APRA Rebelde in Peru. Their successes have been temporary. The Venezuelan guerrillas shook the Betancóurt and Leoni regimes rather thoroughly before they lost their appeal, and the guerrillas in Bolivia led by Guevara caused the leadership of the country some genuine concern. No one can confidently predict that guerrilla forces cannot overthrow the existing governments in Latin America. Too many of these represent the interests of only a small political class, and any predictions of unbroken stability would be unwarranted. The problem for the Soviet Union and also for Castro was whether and to what degree such guerrilla movements should be supported. The interests of Castro and the Soviet Union differed on this issue as they did on others.

After the missile crisis, Castro became convinced that the Soviet Union had been, and might again be, unreliable in protecting Cuba from American pressure or even from intervention. Until and even after February, 1965, when Soviet aid to North Vietnam became significant, Castro's representatives at international communist conferences always took much stronger positions supporting Vietnam than did the Russians themselves.

Castro's security problem was how to enhance his strategic position on the southern continent. The only solution he could hit upon was to emerge from his isolated, pariah position by promoting successful socialist revolutions in other Latin American countries, where the new governments would be led by a Castroite communist party rather than by a traditional communist party. Even though not every attempt might succeed, Castro hoped that some would. In any case, he could think of no other way to buttress his position. When it became clear that the prospects for successful revolution were not as good as he had once believed, he shifted to a policy of promoting more Vietnams. Guevara took the lead and became the symbol of the new policy. The existence of rebellions in various Latin American countries or countries elsewhere in the world would cause the commitment of American troops on the scale of those in South Vietnam. If this could occur simultaneously in several places, the United States would then be too preoccupied to pay very much attention to Castro. This has been tried but, as we know, so far unsuccessfully.

The Soviet Union in its dealings with Castro and in its negotiations with him on the guerrilla movement has had other goals. First, especially in the early years, the Soviet Union tried to maintain as good relations as possible with Castro because of its fervent desire not to permit the only new socialist state established since 1949 to be overthrown. In December, 1964, a secret conference of all the Latin American communist parties took place in Havana. The results, which were soon published in Cuba and in Moscow, indicated that a compromise on the guerrilla movements had been reached on the basis of local autonomy. Each party was given the right and the duty to decide for itself whether it wanted to support guerrilla warfare or not. Castro apparently hoped that he could persuade more parties to his view than he in fact was able to do. Consequently, the Soviet-Cuban agreement on allowing autonomy to each communist party broke down. Castro was never again to be the host for all the Latin American communist parties. From this time on he was to invite to Havana only the nationalist revolutionary forces on the continent and selected communists. Since Castro issued the invitations, the conferences passed resolutions which supported views to which many of the communist parties of Latin America and the Soviet Union have not subscribed. In recent years Castro and his erstwhile publicist, the young French radical Régis Debray, have accused the Latin American communist parties, and by implication the Soviet Union, of being counterrevolutionary.

The arguments against supporting the guerrilla movements in Latin America are very strong, both for local communist parties and for the Soviet Union. It has already been indicated that if these guerrilla movements that are not communist controlled should win power, the old-line communists could look forward to a future such as that enjoyed by the old-line communists in Cuba. But even before that eventuality, if it should ever come to pass, the old-line communist parties suffer severely from the activities of guerrilla forces. The guerrillas, whether they operate in the countryside or sometimes in urban centers, as in Venezuela and Montevideo, are much harder to locate and apprehend than the old-line communists. Very often when the governments are under pressure because they are not successfully suppressing guerrilla movements, they arrest and imprison old-line communists. Thus the latter have to suffer for a movement that they oppose and that they feel will not succeed in any case. Nevertheless, the communist parties must give grudging verbal support to the guerrillas, because they cannot publicly condemn those who are struggling against the oligarchy with weapons in their hands. However, after the guerrillas fail, the communists and sometimes Soviet commentators are quick to stigmatize them as irresponsible adventurers, as they did after Ché Guevara failed to start a guerrilla movement in Bolivia.

The Soviet Union supports the local Latin American communists not only because it generally agrees with their assessment that revolution is not in the offing, but because of the requirements of the international communist movement. As indicated earlier, people like Suslov feel it urgently important to retain the revolutionary legitimacy of the Soviet Union. They want to show that most communist parties in the world approve the Soviet world strategy rather than the Chinese. An international meeting of communist parties in which pro-Chinese abstainers would be few has been a Soviet objective for many years. The Latin American communist parties, despite their weakness, are important to such a goal, since (as in the United Nations General Assembly) each member, no matter how small his constituency, receives a single vote. The Soviet Union is anxious to keep the communist parties of Latin America obedient to its lead in the international communist movement, and supporting their line on the guerrilla movement is one way of doing so.

Moreover, the Soviet policy toward Latin American states is inconsistent with the support of guerrilla movements. The Soviet Union assumes that every diminution of American power or influence is an automatic accretion to the power and influence of the Soviet Union. Just as the United States believes that East European nationalism is anti-Soviet, the Soviet Union judges Latin American nationalism to be anti-American. Soviet support of Latin American nationalism even on a moderate scale can, it is believed, catalyze and magnify anti-U.S. sentiment. The Soviet Union has therefore sought to establish normal state relations with those Latin American countries where they do not already exist. In many countries, especially those which are in conflict in one form or another with the United States, oppositionists make much of the fact that the United States "forbids" the government in power to have relations with the Soviet Union. Thus, as recently in Peru, people of a quite conservative cast, in their irritation with one aspect or another of American policy, undertake to improve their relations with the Soviet Union. Sometimes the object is domestic political advantage; at others it is to enhance the bargaining position vis-à-vis the United States. Whatever the case, it offers to the Soviet Union a cheap and easy way of reducing the influence of the United States.

Latin American political elites are contemptuous rather than complacent about the role of communist parties. They generally despise them because they have been weak and ineffectual for almost three generations. Many official expressions of anticommunism are uttered for domestic political reasons and sometimes to impress North Americans. Yet Latin American political leaders are loathe to accept Soviet assurances that these parties will not undertake antigovernmental activities. They prefer to demonstrate by action that they can dominate the situation. Thus, when commercial relations were established between the Colombian and the Soviet governments, as the Soviet negotiators arrived, the Colombian communists were ostentatiously arrested and jailed. The negotiations were successfully concluded, thus demonstrating the unimportance of the local communist party and the acquiescence of the Soviet government in its subordination to Soviet-Colombian state interests. Obviously, Castro is furious on such occasions, and rages at Soviet collaboration with the Latin American governments that are not only anticommunist but are also, and more importantly for him, anti-Castro.

Soviet policy toward Cuba will probably continue with few changes. Thus far, despite Castro's insults, Soviet economic support continues in an atmosphere of cool correctness. The general Soviet policy of maintaining socialist governments everywhere applies to the Caribbean area also. Rather than risk the opprobrium and the presumed consequences of losing a socialist country, the Soviet Union is willing to swallow the insults that Castro offers so regularly. In the Caribbean the cost to the Soviet Union of maintaining a socialist country is the injury to its pride and large bills. In Czechoslovakia the cost was the invasion of the country. But in both cases the objective is the same—the preservation of a socialist state. The Soviet Union believes the failure of socialism in Cuba would be politically disastrous; Castro needs Soviet support. This constitutes a community of interest that can withstand conflicts on other issues.

Would the situation change radically if a local guerrilla movement should succeed? Such a situation would present a great many problems to the Soviet Union. The ideal outcome of such a victory would be the control by the local communist party of the movement, no intervention by the United States, and a successful program of economic development not requiring Soviet support. Such a combination of circumstances, however, is extremely unlikely. The communist parties in Latin America, as in other parts of the world, are no longer the most radical and the most vigorous of political forces; they are outflanked by more activist movements so that a successful guerrilla movement in Latin America would probably not be led by communist parties accepting the authority of the Communist Party of the Soviet Union. However, if the United States should intervene against a movement it judged communist, whatever its true nature, the Soviet Union would have to choose between passively watching the United States overturn such a movement or confronting the United States and defending the movement. The Soviet Union was spared this difficult choice in the Dominican situation, because the United States intervened too quickly for any commitments to have been forced upon the Soviet Union. The latter would prefer to avoid such choices, and, if most specialists on Latin America are correct in believing that guerrilla movements are on the wane, it will continue to be spared.

In Asia Soviet policy is largely shaped by its fear of China. Since about 1959 or perhaps 1960 the Soviet Union has been trying to contain China. Often an action originally undertaken to deny an area to Western influence has become largely anti-Chinese. Soviet policy in Indonesia is a case in point. After the failure of what was generally believed in Indonesia to be a CIA-inspired rebellion, American influence in Indonesia was at a low ebb. Shortly thereafter (in 1960) the Soviet Union began a program of resupplying the Indonesian government with extensive military equipment estimated at about $1 billion. This was an obvious effort to prevent the United States from patching up relations with Indonesia by assuming the responsibility for the supply of its military forces. Many American specialists on the Far East felt that assisting the Indonesian military would have created a counterpoise to Sukarno's leftward drift. By pre-empting the United States in such an effort, the Soviet Union kept U.S. influence out of Indonesia.

However, the strengthening of the Indonesian armed forces in the person of General Nasution, the hero of the suppression of the communist revolt of 1948, had obvious implications for the Communist party of Indonesia (PKI). By ostentatiously decorating General Nasution on one of his trips to the Soviet Union, the Soviets made it clear that the interests of the Indonesian Communist Party had to yield to the Soviet goal of displacing the United States. Not surprisingly, the PKI moved closer and closer to the Chinese line, repeating many of the Chinese interpretations of the international situation. The PKI believed it possible to take power in installments without violence, but this difference in emphasis did not hinder the establishment of good relations with the Chinese. During the crisis that erupted when Sukarno was believed to be mortally ill, the Indonesian army, strengthened militarily and politically by Soviet aid, suppressed the Indonesian communists, either slaughtering or permitting the slaughter of thousands of communists and their families. It is probably going too far to say that the Soviet Union is indifferent to the fate of the PKI, but it did change the balance of forces within Indonesia so that the communists were weakened. The Soviet Union has sought to maintain good relations with the new regime, which has destroyed one of the two largest nongoverning communist parties in the world. One can speculate with reasonable confidence on the rationale for this behavior. The Soviet Union does not want to leave a free field for the United States in Indonesia, and it also wants to keep Indonesia out of the sphere of Chinese influence. In the second goal, its interests overlap with those of the United States.

Much the same pattern is to be discerned in India, though there the communist party has not suffered such cruel repression. As Indian-Chinese relations steadily deteriorated over the Tibetan issue, the Soviet Union moved from a posture of intermediary between the two to neutrality, and finally, when the Chinese invaded India in 1962, to a position of support of the Indian side. Since that time the Soviet Union has continued its program of economic aid to India and has added to it some military assistance. This development in Soviet policy is best understood in the larger context of a Soviet plan to contain China. Thus in India Soviet and American interests are common. Both powers want to support a stable Indian government, for otherwise they fear that India would dissolve and thus create an opportunity for pro-Chinese communist parties like the Bengali to seize power and become allies of the Chinese. To this end, economic and military aid is proffered to the Indians by both the United States and the Soviet Union. Outside Asia, Soviet policy competes with capitalist countries for influence. In Asia it is basically a contest with the Chinese.

Soviet activity in Indochina constitutes at once a confirmation and a modification of this generalization. Until February, 1965, Soviet policy in Indochina might have been interpreted as part of the general anti-Chinese pattern. The precise course of the U.S.-Soviet-Chinese-North Vietnamese-South Vietnamese relationships cannot yet be traced with confidence. Thus far the available source materials illuminate only particular points in this complex relationship. It is now clear that in 1960, for example, the communists in South Vietnam wanted to step up the level of their operations against the Diem government, and that they were able to overcome the objections of the North Vietnamese Communist Party. In general, the Chinese have supported the South Vietnamese communists, and the Russians have supported the North Vietnamese Communist Party, which in the early period wanted to concentrate on socialist construction in North Vietnam. Khrushchev in all his discussions of the struggle for national liberation was careful to describe the Indo-Chinese struggle as having been crowned by victory in 1954. This public posture reflected the caution which generally characterized his policies in the area. There were important exceptions, however. For example, during the Laos crisis the Soviet Union made a major effort to supply the Pathet Lao and the neutralists through North Vietnam.

The United States had sharply altered its course because it had come to realize that the South Vietnamese regime was in critical danger. It was the vulnerability of its client rather than any sharp change in the strategy of the National Liberation Front which frightened the United States into action. The analogy to the situation in Eastern Europe is striking. Neither the Soviet Union nor the North Vietnamese, in all probability, can guarantee the survival of the South Vietnamese regime any more than the West Germans can guarantee the communist regimes in Eastern Europe. Whether the United States was impelled by "defensive" or "offensive" motives, the Soviet Union had to deal with the fact that a socialist ally was under attack. It is not clear whether the Soviet arrangements for the military and economic support of North Vietnam were made contingent upon an American escalation of the war or without conditions in the hope that the Soviet Union could earn some of the credit for the expected collapse of the South Vietnamese government. Whatever the case, the Soviet Union accepted the risk of embroilment with the United States in its support of North Vietnam.

The American authorities however were also eager to avoid embroilment with the Soviet Union and did not interfere with the latter's supply of air defense equipment, surface-to-surface rockets, and large-scale economic aid. Although the United States and the Soviet Union had divergent hopes and expectations for the outcome of the war, they shared a common interest in not coming to blows in the area. They both had expectations that they might come to mutually desirable agreements in Europe. In addition, the United States hoped that the Soviet Union might play the role of intermediary whenever an opportunity to conclude the war on a negotiated basis might present itself. The very fact that the Soviet Union was supporting the North Vietnamese made its role as an intermediary more likely to be valuable. Thus in a peculiar way, when the Soviet Union began to contribute measurably to American military difficulties in Vietnam, it also expanded the area of mutuality of interest with the United States. The Soviet intervention in Vietnamese affairs constitutes one of the few successes in foreign policy of Khrushchev's successors. Though the Chinese were largely responsible for supplying small arms to the Vietnamese, the Soviet Union cannot be denied an important share of the credit for the successes of the North Vietnamese and, therefore, of the National Liberation Front, too. It must be noted, however, that in the earlier years the latter had held its own with extremely primitive weapons. But in any case the Soviet Union by its association with the Vietnamese struggle since 1965 has somewhat refurbished its credentials as the world leader of revolutionary forces and has very much improved its reputation among Far Eastern communists.

It may perhaps be useful to go somewhat beyond Soviet interests in underdeveloped countries in the Far East and deal with Soviet policy toward the area as a whole. As has been earlier indicated the chief Soviet concern is with a nominal ally, mainland China. An anti-Soviet China not only challenges the Soviet self-image as leader of a system of socialist states, but also creates problems for Soviet security. China, in the foreseeable future, will not be able to contemplate the initiation of war with the Soviet Union in the expectation of a victory which would force Soviet territorial or other concessions. But the converse does not apply. The Soviet Union cannot contemplate a war against the Chinese whose victorious outcome would bring Chinese acquiescence in Soviet wishes. It is no more possible for the Soviet Union to conquer and occupy China than it is for the United States to pacify South Vietnam, or for the Israelis to occupy Egypt. Although the Soviet Union is many times stronger than China, it cannot use force to bend her to its will as it is bending Czechoslovakia. China, therefore, is immune from the ultimate sanction of Soviet occupation. On the other hand the Chinese can impose heavy security costs upon the Soviet Union. The small Chinese capability in missiles equipped with nuclear weapons clearly represents a security problem for the Soviet Union. (It is dubious that it represents anything like the same problem for the United States.) Soviet conventional forces have to be in a state of high readiness to prevent unilateral Chinese "rectification" of the joint border.

Quite naturally the Soviet Union hopes that with a change in the internal regime in China, at least correct relations can be restored. Soviet discussion of the matter indicates that the best opportunity for the improvement of Sino-Soviet relations will be in the post-Mao period. Then the resumption of the effort to industrialize China will lead to a rapprochement with the Soviet Union which will again offer economic cooperation and perhaps even assistance. If, however, China has meanwhile established good relations with Japan or even the

United States, the main inducement to a change in the Chinese policy toward the Soviet Union will have been removed. Soviet preoccupation with this possibility is expressed in the frequent charges to be found in the Soviet press that China is not cooperating in a common policy of support to North Vietnam.

The Soviet Union wants to keep China in isolation and fears that China may exploit the many differences between the United States and the Soviet Union and between the Soviet Union and Japan to isolate the Soviet Union in the Far East. Soviet policy in the Far East tries to deal with these fears and, at the same time, with the over-all purposes of Soviet policy. By its support of the North Vietnamese the Soviet Union seeks to, and has partially succeeded in, isolating China from North Korea, Vietnam, and other Asian communist parties. At the same time, however, by gaining U.S. acceptance of the notion that Soviet involvement in North Vietnam gives the Soviet Union greater leverage in bringing about a settlement of the Vietnamese war, the Soviet Union keeps its lines to the United States open. The Soviets probably realize that the settlement of the Vietnamese war and the withdrawal of sizable U.S. forces from the mainland of Asia is a necessary condition for a U.S.-Chinese rapprochement, which they fear. But short-range necessities dictate the continuation of the mediation effort.

As a further hedge against the re-entry of China into the world diplomatic system, the Soviet Union has been courting the Japanese by the insistent offer of wide-ranging commercial concessions in Siberia. One gets the impression, however, that the Soviet haggling over terms and their unwillingness to return conquered territory to Japan earlier rather than later has made progress slow.

The future of the Soviet position in the Far East is a function of a whole set of variables: the direction of Chinese internal policy, the development of Japanese foreign policy, and the nature of the settlement in Vietnam. In many ways the first two variables are a function of the third. At the two extremes, China can either view the United States as a country which has learned its lesson and withdrawn from the mainland of Asia, and which can be exploited as a counterweight against the Soviet Union, or China can continue to regard the United States as hostile and capable of wounding China grievously at very short notice. Similarly the course of Japanese policy will be significantly influenced by American policy in Vietnam. Either a precipitate U.S. withdrawal from the Western Pacific or a failure to conclude the war will probably have a similar effect—a Japanese conviction that they cannot rely on the United States and that they must deal with their Asian neighbors on their own.

Probably the determining factor in U.S. policy in Vietnam will be American domestic politics, and here the Soviet Union has only marginal opportunities to influence the outcome. In the Far East, as elsewhere in the world, Soviet opportunities and limits are functions of the policies and politics of the United States.

7. Conclusion

The men in the Kremlin must be deeply disappointed with the state of international relations. True enough, the Soviet Union need no longer be genuinely concerned about its physical security, but little else positive can be said. The Soviet Union has been transformed from a vulnerable state to the second most powerful military power, obviously strong enough to deter whatever impulse to initiate a nuclear war might exist in the United States. Instead of existing in fearful isolation, the Soviet Union is now one of a whole system of socialist states stretching from the China Sea to the Baltic and to the Mediterranean. Instead of being restricted in the exercise of its influence to countries bordering on the Soviet Union, it is now a global power with influence and interests in almost every country in the world. But the burden of the nuclear balance with the United States is terribly heavy, since mutual misperceptions and the necessities of internal politics in both countries make the maintenance of the arms balance ever more costly. Moreover, the Soviet Union has to deal with the prospect that, even if an agreement with the United States, tacit or formal, could be reached on reducing the arms burden, a similar agreement with China is further in the future.

The other socialist states burden rather than support the Soviet Union. The Soviet Union bears more than the responsibility of a hegemonial power in a traditional alliance system. In addition to the responsibility for the security of its allies, it is responsible for the preservation of the socialist system in each one. In the Soviet estimate, failure to do so would have the most deleterious consequences for its international and domestic position. In any given year, one or another socialist country is suffering a severe political or economic crisis, and the Soviet Union feels called upon to intervene by force, as in Czechoslovakia, or to support it economically at great cost, as in Cuba and Vietnam. Though it might be realistic to hope for an end in Vietnam, it seems oversanguine to expect that the socialist states of Eastern Europe will become politically and economically stable. While Soviet involvement in the affairs of Nigeria, Peru, Pakistan, and India may salve egos bruised in other quarters, the acquisition of a train of demanding clients is only a burden. In the nuclear age, extending the list of one's clients does not enhance security, and it empties the treasury.

Many of the burdens borne by the Soviet Union are unnecessary and derive from feelings of political vulnerability. Diversity in the socialist regimes in Eastern Europe or even the abandonment of socialism in one of these countries need be no more a disaster for the Soviet Union than socialism in Cuba has been for the United States. But such a relaxed posture cannot be expected until important political changes occur within the Soviet Union and a new leadership comes to power, one which does not identify its own security with the preservation of an international socialist state system. The prospects for a more confident and internally more successful Soviet political leadership seem poor in the short range but good in the long. Such a leadership with a reduced fear of its own vulnerability would be, as has been argued in these pages, less inclined to vigorous and ultimately futile efforts to keep the communist international system unchanged. It would also realize the slight advantage to be derived from extending its influence in third areas, thus reducing the risk of confrontation with the United States, which at present seems prepared to tolerate and encourage the development of economic and political heterogeneity in these areas. A more confident and relaxed Soviet leadership would even have better prospects of coming to an understanding with Communist China.

It is obviously in the American interest that Soviet political life develop in this direction rather than the opposite. The United States can influence but not effect this development. Much depends on the successors to the present group of Soviet leaders, who entered political life in the aftermath of the great purges and who survived by being circumspect and not pressing for change. The present leaders therefore are not likely to realize that their own political position and the security of the Soviet Union are not dependent on rigid maintenance of the status quo in socialist countries. Nor are they likely to realize that the wide extension of Soviet influence abroad will help but little in the primary problems of relations with socialist allies. Perhaps the next generation of Soviet leaders may be better. The emergence within the present leadership of less parochial and more confident elements nourishes hope.

The key policy question is whether the United States by its actions can encourage the growth of a sounder Soviet leadership. The postwar history of Soviet-American relations suggests that the United States can usefully influence Soviet domestic politics. But the dynamics and even the facts of Soviet internal politics are too imperfectly understood to make playing Soviet domestic politics on a day-to-day or week-to-week basis feasible. For example, as pointed out earlier in these pages, even now, as in 1962, it is not clear whether a "concession" on West Berlin would have stimulated a counterconcession or Khrushchev's appetite.

The prospects for U.S. influence on Soviet internal politics lie in much larger and more general measures. The continuation or the conclusion of the Vietnamese war, the funding or the postponement of the Safeguard system, the encouragement or discouragement of a West German initiative for a Central European settlement are the areas in which we have opportunities to influence Soviet policies in desirable directions. Sometimes the Soviet Union will be inhibited from exploring an opportunity out of preoccupation with its own vulnerabilities. In such cases the United States can do little but wait for the propitious time.

But the United States can divest itself of exaggerated fears of its own vulnerabilities. The Soviet Union is not going to acquire a first-strike capability in the foreseeable future. (Nor are we for that matter.) Technological improvements are not likely to invest either side with a long-term preponderance in strategic strength. The experience of the last twenty-five years has been that each side has been able to acquire in fairly short order the weapons systems the other initiated. Moreover a positive aspect of the spiraling arms race is that the strategic balance has become "superstable." Each side now owns so many nuclear weapons and delivery vehicles that the successful employment of only a fraction would produce unimaginable horror. No technological improvements now contemplated can so reduce the fraction that a meaningful victory could be envisaged and the initiation of war undertaken on any rational, albeit wicked, calculus.

But even if no contemplated technical improvements can alter the technical balance significantly, what about as yet unimagined prodigies? The United States at least can draw confidence from the realization that its superior economic and technological bases make it possible to overtake and surpass the Soviet Union in new weapons. In the only important Soviet "first," ballistic missiles, the Soviet program started eight or nine years before the American.

What, says the doubting Thomas, of the political utility of military superiority? Communist states increased most in number when the United States had a monopoly of nuclear weapons. Cuba, the latest addition to the communist system, entered at a time when the Soviet Union had an extremely marginal air-nuclear capability to reach the

United States and no missile capacity of comparable range. The most vigorous Soviet actions (like our own) have been in response to vulnerabilities within the system rather than to threats from without. Fears of weakness rather than fantasies of power have been the prime movers.

For several years it has become increasingly clear that international communism is not a threat to the Western system but the Achilles heel of the Soviet Union. With the exception of Vietnam no other countries seem likely to become communist, and if some unlikely prospects do enter the system, they will probably be indigent and weak. The task of maintaining the status quo in every socialist country is the task of Sisyphus, because the Soviet Union, ridden with fears of disintegration, narrowly defines the limits of permissible change within a communist state. The impossible task of preventing change in a host of countries will exhaust the psychic energies, if not the physical resources of the Soviet Union. But American preoccupation with galloping disintegration seems to be more a feature of the past than the future. Except for Vietnam, the United States is no longer everywhere committed to the maintenance of the status quo.

The realization that the Soviet Union is politically and economically weak does not mean that the United States can be satisfied to simply wait for the once feared opponent to fall into desuetude. It does suggest, however, that the vulnerabilities and rewards are within our own system and that the future is ours to shape.

Part 2

THE CONDITIONS

4

THE DOMESTIC SCENE

Francis E. Rourke

When the Cold War began in the years immediately following World War II, American diplomacy was haunted by the fear that public opinion would refuse to sustain the commitments abroad that national security required. This fear had its origins in the memory of the post-World War I period, when a mood of disillusionment with foreign involvement prevented American participation in the League of Nations and led to a long period of withdrawal from an activist role in world politics.

In the interval between the two world wars, the events associated with the rejection of the Versailles Treaty by the U.S. Senate and the "return to normalcy" in the presidential election of 1920 had an abiding effect upon the behavior of American politicians. Even the most internationalist American president of this era, Franklin D. Roosevelt, moved with great caution on the diplomatic front, under what appeared to be the constant apprehension that public support would desert him as quickly as it had Woodrow Wilson after his return from the Paris peace conference in 1919. Roosevelt himself had, after all, been a victim of the Republican landslide in 1920, when he was a vice-presidential candidate on the Democratic ticket.

In the light of this historical background, what is most remarkable about the record of American diplomacy since World War II is the strength and continuity of public support for involvement abroad. This support has permitted a worldwide expansion of American responsibilities in foreign affairs, through participation in international organizations and the negotiation of formal and informal alliance systems in both Europe and Asia. On more than one occasion since 1945 segments of the public have been even more enthusiastic in their support of intervention abroad—when suggested, for example, by the Eisenhower administration's rhetoric on "rolling back the iron curtain in Eastern Europe"—than administration officials themselves.

Fears that the post-World War II era would see a return to isolationism thus proved to be unfounded. In the face of what Americans regarded as an aggressively expanding communist threat around the world, an internationalist consensus quickly emerged, and, by the time the great debate over Vietnam began in 1965, the term "isolationist" had become one of the harshest epithets on the domestic political scene. As this movement from isolationism to internationalism occurred, fear of public opinion as a constraint upon the conduct of foreign policy tended to recede. Indeed, it has become increasingly common for observers to regard domestic opinion as imposing few if any restrictions upon the decisions of officials responsible for foreign affairs.[1] On the other hand, the foreign policy process has not evolved into a system in which the president has been completely freed of any limitations from domestic politics in making his decisions. What the record of events since 1945 actually suggests is that, while successive American administrations have enjoyed great latitude in foreign policy, the actual use of presidential discretion has been hedged about by very formidable restrictions in the domestic political arena.

One set of restrictions is rooted in the power of public opinion. Although the public has remained generally quiescent as foreign policy has moved from an isolationist to an internationalist mode, it nevertheless has retained the capacity to intervene decisively in foreign affairs when the occasion requires through reprisal at the polls. The careers of two Democratic presidents, Harry S. Truman and Lyndon B. Johnson, foundered during this period largely as a result of their handling of executive responsibilities in foreign affairs.

Another source of restraints under which presidents have operated since World War II is the variety of governmental and nongovernmental institutions that have retained the capacity to affect the use of executive power in foreign affairs. The number of such institutions has actually expanded during the past two decades, as the Cold War has seen the establishment of additional centers of power in government bureaucracy and brought new segments of the community into positions of influence in foreign policy. While presidential primacy re-

---

1. As early as 1950, Gabriel Almond noted that "the decline of isolationism has widened the scope of discretion of the opinion and policy elites." *The American People and Foreign Policy* (New York: Harcourt, Brace and Company, 1950), p. 88. This conception of public opinion as being highly permissive in the area of foreign affairs has become even more pronounced in recent years. See Samuel P. Huntington, *The Common Defense: Strategic Programs in National Politics* (New York: Columbia University Press, 1961), pp. 234–51, and Kenneth N. Waltz, *Foreign Policy and Democratic Politics* (Boston: Little, Brown and Company, 1967), especially pp. 267–97.

mains today, as in 1945, a dominant characteristic of the process through which the United States makes its foreign policy, the system has by no means evolved into an executive monopoly of power.

This survey of the relationship between foreign affairs and domestic politics over the past quarter of a century examines both the role of public opinion in the foreign policy process in the United States and the way in which presidential decisions in foreign affairs have been influenced by other institutions in and out of government. These various forces have affected foreign policy either by actually exerting pressure on the president as he makes his decisions, or by their very presence inducing him to take their views into account even in the absence of such pressures.

1. Public Opinion and the Foreign Policy Process

While the public has usually been prepared during the last two decades to support the government's foreign policy, this delegation of power has by no means been an irrevocable surrender of authority.[2] Instead, there has been an implied contract underlying the consent of the governed with respect to foreign policy decisions, a contract which, in the hallowed tradition of John Locke, has been a conditional one. The public has supported American foreign policy since World War II as long as it appeared to be yielding tangible results, or, in the absence of such results, did not impose what the electorate regarded as burdensome costs. When these conditions were not met, a serious erosion in public support began to appear. Twice during this period, once in 1952 and again in 1968, presidents have been confronted with sharp division in the electorate and imminent defeat at the polls as a result of their record in foreign affairs.

Since World War II the events which have unquestionably tested the outer limits of public support of foreign policy have been the occasions when the administration in power in the United States saw fit to engage in military intervention abroad. Such acts of intervention have been high-risk ventures on the part of American presidents. They have always been somewhat unpredictable in their benefits and have stirred widespread public concern about their moral, economic, or political costs. Such cases occurred in Korea in 1950, in Lebanon in 1958, in Vietnam over a long period of time but on a massive scale beginning in 1965, and in the Dominican Republic in that same year.

2. The "public" in this context refers to the general or mass public, as distinguished from so-called "attentive" publics—smaller groups of individuals who concern themselves with foreign policy as a whole or in part on a continuing basis.

Each of these acts of military intervention triggered extensive debate, and in the case of Vietnam prolonged and acrimonious controversy, among the foreign policy elites outside the administration—in Congress, the universities, and the news media. However, the public at large gave the government firm and even enthusiastic support at the beginning of every episode, and, with respect to Lebanon and the Dominican Republic, this support did not waver substantially during the comparatively brief period when the intervention was in effect.[3]

When, however, in the cases of Korea and Vietnam the intervention did not seem to indicate a successful outcome, and when in addition the costs began to mount in terms of casualties abroad and disruption at home—reserve call-ups, expanded draft calls, and the like—the consensus of public support began slowly but surely to erode. At this point critics of the president have begun to find a mass audience when they attacked the goals of executive policy. As long as that policy seemed reasonably successful or did not seriously inconvenience the public, the role of the critic has very often been that of the proverbial voice crying in the wilderness.

Of course the influence of such critics has not entirely depended on the extent to which their views enjoyed public support. In this period as in earlier times, the members of critical elites have retained the capacity to influence officials responsible for foreign policy by the force of their arguments or direct pressures rather than their ability to mobilize public support. Indeed, the policies of every president since 1945 have been developed or modified in response to such influence. For example, the periodic decisions to engage in military intervention abroad have been rooted in conceptions of the security of the United States that outside elites as well as government officials have been instrumental in developing.[4]

The conditions of the contract between the government and the general public in the area of foreign policy since World War II suggest that time is a critical factor in determining whether a president will be successful in holding on to public support. The lesson of the last twenty years has been that military intervention abroad, for example, should achieve its intended results very rapidly—before costs begin to mount or become visible—and that the situation most to be avoided is a protracted stalemate following intervention. Many of the

3. On public support of the Dominican intervention, see the *Gallup Political Index*, Report No. 7, December, 1965, p. 7.

4. For an analysis of the dialogue among elites and its effect on foreign policy during this period, see Chapter 2 of this volume.

members of the Senate Foreign Relations Committee who were opposed to administration policy in Vietnam in the 1960s were no less
critical of American intervention in the Dominican Republic during
that same period. But in the Dominican case, American military action
succeeded so quickly in suppressing what was alleged to be a communist attempt at seizing power that critics had small chance to make
themselves heard. As this comparison reveals, success has tended to
bury all misgivings on the part of the public regarding the wisdom of
American military intervention abroad.

Of course, the military involvement in Vietnam prior to 1965 was
also a minimal one from the point of view of the burdens it imposed
on the public. If this intervention had remained at the low level it
attained under the Eisenhower administration, or even at the expanded
stage it reached under President John F. Kennedy, it is doubtful
whether Vietnam could ever have become a major issue in American
politics, even though the results achieved by intervention remained
somewhat inconclusive. It was the escalation of costs added to the
indeterminacy of results that finally triggered the crisis in domestic
politics over the Vietnam War in the late 1960s.

During the period immediately following the build-up of American
forces in Vietnam in 1965, President Johnson pursued a strategy of
keeping the visible burdens of the war as low as possible. There was
no call-up reserves, the selective service system allowed student or
occupational deferments to the great majority of the eligible males in
the upper and middle classes of American society, and the apparent
fiscal burdens of the war were kept low by avoiding a tax hike and
publicly minimizing the extent to which the war would increase defense expenditures. From the point of view of domestic politics, the
expanded war under Johnson was handled with great skill in its early
stages.

These tactics were, however, best suited to maintaining domestic
support for a short war. If there had indeed been "light at the end of
the tunnel" by the end of 1967, as the administration continued to
hope, criticism of the Vietnam War would have remained a constant
source of annoyance to the administration but would not have fatally
weakened it in terms of public support. However, by early 1968 the
grace period had elapsed for the Johnson administration. The Tet
offensive starkly pointed up how far American forces were from bringing the war to a victorious conclusion, and by this time the domestic burdens of the war could no longer be concealed. Some reserve
units were mobilized, a tougher policy on draft deferments was put
into effect, a surtax on incomes was authorized, and the swelling size

of the defense budget forced the curtailment of a number of domestic programs, cutbacks that were painful in their effects on varied segments of the community.

However, even this growing disaffection did not strip the Johnson administration of substantial public support for its Vietnam policy. Quite to the contrary, public opinion polls continued in 1968, as they had in previous years, to find a majority of the public aligned behind such specific administration proposals on the war as the refusal to halt the bombing of North Vietnam.[5] What happened was that the public, while continuing to give lip service to the support of current Vietnam policy in its answers to pollsters, also began to indicate in a variety of other ways that the administration's entanglement in Southeast Asia had become a serious liability in domestic politics.

For one thing, the polls began to show a marked rise in the number of Americans now prepared to agree that our initial intervention in Vietnam had been a mistake, as well as a continuing decline in the public's rating of the competence with which the President was doing his job. Between August, 1965, and April, 1968, the segment of the public that regarded American military intervention in South Vietnam as a mistake rose from 24 to 48 per cent. Over the course of the same period, the percentage of the public approving President Johnson's performance in office dropped from 65 to 41 per cent.[6]

Even more serious from the point of view of practical politics, candidates opposing the war began to run strongly in primary and special elections, or, as in the case of Senator Eugene McCarthy in New Hampshire, ran even with the President in a presidential preference primary in which the administration made a major effort to achieve a decisive victory. In American politics it has been cold comfort to a party in power to find its stand on foreign affairs supported by a majority of the voters in public opinion polls, when these same voters were repudiating it in the election booth on what appeared to be foreign policy issues.

To be sure, not all the Johnson administration's difficulties in 1968 were traceable to the Vietnam War. Disorder in the cities associated with tensions arising from racial desegregation—more generally re-

5. For data on the widespread public support of the bombing of North Vietnam (prior to the partial suspension ordered by President Johnson in March of 1968) see the *Gallup Opinion Index*, Report No. 33, March, 1968. See also the summary report on public opinion regarding the Vietnam War in the *Gallup Opinion Index*, Report No. 30, December, 1967, pp. 6–40.

6. See *Gallup Opinion Index*, Reports No. 35, May, 1968, p. 21; No. 24, June, 1967, p. 3; and No. 38, August, 1968, p. 1.

ferred to as the "law and order" issue—had become a major source of public dissatisfaction in the domestic area. The Johnson administration might well have been in serious trouble in 1968 even if there had been no Vietnam War. The least that can be said with respect to the impact of the war is that it seriously split the Democratic Party, then in power, adversely affecting its public image and its capacity to cope with such problems of domestic policy as the issue of civil disorder. It should also be noted that the polls continued to show that the voters identified the Vietnam War as their major concern in 1968, so that, while it cannot be proved that Vietnam was the most important issue in the 1968 election, the voters themselves were certainly prepared to say that it was throughout the year.[7]

The conditional nature of the support the American public has given to the government in foreign affairs over this period has been evident in areas other than military involvement abroad, although, as the issue that may eventually impose the heaviest costs upon the voters, armed intervention in other countries has put public support of foreign policy to the most severe test. However, the operation of other international programs during this period—most notably, foreign aid—has also illustrated the conditions under which public support for foreign policy begins to atrophy.

When the foreign aid program was first introduced immediately following World War II, it was a considerable success. Its object was to bring about the economic recovery of the principal states of Western Europe, and these states were generally able to make quick and effective use of the financial aid given them. However, as this policy of international economic assistance was transferred to the underdeveloped nations of the world in the early 1950s, it steadily lost public support in the United States. It proved much more difficult to demonstrate the beneficial effects of foreign aid in backward as opposed to industrialized societies, and it was impossible to predict when, if at all, such programs would no longer be needed. When foreign aid was confined to Europe, it met the conditions necessary for public support of foreign policy: the programs achieved discernible results without entailing interminable expenditures. When applied in Asia, Africa, or Latin America, on the other hand, the programs could not meet these conditions, and slowly but surely they lost favor with the public.[8]

7. See, for example, the *Gallup Opinion Index*, Report No. 38, August, 1968, p. 15.

8. See Louis C. Gawthrop, "Congress and Foreign Aid" (unpublished Ph.D. dissertation, The Johns Hopkins University, 1962), especially p. 299.

The kind of test that the public has applied to foreign policy since 1945, that it achieve results without exorbitant costs, represents a standard that is essentially pragmatic in character. In this period Americans have been severely indicted for being excessively legalistic or moralistic in their approach to international politics.[9] This may be a fair criticism of the orientation of certain elites that have been dominant in foreign affairs, since the conduct of American diplomacy has always been subject to heavy influence by lawyers, for example; but it fails to recognize the extent to which the attitudes of the public at large have been shaped by purely practical considerations. Noteworthy in this regard is the fact that much of the controversy over the Vietnam War among elites in the United States tended to focus on legal or moral questions, while public disenchantment with the war seemed finally to stem from a growing conviction after the Tet offensive that it was impractical to try to win this kind of conflict.

As a result of the contract with the public in the area of foreign affairs, successive presidents have enjoyed extensive latitude in the day-to-day conduct of American diplomacy since 1945. Within the limits indicated, the public has been highly permissive with respect to the policies it has been prepared to support. On a great many issues of international politics, the public has had either no opinion or opinions of very low intensity, thus supplying the administration with a spacious zone of public indifference in which it has been free to act at its own discretion. And the public has commonly been prepared to give the government enthusiastic support in situations that officials chose to define as perilous from the point of view of American national security.

Indeed, this support has often seemed strongest on precisely those occasions when the wisdom of official decision-making was most in doubt. During the Eisenhower administration the suppression of the Hungarian uprising by Soviet troops appeared to enhance Republican prospects in the 1956 presidential election, even as it underscored the futility of the administration's previous commitment to "liberate

9. This indictment is presented in its most stringent form in Hans J. Morgenthau, *In Defense of the National Interest* (New York: Alfred A. Knopf, Inc., 1952), and George F. Kennan, *Realities of American Foreign Policy* (Princeton: Princeton University Press, 1954). The myth of American innocence in foreign affairs may not be entirely subscribed to in parts of the world, such as Latin America, where an American talent for hardheaded and sometimes cold-blooded *realpolitik* has been very much in evidence. Between 1945 and 1968, for example, there was the participation by the CIA in the overthrow of the Arbenz government in Guatemala in 1954, the invasion of Cuba at the Bay of Pigs in 1961, and the American intervention in the Dominican Republic in 1965.

the captive peoples" of Eastern Europe. Five years later, President Kennedy's support by the public reached dramatic highs at the time of the abortive American-sponsored Bay of Pigs invasion of Cuba by exile groups and the crisis following the emplacement of Soviet nuclear missiles in Cuba in 1962, although each of these events seemed to raise serious questions regarding the skill with which affairs with Cuba were being handled by the Kennedy administration.[10]

Yet, while public opinion has thus seemed quite malleable in the area of foreign policy, it would not be correct to say that it has been equally plastic with respect to all policies that presidents have tried to inaugurate. Some have in fact evoked a good deal more resistance than others, and have required therefore considerably more salesmanship on the part of administration spokesmen. While such salesmanship has usually been successful, the need to undertake it testifies to the uneven nature of public deference to the government on foreign policy issues.

It is quite clear, for example, that proposals for taking a hard line toward what is regarded as communist expansion abroad have triggered more instantaneous support than proposals for détente with the Soviet Union. The intense antagonism toward communism that has existed in the United States since World War II can hardly be exaggerated. As Gabriel Almond has pointed out: "Every group of any significance in the United States feels itself to be threatened by this movement. . . . The believing Christian, the trade unionist, the democratic Socialist, the liberal, the conservative—all save a small sector of the population—experience Russian and Communist pressure as a grave threat to fundamental values."[11]

Hence it took a good deal more educational effort on the part of President Kennedy to arouse public support for acts of accommodation with the Soviet Union, such as the nuclear test ban treaty in 1963, than it did to mobilize public hostility in confrontations with the Soviets during the Berlin and Cuban crises. Still, it is instructive to note that in the case of the nuclear test ban treaty, as in similar acts of ac-

10. Of course, the public support engendered by any foreign policy crisis may be of a short-run character—a "rallying around the flag" for the brief period of the emergency—that may well be followed by a dip in the administration's popularity if the conviction spreads that the country has actually suffered a defeat in international politics.

11. See Almond, *The American People*, p. 17. However, it can also be argued that policies that appear to involve concessions to any other state, whether communist or not, will always be more difficult to sell the public than programs that do not require such acts of accommodation.

commodation since 1945, the administration was eventually able to win the public over to its side, even in the face of strong opposition. While certain kinds of policies have required more explanation than others, the public has generally been disposed to give the president's case more weight than it has assigned to arguments by his critics, even though it may have had misgivings about proposals that an administration was putting before it.

It has been a continuing advantage to presidents in situations in which such salesmanship has been required that anticommunism has by no means been the only appeal in foreign policy to which the public has responded since 1945. The cause of international peace, or perhaps more accurately, the avoidance of nuclear war has been of at least equal potency. The movement toward détente with the Soviet Union, which has waxed and waned since World War II, has been justified time and again by American presidents on the grounds that the single greatest imperative in international politics today is the avoidance of a nuclear conflict between the two superpowers. Hence, while anticommunism has often seemed the indispensable cement for holding together the consensus of public support for internationalism since World War II, it has not been a barrier against accommodation with the communist world. Presidents have had at their disposal equally powerful symbols for mobilizing public support for firm or conciliatory policies toward communist adversaries abroad.

In describing the character of the recent relationship between the government and mass opinion, it should be noted that often in the past the policy maker's chief concern has not been with public opinion in general but rather with the views of certain narrow but intensely interested segments of the community. Prior to World War II, foreign policy was frequently subject to heavy pressure by powerful groups in areas in which the general public itself was largely indifferent. This was particularly true in the area of foreign trade, when economic groups lobbied vigorously and often successfully against trade arrangements they regarded as disadvantageous to their interests, or with respect to issues involving significant nationality groups in the United States, when ethnic groups in this country sought to shape American policy toward their homeland.

However, it is questionable whether pressure groups of this traditional kind have been a major source of influence upon foreign policy since 1945.[12] There have been vast areas of decision in foreign affairs

12. For a careful analysis of this problem and for extensive bibliographic data, see Bernard C. Cohen, *The Influence of Non-Governmental Groups on Foreign*

in which no significant pressure group structure has existed, or in which interest groups have had minimal influence. Moreover, the role of such groups has even been declining in the areas in which they have historically exterted their greatest influence—international trade and nationality issues. E. E. Schattschneider has measured the deterioration in the influence of the economic protectionist lobbies in American politics in recent times by the "astronomical distance" that separated the political atmosphere surrounding the Hawley-Smoot Act of 1930 from the climate of opinion that prevailed when the Trade Expansion Act was passed in 1962. By 1962 the influence of protectionist groups was far below what it had been three decades earlier.[13]

Certain forms of ethnic pressure upon foreign policy have also continued to recede, as members of the groups involved have been assimilated into the general fabric of the American community. There are, however, notable exceptions. For example, Jewish groups in the United States have been very active in their efforts to maintain American support for the state of Israel in its periodic confrontations with the Arab world since World War II. During this period there has also been heightened political activity by organizations representing minority groups with homelands in the countries in Eastern Europe under Soviet domination. However, while these groups have affected American policy in the Middle East and Eastern Europe, they have certainly not controlled it. Witness, for example, the refusal of the Eisenhower administration to support the joint efforts by the British, French, and Israeli governments to bring down the Nasser regime in Egypt in 1956, and the de facto acceptance by the U.S. government since World War II of the reality of Soviet domination over Eastern Europe.

It should also be noted that the State Department has remained in the advantageous position of being able to initiate as well as respond to the pressures of organized groups. In 1947, for example, the Department helped establish a citizens' committee to mobilize public

Policy-Making (Boston: World Peace Foundation, 1959). Cohen concludes that "despite frequent assumptions to the contrary . . . interest groups seem to have considerably less effect on foreign policy than they do in the domestic realm" (p. 6). This finding is confirmed by an even more recent study, Lester W. Milbrath, "Interest Groups and Foreign Policy," in James N. Rosenau (ed.), *Domestic Sources of Foreign Policy* (New York: The Free Press, 1967), pp. 231–51. Milbrath describes the influence of interest groups on foreign policy as "slight" (p. 251).

13. E. E. Schattschneider, review of "American Business and Public Policy," by Raymond A. Bauer, Ithiel De Sola Pool, and Lewis Anthony Dexter, *Public Opinion Quarterly*, XXIX (Summer, 1965), pp. 343–44.

support for the Marshall Plan, and a similar group was formed by President Johnson in 1967 to win public backing for his Vietnam policy. When involved in this way in the organization of what might be called government front groups, administrations have adroitly combined the arts of manipulation with the norms of democracy by helping to create the public opinion they are assumed to be reflecting.[14]

As noted earlier, the electorate has accepted a subordinate position in the area of foreign policy since 1945, but from the government's viewpoint it has retained a reserve power of awesome dimensions by virtue of the fact that political parties and officials must periodically submit their policies to public approval or disapproval at elections. As a result, officials charged with responsibility for foreign relations have known that, in exercising the discretion they are so freely granted today, they may reap a harvest of unpopularity at the polls at some future date. This knowledge has been a continuing limitation upon their behavior. Policy makers have been forced to anticipate in their calculations what the public reaction to a decision will be once its consequences have been felt, though the officials themselves have not been certain what these consequences will be.

Of course, the existence of this latent power of the public has also offered a standing invitation to elected officials to undertake activities in foreign affairs that will enhance their prospects on election day. The history of summit meetings between the United States and the Soviet Union since World War II suggests that, in the American perspective at least, such meetings have often been more useful in terms of domestic politics than foreign policy outcomes. These meetings have cast each president since World War II as a highly visible protagonist of the nation and have identified the political party in power with the cause of international peace. Their role in domestic politics has made such meetings highly valuable for all American presidents, however little effect they may have had upon the relations among the states involved. By all accounts, one of President Johnson's bitterest disappointments in his closing months in office was his inability to arrange a second summit meeting with Soviet leaders before leaving the presidency. Such a meeting would have underlined his commitment to a peaceful international order and softened the warrior image in which he had been cast by the Vietnam War.

There are those who contend that recent efforts to harvest domestic

14. See Francis E. Rourke, *Bureaucracy, Politics and Public Policy* (Boston: Little, Brown and Company, 1969), pp. 16–17.

political advantage from activities like summit meetings have had very harmful consequences for American interests abroad. These efforts have been described by George F. Kennan as "the worst phenomena of American diplomacy ... the abuse of external relations of our people as a whole for the domestic political advantage of a single faction or party."[15] Kennan's comment here reflects his long experience as a professional civil servant whose natural tendency is to feel that blundering politicians hamper the development of sound policy. There is truth in this point of view, but clearly it is not the whole truth. While summit meetings in recent times have been in part political stunts, they have also served as a means of liberating the president's perspective on foreign policy from the everyday routines and organizational traditions of the State Department. President Kennedy, among others, felt it of vital importance that foreign policy be rescued from the vices of bureaucracy as well as from those of politics.[16]

The deferential attitude in foreign affairs that the public has exhibited toward the government since World War II has various roots, not least in importance the fact that the administration in power has been the primary source of information on foreign policy and that the public has evaluated the credibility of this source very highly. Research on how voters form their opinions has shown that the ability of information to influence opinion turns very largely on the reputation of its source,[17] and there is no source of data on what is going on outside the United States to which the average voter has given greater credence than his own government.[18]

To be sure, the record since 1945 also suggests that an administra-

15. *New York Times*, September 22, 1968, p. 3.

16. See the chapter on "The Reconstruction of Diplomacy" in Arthur M. Schlesinger, Jr., *A Thousand Days* (Boston: Houghton Mifflin Company, 1965), pp. 406–47.

17. See Robert E. Lane and David O. Sears, *Public Opinion* (Englewood Cliffs, N.J.: Prentice-Hall, 1954), pp. 43–56.

18. Though more pronounced in foreign affairs, this credibility is a general characteristic of governmental communications. As a congressional committee long ago pointed out: "The average citizen ... assumes his Federal Government to be objective, impartial, and fair in its information services. ... Whereas the individual might reject propaganda coming to him from other sources, he is more likely to be receptive to it when it is offered in the guise of 'information' which comes through official channels." See U.S., Congress, House, *Twenty-Third Intermediate Report of the Committee on Expenditures in the Executive Departments*, 80th Cong., 2d Sess., December 31, 1948, H.R. 2474, p. 7.

tion may weaken its power over public opinion if it allows too large a "credibility gap" to open up with respect to its own communications. Whenever this has occurred, the reputation of alternative sources of information with the public has been increased. During the Vietnam War, for example, the Johnson administration lost some of its credibility in foreign affairs, partly because of the inaccuracy of its many forecasts on the course of the war in Southeast Asia, but partly also because of the rather transparent deceptiveness that characterized the President's style of handling foreign as well as domestic politics. This credibility gap provided an opportunity for the news media (especially the major television networks) and congressional committees (most notably the Senate Foreign Relations Committee) to gain a much wider audience for their own quite different version of the events that were taking place in Vietnam.

While the administration's hegemony as a source of information was challenged during the Vietnam War (more seriously than in any similar period of armed conflict abroad in recent American history), it was never overcome. What is more important, at the decisive junctures at which major choices of policy were being made, it was the administration's presentation of the facts that controlled public opinion. For example, when the first attack by American aircraft upon North Vietnamese territory was launched in 1964, it was the President's account of what had occurred to provoke this attack that elicited the widespread support this action received from the public. It was only some years later that investigations by Congress and newspaper reporters raised questions as to whether American destroyers had really been in international waters, as claimed by the President, and whether there had indeed been attacks on American warships sufficient to justify the reprisal measures taken.

All these doubts, however, were stirred long after the hostilities in the Tonkin Gulf had taken place. By that time the war had escalated, American planes were bombing North Vietnam every day, and there were more than one-half million American troops in South Vietnam. The question of what had actually happened in the Tonkin Gulf seemed more relevant to history than to present policy. The problem on which the administration was now able to forcus attention was the safety of American forces in South Vietnam, and critics who questioned the administration's veracity were easily put on the defensive by the charge that they were endangering American troops. What this cycle of argument suggests is that the ability of an administration to manipulate public opinion in foreign affairs is quite substantial. Moreover, the advent of new media of communication, such as television, played a major role in strengthening such power up until Vietnam.[19]

Perhaps the best evidence of the extent to which the public has deferred to the authority of the government in the field of foreign policy since World War II is the fact that it has accepted policies the government had put into effect, though it had rejected them when they were originally proposed by sources outside the administration. While the bombing of North Vietnam by the United States was going on, a number of critics of the Vietnam War suggested that a cessation of the bombing would be a first step toward negotiations that might end the war. The American public repeatedly supported the government in its refusal to stop the bombing. However, at virtually the same time, an equally impressive majority gave an affirmative response when asked if they would approve if the government itself should end the bombing and withdraw from Vietnam.[20]

In view of the latitude the general public has allowed the government in international politics since World War II, the major decisions on foreign policy during this period have characteristically involved a dialogue among elites, with occasional participation by "attentive" groups of citizens actively concerned with foreign affairs. This dialogue has usually been initiated at the White House, as, for example, when officials around the president defined Soviet pressure on Berlin in 1959 or the imminent collapse of the South Vietnamese government in 1964 as posing a fundamental threat to American security. On occasion, however, it has been triggered by a challenge to the president from members of the opposition party in Congress—as was partially the case in the Cuban missile crisis in 1962—or from members of the president's own party, as occurred during the course of the war in Vietnam in 1968.

To an increasing extent since World War II, foreign policy decisions related to national security have also been affected in a major way by the bureaucratic elites concerned with foreign affairs, particularly high-level officials in the defense establishment. Moreover, groups outside of government have begun to play a significant role in these discussions in recent years, as the foreign policy consensus that had

19. For a comparison of the government's capacity to manipulate public opinion in foreign and domestic policy, see Francis E. Rourke, *Secrecy and Publicity: Dilemmas of Democracy* (Baltimore: The Johns Hopkins Press, 1961), pp. 204–7.

20. See the public response to the bombing of North Vietnam as measured in the *Gallup Opinion Index*, Report No. 33, March, 1968, p. 7, as compared with the poll reported in the *Gallup Opinion Index*, Report No. 34, April, 1968, p. 16.

held together so long began to erode under the impact of the Vietnam War. The section that follows examines the interaction among these varied groups in the making of foreign policy since World War II—subject always to the latent power of the public to condition the decisions that could be made.

2. Domestic Politics and Decision-making in Foreign Affairs

From 1945 through 1948 the president remained at the hub of the system through which foreign policy decisions were made in the United States. Whenever other leaders or groups participated in shaping foreign policy, they did so mainly by exerting pressure on the president, either by influencing his decisions beforehand or by mobilizing support or opposition to them afterward. While foreign policy was by no means the president's exclusive preserve during this period, the interval between his power and that of his nearest competitor was a wide one. This situation is not likely to change. Presidential ascendancy over foreign policy in the United States is firmly rooted in constitutional tradition, the realities of domestic politics, and the imperatives of the international environment.

Thus since 1945 the dialogue on foreign policy has either been stimulated by, or has ultimately involved, a challenge to presidential authority. In the political sphere, such confrontations have usually come from the opposing political party or, as occurred in 1968, from members of the president's own party. The institution in which such challenges have usually been mounted is Congress—more particularly, those fortresses of legislative influence, the congressional committees having powers relating to foreign affairs.

On the surface, combat between the two major political parties may not seem to have been a significant source of difficulty for presidential authority over foreign policy since World War II. Both Democrats and Republicans paid frequent homage to the doctrine of bipartisanship in foreign affairs, and at moments of crisis the leaders of both parties rallied behind the president to defend what he defined as vital national interests. Periodically, presidents have also been able to reinforce this tradition of unity through bipartisan appointments to executive office, as for example, President Truman's appointment of Robert Lovett as Secretary of Defense in 1951, or President Kennedy's selection of Douglas Dillon as Secretary of the Treasury in 1961—a move heavy with significance for foreign affairs because of the acute problem of balance of payments in international trade.[21]

21. A study of presidential appointments to executive office notes that "appointments from the opposition party were much more likely to be made to agencies

While foreign policy since World War II has thus been diminished as an issue in party politics by this tradition of bipartisanship, it has by no means been eliminated from the calculations and strategies of presidents and party leaders. In every election since 1945, the question of America's standing in the world or the problems the nation faces abroad have figured at least covertly in the appeals directed at voters by candidates for national office. This has more frequently been the case in presidential than in congressional contests, which have commonly been conducted on local or domestic issues. For legislative candidates, "standing behind the president" has been a convenient posture on foreign policy questions, though many politicians of both parties have been careful to take a stance as far behind the chief executive as possible, so as not to be hit by any of the falling debris in the event that his policy collapses.

In the six presidential elections since 1945, however, foreign policy has inevitably played a major role, if only because the emergence of an internationalist consensus during this period has required each presidential candidate to persuade the voters that he is better qualified than his opponent to handle the nation's foreign affairs. Since World War II competence in international politics has been a large part of the image of effectiveness a prospective chief executive has had to radiate to the public in order to become a credible choice for the presidency. And, although it cannot be conclusively demonstrated, several presidential elections during this period seem clearly to have been affected in a major way by public concern over foreign policy.

For example, the defeat of Adlai Stevenson in 1952, as well as that of Hubert Humphrey in 1968, were commonly linked to the disfavor in which the public held the performance in foreign policy of their immediate Democratic predecessors. In his successful campaign in 1960, President Kennedy laid great stress upon what he alleged to be the deterioration of this country's international position during the last years of the Eisenhower administration. Moreover, the margin of President Eisenhower's victory in 1956 is widely believed to have been increased by public concern over foreign policy in the wake of the Hungarian uprising and the Suez crisis, and the belief of the electorate that Eisenhower was better qualified than his opponent to deal with these problems.

So, while each president since 1945 has drawn strong support from rival party leaders during crises in foreign policy, each has also been

concerned with foreign relations and defense than to other agencies." David T. Stanley, Dean E. Mann, and Jameson W. Doig, *Men Who Govern* (Washington, D.C.: The Brookings Institution, 1967), p. 25.

keenly aware of the fact that missteps on his part could easily redound to the advantage of his political adversaries. From the point of view of this opposition, however, caution has certainly been the watchword in challenging presidential authority. For one thing such challenges always have an element of *lèse-majesté* about them, offensive to the dignity of the country as well as its chief executive. Moreover, since the president commands such a vast bureaucratic establishment in foreign affairs, it has been hard for his critics to convince the public that their sources of information are better than his. When Senator Kenneth Keating of New York disputed President Kennedy's claim that there were no offensive Soviet missiles in Cuba in 1962, it was difficult for the public to credit the idea that a mere senator could know more about this subject than the president himself.

In any case, it has not always been advantageous for critics of the president to be proven right by events. It was not Senator Keating's Republican Party but President Kennedy's Democrats who benefited politically when it was finally discovered that medium- and intermediate-range Soviet missiles had indeed been emplaced in Cuba. From the point of view of domestic politics, all this discovery did was to enable President Kennedy to gain public credit for their removal. In the congressional elections shortly thereafter, the Democratic Party scored a moral victory by losing fewer House seats than in any previous mid-term election, and the Republicans charged that they had been "Cubanized."[22] Critics of President Johnson's Vietnam policy did not always fare much better during the 1960s. Indeed, two of the President's sharpest critics, Senators Wayne Morse of Oregon and Joseph Clark of Pennsylvania, were defeated in their efforts to obtain re-election to the Senate in 1968. However, the exact impact of Vietnam upon congressional elections is not clear, since many opponents of the war were also successful in their election campaigns, including Mark Hatfield in Oregon in 1966 and Senator William Fulbright in Arkansas in 1968.

The fact of the matter is that in foreign affairs there have been more promising strategies open to a president's political opponents since 1945 than direct challenges to his authority. The strategy most often employed has been to concede the president some measure of immunity from criticism in matters relating to international politics, while

22. Prior to 1962, the party in power in national politics had lost an average of thirty-eight seats in mid-term congressional elections. In the 1962 elections the Democrats lost only four seats in the House of Representatives, and actually picked up four seats in the Senate. See *Congressional Quarterly Almanac*, Vol. XVIII, pp. 1029–30.

attacking with great vigor the conduct of his chief advisors, especially the Secretary of State. Hence the drumfire of Republican criticism leveled against Secretary of State Dean Acheson in the Truman administration after 1949, and the assault by the Democrats against John Foster Dulles during the Eisenhower years. While this strategy has made the office of the Secretary of State something of a scapegoat in domestic politics, it has been a useful convention from the point of view of the opposition, and it has not been without value to presidents themselves.

Another successful gambit followed by the party out of power has been to line up behind the president in the goals he has been trying to achieve while remaining severely critical of the means he is employing in pursuit of his objectives. This was the path followed by many Republican leaders during both the Korean and Vietnam Wars, and the results of the 1952 and 1968 elections suggest that there is much to be said for this course of action as a means of winning presidential contests.

Perhaps the most advantageous of all situations for the party out of power has appeared when the burden of challenging the president was assumed by members of his own party. Samuel Lubell has argued that the major controversies in American political life take place not between the two parties but within the majority party.[23] This proposition can find no better illustration than the fight over Vietnam that embittered American politics between 1965 and 1968. This controversy was centered in the Democratic Party, and it left the Republican candidate for the presidency in 1968, Richard M. Nixon, in the fortunate position of being able to benefit from the dissatisfaction with the Democratic administration which criticism of the war both aroused and reflected, without himself bearing the onus of having to attack the President.

In the last analysis it is very difficult to know how deeply a president's decisions on foreign affairs have been affected by considerations stemming from party politics since 1945. It is possible, for example, to interpret major decisions in the Korean War in terms of domestic pressures. The free hand President Truman gave General MacArthur in 1950 to pursue communist forces to the uppermost reaches of North Korea may well have resulted from Truman's fear that any restraints he imposed on MacArthur would give Republicans the opportunity to charge that the Democrats had foregone the opportunity for a decisive

23. Samuel Lubell, *The Future of American Politics* (New York: Harper & Bros., 1951), pp. 200–5.

victory over the forces of communism. The decision in the same year to use the Seventh Fleet to protect the island of Formosa from invasion by Chinese communist forces can also be read as a response on Truman's part to domestic pressures. At that time the Truman administration was under heavy fire from Republican charges that it had allowed the communists to take over the Chinese mainland.

Similarly in 1961 President Kennedy allowed the plan for the invasion of Cuba by anti-Castro exiles to go forward after he took office. The result was the humiliating defeat inflicted upon the American-sponsored invasion at the Bay of Pigs. Part of Kennedy's acquiescence in this ill-fated venture may well have lain in the fact that a veto of the invasion would have exposed him to the Republican charge that he had missed a golden opportunity to bring down the Castro regime. Kennedy's vulnerability to this charge was particularly acute, because plans for the invasion began secretly during the Eisenhower administration and thus were known to his Republican opponents.

President Johnson's decision to intervene in the Dominican Republic in 1965 can likewise be traced to fears of the adverse consequences that might ensue for the Democratic Party if the communists were allowed to take over another country in the Western Hemisphere—a possibility that some administration officials believed to be imminent. In addition, the whole conduct of the Vietnam War by the Johnson administration is open to interpretation in terms of partisan political considerations. In the face of a possible communist take-over in South Vietnam in 1965, and the domestic political repercussions that might have ensued, the decision to move American combat troops into the South may be regarded as an effort to protect the Johnson administration at home as well as the regime in Saigon.

Moreover, while the decision to begin bombing North Vietnam in 1965 was defended by the administration on the grounds of its military value, it can also be viewed as a step taken to stifle potential Republican critics who might otherwise have charged the administration with failing to take the steps necessary to safeguard the American troops then being sent into the South. During the Korean War President Truman had frequently been assailed by Republicans for allowing the communists to enjoy a northern sanctuary in China from which they could launch attacks upon American troops in South Korea.

A similar sensitivity to Republican criticism may have been partly responsible for President Johnson's decision in 1968 to begin deployment of a "thin" ballistic-missile defense system in the United States. With the presidential campaign of 1968 then in the offing, the President could little afford, on top of his troubles in Vietnam and the

civil disorder in American cities, to furnish Republicans with an opportunity to charge that he had allowed a security gap to develop in the
nation's defense against a nuclear attack. A similar "missile gap"
charge had been used very successfully by the Democrats in the 1960
presidential campaign.

While all these interpretations are possible, none is necessarily true.
Considerations of party politics may actually have been of negligible
importance in each of these decisions, as compared to forces emanating from the international environment. What we do know, however,
is that the men elected president of the United States by that fact alone
give evidence of a keen sensitivity to currents of public opinion. It
would be incredible if they had given no consideration at all to domestic political effects in making foreign policy decisions between 1945
and 1968.

What has been particularly noteworthy since 1945 and certainly
not without significance about each of these cases in which party politics may have had an impact upon decision-making in foreign affairs
is that they all concern Democratic presidents faced with the possibility of being charged by their Republican adversaries with insufficient toughness in their anticommunist posture. A variety of events
during the 1940s made the Democrats vulnerable to Republican
criticism on this score, including the record of wartime collaboration
with the Soviet Union under President Roosevelt between 1941 and
1945, the agreements reached at Yalta and elsewhere (which seemed
to many critics to be more advantageous to the Soviets than to the
United States), and the fall of China to the communists during the
Truman administration.

It is thus possible to trace many of the decisions of Democratic
presidents in the Korean, Dominican, and Cuban episodes to their
susceptibility to the Republican charge of being "soft on communism."
If this is a valid interpretation, then many of the most significant developments in the Cold War since World War II have been influenced
by pressures originating in competition not only between the United
States and the Soviet Union but also between the Democratic and Republican Parties. Certainly it is clear that the balance of power in
party politics at home as well as the balance of power abroad has been
a major preoccupation of every president in recent times.

At the same time, however, it is possible to identify some moves by
presidents during this period as being taken with the expectation that
they would arouse strong public hostility within the country. President
Truman's removal of General Douglas MacArthur from his command
in the Far East was the outstanding occurrence of this kind between

1945 and 1968. Truman could not help but know that he was presenting his opponents with a gilt-edged issue in relieving MacArthur, but
he decided to do so nonetheless, presumably because he believed the
step was necessary to advance the security and the diplomatic interests of the United States.

One conclusion that a review of the years between 1945 and 1968
makes abundantly clear is that partisan political considerations were
not a major hindrance to the relations between the president and Congress in the development of foreign policy. The unhappy memory of
Woodrow Wilson's struggle with the Senate over the League of Nations had created the widespread expectation after World War II that
the normal institutional conflict and jealousy which the Constitution
deliberately encouraged between executive and legislative officials
would be exacerbated when the two branches of government were
controlled by different political parties. In point of fact, however,
there were eight years in which the Democrats and the Republicans
controlled opposite branches of government (1946–48 and 1954–60),
and these years witnessed as much productivity and cooperation in
foreign policy between president and Congress as in any other period of
time.

Indeed, it can be argued that pressures for cooperation and agreement were strongest during the years when the parties divided control
over the two branches of government. Such situations have provided
both president and Congress with a strong incentive to shun the appearance of putting party ahead of country, and this has induced the
executive to be more careful to consult with the legislature, and Congress to go out of its way to avoid charges of obstructionism. In the
1946–48 period the Republicans in Congress were looking forward with
confidence to victory in the 1948 presidential election, and they were
anxious to avert any criticism that they were standing in the way of
American involvement abroad which the security interests of the nation required. The product of this mood of cooperation was one of the
most successful ventures in postwar foreign policy—the European recovery program.

Similarly, between 1954 and 1960 the Democratic leaders in Congress—Lyndon B. Johnson in the Senate and Sam Rayburn in the
House—emphasized bipartisan cooperation with the president in their
approach to foreign affairs, partly because they were aware of the
esteem with which President Eisenhower was held by the electorate,
but also because they were determined to avoid any charge that the
Democrats in Congress were guilty of irresponsible conduct. Obviously, they intended to put this Democratic record of good behavior
to advantage in the 1960 presidential election.

Conflict between president and Congress over issues of foreign policy was actually most severe when both branches of government were controlled by the same party. In such situations the majority party has often behaved as though it had been liberated from the restraints under which it operated when it was in the uncertain position of dealing with a president of opposite political persuasion. Two of the periods of most acute conflict over foreign policy issues in recent history were between 1952 and 1954 and 1965 and 1968, when first the Republicans and then the Democrats controlled both branches of government.

During each of these periods factionalism within the majority party proved to be a much more divisive force in foreign affairs than competition between the two major parties. Between 1952 and 1954 the Eisenhower administration was faced with a continuing challenge from the conservative wing of the Republican Party, which had been defeated at the 1952 presidential convention but was still strongly entrenched in Congress. The Johnson presidency was bedeviled after 1965 by the defection of a substantial segment of the Democratic Party over the issue of the Vietnam War. Both the Democratic majority leader of the Senate, Mike Mansfield of Montana, and the chairman of the Senate Foreign Relations Committee, J. William Fulbright of Arkansas, were leading critics of their own president's policies in Southeast Asia. Although President Johnson identified these attacks with the Kennedy wing of the party, his sharpest critic, Senator Eugene McCarthy of Minnesota, was himself an antagonist of the Kennedys.

In the light of this record, the prospect in 1969 of some years of divided government did not in itself auger any serious discord in the relations between president and Congress over issues of foreign policy. What did, however, suggest the possibility of such conflict was the increasing dissatisfaction of Congress with its subordinate role in foreign policy as the Vietnam War continued. By 1968 the Senate Foreign Relations Committee, long the linchpin of cooperation between president and Congress in foreign affairs, had become a citadel of opposition to executive policies in international politics. This hostility was in large measure a product of what the committee considered to be the Johnson administration's deception in both the Dominican and Vietnam episodes, and of the refusal of high executive officials to testify in public before the Committee.

Responsive as it is to public discontent, Congress was most disturbed in its relations with the president between 1945 and 1968 when his policies seemed likely to impose substantial burdens on the voters back home. Military intervention abroad during this period, as in

Korea or Vietnam, thus had the effect of heightening the tension between the two branches of government. At the same time, however, such involvements also imposed strong pressures for cooperation. The need for domestic unity in confronting a foreign adversary and the necessity of backing up American troops overseas greatly limited the ability of Congress to express open opposition to the executive at times of international crisis. This was especially true after presidents began to secure the passage of congressional resolutions giving them authority to take military action in various parts of the world if they should deem it necessary to repel aggression.

The fact that Congress was thus deprived of choice in many phases of foreign policy produced a frustration that greatly affected its behavior during this period. It helped to account for much of the difficulty the foreign aid program experienced in the legislature. In a variety of other areas in which the president required the cooperation of Congress, he was able to tie its hands by linking his request for legislative action to indispensable requirements of military security. In foreign aid, however, this rationale was more difficult to sustain, and Congress, faced with an all too rare opportunity to dispose of a resource needed in foreign policy at virtually its own discretion, responded with a stubborn recalcitrance that made this the most difficult of all areas of legislative-executive relations during the period.

However, congressional dissatisfaction with a captive position in foreign affairs also found other, more constructive expression. Most notably, it led to an extensive use of the legislature's investigative power, as a means of exposing both the shortcomings of existing policy and the possibility of pursuing alternative courses of action in foreign affairs. The most celebrated of these congressional inquiries were the hearings on the Vietnam War conducted by the Senate Foreign Relations Committee. Televised nationally, these hearings provided congressional critics of the war with an opportunity to vie with the president in using the power of publicity to mobilize public support. Previous to this time, the mass media had increasingly served as instruments by which the president rather than Congress molded public opinion in foreign affairs.

Much less visible to the public, but also of great importance, were the hearings conducted during this period by the Jackson subcommittee on national security policy making. These hearings exposed the process of forming foreign policy to a public scrutiny more wideranging than it had ever before received. This kind of independent inquest into executive performance did much to elevate the standing of Congress as an institution capable of making a positive contribution to the development of foreign policy. In the years immediately following World War II, the image of congressional participation in foreign affairs, especially in liberal circles, was in large part a negative one—framed as it was by the vendetta in Congress in the early 1950s against State Department personnel involved in shaping American policy toward China when the communist government came to power in that country.

However, by the 1960s, especially though not entirely because of the Vietnam War, it was coming increasingly to be recognized that legislative surveillance was indeed a very useful part of the foreign policy process in the United States. As a result, there was in fact a very substantial shift in the attitudes of liberals and conservatives on the respective roles of president and Congress on foreign policy. In the earlier years of this period, conservatives were characteristically hostile toward presidential ascendancy over foreign affairs. Witness the struggle over the Bricker amendment to the Constitution in the early 1950s, when conservative forces unsuccessfully attempted to trim the president's power in this area by restricting his capacity to reach understandings with foreign powers through executive agreements which did not require congressional approval. Liberals fought this proposal, as they did other attempts to limit presidential supremacy over foreign policy during this period.

However, by 1968 Congress had become a bastion of liberal opposition to the Vietnam War, and for the first time since 1945 the faith of liberals in the beneficial effects of presidential power in foreign policy was seriously shaken. Conservatives, on the other hand, were mainly aligned behind the president in foreign policy controversies during the 1960s. The period from 1945 to 1968 thus brought an evolution, if not a revolution, in political attitudes, as conservatives became progressively less hostile toward executive power in foreign affairs, and liberals increasingly more so.

It would, however, be erroneous to identify Congress entirely with liberal criticism of American intervention abroad, either in Vietnam or elsewhere. Congress also provided an institutional outlet for some of the most militantly conservative attitudes toward American foreign policy during this period, in the sense at least of aggressively anti-Soviet positions. More often than not, influential legislators, especially those in positions of leadership on committees dealing with military appropriations, were pushing the executive toward higher levels of defense expenditures. In some cases Congress even authorized appropriations for weapons systems which the executive refused to develop. As a result of growing linkages among legislators, defense contractors, and Pentagon officials, Congress was a major source of conservative as well as liberal pressures on foreign policy from 1945 to 1968.

There are some grounds for describing this era as one in which the foreign policy of the United States was "bicameralized"—made subject, that is, to the authority of the House of Representatives as well as the Senate. Certainly it is true that the increased dependence of foreign policy upon supportive legislation, especially appropriation acts, gave the House an importance in this field that it did not possess during earlier periods of American history. At the same time, however, the power of the Senate was not appreciably diminished by this increased intrusion of the House into the arena of international politics. If the power of the House has grown during this period as a result of its increasing involvement in foreign affairs, that of the Senate has expanded even more.

There is perhaps no better index of the growth in status of the upper chamber of the legislature in American politics than the fact that by 1968 the Senate had become the chief recruiting ground for presidential candidates in both the major political parties. Between 1960 and 1968 all the men nominated for the presidency by both the Democrats and the Republicans had previously acquired national preeminence as U.S. Senators. What this experience suggests is that the relationship between the House and the Senate is not necessarily one in which the growth in power of one branch of the legislature occurs at the expense of the other—in foreign affairs or in other areas of policy.

3. Bureaucratic Power and Foreign Policy

Of all the developments since 1945 which have affected decision-making in foreign affairs and the pattern of influence to which presidents are subject, none is more striking than the appearance of a vast and complex bureaucratic apparatus with responsibilities in the field of foreign policy. When the postwar period began, there was widespread apprehension that the effectiveness of the United States in foreign affairs would be greatly hampered by the weakness of its administrative establishment, thinly manned as it was and lacking a long tradition of participation in international activity.

However, by 1968, it was quite apparent that these earlier fears had been exaggerated. The bureaucratic organization necessary to carry on American activites abroad had been created partly through an enlargement of the State Department, but much more significantly through the assignment of responsibilities in the international sphere to a variety of other agencies in the national government. This growth was made necessary not only by the expansion of American commitments overseas but also by the emergence between 1945 and 1968 of a vast number of new states in the underdeveloped regions of the world, with which diplomatic and other contacts had to be maintained.

As a result, the problems America faced in 1968 with respect to its administrative establishment in foreign affairs were primarily those of a mature rather than an infant bureaucracy. In recent years there has been, for example, a constant search for an organizational design that will provide adequate avenues of coordination among the diverse agencies now involved in the foreign policy process. As the State, Defense, and Treasury Departments, the Central Intelligence Agency, the Atomic Energy Commission, and a host of other agencies became participants in foreign affairs, it has been increasingly essential to find ways and means of keeping the policies and activities of these agencies in concert. Foreign policy has been confronted with the perennial hazard that the activities carried on by one agency, such as the U-2 "spy flight" launched by the CIA over the Soviet Union in 1960, would nullify other international ventures such as the summit meeting in Paris that coincided with this aerial reconnaissance mission.

However, coordination requires elaborate procedures for consultation, clearance, and committee decision. A chief result of the efforts since 1945 to eliminate the mishaps of inadequate coordination has often been the establishment of cumbersome routines that seemed to sap foreign policy of vitality and prevent a rapid response to changing conditions. Between 1961 and 1963 high officials in the Kennedy administration often found themselves at loggerheads with the bureaucratic apparatus in foreign affairs, because of its apparent inability to move quickly in periods of crisis or to change traditional Cold War attitudes. Thus efforts to restructure the organizational system through which foreign policy has been carried on in recent years have oscillated between attempts to improve coordination so as to eliminate mistakes, and efforts to allow administrative units more operational autonomy in order to enhance their ability to achieve results.

One seemingly irresistible trend in the administration of foreign affairs since World War II has been the continuing decline in the authority of the State Department in international activities carried on by the United States. This development had begun as early as the 1930s, and was greatly accelerated during World War II, when President Franklin D. Roosevelt relied mainly on personal envoys or his military advisers in conducting foreign policy. Cordell Hull's role as Roosevelt's Secretary of State was chiefly that of maintaining support in Congress for Roosevelt's foreign policy.[24]

The decline in the State Department's influence has been even more pronounced since 1945. As the Cold War began and American military commitments around the world proliferated, the Department of Defense assumed a commanding position in international activity, and the expertise of the military official in foreign policy began to rival that of the diplomat. No less impressive was the rise in power of the CIA, as the gathering of information related to American national security and the conduct of clandestine operations abroad for the first time became major aspects of American international activity. Thus over the period 1945–68 a national security apparatus emerged in which the State Department often found itself playing an inferior role.

As international economic activities, particularly monetary and fiscal problems, have assumed increasing importance, the Treasury Department has also come to have a major voice in the development of foreign policy. Moreover, disarmament negotiations with the Soviet Union, such as the meetings prior to the nuclear test ban and nonproliferation treaties, have turned essentially on the advice and counsel of scientists rather than diplomats. This has enabled agencies like the Atomic Energy Commission to take a leading part in some of the most important international conferences since World War II.

Perhaps the major blow to the position of the State Department as the nominal administrative channel for the conduct of American foreign policy was the establishment of central offices close to the president charged with responsibility for coordinating and setting priorities in the field of foreign policy. The National Security Council, in which the Secretary of State is but one of several members,[25] is the formal institutional channel through which such coordination has been carried on since this agency was first established in 1947. Equally significant, however, has been the appointment on the White House Staff of the President's Special Assistant for National Security Affairs. In a position of close proximity to the president, this advisor has been in a strong position to compete for influence over foreign policy with the State Department, particularly under a president like John F. Kennedy,

24. See Richard F. Fenno, *The President's Cabinet* (Cambridge: Harvard University Press, 1959), pp. 173–77, 204–6.

25. Under the terms of the statute by which it was created, the National Security Council has only five members, but as many as twenty officials may actually attend its meetings. See Harry H. Ransom, *Can American Democracy Survive Cold War?* (Garden City, N.Y.: Doubleday & Co., 1964), pp. 31–32.

who preferred such personalized channels of advice to institutional mechanisms like the State Department.

The emergence of this vast administrative establishment in national security affairs has been a Promethian development from the point of view of the president's command over foreign policy since 1945. On the one hand, it has provided chief executives with an invaluable resource for maintaining the "information gap" that has been a chief basis of their supremacy over Congress in the field of foreign affairs. The rise of a supporting bureacracy has increased the number and the variety of experts presidents could tap to buttress the authority of their own pronouncements in foreign policy. In this respect it has represented a substantial political gain for the president, and a distinct disadvantage for his opponents, in both the rival party organization and his own.

At the same time, however, the new and expanded agencies in the foreign policy field have also acquired an independent power of some magnitude over foreign policy. A major source of this power has been the ability of executive officials to shape the views of the president through the advice they give, sometimes in ways that have been disastrous for him. There have been dramatic episodes since World War II when presidents were badly misled by the advice of their administrative subordinates. In the case of the Bay of Pigs invasion in 1961, for example, President Kennedy received highly erroneous predictions from intelligence agencies regarding the events that would ensue once the refugee force had been landed in Cuba.

The strength of the bureaucratic apparatus created in the field of national security since World War II has been evident not only in the initiation of but also in adherence to policies, once they have been decided upon. After the initial presidential decision to intervene in South Vietnam, the American officials and agencies associated with the Saigon government, especially the military organizations, became the strongest protagonists for maintaining and expanding the American commitment in that beleaguered country. In the European theatre, the MLF plan for sharing nuclear weapons with the other NATO countries undoubtedly endured long after its unacceptability to the affected countries had become clear, largely because American bureaucrats identified with this proposal continued to lobby for it at high echelons of government.

Perhaps the most formidable of all aspects of bureaucratic power since World War II has been the ability of agencies in the national security field to form alliances with other groups in the domestic political arena, thus adding political muscle to bureaucratic organization as sources of influence upon foreign policy. Easily the best-known of these alliances is the "military-industrial complex" that has figured so largely in political controversy in recent years. This alliance is alleged to draw together in a concert of attitude and action the executive agencies that have the power to hand out defense contracts, the business firms whose profits are based on such awards, trade unions that depend on defense spending for jobs for their members, community groups that see military installations and defense plants as contributing to the prosperity of their local economy, congressmen whose public standing derives from their identification as protagonists of a strong military establishment, and a variety of assorted "defense intellectuals" from universities and private research organizations who are employed by the government to provide cerebral support for Cold War activities.

The emergence of this military-industrial complex has clearly been one of the most striking developments in the domestic setting of foreign policy since World War II. It has given agencies connected with national security a degree of support in the domestic political system that sharply contrasts with the comparatively isolated political position of the armed forces in the 1930s, and it has created strong vested interests in American involvement abroad, inasmuch as these overseas activities have provided career advancement for officials in both military and civilian agencies, as well as opportunities for service and profit abroad for a wide variety of nongovernmental organizations and individuals.

The influence this military-industrial complex has exerted over foreign policy has not, however, been unlimited. For one thing, it has not been a monolithic force in foreign affairs. If the power of all the agencies in the national security establishment had been added together during this period, it would have represented an awesome force in foreign policy decision-making, before which even the authority of the president might have been impotent. The fact of the matter is that the agencies in this defense complex have often been sharply divided in their views, each counteracting rather than reinforcing the influence of the other. This division of opinion was quite evident at the time of the nuclear test ban treaty in 1963. Moreover, on issues of defense strategy, presidents have usually been able to find some support among the various branches of the armed forces for virtually any course of action they chose to follow since World War II.[26] In short, the military-industrial complex has been a family of organizations with competitive as well as complementary interests throughout this period.

26. Huntington, *The Common Defense*, pp. 113–15.

In any case, the recent growth of expenditures for national defense has been traceable not only to the manipulative activities of a defense complex but also to the simple fact that there has been overwhelming public support for spending prodigal amounts to assure the physical security of the country. As a matter of fact, the public has been prepared since 1945 to make even larger expenditures for national defense than officials have felt it necessary to recommend. Public pressures for economy have mainly been directed at domestic programs during this period. Among expenditures for national security, only foreign aid—an area of activity dimly related in the public mind to the nation's safety—has been subject to strong pressure for economy. The notion advanced by some defense strategists (most notably by Robert S. MacNamara during his tenure as Secretary of Defense between 1961 and 1968) that after a certain point additional expenditures for weapons purchase insecurity rather than security has been far too subtle to gain wide public acceptance.

Moreover, it has not always been certain that programs or courses of action that are strongly supported within the military-industrial complex will necessarily be adopted. For example, proposals for universal military training were strongly advocated by the military in the period immediately following World War II, but they were defeated by a coalition of religious and educational organizations, in spite of the fact that the public at large strongly favored such a UMT program.[27] In legislative struggles, peace groups have often been stronger during this period than might have been predicted from the degree of public support they have enjoyed.

Since President Johnson's escalation of the Vietnam War in 1965, a coalition of groups opposed to the military-industrial complex has emerged in domestic politics. This coalition has a strong interest in cutting back the level of defense expenditures so as to make it possible to allocate additional funds to domestic purposes, especially in the inner-city areas of the country for the benefit of Negro and other disadvantaged groups. This urban coalition, which has civil rights groups as the core of its organized support, has urged the view that an expansive role for the United States in preserving "order" in Asia and elsewhere commands resources and energies that might be better used to eliminate poverty at home and the domestic tensions to which it gives rise.

In the 1950s, the primary check upon a rising level of expenditures for national defense had been the fear of conservatives that too high

27. Almond, *The American People*, p. 104.

a level of defense spending would unbalance the budget and lead to what Secretary of the Treasury George Humphrey described in 1956 as a hair-curling depression. This brake upon defense spending was essentially removed with the arrival of the Kennedy administration, which was willing to accept a deficit in the national budget if it was required to stimulate the domestic economy. The "new economics" thus eliminated the chief restraint that had previously operated as a check upon expenditures for national security, and by so doing helped to accelerate the rate of defense spending in the Kennedy and Johnson administrations.

However, the change in the perspective of liberal politicians during the 1960s was a startling one. As the decade began, leading Democratic spokesmen, including President Kennedy, were determined that this country should gain ascendancy over the Soviets in missile weaponry and were convinced that much stronger conventional forces were needed to deal with crisis situations below the threshold of nuclear confrontation. As it ended, liberal fears that military expenditures would inhibit attention to domestic problems had replaced conservative concern for economy in government as the chief deterrent to defense spending. The civil rights movement and the Vietnam War had thus combined their effects so as to "radicalize" the liberal forces in American politics.

Thus in recent controversies over American foreign policy there have been two major centers of political power. One is the military-industrial complex, in which there are substantial groups with both strong ideological convictions and large self-serving institutional interests in the perpetuation of an imperial role for the United States in preserving world order. The other is a loosely organized coalition of liberal groups with a deepening conviction that domestic reform rather than foreign policy should be the primary item on the political agenda, and the skeptical suspicion that American intervention abroad in the interest of world order has chiefly the effect of obstructing social and economic reform in other societies. Needless to say, segments of this coalition also have vested interests in channeling government expenditures into such domestic programs as urban rehabilitation.

The institutional locus of the military-industrial alliance has been easy to identify, centered as it is in the Pentagon and the vast system of defense industries, which together have the power to dispose of eighty billion dollars annually—more than one-third of the national budget. And this complex has behind it the momentum generated by the fact that it supports defense policies that have matured over the course of two decades and have sunk deep roots into American society.

Any appreciable shift from the internationalist policies of the past, particularly from the high level of defense spending to which these policies have given rise, would cause severe dislocations within the American economy.

There has been perhaps no better indication of the extent to which this defense spending has been built into the expectations of the American community than the fact that so much local resentment has been aroused in recent years by the closing of military installations in the United States, however outmoded or unnecessary a facility may be for defense purposes. Equally painful has been the reaction when a defense contract with a local industry was canceled, or when an expected award went instead to a firm in another community. It has been responses of this sort which have led many observers to the wry conclusion that America's global commitments serve too many domestic functions ever to be abandoned. In a great variety of ways the domestic economy has come to live off the nation's foreign policy.

The institutions with which liberal criticism of foreign policy has been chiefly associated represent a much less cohesive set of organized interests than the military-industrial complex. There are, however, a number of agencies in the national government from which opposition to a high level of defense spending and the policies associated with it can be mobilized, as, for example, the Arms Control and Disarmament Agency in the State Department, whose concerns and recommendations envisage a cutback or at least a deceleration in defense expenditures.

The Disarmament Agency is not, however, the only part of the bureaucratic apparatus whose interests conflict with the fiscal and organizational might of the Pentagon. There are a great number of agencies in the domestic sphere which in recent years have seen their own appropriations scaled down because of the needs of the defense establishment. The Department of Health, Education, and Welfare, along with the Department of Housing and Urban Development and the Office of Economic Opportunity, have been the agencies most immediately and adversely affected by the cutback in expenditures for urban-oriented activities since the escalation of the Vietnam War. Bureaucrats in such agencies often identify with the needs of their own impoverished clientele rather than with the foreign policies of the government that employs them.

Agencies concerned with scientific research, such as the National Science Foundation and the National Institutes of Health, were also hurt by cutbacks in nondefense expenditures resulting from Vietnam. Indeed, research and development activities in all segments of the national bureaucracy, including the Department of Defense, suffered similiar reductions in appropriations, thus indicating the extent to which conflicts can occur within the military-industrial complex itself— as funds for financing the Vietnam War were withdrawn from defense-related research activity.

In any case, the widespread conception in radical politics of the national bureaucracy as a monolithic establishment which gives primacy to defense rather than domestic needs is highly oversimplified. There are officials in the Department of Housing and Urban Development, for example, who have been as vigorous in advocating priority for domestic programs as any of the contemporary spokesmen of the New Left.

Inevitably, however, bureaucrats are restricted in the extent to which they can publicly oppose the policies of the government of which they are a part. In the 1960s the real center within the governmental structure of opposition to American policies in Vietnam and elsewhere which seemed to overextend the nation's responsibilities in international affairs was the Foreign Relations Committee of the U.S. Senate. Under the chairmanship of Senator Fulbright, the committee provided a rostrum from which both senators and witnesses could voice well-publicized objections to the course of American foreign policy, or to what Fulbright himself called the "arrogance" of power—"the tendency of great nations to equate power with virtue and major responsibilities with a universal mission."[28]

It is possible that substantial debate over Vietnam or other issues would have taken place even without the Senate Foreign Relations Committee as a forum for discussion. It is very clear, however, that the Committee played an enormously important role in legitimizing and reinforcing public dissent in successive crises during the 1960s, including, besides Vietnam, the Bay of Pigs in 1961 and the American intervention in the Dominican Republic in 1965. As a governmental institution, the Committee's pronouncements have carried considerably more authority with the public than has dissent from the nongovernmental sector of society. Senators are (more so in the public mind perhaps than in fact) privy to official information denied to outsiders. The fact that the Committee could reach the negative conclusions it did about American policy in Vietnam was highly significant in persuading people outside of government that their own misgivings were justified.

28. J. William Fulbright, *The Arrogance of Power* (New York: Random House, Inc., 1966), p. 9.

Over this period the media of mass communication have also done much to stimulate dialogue and dissent on issues of foreign policy.[29] Because of the mass audience they command, the television networks have played a particularly important role in this respect. The Johnson administration often traced its domestic difficulties over the Vietnam War to the amount of coverage the action on the battlefield received on television. In point of fact, however, the communications media exercised influence over public attitudes toward Vietnam in a great variety of other ways as well, by covering the activities of dissenting groups, providing a platform for critics of official policy, and airing versions of the facts that were at variance with the views articulated by government agencies.

Newspaper criticism of the Johnson administration's handling of the Vietnam situation was also widespread and helped account for the administration's loss of public support. Perhaps the major blow it suffered in this respect was the defection of the *New York Times*, which up until Vietnam had been steadfast in its support of the main outlines of American foreign policy in the decades following World War II. While the *Times* is not read by anything resembling a mass audience, it does have an enormous circulation among so-called opinion-makers, members of elite groups who take their cues on matters of foreign policy from the *Times* and who are in a strategic position to influence the opinions of others.

In summary, therefore, it can be seen that while the emergence of a bureaucratic apparatus in the national security field—with its civilian support groups in the military-industrial complex—has provided a basis of institutional support for conventional Cold War attitudes, it has also generated activity on the part of countervailing forces. The Vietnam conflict, whatever judgment of it may finally be made, has clearly demonstrated that even twenty years of consensus politics in support of the Cold War could not obliterate the capacity of Americans to carry on a spirited and wide-ranging debate on foreign policy regarding relations with the communist world. Thus, while Vietnam has been a trial for American democracy, it has also been a tribute to it. Although the administration tried fitfully to silence dissenters with demands for unity in the face of foreign adversaries, these efforts seemed if anything only to stiffen the opposition of its domestic foes.

---

29. For an analysis of the role of the media in foreign affairs since World War II, see Bernard Cohen, *The Press and Foreign Policy* (Princeton: Princeton University Press, 1963), and James Reston, *The Artillery of the Press* (New York: Harper & Row, 1967).

The American experience during the Vietnam years has thus decisively refuted the expectations of those who felt in the late 1940s and early 1950s that a prolonged involvement in the Cold War would so militarize and bureaucratize this country as to turn it into a "garrison state" in which the armed forces would become dominant and traditional freedoms would gradually disappear.[30] These fears were reinforced by the period of McCarthyism American society went through in the early 1950s, when a climate of opinion hostile to civil liberties did appear as a result of events connected with the Cold War, particularly Soviet espionage in the United States and the Korean conflict.

Whatever else may be said about the United States as the year 1969 began, it was certainly not a society in which dissent was no longer possible. Indeed, the theme of President Nixon's inaugural in 1969—"bring us together"—is an accurate indication of the view of most political leaders, that what the country most needed and desired in the years ahead was a relief from disunity and discord.

4. American Attitudes toward Foreign Policy

While the years since World War II have represented in many respects a period of continuity in American diplomatic history, they have also been marked by several major transitions in fundamental American attitudes toward foreign policy. As noted earlier, the period began with liberals determined to uphold the president's authority in foreign policy and sharply critical of conservative efforts to force the chief executive to share his power with the Congress. When it ended, many liberals were bitterly disillusioned with the use President Johnson had made of his executive power in foreign affairs during the Vietnam conflict, and sympathetic to proposals by Senator Fulbright and others that presidential power be made subject to closer congressional surveillance. Conservatives in the meantime had lost much of their concern over the President's ascendancy in determining American foreign policy.

Moreover, at the beginning of this era liberals were at the spearhead of the movement to involve the United States in international activities, as they had been since Woodrow Wilson's day. By its end, they were hanging back to an extent not seen in American politics since the Spanish-American War. Political support for American in-

30. This theme was initially developed by Harold Lasswell before World War II and reiterated in a number of writings since that time. See, for example, Harold Lasswell, *National Security and Individual Freedom* (New York: Harper & Bros., 1950), pp. 23–49.

tervention in Vietnam and elsewhere in Asia was strongest among conservatives, who had always been prepared to see the United States more actively involved in Asian than in European politics. Even in the 1930s, when isolationist sentiment was rampant, it was primarily directed at keeping America from becoming entangled in European problems.

Even more remarkable was the contrast between 1945 and 1968 in attitudes regarding the relationship between foreign and domestic affairs in the United States. As noted at the outset, the predominant fear in the years immediately following World War II was that foreign policy would be neglected as the society turned inward toward domestic concerns. But in the late 1960s, as America was drawn into deeper involvement in Southeast Asia, the argument was increasingly heard that the United States was neglecting its domestic needs for the pursuit of power and prestige abroad. A society that in the 1940s had been regarded as far too insular in its perspective seemed to many by the late 1960s as excessively cosmopolitan in its orientation.

As important as any other factor in bringing about this change in attitudes was the growing recognition that America did indeed have serious domestic difficulties. In the late 1940s and the 1950s, there was a widespread conviction that the United States had solved the problem of poverty at home and was moving, if much too slowly, toward a solution of the long-standing grievances of the Negro population. This feeling of satisfaction with domestic affairs helped sustain and justify the concentration upon problems of foreign policy throughout the first decade of the Cold War.

By the 1960s, however, this sense of domestic well-being began to dissolve. Civil-rights organizations, first in the south but eventually in the north as well, were able to dramatize the fact that Negroes were lagging far behind whites in enjoying the new affluence of American society. The publication of studies like Michael Harrington's *The Other America* highlighted the condition of substantial segments of the population who were experiencing one of the most difficult of all human situations—a life of poverty in the midst of plenty. It was in the wake of these developments that first President Kennedy and then President Johnson began to develop plans for the "war on poverty" at home that was eventually to supplant the Cold War abroad as an object of primary concern for many members of their own Democratic Party.

By the end of the 1960s it was also clear that anticommunist sentiment had lost some of its potency as a justification for American intervention abroad. It was not that Americans had become any more favorably disposed toward communist ideology and institutions than in earlier times. It was simply that after more than twenty years of living in the same world with communist states, the public had become resigned to the inevitability, though by no means the desirability, of accommodating to their presence.

In the early phases of the Cold War there had been some expectation of not only containing but also "rolling back" communist power in Eastern Europe. However, by the 1960s it was apparent that these expectations had little prospect of being realized. At the time of the Hungarian uprising in 1956, there was at least some public sentiment in favor of taking action in support of the "freedom fighters" in Budapest. In 1968, when the Soviets occupied Czechoslovakia, the inability of the United States to involve itself directly in such Eastern European developments had become clear, and the response of the American government to the Czechoslovakian crisis was a tepid one. There is no better indication of American acceptance of the permanence of communist power in the world than the contrasting reactions in the United States to the events in Budapest in 1956 and in Prague in 1968.

The passage of time thus deepened Americans' awareness that it would be necessary to share the world with unpleasant communist neighbors for the foreseeable future—indeed, to share the Caribbean with one such neighbor less than ninety miles from the American coast. The acceptance of this condition was perhaps made easier by the fact that the communist states had begun in the 1960s to quarrel so markedly among themselves. A collection of communist societies beset by internal ideological disputes seemed much less menacing to Americans than what appeared to be the monolithic communist apparatus in the early 1950s.

Also of great importance in reshaping American attitudes toward foreign policy was the emergence in the late 1960s of a generation that was not as preoccupied with the menace of Communist expansion as its parents had been. In part this was a matter of disillusionment with the Cold War. In many underdeveloped societies, the effort to contain communist power had led to American support of military regimes, mainly because the military was the only institution other than the communist party with a nation-wide organizational capability. The rise of military power was most apparent in Latin America, but perhaps its most disheartening manifestation was in Greece—in whose behalf the United States had ostensibly begun its containment policy in 1947—which came under the control of a military junta in 1967.

Moreover, idealistic segments of the new generation of Americans were less interested in international activity simply because other matters now seemed more important to them. In the early 1960s enthusiasm for the effort to modernize underdeveloped nations led many young Americans into the Peace Corps, but by the end of the decade even this degree of involvement in the international sphere had become less fashionable. Problems associated with racial injustice in America or the task of reconstructing cities now claimed an increasing portion of the moral energy and crusading zeal of Americans.

Indeed, by the late 1960s the feeling had developed among much broader sectors of American society than the young or idealistic that American participation in the Cold War for two decades had produced a hypertrophy of foreign policy. Burning questions at home were receiving less attention than secondary or tertiary issues abroad. The Vietnam War was the event that did most to generate this conception of an America excessively preoccupied with international situations that might better be treated with a kind of "salutary neglect" by the United States. When the decade drew to a close, the proposal to deploy an antiballistic missile system in the United States had become a major center of controversy, as the ABM program came under bitter attack as a needless and costly escalation of the arms race.

This hypertrophy of foreign policy, if it can correctly be called that, may be traced to two major forces operating in the domestic political arena. The first was the fear by men elected to office that any evidence of their being less vigilant than their competitors in pursuing national security goals in an age of widespread anxiety over nuclear war would lead to their swift departure from office. Inevitably, the political sensitivity of national security issues in domestic politics led to an acceptance of an "overkill" capacity—the extension of American commitments abroad or the development of weapons systems beyond the point needed to assure the defense of the country.

Also important in giving national security policy its overwhelming momentum was the pressure exerted by the government agencies concerned with this area of policy. Since World War II these bureaucracies have been in a strategic position to inflate national security needs in order to advance either their expansionist goals as organizations or the career ambitions of their members. "Created by wars that required it, the machine now created the wars it required."[31]

The reaction against this exaggerated preoccupation with foreign policy in the late 1960s led to considerable speculation as to whether the United States was returning to the kind of isolationist posture it had presumably left for all time in World War II. These fears were

31. Joseph Schumpeter's description of the military bureaucracy in ancient Egypt, as quoted by Arthur Schlesinger, Jr., in "Vietnam and the End of the Age of Superpowers," *Harper's Magazine* (March, 1969), p. 43.

partially triggered by the Johnson administration in an effort to discredit opponents of the Vietnam War, who were often linked by administration spokesmen with the appeasement policies of the 1930s. But the apprehension was also based on the fact that critics of American foreign policy in the 1960s did use arguments reminiscent of pre-World War II isolationism, especially the proposition that American influence in the world could best be achieved by the example this country set of peace and prosperity in its domestic life.

The fact is, however, that American society in the 1960s did not provide a setting appropriate for the revival of the kind of isolationism that prevailed in the 1930s. This sentiment in the earlier period rested on the belief that America could be insulated from world affairs. Its strongest base was in rural America, where events abroad had the least impact in the United States. But this insular segment of the country shrank dramatically in size as the society became increasingly urbanized in the period following World War II.

The insular attitudes of the 1930s also rested in good part on the attachment of ethnic groups in the United States to one of the Axis powers or their hostility toward the British empire, with which American intervention in Europe would be chiefly associated. When the main antagonist of the United States became the Soviet Union, these traditional ethnic allegiances no longer operated against American intervention in Europe.

However, the gap between the 1930s and the contemporary situation exists not only because the social order no longer exhibits characteristics that sustained isolationism in the earlier period. An even more important distinction is the fact that internationalist attitudes now rest on pervasive patterns in American society that did not exist in the 1930s. The population of the United States is better educated, it travels more, and its attitudes are shaped by the media of mass communication, which promotes a sense of involvement in international events.

Moreover, as has been noted before in this discussion, large segments of the labor force now benefit economically from one or another aspect of American involvement in world politics. While critics of American activities overseas have often complained that these programs divert resources from domestic needs, it is no less true that they provide a livelihood for great numbers of Americans employed in defense industries or other activities stemming from American involvement abroad. Thus any substantial cutback in the U.S. international role would have threatening implications for Americans that it did not have in the 1930s.

There is in short no real social, economic, or political basis for anticipating a revival of traditional isolationism as a major force in American politics in the immediate future. Periodically since World War II, movements of disenchantment have developed with respect to America's participation in international life. Prior to the intervention in Vietnam, these moods were largely a product of right-wing resentment of the failure of our European allies to carry their share of the defense burden, or fear that participation in international organizations might jeopardize the sovereignty of the United States over its own internal affairs. Since Vietnam, disillusionment with internationalism has increasingly been found on the left or even at the center of the political spectrum.

These moods of isolationism like so many political phenomena in the United States, have been evanescent in character. Who now can remember the right-wing campaign for the Bricker amendment in the early 1950s? Equally difficult to remember in the future may be some of the calls for American withdrawal from world politics that emerged in the late 1960s, as protests against the Vietnam War swelled into civil disorder. Critics of the war as well as its defenders often tended to stake out more extravagant positions on the meaning of Vietnam than were justified by the rather unique circumstances of that conflict.

Moreover, periodic surveys of public opinion since World War II clearly reveal a continuing rejection of isolationism as a course of action appropriate for the United States in foreign affairs. When asked the question on the Gallup Poll, "Would it be better for the United States to keep independent in world affairs—or would it be better for the United States to work closely with other nations," the American public has consistently supported the idea of international collaboration by majorities ranging from 72 to 82 percent.[32]

To be sure, it is possible to see a revival of isolationism today, if it is defined as the belief that a nation should limit its involvements abroad, particularly military commitments, and avoid what some consider to be hyperactivity in international affairs. However, it seems more accurate to characterize this outlook as some form of revisionist internationalism, since it has been accompanied in the 1960s by a strong commitment to American participation in international organizations, a recognition of the impact of events abroad upon the United States, and an eagerness to use American economic and technical resources to help impoverished societies.

Many of the more influential critics of the Vietnam War have ex-

32. See *New York Times*, February 23, 1969, p. 43.

hibited just such a pattern of attitudes. Their criticism of the war has reflected not a "neo-isolationist" longing for an America separated from the impact of external events but a keen sensitivity to world opinion and the conviction that the country's participation in the war damaged its standing abroad. Whether or not this belief is supported by the facts, it is certainly a far cry from the hostility to international involvement that characterized American isolationism during the 1930s.

Indeed, it is possible to interpret the fissure that appeared in the internationalist consensus in the late 1960s as the death knell of old-style isolationism. In the years immediately following World War II internationalists of all varieties had been linked by their fear of an isolationist revival. The fact that they now permit themselves the luxury of disputes over how far and through what channels intervention should be carried on may be taken as a sign that they no longer regard an isolationist resurgence as a serious possibility.

5

THE MILITARY ISSUES

Robert E. Osgood

1

From the United States' standpoint, the politics of the Cold War have been heavily suffused with military concerns. They have been punctuated by American participation in two large local wars and by a number of crises in which American armed force played a critical role overtly or in the background. These concerns have reflected some of the major preoccupations of the last twenty years: the avoidance of nuclear war, disarmament and arms control, the strategy of containment, the security and cohesion of NATO, the restraint and reassurance of West Germany, the prevention of nuclear proliferation. They have evoked a remarkable outpouring of strategic doctrine and analysis—most notably by nonmilitary men—and this outpouring has spilled over into allied states and, to some extent, the Soviet Union.

Many of the most imaginative—though not necessarily successful—policies and programs sponsored by the American government have been in the military field: the Baruch disarmament plan, the "open skies" arms control proposal, the Strategic Air Command ground and airborne alert force, the seaborne Polaris nuclear retaliatory force, safe and secure command and control over nuclear weapons, the proposed multilateral nuclear force (MLF), and the formulation and implementation of a strategy of controlled and flexible response. Some of the most important controversies in American foreign policy have revolved around the commitment, deployment, use, adequacy, and control of American military power: the North Atlantic Treaty, the B-36 and aircraft carrier controversy, troops for Europe, the strategy of "massive retaliation," the "bomber gap" and "missile gap," and the nuclear test ban. Three American military interventions—the Korean War, the Dominican intervention, and the Vietnamese war—have dominated opinion and politics in their time and greatly affected the course of American policy.

Yet now the intense military concerns of the past seem relatively remote and quiescent. The stubborn remnants of the Vietnamese war and the issues of ABM, MIRV, NPT, and the strategic arms limitation talks excite some public discussion and remind us that military concerns are a continuing feature of our external affairs. But the discussion does not go to the roots of strategic doctrine or American foreign policy, like some of the earlier debates. Does this mean that the previous excitement over military issues was only part of adjusting to the novelty of nuclear weapons and other technological changes and that the major adjustments have now been made? Does it mean that these issues were largely bound up with one transitory period of international tension in which military security and the avoidance of nuclear war were for a while foremost concerns? Is the present quiescence of military issues likely to last long, or is it merely a lull before new political and military developments reactivate military concerns? More specifically, in what respects are the military issues, theories, and policies of the last two decades obsolete; in what respects are they of lasting significance; and what new issues may arise? The present relative lull in the generation of military concepts and controversies provides an opportune moment to assess forthcoming military issues in light of a reassessment of the past.

An assessment of the military issues should begin by recognizing that one of the most significant developments in military affairs since World War II is a change of attitude toward the objectives and uses of armed force. This change has come to dominate American military policies and promises to prevail, because it reflects the terrible realities of the nuclear age. According to the common American view before World War II, the only war the United States might fight would be a total war to protect American territorial security; the principal objective would be to defeat the enemy by destroying his armed forces and his ability to support them, after which an "unconditional surrender" would be exacted. From this view it followed that the ultimate requirement of military preparedness was the capacity to win a total war. But in the nuclear age a different view has emerged, reinforced by the impact of World War II and the memory of World War I. According to this view, no one could win a total war because, for any state, the extent of devastation incurred would far outweigh the value of defeating the adversary; but the United States might nevertheless have to fight local wars for limited objectives, even though American territorial security were not directly threatened. From this view, it followed that the principal objective of preparedness was to deter attacks that might lead to general war, but also that it was scarcely less important to deter, or if necessary to resist, local aggressions of smaller scope.

Consistent with this new attitude was a change of emphasis in the standard of military sufficiency. In the last decade there has arisen a strong disposition to view the objective of strategic preparedness less as the achievement of a superior capacity to fight a general war than as the achievement of a stable military balance conducive to mutual deterrence, moderation of the arms race, and avoidance of war by accident or misapprehension of military intentions.

This change of attitude toward the objectives and use of armed force will almost surely outlast the particular context of military technology and international politics in which it arose, but the particular strategies, policies, and programs designed to implement it cannot remain static in a changing technological and political environment. To assess the likely and desirable changes and continuities in these strategies, policies, and programs, we shall examine the strategic balance with the Soviet Union, the military restraint of Communist China, the formulation and application of the strategy of flexible and controlled response, and arms control, in each case taking into account prospective developments in military technology and international politics.

2

In the first years of the Cold War, American military strategy and preparedness were directed almost entirely toward deterring the Soviet Union from invading Western Europe or striking the United States. Deterrence was thought to depend critically on America's temporary nuclear monopoly, then on its nuclear superiority, and on its resulting capacity to win another world war. But the American and Soviet achievement of vastly more powerful thermonuclear warheads in the early 1950s, together with their acquisition of long-range missiles in the late 1950s, convinced American and—eventually, though less clearly or universally—Soviet leaders that a general war involving homelands could no longer be won in the way that such wars had been won before the invention of nuclear weapons. Rather, such a war would be a mutual catastrophe. Logically, it followed that the chief requirement of a strategic force was not quantitative parity or superiority in warfighting capability but a capacity to inflict enough retaliatory damage to deter a nuclear attack. But this logic was not universally accepted in either country.[1]

1. In the Soviet Union Khrushchev was the principal voice conveying official recognition that a Soviet-American war would be so mutually devastating as not to be a useful instrument of national policy. As in the United States under the Eisenhower-Dulles administration, his assertion of this position went along with his emphasis upon nuclear striking power as a substitute, to some extent, for ex-

The implications of this logic for American strategy went beyond the requirements of deterring a nuclear attack to affect another function of strategic deterrence, the deterrence of attacks and threats of attacks upon other states.

In the first place, the function of a strategic force was and still is more than the deterrence of a surprise attack. The United States has relied heavily on its strategic nuclear force, supplemented by tactical nuclear weapons and a minimum capacity for local resistance, to deter the Soviet Union from small-scale nonnuclear aggressions against U.S. allies. This is called "extended deterrence" in strategic parlance.[2]

In the second place, both the United States and the Soviet Union regard their strategic forces as crucial psychological levers for their respective interests in crises and diplomatic encounters. These functions, to be effective, presuppose one side's residual fear that its nonnuclear incursions may lead the other side to start a nuclear war. Yet neither side now possesses a nuclear capability that would make such a first strike anything but self-defeating.

The Soviet Union has never enjoyed a ratio of strategic power that would enable it to strike the United States without in retaliation being destroyed as a modern industrial nation. Until the deployment of Soviet ICBMs in the early 1960s the United States was probably able to knock out enough Soviet strategic weapons on a first strike to escape extreme devastation, though for a decade American leaders had portrayed the inevitable result of any nuclear war as virtually the end of civilization for both sides.[3] Inevitably, however, the growing numbers

---

isting conventional and general purpose forces. But both the doctrine and the policies that accompanied this emphasis have been the object of vigorous and continuous dissent by some Soviet military men, who insist that a nuclear war can be won in the traditional sense and that the Soviet Union needs strategic parity or superiority (as well as superiority in ground forces) to deter the United States, protect Soviet interests against American pressure, and win a European war if necessary. Roman Kolkowicz, *The Dilemma of Superpower: Soviet Policy and Strategy in Transition* (Washington, D.C.: Institute for Defense Analyses, October, 1967).

2. Extended deterrence refers to the deterrence (by virtue of one's capacity to strike the adversary directly) of hostile actions that one state might take against other states. Soviet dependence on the threat of a nuclear response to American actions against Soviet allies and friends was never as explicit as the comparable American dependence. In general, Soviet nuclear threats against the United States were couched in terms that implied that, if the United States offered armed resistance to Soviet moves against American allies and friends, it would incur the risk that the resulting conflict would become nuclear.

3. How much retaliatory damage a government could tolerate without regarding the value of striking first as nullified—an amount commonly called "unaccept-

and the invulnerability of American and Soviet missiles in the 1960s undermined the feasibility of either side's achieving a reliable, rationally usable, first-strike capability.[4] To some indefinite extent these developments also undermined the credibility of either side's resorting to a nuclear first strike. In any event, they greatly increased the uncertainty about the extent of retaliatory damage that any government contemplating a nuclear first strike must take into account, and this uncertainty is itself a powerful deterrent when the damage might well be catastrophic.

In the United States, the first serious effort to adjust its military strategy and forces to this novel situation took the form of trying to strengthen nonnuclear forces as a means of reducing America's dependence on extended deterrence. The Kennedy-McNamara administration made this effort the centerpiece of its military program. In Western Europe, however, where dependence on extended deterrence was heaviest, the success of this program in terms of actual capabilities was limited by economic and domestic political contraints in the European states against their expenditures for local defense, and by their

---

able damage"—is, of course, a subjective judgment depending on many circumstances. In his annual "Posture Statements," McNamara estimated that the Soviet Union would generally regard the destruction of about one-fifth to one-fourth of its population and one-half of its industrial capacity as intolerable. If a comparable standard were applied to the American government, it would follow that a first-strike capability, in order to be rationally useful, would have to confine Soviet retaliatory damage to a level that McNamara regarded as practically unobtainable. In 1968 he calculated that by the 1970s, only if the United States deployed a $22-billion ballistic-missile defense and the Soviet Union failed to respond with multiple warheads, penetration aids, and additional mobile missiles, could the United States expect to receive less than forty million fatalities after striking first. *Statement of Secretary of Defense Robert S. McNamara before the House Armed Services Committee on the Fiscal Year 1969–73 Defense Program and 1969 Defense Budget*, p. 64. Still more conservatively, he defined a rationally usable first-strike capability as one that could "substantially eliminate" the attacked nation's retaliatory second strike.

4. According to McNamara's figures, either the United States or the Soviet Union could inflict 120 million immediate deaths on the other and destroy 75 percent of the other's productive capacity. Beginning in the late 1950s, the invulnerability of nuclear striking forces to destruction by a nuclear first strike has been greatly increased through dispersal, warning systems, airborne alert, mobility, concealment, and the hardening of sites. Early intercontinental missiles were vulnerable because they were liquid-fueled and above ground, but by 1960 the mainstay of a relatively invulnerable American missile force was the growing fleet of nuclear submarines carrying Polaris missiles. The Soviet Union did not begin hardening and dispersing its missile forces until after 1963. In 1968 it began to deploy a fleet of Polaris-type, submarine-launched missiles.

declining apprehension of a Soviet military threat. Significantly, however, this did not lead the government to try to enhance the credibility of an American first strike against local communist aggression. In fact, the American government, increasingly cautious in the face of growing Soviet retaliatory strength, openly renounced pursuit of a first-strike capability, and it even ceased to talk of a first-strike strategy. In increasingly unambiguous language, Secretary of Defense McNamara pronounced a first-strike capability to be unobtainable, and, except for a momentary emphasis on "damage limitation,"[5] he declared that a capability for "assured destruction" (that is, the infliction of unacceptable damage in response to a nuclear first strike) was the determining objective of America's strategic weapons program. Whereas Dulles had stressed America's reliance on "massive retaliation," and the American government throughout the 1950s had felt compelled repeatedly to assure West Germany and to persuade the Soviet Union that the United States would defend its allies against conventional aggression with nuclear weapons if necessary, President Kennedy and Secretary McNamara soft-pedaled the threat and strategy of a nuclear first strike, and stressed instead the necessity of a "flexible and controlled response."

Thus the military security of America's European allies remains almost as dependent as ever on the deterrent effect of a nuclear capability that would be avowedly self-defeating for the United States to use in their behalf. Americans, like their allies, generally find this anomalous position quite acceptable, at least as long as the Soviet military threat appears to be quiescent. For they regard the mutual capacity of the two superpowers to destroy each other in any nuclear war, no matter who strikes first, as the best assurance of peace, and they assume that the fear of nuclear war would arise in even the smallest clash of Soviet and American forces, because of the danger that such a clash would expand.

On the other hand, the implications for specific military policies and for programs of this situation of virtual parity in deterrence of a nu-

5. Damage limitation was McNamara's term for limiting, through offensive and defensive strategic weapons, the Soviet capacity to damage the United States in a nuclear war. In 1962, when he first formulated this objective in terms of a counterforce capability to blunt Soviet striking power in a no-cities exchange, he may have envisaged bolstering deterrence by rendering a nuclear exchange more nearly rational to carry out. But he subsequently made it clear that a damage-limiting capability would have no effect on deterrence (either first-strike or second-strike); nor would it mitigate the Soviet Union's ability to destroy the United States. By 1964 the McNamara budget had de-emphasized damage limitation and re-emphasized dependence on assured destruction.

clear first strike are not so readily agreed upon. In this respect, indeed, present technological and political trends seem destined to raise new controversies, or at least intensify old ones, for they pose insistent questions about the nature and requirements of the bipolar strategic balance, and particularly about the meaning, feasibility, and utility of American strategic military superiority.

3

American strategic military policies have been a response to the imperatives of containment in a largely bipolar contest. The primary objective of containment was always to achieve such countervailing power at points of Soviet pressure as to induce the Soviet Union to refrain from forcibly changing the status quo and eventually to moderate its conduct of foreign affairs. At first, American military planners regarded the distribution of strategic power needed for containment as primarily a superior capacity to devastate the Soviet Union—that is, a capacity to inflict far more damage on the Soviet Union than the Soviet Union could inflict on the United States. For this purpose SAC's nuclear bombers would compensate for NATO's inferiority in conventional forces. To enhance the credibility of nuclear retaliation against a non-nuclear attack in Europe, tactical nuclear weapons were added in the early 1950s, and a somewhat more effective conventional resistance capability was created during the early 1960s; but there was no effort to overcome Soviet superiority on the ground.

With the growing recognition of the unacceptability of nuclear war and the increasing stress on an invulnerable second-strike capability as the mainstay of deterrence, the emphasis in American military thinking shifted from maintaining superiority in war-fighting capabilities to stabilizing mutual deterrence, though the United States retained quantitative superiority in strategic weapons. Stabilizing the military balance required minimizing the risk of inadvertent war that was inherent in the possibility of a hair-trigger response. One way to minimize the risk was to seek reciprocal assurances against surprise attacks and to develop techniques, devices, and procedures to prevent accidents and political miscalculations. From this concern with a stable military balance, which became established doctrine in the latter years of the Eisenhower administration, it was an easy step to McNamara's renunciation of a first-strike capability altogether as the Soviet Union's second-strike capabilities increased. But it was a wrenching step, especially for some congressmen and military men, to the equally logical abandonment of superiority in war-fighting capability as the criterion of strategic preparedness; for this contravened ingrained notions of military security as well as America's pride in its military prowess. Nonetheless, this is the course that Secretary McNamara took. Though he tried to soften the impact by asserting America's maintenance of quantitative superiority in striking power, his rationale for strategic programs refuted the value of such superiority.

At the beginning of his tenure, in the wake of Democratic charges that the previous administration had not provided against an approaching missile gap, McNamara expanded America's missile program, despite the discovery, hailed by President Kennedy, that the United States enjoyed at least a four-to-one superiority in intercontinental striking forces, which enabled it to inflict more damage on the Soviet Union in a second strike than the Soviet Union could inflict in a first strike. McNamara later changed his tune from hailing American strategic superiority to stressing only sufficiency as the objective, and this within a nuclear balance that gave either side the capacity to devastate the other. He regretted having contributed to the "mad momentum" of the arms race by initiating, on the basis of an overestimate of Soviet intentions to produce ICBMs, defense increases to which the Soviet Union had responded in kind.[6] By the end of his tenure he had clearly revealed that his primary objective, far from being the maintenance of America's strategic superiority, was the stabilization of mutual deterrence on the basis of virtually equal second-strike capabilities, while slowing down the arms race so as to avoid the superfluous, expensive, and possibly provocative accretion of strategic weapons.[7]

Just as the American government had reached this position on the strategic balance in the late 1960s, the Soviet Union posed the first

6. McNamara's views are contained in many interviews, public statements, and official testimonies, as well as in his annual posture statements. They are extracted and summarized in two books: William W. Kaufmann, *The McNamara Strategy* (New York: Harper & Row, 1964) and Robert S. McNamara, *The Essence of Security* (New York: Harper & Row, 1968).

7. McNamara's position on superiority can be summarized as follows: (1) The realistic measurement of superiority is not gross megatonnage or numbers of missile launchers, but the number of separate warheads that can be delivered with accuracy on individual high-priority targets with sufficient power to destroy them on a retaliatory second strike. (2) The United States possesses a superiority over the Soviet Union by this criterion of about four to one, and will continue to maintain superiority as far ahead as can be realistically planned. (3) But this superiority is greater than the government planned (because the Soviet Union did not produce as many ICBMs as the United States estimated it might in 1961) and more than is required for assured destruction. (4) Moreover, this superiority does not effectively translate into political control or diplomatic leverage; but it has fueled the "action-reaction phenomenon" of the arms race, manifested most recently in substantial increases in Soviet offensive forces.

genuine challenge to American strategic superiority as measured by common quantitative comparisons. This was the result of several developments: (1) After the Cuban missile crisis the Soviet Union not only increased its total defense outlays (especially in 1966 and 1967) but also substantially increased the proportion of its defense expenditures allocated to offensive and defensive strategic weapons, while the United States in the same period decreased its expenditures on strategic weapons, absolutely as well as proportionately.[8] (2) As a result, the Soviet ICBM force about tripled from 1965 through 1968, while the numbers of deployed American ICBMs and submarine-launched ballistic missiles leveled off.[9] (3) In addition, the largest Soviet missiles carry much larger payloads than American missiles (which, among other possible advantages, permits the Soviet Union to install more warheads on each missile); and the new generation of solid-fuel Soviet missiles, like their American counterparts, have a greatly improved accuracy (which threatens the invulnerability of even the most hardened sites for land-based missiles). (4) Finally, Soviet deployment of antiballistic missiles (ABMs), although initially confined to the Moscow area, might portend a larger deployment that would degrade America's second-strike capability.

On the other hand, the United States decided in September, 1967, to deploy a "thin" ballistic-missile defense (BMD) system, called

8. See U.S., Congress, House, Subcommittee on Appropriations, *Department of Defense Appropriation, 1966,* 89th Cong., 1st Sess., Part 4.

9. In 1967 American ICBMs, of which there were 854 in 1965, leveled off at 1,054. Ballistic-missile submarines deployed, with 16 missiles each, went from 27 to the programmed level of 41 in the same period and leveled off. Strategic bombers declined from 710 to 646 and would decline about another 200 by the mid-1970s. From 1965 to 1967 Soviet ICBMs increased from 270 to 720 by some estimates and to 450 by others (depending somewhat on estimates of how many were actually operational). There were sites for roughly 1,000, and the Soviets were producing from 150 to 200 a year. In 1969 the number of Soviet ICBMs was expected to equal or surpass the number of American ICBMs. In addition, the Soviet Union had flight-tested a fractional orbital bombardment system (FOBs). Soviet nuclear-powered ballistic-missile submarines with three missiles each, of a range capable of hitting all but the most centrally located American cities, have increased from 40 to 50 in the past three years. In 1968 the Soviets were beginning to deploy nuclear submarines with 16 Polaris-type missiles aboard, which could give them a force comparable to the Polaris fleet by the mid-1970s. Strategic bombers (not counting medium-range bombers, which can be refueled in the air) have declined from 200 to 155. The Soviet figures are estimated conservatively on the basis of somewhat divergent data published in the Institute of Strategic Studies' annual *Military Balance, Jane's Fighting Ships,* and congressional testimony. See also: U.S., Congress, House, Committee on Armed Services, *The Changing Strategic Military Balance,* 90th Cong., 1st Sess., July, 1967.

Sentinel, against the prospect of Chinese ICBMs in the early 1970s; and this system, as its congressional advocates pointedly emphasized, could be expanded to protect American cities and missiles from Soviet attacks as well.[10] Equally important, the American government was prepared to install in a few years, before the Soviet Union could do so, multiple warheads (called MIRV for multiple independently targeted re-entry vehicles) in long-range missiles, beginning with Minuteman III and Poseidon, which is programed to replace Polaris. This would have the effect of quickly multiplying the number of potential strikes that could be delivered on separate targets. McNamara was confident that these measures, together with penetration aids and improved missiles, could preserve America's assured-destruction capability even against an extensive and effective Soviet BMD system. But he was disinclined to program measures that would upset the military balance and accelerate the arms race, unless it were clear that the Soviet Union was going ahead anyway with programs that would jeopardize America's capability for assured destruction.

Those who agreed with McNamara's emphasis on stabilizing the military balance and holding down arms expenditures asserted that, if the United States and the Soviet Union went ahead with MIRVs and ABMs, the United States or even both powers might upset the stability of the bipolar balance by acquiring or threatening to acquire first-strike capabilities. In any event, they charged, if either state deployed new ABM systems or installed MIRVs, the arms race would greatly accelerate. And they pointed out that, even in the current state of the arms race, President Nixon was likely to be presented by the Joint Chiefs with a military shopping list totaling $100 billion to $110 billion, a sum that was from $20 billion to $30 billion higher than the existing defense budget.[11]

The critics of McNamara's position, on the other hand, charged that American security was already endangered, because Soviet leaders were determined to gain strategic superiority, or at least parity, while

10. In March, 1969, President Nixon decided not to go ahead with this system but to authorize only a minimal Safeguard system designed primarily to protect two ICBM sites, which, however, might be expanded and modified following annual reviews of technical developments, the Soviet and Chinese threat, and the status of any arms talks.

11. In addition to expenditures for the Sentinel system, the shopping list was said to include expenditures for a new strategic bomber, a much larger successor to the Minuteman missile (Minuteman III), a new sea-based successor to the Polaris missile, both in new submarines and on surface ships (Poseidon), and a new continental air defense system. New York Times, December 19, 1968, p. 30.

American leaders were deliberately forfeiting it.[12] They pointed to the increasingly conspicuous Soviet political presence in the Near East and its naval presence in the Mediterranean, Soviet assistance to North Vietnam, and Soviet armed intervention in Czechoslovakia as evidence that the Soviets were more interested in maintaining and advancing their whole power position than in stabilizing the military environment and reducing international tensions. Therefore, to grant the Soviet Union parity could only encourage a more aggressive and adventurous Soviet policy.

4

This controversy about the ratio of American to Soviet strategic power, though subdued compared to previous controversies on military issues, sharpened the impact of portentous technological developments and disturbing trends in Soviet defense and foreign policy. It confronted the Nixon administration not only with specific military decisions but also with fundamental choices of military concept on which such decisions should be based.

One concept at issue is that of superiority; but the controversy over superiority goes deeper than its articulation. Just to pose the arguments about strategic policies in terms of the concept of superiority, with all its inherent ambiguity in the nuclear age, conceals some of the underlying issues. McNamara was correct in emphasizing that the proper standard of strategic preparedness is not a quantitative or even a quantitative-qualitative comparison of bombers, missiles, warheads, or other isolated components of military power, but rather sufficiency of strategic forces in the aggregate from the standpoint of fulfilling

12. Congressional and military critics principally cited two indices of America's fading superiority: the total megatonnage carried by strategic weapons and the numbers of strategic vehicles. They emphasized the danger of an extensive Soviet BMD deployment combined with continued increases in Soviet offensive missiles. But their strategic objectives and premises were not so clear. In general, they emphasized the maintenance of an adequate second-strike force and argued that this required a capacity not only to inflict unacceptable damage but also to win a nuclear war, even if winning meant only that the United States would end the war in better condition than the Soviet Union. The principal function of superiority, however, was not actually to win such a war (which most conceded would be devastating) but to prevent Soviet leaders from acting more adventurously because they thought that the United States was determined to avoid war at all costs. For extreme statements of this view, see General Curtis Lemay, *America Is In Danger* (New York: Funk & Wagnall, 1968) and General Thomas S. Powor, *Design for Survival* (New York: Coward-McCann, 1965). For a more moderate exposition, see William Kintner, *Peace and the Strategy Conflict* (New York: Frederick A. Praeger, 1967).

specific functions. Therefore, determining what functions are feasible and desirable is logically prior to determining the composition and quantity of strategic forces.

There is general agreement that assured destruction, as McNamara defined it, should be the primary function of strategic forces. For this purpose the U.S. capacity to inflict unacceptable damage on the Soviet Union after receiving a Soviet nuclear attack is essential; but the capacity to defeat or disarm the Soviet Union in a nuclear war while keeping damage to the United States at an acceptable level, although desirable, is neither essential nor attainable. Given the immense uncertainty about the actual consequences of employing so many fearful weapons that have never been used in war, and some that have never been adequately tested (for example, antiballistic missiles), it would be incredible folly for one superpower to strike the other on the assumption that it could escape unacceptable retaliatory damage. Nor could it compensate for such damage by inflicting greater damage on the enemy.

There is less agreement on whether the composition and quantity of strategic forces should be governed by the function of damage limitation. The most ambitious strategy of damage limitation—holding open the option of avoiding cities in a nuclear exchange—seems prudent, even if the prospect of its actually working is improbable. For one should not dismiss the possibility of a nuclear exchange arising from circumstances (involving, for example, some miscalculation of intentions or responses) that would impel both sides to stop far short of maximum devastation. Some strategic counterforce capability beyond what is required for assured destruction may be useful for this purpose in order that both sides may avoid eroding their ultimate deterrent against countercity exchanges. It may be useful anyway, in order to blunt Soviet striking power. On the other hand, the growing invulnerability of Soviet forces and the slight prospect that anything but the most limited nuclear exchange could be kept below acceptable levels of destruction severely limit the utility of major expenditures on offensive missiles for damage limitation. Indeed, the marginal surplus of strategic striking power needed to assure an adequate second-strike capability may be enough for the extent of damage limitation that one can reasonably expect offensive missiles to achieve. Whether ABMs should be deployed for damage limitation is another question, which we shall consider in the context of their other functions and effects.

The function that would call for the biggest change in strategic forces, if the United States were seriously to pursue it, would be a first-strike capability. One can argue that such a capability, in the absence of much greater local resistance forces, is necessary to restore the credibility of extended nuclear deterrence—the principal deterrent that the United States and its European allies must rely upon against limited nonnuclear incursions. Otherwise, we are at the mercy of Soviet good intentions and Soviet fear that any armed conflict in Western Europe will grow into a nuclear war. The trouble with this argument is not that a first-strike capability would be undesirable because it would raise the risk of a Soviet pre-emptive attack, which is quite unlikely, or even that it would accelerate the arms race, which is probably true, but rather that, as an option that is significantly credible or likely to be used, it is unobtainable at a reasonable cost, if at all.

Let us posit the unlikely prospect that the United States would be able to reduce the expected damage from a Soviet retaliatory strike by 50 percent, if it were willing to increase its defense expenditures a great deal. Then the pertinent question would be not one of capability but of value in relation to cost. How would such a first-strike capability change the existing balance of power in real terms? To what additional degree and under what circumstances would such an estimated capability, with all its terrible uncertainties, embolden the American president to initiate the use of nuclear weapons or enable him to convince the Soviet leaders that he might do so? How would such a capability affect Soviet behavior? Obviously, the answer to such questions depends on many factors other than the strategic military balance; but, judging from the historical evidence, the correlation between the efficacy of America's first-strike force and its deterrent capacity (or the will and nerve of the president) is highly problematical, if not altogether nonexistent.[13] It provides no basis for supposing that the results of trying to achieve a first-strike capability would come close to justifying the effort.

The argument for superiority rests heavily on its alleged necessity for another function of strategic forces, a function that is even more dependent on subjective judgments but is not implausible or unfeasible. This function is the general support of national policy in conflicts short of war. It is based on the supposition that quantitative superiority in the most powerful weapons has a general psychological impact beyond its utility as a deterrent, that it discourages an aggressive Soviet policy and bolsters American prestige and policy against Soviet pressure, particularly in crises. In this shadowy realm of conflict, some simple,

13. Comparing the period in the 1950s, when the United States had a first-strike capability, with the period since then, one would have to conclude that this factor made no discernible difference with respect to the outbreak and the outcome of Soviet-American crises, but that other factors were decisive.

crude measures of superiority may have an effect, if only because the adversary thinks that they do. Thus Soviet leaders, it is argued, believe that the United States has exploited its strategic superiority to bolster political adventures in the Middle East, Southeast Asia, and elsewhere. By the same logic, Soviet leaders may believe that they could play a more adventurous game and reduce the risk of American intervention if they could convince Americans and others that the Soviet Union held strategic superiority. It would follow that, in order to restrain the Soviet Union, it is necessary to prevent it from achieving superiority, or the impression of superiority, by whatever criteria seem persuasive.

There is some evidence for this proposition, but it is not conclusive.[14] The history of the Cold War reveals no definite cause-and-effect relationship between the nature of the strategic balance and the American or Soviet will or ability to pursue foreign policies in the face of the other's opposition—except for the obvious necessity for caution imposed on both states by their mutual fears of a nuclear confrontation. And, clearly, many other factors count as much as or more than the strategic balance; for example, the relative value of the interests at stake, the local conventional balance, the quality of national leadership, domestic opinion and politics, and the whole political context of crises. Yet, since the Soviet Union has never actually enjoyed even quantitative parity in strategic striking power, one cannot be sure how its attainment of superiority would affect its behavior.[15] Probably

14. Soviet leaders have sought political advantages in claiming technical, qualitative superiority and vast destructive capability for Soviet ICBMs. Soviet military leaders have been particularly insistent on attaining this kind of superiority. Evidently they regard such superiority as serving a variety of policy purposes, among which imposing nuclear constraints on American opposition to Soviet moves is prominent. Therefore, a convincing Soviet superiority might encourage an aggressive foreign policy. See, for example, the analysis by Arnold L. Horelick and Myron Rush of Khrushchev's effort to use Soviet Sputniks, ICBM production claims, and the missile-gap controversy to convey the false impression of a shift in the balance of strategic power toward the Soviet Union, and to exploit this impression as the underpinning for a more aggressive foreign policy, particularly in Berlin. See their *Strategic Power and Soviet Foreign Policy* (Chicago: University of Chicago Press, 1965). It is notable, however, that Khrushchev's deception failed. It failed to intimidate the American government and provoked the Kennedy administration's revelation of American quantitative and qualitative superiority in nuclear striking power. Moreover, nothing in the history of this incident warrants the inference that Khrushchev would have come closer to achieving his policy goals if his various claims of Soviet strategic power had been true.

15. Some contend that Soviet parity or superiority would include Soviet leaders to be more relaxed and less aggressive in their conduct of external affairs, since

some quite unsophisticated notions of what constitutes military superiority (notions carried over from earlier, prenuclear arms races) count for something in contemporary international competition. So, even if ratios of strategic power are of purely symbolic significance, they might nevertheless be crucial. Yet in practice we cannot know enough about the decisive measure of symbolic superiority or the correlation between such superiority and the behavior of the superpowers to warrant making the quantitative American-Soviet ratio in any particular strategic weapons the primary guide to America's strategic program. To do that would mean subordinating all the more compelling criteria of military strategic sufficiency to highly subjective, uncertain, and ephemeral suppositions.

5

If the foregoing analysis is a correct view of the feasible and desirable functions of strategic forces, then the significant issue in terms of development, production, procurement, and deployment of strategic weapons against Soviet forces is not whether to seek or abandon superiority, but rather how much of what kinds of strategic weapons is enough for assured destruction, with perhaps an extra margin for damage limitation. In meeting this issue the most important weapons developments about which decisions have to be made for the 1970s are the MIRV and the BMD. Such decisions should be made not only in light of technological and cost-effectiveness considerations but also in light of an assessment of Soviet foreign and defense policies, the nature and scope of American commitments, and the foreign and domestic objectives that compete for public expenditures.

If the principal function of American strategic forces is assured destruction, the United States can afford to make the relevant decisions on the basis of firm evidence of Soviet military production and deployment, rather than to assume the worst (as in the past) and rush into a program that turns out to be an overreaction. For a large, active, imaginative research and development program—combined with the present surplus of retaliatory forces and the high quantity and diversity of strategic weapons—minimizes the risk of the Soviet Union's suddenly achieving a first-strike capability, and it permits the United States to defer to the need for increased domestic expenditures.

---

they would not be under the compulsion of the past, which reached its culmination in the Cuban missile crisis, to offset American superiority and compensate for Soviet inferiority by means of adventures in either the political or military realm. But there is no more evidence for this proposition than for its opposite, and it is a risky basis for policy.

In the absence of an effective arms-control agreement (which we discuss later), one must expect, while trying to prevent, the substantial incorporation of MIRVs and ABMs in American and Soviet strategic forces—eventually. This will undoubtedly compound the uncertainties of calculating security requirements and start a new phase of the arms race. Yet if this development takes place gradually and moderately and with the proper expectations, it need not have adverse consequences beyond the money regrettably spent in running the arms race just to stay in the same place.

The effectiveness of ABMs in protecting cities against various penetration devices and tactics (especially tactics designed to overload defensive systems and saturate targets) would be extremely difficult to determine precisely, even if tests with atmospheric nuclear bursts were not proscribed by the nuclear test ban. The difficulty of knowing the requirements of a second-strike force, when visible missiles might hold an unknown number of warheads capable of attacking separate targets with great accuracy, is obvious. But, if these uncertainties are symmetrical and if both sides are known to have a sufficient number of mobile, concealed, superhardened, or ABM-protected missiles to discourage pre-emptive nuclear strikes, the effect might simply be to increase the reluctance of either side to strike first. In any case, it is quite improbable that moderate deployments of MIRV missiles and ABMs would make either side more willing to incur the risks of using nuclear weapons. It is somewhat less improbable, however, that one or both sides might fear this possibility.

Therefore, in order to avoid rapid and provocative changes in the strategic balance and to forestall unnecessary competitive arms expenditures, it is important that the United States go no further or faster with its MIRV deployments than is clearly essential to preserve an assured destruction capability against moderate estimates of Soviet offensive and defensive capabilities in the 1970s. In this respect it should be noted that, according to the Defense Department's estimates, the United States already has a great deal more than enough second-strike capability, even if the high level of assured destruction that is prescribed is essential.[16]

16. According to McNamara, American alert forces alone and without MIRV carry more than 2,200 warheads with an average yield of one megaton each, but a mere 400 of these weapons delivered on target—all of them having "devices that ensure penetration of Soviet defenses"—would be sufficient to destroy over one-third of the Soviet Union's population and one-half of its industry. McNamara, *The Essence of Security*, p. 54. According to Secretary of Defense Clifford at a Pentagon news conference on October 25, 1968, the United States has 4,206 deliverable strategic weapons, the Soviet Union, 1,200.

The proper function of a BMD system deployed to protect cities is not to enhance the credibility of a first strike but to limit damage from a strategic nuclear war or from a limited nuclear strike resulting from a political miscalculation.[17] It would have no appreciable effect on one's own assured-destruction capability except insofar as it also protected missiles. But can ABMs substantially limit damage, and would they be worth the expense?

The arguments against a very expensive (say, $40 billion to $60 billion) BMD system intended to provide maximum protection of American cities are not necessarily compelling against a much more modest system. A maximum system, especially if installed at a rapid pace, might well provoke offsetting countermeasures—such as offensive missiles, penetration aids, multiple warheads, bombers, FOBS (fractional orbital bombardment systems), and cruise missiles to fly under BMD radars—which would cost more in their acceleration of the arms race and associated political tensions than the estimated reduction of damage would be worth. But a BMD system designed to reduce deaths by 15 or 20 percent might achieve its objective without the ill effects of the more extensive system and without inciting the Soviet Union to nullify it.[18] One may infer from the Soviets' attitude toward their own ABMs and defensive weapons generally that they would not regard such a system as provocative or as a threat to Soviet deterrence that had to be offset with strategic increases.[19] Therefore, the United

17. BMD protection for cities might have some of the same effect as retaliatory offensive weapons in deterring a first strike, since it would make it more difficult for the Soviet Union to count on inflicting overwhelming civil damage—evidently one of the Soviet objectives on a first strike. The Sentinel system was an area-defense system based primarily on the Spartan long-range exoatmospheric interception missile, with a small number of Sprint point-defense, short-range, atmospheric interception missiles to be added later. But whereas the Sprints would be deployed principally to protect ABM radars according to the Sentinel concept, an effective system for the protection of missiles would have to depend primarily on point defense. In some respects such a system might be a better response than MIRV to Soviet BMD increases, since, given the Soviet defensive-mindedness, it would be less likely to induce a Soviet counteraction and would not threaten the Soviet assured destruction capability. By the same token, it would also be better than increasing offensive capabilities as a way to preserve America's second-strike capability against Soviet MIRVs.

18. Donald G. Brennan argues for this point of view and against the proposition that every BMD increase should or will be offset by offensive increases and improvements in D. G. Brennan and Johan J. Holst, *Ballistic Missile Defense: Two Views* (Adelphi Papers, No. 43; London: Institute of Strategic Studies, November, 1967).

19. Analysts of Soviet military policy have observed the special emphasis placed on defense, including strategic defense—an emphasis presumably stemming from a combination of historic military experience, special service interests,

States and the Soviet Union might both deploy minimal ABM systems that would provide good protection against limited nuclear strikes resulting from miscalculation and some assurance of reducing damage in a larger nuclear war by 10 or 20 percent, and yet not raise expectations of reducing damage so much as to make the resort to nuclear weapons more attractive to either. The capacity of BMD to save lives and limit destruction would be principally valuable as an end in itself. On the other hand, deploying anything beyond a minimal BMD system on the supposition that the Soviet Union would not offset it would be an expensive gamble in view of the inherent dynamics of arms competition and the prospective ease of offsetting ABMs with offensive devices and strategies.[20]

In light of all these considerations, if the United States and the Soviet Union cannot reciprocally avoid deploying MIRVs and additional ABMs altogether, the United States ought to gear its offensive and defensive missile policies to the objective of encouraging as limited and gradual an ABM deployment on both sides as possible. It follows that the American response to Soviet BMD ought not to be based on the worst assumptions about the scope of its intended deployment and that the United States ought not to operate on the assumption that every increase of Soviet defensive capabilities automatically requires an increase in America's offensive capabilities.

6

As the foregoing account indicates, America's military strategic policies have developed entirely in the context of its relations with the Soviet Union and have been almost exclusively concerned with the security of the United States and Western Europe. America's concern with other nuclear states, actual or potential, has been confined to "nuclear sharing" with allies, limiting the existing nuclear forces by arms control, or preventing the emergence of new nuclear forces. It has not begun to consider the many problems that may be posed in

---

and fear of an American surprise attack. One aspect of this emphasis is the Soviet insistence that, contrary to American views, the protection of Soviet cities would not disturb the strategic balance so as to require the United States to deploy offsetting ABMs. In any case, the composition of Soviet strategic forces, as opposed to the magnitude of the Soviet strategic program, seems to be more responsive to special Soviet strategic concepts and to service politics than to American weapons programs.

20. The argument that offensive tactics and cheap penetration aids could nullify the effectiveness of even a light ABM system is presented by Richard L. Garwin and Hans A. Bethe in "Anti-Ballistic Missile Systems," *Survival*, X (August, 1968), 259–68, reprinted from *Scientific American* (March, 1968).

a decade or so by the necessity of managing America's strategic force in a multipolar nuclear system. Thus American military planners until recently have not been concerned about the strategic balance with Communist China, since the prospect that China could launch nuclear strikes against American allies and friends in Asia, let alone the United States itself, was remote. But this situation is changing. Now China is expected to have developed an operational MRBM force by the early 1970s, and an operational ICBM force by the late 1970s. This raises the question, which will have policy significance before long: How should the United States counteract China's nuclear capability?

One issue is whether, and, if so, how, the United States should try to maintain the credibility of its first-strike capability against China. It might wish to do so in order to protect allies and friends against China's nonnuclear incursions and "nuclear blackmail," to maintain a pre-emptive option against prospective Chinese attacks on the United States, or perhaps in some circumstances to knock out China's vulnerable nuclear installations.

One must expect a growing Chinese MRBM, and especially an ICBM, force to diminish the credibility of an American first strike in the eyes of China and in the eyes of states that might be the object of Chinese incursions and pressure. How significantly credibility will be weakened may not depend primarily on the physical magnitude of America's first-strike capability. After all, the United States has applied remarkable constraints on the use of its nuclear weapons against China or China's allies, even when China had no capacity for nuclear retaliation. In two large wars involving American forces (one with China in Korea, the other with China's ally in Vietnam), the United States refrained from using even tactical nuclear weapons. One might expect these constraints to be relaxed somewhat, if the fear of the Soviet Union's backing China with nuclear weapons continues to diminish while China challenges American interests more directly with military attacks. However, the problem of maintaining the credibility of America's first-strike capability in Asia in the face of a growing nuclear force will continue to be of quite a different order than the same problem was against the Soviet Union in Europe. In Asia the value of interests for which the United States would take risks of nuclear war is less than in Western Europe. In Asia there is no institutionalized embodiment of these interests comparable to NATO, with its American commander and American forces in the area. Moreover, the United States is apt to consider unacceptable a much lower level of Chinese retaliatory damage when incurred in defense of Asian interests.

This is not to say that America's nuclear capability will cease to deter China from taking direct military actions against Asian states— China's caution in this respect has been notable—but only to observe that perceptions of the interests and alignments of states are going to have more effect on the efficacy of that deterrent in the next decade then the objective capability of America's strategic force. Nonetheless, if China, under the cover of its growing nuclear capability, should be tempted to play an aggressively active role in Asia, the credible capacity of the United States to protect Asian states from nuclear blackmail might be essential to Asian security.[21] For this purpose an American BMD to limit damage from a hypothetical Chinese attack on the United States or to protect Asian states directly (if seaborne ABMs should prove practicable) could be a useful complement to a vigorous deterrent policy.[22] Whether such a system promises to be sufficiently effective to warrant the cost of installing it is a more complicated and less calculable question. The choice of an anti-Chinese BMD is further complicated by the problem of gauging its effect on the military balance, on arms competition, and on diplomatic relations with the Soviet Union. It is doubtful that anything beyond a very thin ABM system can be distinguished from an anti-Soviet deployment.

No one questions the value of maintaining a capability for assured destruction against a Chinese first strike, but this presents no material problem to concern American military planners in the next ten years or so.[23] Any Chinese first strike against the United States, even a preemptive strike, would be truly irrational. The prospect of such a strike is too slight to justify deployment of a BMD. Therefore, the justification for an anti-Chinese BMD depends very much on whether

21. Nuclear blackmail is an ambiguous term. It is used here to refer to pressure of various kinds exerted by China against Asian states under the implicit threat of nuclear attack. To counteract this kind of pressure, the United States will be in a better position if it can convince China, the states that may be the objects of Chinese pressure, and itself that it could strike Chinese nuclear forces without incurring more than minimal nuclear retaliatory damage.

22. Secretary McNamara estimated that the Sentinel system, facing a relatively primitive Chinese attack in the 1970s, could hold American fatalities below one million. McNamara, *Statement on Fiscal Year 1969–73*, p. 63. Garwin and Bethe contend, however, that by the time the Chinese ICBM is deployed it will have devices to counteract the Sentinel system. Garwin and Bethe, "Anti-Ballistic Missile Systems."

23. McNamara estimated that a relatively small number of warheads detonated over fifty Chinese cities would destroy half of the urban population and more than one-half of the industrial capacity, as well as most of the key governmental, technical, and managerial personnel and a large proportion of skilled workers. McNamara, *Statement on Fiscal Year 1969–73*, p. 50.

the United States anticipates playing an active countervailing role against an aggressive China determined to extend its influence and control in Asia in the most forceful way.

In any case, however, the primary issues of military strategy and policy that arise from China's power and behavior are not in the realm of the strategic nuclear balance, but are rather in the realm of limited-war strategy and policies, to which we now turn.

7

America's traditional approach to war and military preparedness has undergone as radical a change of attitude in the realm of local deterrence and defense as in the realm of the strategic balance. This change is marked by the great attention Americans have devoted to limited war and, more broadly, to the strategy of flexible and controlled response.[24] In spite of the formidable antipathy toward the concept of limited war during the Korean War and the Eisenhower-Dulles administration, the rationale of limited war has gained widespread acceptance in the United States and, to a somewhat lesser degree, in allied countries. In the 1960s the United States went far in implementing the concept with strategies, weapons, and organization.

The detailed elaboration of a strategic doctrine of limited war, the formulation of specific plans for carrying out this doctrine, and the combined efforts of government, the military establishment, and private analysts and publicists to translate the doctrine into particular weapons and forces are developments peculiar to the nuclear age. They are products of the profound fear of nuclear war and the belief that

24. One symptom of the increased acceptance of the concept of limited war is the increased ambiguity of the term, since the concept of controlling war within rational limits relevant to specific political objectives has come to be applied to *any* kind of war, even one involving a nuclear exchange. A limited war is generally conceived to be a war fought for ends far short of the complete subordination of one state's will to another's and by means involving far less than the total military resources of the belligerents, leaving the civilian life and the armed forces of the belligerents largely intact and leading to a bargained termination. Although a war between nuclear states might conform to this definition, the term limited war is generally applied to relatively more likely local nonnuclear wars, in which the superpowers do not confront each other directly. The difficulty of defining limited war arises partly because the relevant limits are a matter of degree and partly because they are a matter of perspective, since a war that is limited for one belligerent might be virtually total from the standpoint of another on whose territory the war is fought. Furthermore, a limited war may be carefully restricted in some respects (for example, geographically) and much less in others (for example, in weapons, targets, or political objectives).

the limitation of war must be carefully contrived, rather than left to inherent limitations upon military capabilities.

On the most general level the conception of limited war surely remains relevant—indeed, imperative. On grounds of morality and expediency alike, it is essential that states—especially nuclear states—systematically endeavor to control and limit the use of force where force is unavoidable. The fact that American public officials and spokesmen now generally take this for granted, while a little over a decade ago high government officials commonly asserted that, once war occurs, it has no limits save those determined by the capacity of the belligerents to gain a military victory, must be regarded as a major and probably lasting triumph of reason over viscera. But not much about the feasibility and utility of particular kinds of limitations in specific conflicts, whether with respect to deterring or fighting a war, can be deduced from the general rationale of limited war.

Moreover, in reassessing limited-war thinking, one must bear in mind the prospect that it may—and, indeed, should—change in some respects as the context of events within which it arose changes. Limited-war concepts and policies arose in a period in which the Cold War expanded to Asia, and the Soviet Union was achieving the capacity to inflict terrible damage on the United States in any nuclear exchange. They first blossomed in response to the Korean War. Limited-war thinking flourished out of office during the Eisenhower-Dulles administration, but at the same time the government quietly began to translate it into planning and programs. The motivation and appeal of limited-war strategy in this period were basically twofold: on the one hand, the desire to mitigate the danger of nuclear war; on the other hand, the desire to support the policy of containment more effectively. The underlying disposition in both respects was to bring force under control as a rational instrument of policy, but the motive for control has been a combination of fear and determination in different admixtures and at different times and in different minds.

In the course of applying the concept of limited war to changing international circumstances, it has become apparent that these two objectives might lead to different policy conclusions, depending on whether one emphasizes effective containment or the avoidance of nuclear war. They might lead to different conclusions not only about particular strategies, which were copiously examined and discussed, but also about two issues that were scarcely discussed at all by proponents of limited war: (1) when or whether to intervene in a local war and (2) the proper intensity and scope of intervention.

Even more important than the two objectives of limitation in shaping views on these questions were certain premises about the international and domestic political environment which have been relatively neglected in limited-war thinking. These premises concern: (1) the nature of the communist threat and its bearing upon American security, (2) the willingness of the American government and people to sustain the costs of fighting aggression, and (3) the identity and behavior of potential adversaries.

Limited-war thinking has been conditioned by a period in which the overriding objective of American policy was to contain international communism by preventing or punishing external and internal aggression, even in intrinsically unimportant places. Proponents of limited-war strategy sought to strengthen containment. They hoped to make deterrence more credible and to bolster allied will and nerve in crises, like the one arising over access to Berlin. They argued their case as strategic revisionists seeking to save American military policies from the thralldom of misguided budgetary restrictions imposed at the expense of security needs. Conscious of America's superior economic strength and military potential, they rejected the thesis of the Eisenhower-Dulles administration that the United States would spend itself into bankruptcy if it prepared to fight local aggression at places and with weapons of the enemy's choosing.

With the advent of the Kennedy administration the revisionists came into office. Responding to a dominant theme in Kennedy's campaign, they were determined to fill the military gaps in containment. The United States, according to this theme, was in danger of losing the Cold War because the government had not responded to new conditions, including the shift of communist efforts to the Third World. The most dramatic evidence of America's threatened decline of power and prestige was the prospect of the Soviet Union's gaining the lead in long-range missile striking power, but the missile gap was thought to be part of a wider threat encouraged by misguided American political and military policies that had allegedly alienated potential nationalist resistance to communist subversion in the Third World and forefeited America's capacity to deter or resist local aggression. To safeguard American security and restore American prestige, it would be necessary, among other measures, to build up America's capacity to fight limited wars without resorting to nuclear weapons. If the communists could be contained at the level of strategic war and overt local aggression, the new administration reasoned, then the Third World would be the most active arena of the Cold War, and guerrilla war would be the greatest military threat.

In office, the Kennedy administration not only increased America's lead in long-range striking power; it also built up America's capacity to intervene quickly with mobile forces against local aggression at great distances, and it emphasized a strategy of "controlled and flexible response." Identifying the most dangerous form of communist expansionism as "wars of national liberation," it created special forces to help combat aggression by guerrillas and concentrated on developing techniques of counterinsurgency.

By 1964, after the Cuban missile crisis and before large numbers of American forces got bogged down in Vietnam, the United States seemed safely superior to the Soviet Union. The only remaining gap in military containment might be closed if the United States could demonstrate in Vietnam that wars of national liberation must fail. In this atmosphere of confidence and determination, there was no inducement to question the premises about the wisdom and efficacy of intervention that underlay the prevailing American approach to limited war. The tendency was rather to complete the confirmation of a decade of limited-war thinking by proving the latest and most sophisticated conceptions in action.

We shall return to the impact of the adversities of Vietnam on American conception of limited war; but before that let us review the development of limited-war thinking that had taken place with respect to Europe and strategic war.

8

Apart from the fascination with counterinsurgency in the early 1960s the great outpouring of strategic imagination in the United States was inspired by efforts to deter or fight hypothetical conflicts in Western Europe and between the United States and the Soviet Union. But these conflicts, in contrast to wars in the Third World, seemed less and less likely as time passed and détente set in. So in this area it was not the discipline of war that impinged upon strategic thought but rather the discipline of restrictions on defense expenditures and of changes in the international political atmosphere.

In Europe, as in the Third World, the dominant objectives of limited-war strategy were: (1) to enhance the credibility of deterrence, (2) to strengthen conventional resistance to local nonnuclear aggression, and (3) to bolster the West's bargaining position in crises on the brink of war. These three objectives were integrally related. But the objective of resistance was far more difficult to achieve in Europe because of the greater physical and political obstacles to limitation and the greater strength of potential adversaries.

The effort to formulate a strategy that would combine effective resistance with reliable limitations reached its logical extreme in 1957 with the theories of limited tactical nuclear war propounded by Henry A. Kissinger, Admiral Sir Anthony Buzzard, and others. But these strategies soon died from indifference and incredulity. The difficulty of formulating a convincing strategy for integrating tactical nuclear weapons into limited warfare in Europe evidently remains overwhelming; and, despite continuing efforts in NATO, the interest in doing so has declined as the credibility of the West's using any kind of nuclear weapons first, except in circumstances warranting the risks of general war, has declined.

While the Cold War was relatively warm, the search for a strategy of limited war in Europe enriched the postwar history of military strategy with some ingenious ideas, some of which now seem strangely irrelevant. Strategies for fighting large-scale limited wars (endorsed by Alain Enthoven and, apparently, by McNamara in the early 1960s) were condemned to irrelevance by the unwillingness of any ally to support them with the requisite expenditures and manpower, by the unlikelihood of a war involving such powerful adversaries in such a vital area remaining limited, and by the fear of allied governments that emphasizing large-scale conventional resistance would undermine the efficacy of nuclear deterrence. That left strategies for enforcing short conventional pauses and somewhat raising the threshold of nuclear war (first publicized by General Norstad), strategies seeking to combine static with mobile defense and conventional with tactical nuclear resistance in limited wars resulting from accident and miscalculation (formulated principally by F. O. Miksche and Malcolm Hoag), and strategies of bargaining and controlled escalation featuring nonnuclear and nuclear reprisals and demonstrations (chiefly identified with Herman Kahn and Thomas C. Schelling).

All these strategies were attempts to accommodate the logic of limited war to the realities of limited means. They were also responses to perceived security needs in an international political environment in which it was assumed that the threat of Soviet-supported limited aggression was undiminished—and even rising, according to those who foresaw the Soviet achievement of virtual parity with the United States in the capacity to inflict unacceptable nuclear damage in a retaliatory second strike. But this assumption became much less compelling or was abandoned altogether with the onset of détente, although the conception of "flexible response" and raising the threshold of effective conventional resistance continued to gain adherents and in December, 1967, was finally embodied in NATO's official strategic position. Consequently, though the logic of flexible and controlled response prevailed on paper and in strategic pronouncements, the means to withstand anything more than the most limited attack for much longer than a week were not forthcoming.[25] France's withdrawal from most arrangements for collective defense only made this predicament more conspicuous.

Only the French government rejected the objective of avoiding an automatic nuclear response to a local nonnuclear incursion; but for all governments the objective of deterrence increasingly overshadowed the objective of defense. Yet despite the growing Soviet retaliatory capability, the allies were less concerned than ever about the effectiveness of America's nuclear umbrella, since even a low degree of credibility was regarded as sufficient for deterrence under the new political conditions of détente. In this atmosphere strategic thought tended to revert to the conceptions of the Eisenhower-Dulles period. Proponents of limited-war strategy now took comfort in pointing to the deterrent effect of the danger that any small conflict in Europe might escalate out of control. Considering the nature of Soviet intentions, the value of the stakes, and the integration of tactical nuclear weapons into American and Soviet forces, they were prepared to rely more on this danger and less on a credible capacity to fight a limited war effectively.[26]

One aspect of the limited-war strategy of the Kennedy-McNamara administration underwent a modification that was tantamount to abandonment. The most far-reaching application of the idea of contrived

25. To a large extent the agreement on strategic doctrine transferred disagreement on strategic objectives to disagreements on how to implement them. Moreover, since it would be virtually impossible for allies to agree on precisely what response to take in specific contingencies, and since it would be unwise for any ally to specify in detail its own views on contingency responses, even if it could determine them in advance, there will always be considerable ambiguity about the meaning of flexible response.

26. It is symptomatic that this view found support from Bernard Brodie, an outstanding former champion of local conventional resistance in Europe, who now saw the official emphasis on stressing the conventional-nuclear "firebreak" and increasing conventional capabilities as unfeasible, unnecessary, and politically disadvantageous in America's relations with its allies. Bernard Brodie, *Escalation and the Nuclear Option* (Princeton: Princeton University Press, 1966). Brodie's differences with the official position (which, incidentally, he exaggerated in attributing to it the objective of resisting conventionally a large-scale Soviet aggression) were no less significant for being differences of degree. For they were intended as an antidote to a strategic tendency, just as his earlier advocacy of preparedness for limited conventional defense was intended as an antidote to the Eisenhower-Dulles emphasis on nuclear deterrence in Europe. See, for example, Bernard Brodie, *Strategy in the Missile Age* (Princeton: Princeton University Press, 1959), pp. 335ff.

reciprocal limitation of warfare was the counterforce or no-cities strategy, which was intended to make possible the option of a controlled and limited Soviet-American nuclear exchange. When McNamara first publicly announced this strategy at Ann Arbor in June, 1962, critics charged that it was intended to increase the credibility of extended deterrence. This inference was not unwarranted, since McNamara's statement did reflect his view at the time that a strategic deterrent, to be useful, had to be rational to use. In a few years, however, McNamara came to view the strategy as no more than an option to keep as limited as possible a strategic nuclear war that might result from accident or miscalculation, not as a means of deterring or fighting such a war more effectively. In subsequent statements, McNamara explained the objective of a counterforce strategy as exclusively damage limitation. He also explained the difficulties of inducing the Soviets to fight a limited strategic war in such a way as to cast doubt upon its feasibility.[27] Finally, in successive annual reports on the nation's defense posture, he indicated that considerations of cost-effectiveness dictated an increasing emphasis on the prior objective of assured destruction.

Summing up the fortunes of limited-war strategy with respect to Europe and strategic war, we can say that the basic rationale of limited war seems firmly established in the United States and in allied countries, with the possible exception of France, and that this rationale is to some extent implemented in operational plans, military policies, and weapons. But the high point of limited-war theory—in terms of the inventiveness, thoroughness, and energy with which it was carried out in strategic thought and actual policies—was roughly in the period 1957 to 1963. Since then a combination of economic constraints and détente, together with the inroads of time upon novel plans for hypothetical contingencies that have never occurred, has nullified some of the most ingenious strategies and eroded others, so that limited-war thinking is left somewhere between the initial Kennedy-McNamara views and the approach of the Eisenhower-Dulles administration.

In military affairs, as in international politics, one senses that an era

27. On the one hand, he explained, the Soviet Union would be unlikely to withhold its countercity capability as long as its missiles were relatively scarce and vulnerable; but on the other hand, he acknowledged that as Soviet missiles became more numerous and less vulnerable, the prospects of confining retaliatory damage from them would vanish completely. In any event, in each annual "posture statement," he stated in progressively more categorical terms that there was no way the United States could win a strategic nuclear war at a tolerable cost.

has ended, but one has little intimation of the era that may replace it. Meanwhile, strategic imagination seems to have reached a rather flat plateau surrounded by a bland atmosphere in which all military concerns dissolve into the background.

9

This was the state of limited-war thinking in 1965, when American forces became the dominant element in fighting communist forces in Vietnam. At that time the only really lively ideas were counterinsurgent warfare and controlled escalation.

Some regarded the war as a testing ground for strategies of counterinsurgency. When the United States began bombing selected targets in North Vietnam, ostensibly in retaliation for attacks on American units at Pleiku and elsewhere in the South, some regarded this as a test of theories of controlled escalation. The war in Vietnam should have been a great boon to strategic innovation, since it fitted none of the existing models of limited war, although it contained elements of several; but the lessons derived from the strategies that were tried have been either negative or inconclusive. Yet it is not apparent that alternative strategies would have worked any better. Some critics of the conduct (as opposed to the justification) of the war assert that different political or military strategies and tactics, executed more skillfully, might have enabled the United States to gain its political objectives—primarily, the security of an independent noncommunist government in South Vietnam—more readily. Others assert either that those objectives were unattainable because of the lack of a suitable political environment in South Vietnam—fundamentally, the lack of the rudiments of a national polity—or that they were attainable only at an unacceptable cost, no matter what methods had been adopted.

Akin to this latter lesson is the view that no regime too weak to defend itself against revolution or subversion without American military intervention can be defended with such intervention.[28] But even if this turns out to be true in Vietnam, it will not absolutely disprove that the right kind of intervention at the right time under the right circumstances could provide the indispensable margin of assistance

28. Former Ambassador Edwin O. Reischauer reaches the following simple rule of thumb on the basis of the Vietnam experience: "Any regime that is not strong enough to defend itself against its internal enemies probably could not be defended by us either and may not be worth defending anyway." *Beyond Vietnam: The United States and Asia* (New York: Alfred A. Knopf, Inc., 1967), p. 188. Among other weaknesses of this rule as an absolute prescription, it does not seem to take into account the kind and degree of external support of internal enemies.

for the security of another regime. Nor does the experience in Vietnam tell one how to determine whether a regime can defend itself, let alone how to determine this in time to govern the granting or withholding of American assistance.

Rejecting such sweeping rules of abstention, Hanson Baldwin draws from Vietnam the lesson that future interventions against insurgency, if they are undertaken "under carefully chosen conditions and at times and places of our own choosing," must avoid the sin of "gradualism" by applying overwhelming force (including tactical nuclear weapons, if necessary) at an early stage.[29] Walter Lippmann, on the other hand, concludes that Vietnam simply demonstrates that elephants cannot kill swarms of mosquitoes.[30] Given the general disaffection with the war, Lippmann's conclusion is likely to be more persuasive than Baldwin's. Indeed, though overstated, it contains an important kernel of truth. Once the United States becomes involved in any local war with its own troops, it will tend to use its modern military logistics, organization, and technology (short of nuclear weapons) to whatever extent is needed to achieve the desired political and military objectives, as long as its military operations are consistent with the localization of the war. For every military establishment fights with the capabilities best suited to its national resources, experience, and ethos. In practice, this means that American armed forces and the large nonfighting contingents that accompany them, when engaged in a protracted revolutionary war on the scale of the Vietnamese war, tend to saturate and overwhelm the country they are defending.

If the war were principally an American operation, as the long counterinsurgency war in Malaya was a British operation, the elephant might nevertheless prevail over the mosquitoes, even if it had to stamp out in the crudest way every infested spot and occupy the country. But the war in Vietnam, like every local war in which the United States is likely to become engaged, has been fought for the independence of the country under siege—in this case the country nominally represented by successive South Vietnamese governments. Therefore, despite South Vietnam's great dependence on the United States, the United States is also dependent on South Vietnam. The chief trouble with this situation is that in some of the most crucial aspects of counterinsurgency South Vietnamese forces and officials have been ineffective, and the United States could do nothing about it. More-

29. "After Vietnam—What Military Strategy in the Far East?" *New York Times Magazine*, June 9, 1968.
30. "Elephants Can't Beat Mosquitoes in Vietnam," *Washington Post*, December 3, 1967.

over, where American pressure on South Vietnam might have been useful, the very scale of the United States' involvement has deprived it of leverage, since its direct involvement gave it a stake in the war that militated against the sanctions of reducing or withdrawing assistance.

In one respect Lippmann's metaphorical proposition may understate the difficulty the United States must encounter in trying to apply containment to a situation like the Vietnam conflict. If South Vietnam lacks the minimum requisites of a viable polity, then no amount of leverage or control could succeed in establishing the independence of the country, even if the organized insurrection and its external support were defeated. In this case, the incapacity of the elephant would be more profound than its inability to kill mosquitoes. In this case, when the adversary was defeated, the task of establishing an independent country would have just begun.

The lesson—although it is not universally applicable—seems to be that if a country cannot defend itself from insurrection with assistance short of American regular forces, the United States can probably defend it only at a level of involvement that will contravene its objective of securing the sovereignty of that country; so that even if the United States should defeat the insurgents, it will be burdened with an unviable protectorate. To oversimplify the proposition: Either the United States, in these circumstances, must virtually take over the country and run the war itself at the risk of acquiring a troublesome dependent, or it must keep its role limited at least to guerrilla operations and probably to technical and staff assistance at the risk of letting the besieged country fall.

Hanson Baldwin is probably right in thinking that an early massive intervention can, in some circumstances, achieve a limited objective more effectively than a sustained war of gradually increasing scale, but following this generality as a rule of action would entail great risks of overinvolvement in quasirevolutionary wars. Consequently, to condition American support of a besieged country on its ability to survive at a low threshold of direct American involvement seems like the more prudent strategy. This proposition, however, like others concerning the conduct of local wars, implicitly contains a consideration more basic than strategy and tactics: How important are the interests for which the United States may intervene? For if they are truly vital and the nation understands this, a high-risk strategy is justified, and even under the most unpromising conditions intervention may be imperative. By the same token, a low-risk but long-term (say seven to ten years) strategy of low-level intervention ought to be acceptable if it is more expedient.

America's intervention in Vietnam has suffered from ambiguity on this question of interests. South Vietnam was evidently not considered important enough either to justify an indefinitely protracted intervention or to justify the costs and risks of a scale of intervention that, if undertaken early enough, could conceivably have led to a more successful outcome. If the option of a protracted low-level involvement was militarily practical in Vietnam—which would have been difficult to know without a determined effort to try it—it was evidently politically impractical in the United States. The compulsion to win the war quickly was almost proportionate to its unpopularity. Indeed, probably no American leader would have considered the eventual scale of war worth the costs if he had known the costs in advance. The reason the United States got so heavily involved in Vietnam lies not in its estimate of South Vietnam's importance to American vital interests but in the United States' inability to limit an expanding involvement after it had drifted beyond a certain scale of intervention, combined with repeated miscalculations that military victory was attainable at the existing scale of war or at the next step up the scale. Hence, the United States found itself fighting a small version of World War II without undertaking a commensurate mobilization of its resources and manpower—or of its moral energy. In this sense, the scale and costs of the war were greater than the nation was prepared to sustain.

If the larger lessons of Vietnam concerning the efficacy and scale of intervention are uncertain, the validity and utility of subordinate lessons concerning the strategy of limited war are no more conclusive. Perhaps the strategy that has come closest to a clear-cut failure is controlled escalation, which was applied by means of selective bombing in North Vietnam. But even in this case it would be misleading to generalize about the efficacy of the same general procedure under other conditions. Controlled escalation is a strategy developed principally to apply to direct or indirect confrontations between the United States and the Soviet Union.[31] It envisages influencing the adversary's will to fight and his willingness to settle through a process of "bargaining" by means of a "competition in risk-taking" on ascending—but it is hoped, on the lower—levels of violence, which would culminate in a mutually unacceptable nuclear war at the top of the escalation "ladder." In the spring of 1965 the American government, frustrated and provoked by

31. The concept and strategy of controlled escalation are set forth most fully in Herman Kahn, On Escalation (New York: Frederick A. Praeger, 1967) and Thomas C. Schelling, Arms and Influence (New Haven: Yale University Press, 1966), although both authors developed the idea in earlier writings. Needless to say, neither author believes that controlled escalation was properly applied in Vietnam.

Hanoi's incursions in the South and anxious to strike back with its preferred weapons, put into effect a version of controlled escalation, borrowing language and style from the latest thinking about punitive bargaining.[32] Through highly selective and gradually intensified bombing of targets on lists authorized by the President—incidentally, this represented a notable application of one of the tenets of limited-war theory: strict political control of military operations—the United States hoped to convince Hanoi that it would have to pay an increasing price for aggression in the South. Through this graduated application of violence, the government hoped by tacit "signaling" and "bargaining" to bring Hanoi to reasonable terms. But Hanoi, alas, did not play the game.

Perhaps the experiment was not a true test of escalation, since the punitive nature of the bombing was ambiguous. Indeed, in deference to public protests throughout the world, the United States explicitly stressed the purely military nature of the targets, as though to deny their bargaining function. Perhaps the escalation was not undertaken soon enough or in large enough increments, though it seems more likely that the failure lay in the inherent deficiencies of bombing as a punitive device. Probably the fault lay partly in applying to an underdeveloped country a strategy that presupposes a set of values and calculations found only in the most advanced countries. Perhaps escalation works only when there is a convincing prospect of nuclear war at the top of the ladder. Or perhaps the difficulty lay chiefly in the fact that Hanoi had unlimited ends in the South, whereas the United States had quite limited ends in the North. Whatever the explanation, controlled escalation failed to achieve its objective; and that should be sobering to its enthusiasts, if any remain. Nonetheless, the experience does not prove much about the efficacy of a different strategy of escalation against a different adversary in different circumstances.

Nor does the war convey any clear lesson about the wisdom of denying the enemy a sanctuary from combat in his home base of support for an internal war in an adjacent country. Critics contend that carrying the war to the North violated one of the few clear-cut rules of the game on which limitation might be reliably based, it alienated

---

32. Punitive bargaining, however, was only one of the objectives of the bombing. The government also wanted to raise the morale of the South Vietnamese and to impede the infiltration of men and supplies to the South. General Maxwell D. Taylor, *Responsibility and Response* (New York: Harper & Row, 1967), pp. 26–28; Thomas C. Schelling, *Arms and Influence* (New Haven: Yale University Press, 1966), pp. 170ff.; Tom Wicker, "The Wrong Rubicon," *Atlantic Monthly* (May, 1968), pp. 81ff.

world and domestic opinion, it fortified North Vietnam's determination
to fight for an unconditional victory, and it distracted attention from
the real war—the civil war—in the South, without substantially affecting that war. But advocates of carrying the war to the North argue
that the attrition against North Vietnamese units and logistics was significant and might have been decisive but for self-imposed restrictions
that were unnecessarily confining; that these operations were necessary
to South Vietnamese morale and provided a valuable bargaining
counter for mutual de-escalation; and that the denial of sanctuary is a
valuable precedent for avoiding disadvantageous rules of the game in
the future and may be a useful deterrent against other states that may
contemplate waging internal wars against their neighbors. Moreover,
it can be argued that when a local war cannot be won at a tolerable
cost within the country under attack, the only reasonable alternative
to a dishonorable withdrawal is to engage the source of external
support directly and charge it with a greater share of the costs in
order to secure a satisfactory diplomatic termination of hostilities.

Both the Korean and the Vietnam Wars indicate that the particular
restrictions on military operations will be determined by such a variety
of conditions and considerations that it is almost fruitless to try to
anticipate them in advance. In some conceivable future circumstances,
one can even imagine a sensible case being made for crossing the
threshold that bars the United States from using tactical nuclear
weapons. It is unlikely, however, that the prevailing reaction to Vietnam will be in the direction that Hanson Baldwin advocates, when
he condemns the constraints of gradualism and the "cult" of self-
imposed limitations. The United States may seem particularly compelled, not only by its great material power but also by the nature
of its democratic society and its aversion to long wars for limited ends,
to try to terminate its war as quickly as possible with massive force.
But Vietnam does at least indicate that the United States will go a
long and frustrating way to observe significant self-imposed restrictions
on a war rather than insist on obtaining a military victory by all means
available.[33] It indicates that, even when the nation is "locked in" with

33. One indication of the magnitude of self-imposed restrictions is the number
and kinds of military actions that the United States refrained from taking, but
that it might have taken, to defeat communist forces. In Vietnam as in Korea, a
major restriction was on the number of armed forces mobilized and deployed. In
both wars the United States reached an upper limit on these forces—higher in
Vietnam than in Korea—beyond which it would not go, even if that meant ending
the war on less advantageous terms. Another major restriction common to both
wars was the geographical one, which, in Vietnam, excluded efforts to eliminate

its own troops to an unpromising local war, it will prefer to follow the rule of proportionate response to enemy initiatives rather than incur the immediate risks of massive escalation.

It is significant how weak and ineffectual American all-or-nothing sentiment has been in the Vietnamese as compared to the Korean War. The idea of the United States confining itself to a limited war, which was novel and widely unacceptable in Korea, has been widely taken for granted in Vietnam. Indeed, the most influential American critics have urged more, not less, stringent restrictions on combat, despite the fact that the danger of nuclear war or of Chinese or Russian intervention never seemed nearly as great as in Korea.[34] Those (including some prominent conservative senators and congressmen) who took the position that the United States ought either to escalate the war drastically in order to win it or else to disengage clearly preferred the latter course. Their frustration did not manifest a general rejection of the conception of limited war, but only opposition to the particular way of applying that conception in Vietnam.

Thus the popular disaffection with the Vietnamese war does not indicate a reversion to pre-Korean attitudes toward limited war. Rather, it indicates a serious questioning of the premises about the utility of limited war as an instrument of American policy, the premises that originally moved the proponents of limited-war strategy. In Vietnam the deliberate limitation of war has been accepted by Americans simply from the standpoint of keeping the war from expanding or from the standpoint of de-escalating it, whereas in Korea the desire to keep the war limited had to contend with a strong sentiment to win it for the sake of containment. In Korea the principal motive for limitation was the fear that an expanding war might lead to general war with China or nuclear war with the Soviet Union; but in Vietnam the limits were motivated as much by the sense that the political objective

---

the Cambodian sanctuary or to interdict Chinese and Soviet supplies coming into North Vietnam. Perhaps the most obvious restrictions—such as not bombing civilian targets and ports and not invading the enemy's homeland—were in North Vietnam. Correspondingly, the most obvious limitations of political objectives have applied to North, not to South, Vietnam. Of North Vietnam the U.S. government has asked, essentially, only that it stop supporting the war in the South, materially and with its regular units. But in the South too the American government has become willing to settle for something considerably less than a total victory, without arousing popular protest in the nation.

34. It should be noted, however, that one of the reasons that the danger of nuclear war did not seem so great was that the United States refrained from taking actions, like bombing Haiphong, which seemed to carry too great a risk of Chinese or Soviet intervention, compared to their military or political value.

was not sufficiently valuable and the prospect of winning the war not sufficiently promising to warrant the costs of expansion. This change of emphasis reflects more than the unpopularity of the war in Vietnam. It also reflects the acceptance of limited war as an operational concept in American foreign policy.

Some of the reasons for the strength of sentiment for keeping the war limited, however, bear upon the political question of whether to intervene in local wars at all. These reasons suggest that the specific lessons about the strategy and constraints of limited war that one might derive from Vietnam are likely to be less important than the war's impact on the political premises that underlay American intervention. The war may have become so costly and unpromising that, given its remote relationship to American security, the divisions among communist states and parties, and other changes in the pattern of international conflict, Americans have begun to doubt the validity of the premises on which the government intervened—particularly the premises concerning the need to punish aggression in peripheral points of conflict. At the least, these doubts seem likely to lead to a marked differentiation of interests in the application of containment—a downgrading of interests in the Third World and a greater distinction between these interests and those pertaining to the security of the advanced democratic countries. Possibly, they will lead to abandoning containment in Asia altogether insofar as containment requires armed intervention against local aggression on the mainland. More likely, they will simply lead to a sharper distinction in practice between supporting present security commitments and not forming new ones, and between supporting present commitments with American armed forces when aggression is overt and abstaining from armed intervention in largely internal conflicts. What they seem to preclude, at least for a while, is any renewed effort to strengthen military deterrence and resistance in the Third World by actively developing and projecting America's capacity to fight local wars.

10

Yet it is misleading to reach conclusions about future American military policies on the basis of the nation's desire to avoid Vietnams. For the threat of local wars' impinging upon American interests could arise in many different forms. Thus, while the war in Vietnam seems to be waning and the prospect of similar national liberation wars in Asia is uncertain, the capacity and perhaps the incentive of the Soviet Union to support local wars that might spring from quite different circumstances is increasing. The Soviet will to exploit this capacity will depend, in part, on the American position. If Soviet leaders were to gain the impression that the United States is firmly set upon a course of neo-isolationism and the absolute avoidance of intervention in local wars, they might become dangerously adventurous in the Middle East and elsewhere. The United States would almost surely regard Soviet exploitation of local conflicts more seriously than it would regard another war like Vietnam. So one of the military and political issues facing the United States in the late 1960s is how to respond to the growing capacity of Soviet mobile overseas forces.

Current trends seem destined to provide the Soviet Union with a significantly enlarged capacity to intervene in local conflicts overseas, a capacity of which the United States has heretofore enjoyed a virtual monopoly.[35] The build-up of Soviet naval, amphibious, air, and land forces in this direction has been accompanied by a substantial expansion of Soviet arms deliveries and technical assistance to Middle Eastern countries, as well as to North Vietnam, and the acquisition of technical facilities (although not permanent bases) in several Mediterranean ports. The experience of observing America's large-scale support of South Vietnam and providing North Vietnam with weapons and logistics support has given Soviet leaders a new appreciation of overseas local-war forces. At the same time, Soviet strategic doctrine has assigned a greater role to supporting Soviet interests overseas, both on the sea and in local wars on land. These developments do not portend a mobile overseas capacity that can compete with America's capacity in an armed conflict, but they do provide Soviet leaders with options for intervening in local wars. They provide new levers of influence in the Middle East and elsewhere. And they impose new constraints on American intervention. The greatest danger they pose is that the superpowers will unintentionally become involved in competitive interventions in local conflicts where they lack control and

35. Thomas W. Wolfe, "The Projection of Soviet Power," *Survival*, X (May, 1968), pp. 159–65 (reprinted from *Interplay*, March, 1968); Curt Gasteyger, "Moscow and the Mediterranean," *Foreign Affairs*, XLVI (July, 1968), 676–87; Claire Sterling, "The Soviet Fleet in the Mediterranean," *Reporter* (December 14, 1967), pp. 14–18. Since the Cuban missile crisis, the Soviets have made new investments in large long-range air transports and have built up the naval infantry and amphibious forces, enlarged the merchant marine (including ships configured for military cargo) to put the Soviet Union among the two or three leading maritime powers, and established a greatly augmented naval presence in the Mediterranean, including two helicopter carriers for support of landing operations or antisubmarine warfare. There are no signs, however, that the Soviet government intends to create what the United States regards as a balanced naval force capable of coping with American naval forces.

where the modus operandi of avoiding a direct clash have not been established.[36]

11

The history of limited-war thought and practice in the last decade or so provides little basis for generalizing confidently about the feasibility and utility of particular strategies. Many strategies have never really been put to the test; and where they have been tested, either in deterrence or war, the results have been inconclusive. Moreover, strategies are very much the product of particular circumstances—not only of technological developments but also of domestic and international political developments. This political environment is always changing. Developments that have made some strategies seem obsolete—for example, the impact of détente, domestic constraints, and the balance of payments on strategies of conventional resistance in Europe—might change in such a way as to revive abandoned strategies or nurture new ones. The limited-war strategies appropriate to the international environment of the 1970s—especially if there should be a significant increase in the number and severity of local wars, a more active Soviet policy of intervention in local wars, a more aggressive Chinese military posture, or new nuclear powers—might contain some interesting variations on strategic notions that were born in past periods of intense concern with military security. Changes in military technology, such as forthcoming increases in long-range airlift and sealift capabilities, will also affect strategies and politics of limited war.[37]

Yet one has the feeling, which may not spring solely from a lack of imagination, that in the nature of international conflict and technology in the latter half of the twentieth century there are only a limited number of basic strategic ideas pertaining to limited war and that we have seen most of these emerge in the remarkable strategic renaissance of the past decade or so. These ideas may be combined in countless

36. Gasteyger, "Moscow and the Mediterranean," p. 687.
37. In particular, the C-5A air transports, now coming into operation, and fast-deployment logistics ships, not yet appropriated, will greatly increase the troops, equipment, and supplies that can be lifted from the United States overseas in a short time. Such improvements in airlift and sealift will provide increased capabilities and flexibility in supporting many different kinds of military tasks in remote places at all levels of conflict and in varied physical and political conditions. By reducing or eliminating the need for a standing American presence overseas, they will enable the United States to be more selective in establishing and maintaining bases and commitments. See Robert E. Osgood, *Alliances and American Foreign Policy* (Baltimore: The Johns Hopkins Press, 1968), pp. 137–43.

permutations and combinations and implemented by a great variety of means, but we shall still recognize trip wires, pauses, reprisals, denials, thresholds, sanctuaries, bargaining and demonstration maneuvers, escalation, Mao's three stages, enclaves, seize and hold, search and destroy, and all the rest. But more enduring than any of the strategies, one must hope, is the novel respect for the deliberate control and limitation of force from which they arose.

12

In the field of arms agreements, too, the most notable development has been the widespread acceptance of the control and limitation of force as the principal objective; but, contrary to great expectations in some quarters, the tangible results of this approach have been minimal. Though they will probably continue to be minimal, arms control will retain a significant symbolic value and remain an important expression of a changed attitude toward military competition, which may foster mutual restraint even if it does not produce treaties. It will also remain a major instrument of propaganda through which governments will appeal to the fear of war and the longing for relief from the arms burden, not because they want an agreement, but because they want to advance their special interests in the absence of an agreement.

The principal change in American policy toward arms agreements came in 1955, when the formula of general disarmament, which had followed the demise of the Baruch Plan, was in effect supplanted by the concept of partial arms limitations intended to stabilize the military balance—to moderate arms competition and make it safer—rather than to transform international politics or end the arms race.[38] This was the conception underlying the Eisenhower administration's "Open Skies" proposal of 1955 for surveillance and disclosure of information,

38. The Baruch Plan (1946) dominated disarmament discussions for five years. Its avowed goal was to prevent nuclear war by preventing the production of nuclear weapons. It outlawed nuclear weapons and prescribed international ownership and control of all nuclear material and nuclear-energy facilities, and it provided for international punishment, without any national veto, in order to enforce the agreement. By 1950 Soviet rejection of this plan and second thoughts within the United States government had led to its virtual abandonment. In 1952 the Baruch formula was supplanted, in effect, by proposals for what Khrushchev later called general and complete disarmament through staged, balanced reductions under safeguards. But when the Russians, in May, 1955, surprisingly accepted as the basis for negotiation an Anglo-French memorandum of 1954 based on this concept, the United States felt compelled to abandon a position no longer compatible with the military imperatives of containment, the nuclear standoff, or the requirements of verification (particularly verification of nuclear stocks, which both the American and Soviet governments admitted was unfeasible).

intended to provide mutual assurance against a nuclear surprise attack. It underlay a host of proposals for partial disarmament, such as
the nuclear test ban and a nuclear production cutoff. Despite the tactical use of such proposals for purposes of propaganda and military
advantage, their basic rationale was understood to be arms control, not
disarmament; and their feasibility was understood to depend on
affecting the American-Soviet military balance as little as possible.

By the end of the 1950s this new approach to arms agreements had
pervaded Western thinking. The Russians had adopted partial disarmament, though they rejected the American proposals in detail
(particularly their provisions for inspection and surveillance). Khrushchev's reversion in 1959 to general and complete disarmament
(GCD) and his condemnation of arms control proved to be temporary
and largely rhetorical. The United States formally accepted GCD as
an ultimate objective, but actually used it as a formula for proposing
partial measures only nominally related to staged disarmament. The
arms control dialogue proceeded as before. The arms control approach
dominated the Arms Control and Disarmament Agency (ACDA)
created by President Kennedy in September, 1961. Through the medium of the Eighteen Nation Disarmament Committee, which began protracted discussions of arms proposals in March, 1962, it came
to be generally accepted by nonaligned states too.

The popularity of this approach in the United States sprang from
the same set of circumstances that underlay the popularity of limited-
war thinking, insofar as that thinking was directed toward mitigating
the dangers of nuclear war. But the height of American concern for
arms control—roughly in the period of 1957–62—reflected the height
of anxieties about an American-Soviet war arising from destabilizing
tendencies in the nuclear balance (particularly, the introduction of
vulnerable long-range missiles), the danger of inadvertent nuclear war
(whether because of a technical accident, unauthorized use of nuclear
weapons, or misapprehension of a surprise attack), and the prospect
that local wars and crisis might get out of control. Ironically, the
optimistic expectations about arms control as a major instrument of
peace were eroded by declining anxieties about war. Growing confidence in the stability of the strategic nuclear balance, based on relatively invulnerable second-strike capabilities, new safeguards against
inadvertent war (particularly, improvements in command-and-control
systems), and passage of the Berlin and Cuban missile crises without
war, followed by an atmosphere of détente, tended to blunt the incentives for arms control, except as a symbol of mutual understanding
and concern for peace.

The original enthusiasm for arms control has also been dampened by discovery of the limits to feasible agreements. The demonstrated difficulty of negotiating arms control agreements that would clearly affect the arms race or the nuclear balance made many arms control enthusiasts shift their hopes from treaties to tacit understandings and reciprocal unilateral restraints. According to arms control theory, the United States and the Soviet Union, despite their predominantly conflicting political interests, have a common interest in restraining the arms race and making it safer. Though there is indeed such an area of mutual interest, it has turned out to be far more restricted than was originally hoped, and the difficulties of translating these interests into mutually acceptable formal agreements have proved to be formidable. Moreover, the need for doing so has seemed less compelling as both sides have learned to control the hazards of the arms race unilaterally.

The existence of surplus capabilities for assured destruction against whichever side might strike first and the maintenance of these capabilities at a high level and diversified mix of weapons, backed by large research and development programs, enlarge the range of arms restrictions that might be undertaken without affecting the strategic balance significantly, *if* both states are interested only in adequate second-strike capabilities and seek no advantage in terms of damage limitation or "superiority." But the growing complexity and the dynamic nature of strategic weapons technology have immensely complicated the problem of translating this hypothetical range of restrictions into specific categories, numerical ratios, and qualitative characteristics of weapons. And, despite increased capabilities for unilateral inspection by satellites, electronic means, seismographic devices, and the like, technological innovations are also increasing the difficulties of verifying some kinds of arms restrictions.[39]

It is not surprising, therefore, that the treaty for a partial (atmospheric) nuclear test ban stands out as the most notable of the few agreements that have resulted from more than a decade of international discussions of arms control agreements. The proposal for a nuclear test ban became the focus of the arms control dialogue and propaganda as American and Soviet maneuvers on the field of partial arms limitations proved fruitless and fears of radioactive fallout gained world attention in the late 1950s. But the proposal became so

39. For example, although the number of missiles deployed can be verified unilaterally, the introduction of multiple warheads and rapid changes in the technology of defensive and counterdefensive strategic weapons render numbers of missile launchers increasingly inadequate as measures of strategic power, while posing new and perhaps insuperable problems of verifying qualitative measures and the number of warheads.

heavily involved in the psychological warfare of the Cold War that its ostensible objectives were overshadowed by its symbolic and propagandistic functions. The eventual achievement of the atmospheric test ban in 1963 was more significant as a symbolic initiative toward détente than as a restriction of arms. In fact, it was feasible precisely because it did not seem to have much effect on the American-Soviet strategic balance and arms race, although subsequent concern about the effectiveness of ABMs challenged this impression.[40]

The test ban treaty was hailed as the precursor of other arms agreements, but its very success as an instrument of détente diminished interest in other measures, including the comprehensive (all-environment) test ban from which it was extracted. There have been a few other arms control agreements—the Antarctic Treaty of 1959, demilitarizing the area; the tripartite declaration of 1963 on outer space, proscribing the orbiting of nuclear weapons in space; the Hot Line agreement of 1963, setting up special crisis communication facilities between the United States and the Soviet Union; and the Treaty on the Exploration and Use of Outer Space in 1967, internationalizing and denuclearizing the use of outer space, the moon, and other celestial bodies—but none of these has had the political importance of the test ban. The only other negotiated proposal with comparable dramatic impact was also a treaty purporting, in the words of President Kennedy's deepest aspiration, to "get the [nuclear] genie back in the bottle": the nuclear nonproliferation treaty (NPT).[41]

Preventing the spread of nuclear ownership among nations has been an objective of the United States from the time the Baruch Plan was launched in 1946. It was a major objective of the nuclear test ban. But it was not until the détente of the mid-1960s set in that the NPT became an actively negotiated proposal.[42] By then prospective in-

40. The principal concern pertained to the uncertain effects of exoatmospheric bursts on communications and radar systems and on nuclear warheads.

41. The treaty prohibits nuclear states from transferring nuclear weapons or control of weapons to nonnuclear states. It prohibits nonnuclear states from manufacturing or otherwise acquiring nuclear weapons and from receiving assistance in the manufacture of nuclear weapons. Nonnuclear states are obliged to accept safeguards, in accordance with the International Atomic Energy Agency's safeguards system, for the verification of the treaty's provisions designed to prevent diversion of nuclear energy from peaceful uses to nuclear weapons.

42. Though opposed to the spread of nuclear ownership under national control, the United States has also opposed any nonproliferation treaty that would prevent nuclear "sharing" with nonnuclear states (which is regarded as one method of discouraging proliferation) or the transfer of weapons to nuclear states (which in practice meant Britain, not France). The United States first included nuclear nonproliferation in its disarmament proposals in 1961, following

creases in the spread of plutonium production for civilian energy fore-shadowed such an increase in the number of potential nuclear states as to present the proponents of a nonproliferation treaty with the last best chance to bring such production under international control and inspection. Among the existing potential nuclear powers, only India, Japan, and Israel seem at all likely in the next five or ten years to have such a balance of political incentives over all the disincentives to lead them to a nuclear weapons program. But this is enough to accentuate American fears that, in the absence of an international agreement, the contagion of nuclear acquisition will destroy the present fragile international order that has depended so much on the relatively simple, familiar, bipolar nuclear balance. These fears, although based on abstract suppositions about the political consequences of material capabilities,[43] are understandable, and perhaps, in the long run of twenty-five years or so, even warranted as projections of hypothetical dangers. Of course, proliferation might also promise some advantages—principally, it would permit the devolution of countervailing power against the Soviet Union and China from the United States to friendly states—but a prudent government cannot be expected deliberately to upset a manageable situation for the sake of this kind of problematical advantage.

Is the NPT an effective measure for discouraging proliferation? It is unlikely that a state that would seriously consider producing nuclear weapons—a decision of highest national importance—would sign the treaty, and it is questionable whether it would be deterred from acquiring nuclear weapons if it had signed the treaty. Undoubtedly,

---

Soviet and American acceptance of the "Irish Resolution" in the United Nations, which proscribed dissemination and acquisition of nuclear weapons. But it was not until the plan for a multilateral nuclear force (MLF) was abandoned in 1965 and the "European Option" (that is, holding open the option of a collective European nuclear force) was dropped in 1967 that the road was opened to agreement with the Soviet Union on a nonproliferation treaty. Then President Johnson regarded the NPT as the centerpiece of his peace program, as President Kennedy had so regarded the nuclear test ban.

43. The typically apocalyptic American view of proliferation was asserted by President Kennedy in March, 1963, when he envisaged the prospect of the president in the 1970s being faced with a very dangerous world in which "15 or 20 or 25 nations may have these weapons," and by Secretary of Defense McNamara in October, 1964, when he testified, "You can imagine the danger that the world would face if 10, 20, or 30 nations possessed nuclear weapons instead of the four that possess them today.... The danger to other nations increases geometrically with the increase in the number of nations possessing these warheads." U.S., Congress, Senate, Committee on Foreign Relations, *Hearings, The Nuclear Test Ban Treaty*, 88th Cong., 1st Sess., 1963, p. 47; *New York Times*, October 7, 1964.

the treaty would to some extent inhibit a signatory from deciding to join the nuclear club, but these inhibitions would be qualified by the recognized contingent nature of the signatory's formal adherence.[44] Indeed, official testimony has acknowledged that the treaty would be ineffective without other inducements to nuclear abstinence, such as assurances of protection against aggression or threats of aggression by nuclear states.[45] Such inducements would at least be addressed to immediate national interests, whereas the NPT cannot offer any immediate benefits to potential nuclear states; it can only oblige them to perpetuate their nonnuclear status by a pledge of self-denial while imposing no significant restrictions or obligations on the nuclear signatories, not to mention on France and China, which refuse to sign.[46] But though inducements, whether in the form of guarantees or sanctions, may help to gain a nation's signature to the NPT, they are not likely to preserve its satisfaction with nuclear self-denial, if basic con-

44. The contingent nature of a signatory's adherence to the treaty is manifest in the provision that each party would have the right to withdraw on three months' notice, if it decided that "extraordinary events" jeopardized its "supreme interests." Moreover, before withdrawing, signatories could legally acquire a nuclear option by taking many measures (such as stockpiling plutonium, building up reactor technology, and acquiring delivery vehicles and other nonnuclear components of weapons) that could put them in a position to produce weapons. This would be consistent with the conception of the nuclear test ban which presupposes that the United States and the Soviet Union remain ready to resume testing.

45. American official testimony on a nonproliferation treaty has held that assurances of potential nuclear states' security against nuclear blackmail are necessary to make the treaty effective and that the only credible assurances would be guarantees by five or at least three nuclear powers. Yet officials did not believe that such guarantees were likely. Indeed, in order to placate congressional fears, they at the same time denied that the NPT or any security assurances in connection with it would actually lead to additional American commitments. U.S., Congress, Joint Committee on Atomic Energy, Hearings, Nonproliferation of Nuclear Weapons, 89th Cong., 2d Sess., February and March, 1966, pp. 13, 37, 41, 75, 78, 84, 87, 88; U.S. Congress, Senate, Committee on Foreign Relations, Hearings, Nonproliferation Treaty, 90th Cong., 2d Sess., July, 1968, pp. 17, 56. The superpowers hoped that the Security Council Resolution of June 19, 1968, initiated by the United States, the Soviet Union, and the United Kingdom would serve some of the functions of a guarantee. But the resolution obliges members of the Security Council only to act immediately in accordance with the U.N. Charter in the event of "nuclear aggression."

46. In this respect the NPT suffers from the same deficiency as the Baruch Plan, which seemingly (notwithstanding the unsuspected progress Soviet scientists had already made) would have denied the Soviet Union the opportunity to acquire the capability to make nuclear bombs while perpetuating America's monopoly of this capability. Sensitive to the discriminatory aspect of the NPT, India

siderations of national interest should make a signatory dissatisfied with the treaty's restraints.[47]

The principal deficiency of the NPT, however, is not its inefficacy. In some cases it may add a margin of influence against nuclear acquisition, and its inspection provisions would at least serve as an early warning system. The NPT's principal disadvantage—if one still assumes that its objective is valid—may lie in the effects of trying to attain and then maintain the adherence of some countries to its restrictions. In India, for example, the effort to gain Indian adherence to the treaty, by forcing active consideration of the issues of status and security, has stimulated interest in holding open the nuclear option and has accentuated India's nationalist drive for self-sufficiency. In West Germany the most important consequence of the NPT has been to intensify aversion to the treaty's discriminatory nature, while reinforcing suspicions of American-Soviet collusion against German interests.[48] These costs may be regarded as worth the effort if they result in acceptance. But, added to the political costs of gaining or

---

and other leading states with nuclear potential have conditioned their acceptance of nuclear self-denial on the superpowers' acceptance of nuclear constraints, such as a nuclear production cutoff and a freeze on nuclear delivery vehicles. But it is doubtful that these constraints would, in fact, satisfy the basic complaint of nonnuclear states.

47. West Germany and Japan, as allies, are already guaranteed, but their continued acceptance of the treaty's restraints would probably require additional assurances from the United States. It is doubtful, however, that the United States would offer or that nonallied states would accept comparable security commitments merely for the sake of nonproliferation. And the credibility of any guarantees to nonallied states would be doubtful. Furthermore, as the French, British, and Chinese nuclear forces demonstrate, even alliance is no assurance against nuclear acquisition. The threat of economic and other sanctions against friendly states that acquired nuclear weapons would probably only stimulate their drive for nuclear weapons without imposing any serious material obstacles to a nuclear program. Moreover, it is doubtful that the United States would thus subordinate other foreign policy considerations to the objective of preventing nuclear acquisition.

48. Clearly, the major Soviet interest in the NPT is to build special obstacles against West Germany's access to nuclear weapons in any form and, more broadly, to restrict nuclear sharing in NATO, particularly insofar as it might enhance West Germany's participation. One of the major arguments for the NPT in the United States is that it is necessary to alleviate Soviet fears of West Germany, however unwarranted they may be, and thus pave the way for further measures of détente. Whether or not this argument is based on a valid supposition or a correct set of priorities, it is bound to entail considerable political liabilities in America's relations with Germany. These liabilities seem particularly onerous in light of the fact that the Soviet Union wants the NPT for special political reasons and yet pays nothing for the benefit.

trying to gain the nonnuclear states' acceptance of the NPT, one must anticipate the political costs of keeping the signatories satisfied after acceptance. For it is clear that if India, for example, should sign the treaty, it would do so on conditions, explicit or otherwise, that would occasion periodic reassessment and impose certain claims on the United States and possibly the Soviet Union in order to preserve a balance of incentives for nuclear abstinence.

If the NPT is not consummated, considerations like these might lead to a reassessment of America's single-minded commitment to a simple negative instrumentality to cope with a variety of specific cases. Whether or not the NPT is finally signed by the most important potential nuclear states, the American government should, in time, discover that American interests are better served by a more diversified policy toward proliferation. If the objective is to dissuade a particular state from producing nuclear weapons, it should be evident that a nonproliferation treaty is just one of a number of possible measures—guarantees, compensations, rewards, sanctions, and protections (including BMD)—to be used with discrimination according to their effectiveness and political effects in particular circumstances. The problem of dissuading allies, moreover, should be treated differently from the problem of dissuading nonaligned states, let alone enemies.

In no case, however, can the United States afford to subordinate all other political considerations to nonproliferation. A rigid stand on nonproliferation is apt to be as inept for dissuading states that find compelling reasons to acquire nuclear weapons as for punishing states that have already undertaken nuclear programs. In these cases the United States will have to consider whether it is not wiser to give material assistance in order to preserve American influence and promote a safe nuclear force or a stable local balance rather than to remain aloof or hostile. It will have to decide whether to undertake or reinforce technological and political cooperation with, and guarantees to, the near-nuclear or nuclear-fledgling state, or whether to dissociate itself from that state, or perhaps start building countervailing power to restrain it. In the specific cases of India and Japan it may eventually have to decide—but probably not in the next five years—whether American interests in Asian security and order are not better served by one or two friendly nuclear counterpoises being added to a pattern of countervailing power, in which otherwise the United States alone (perhaps supplemented in some special circumstances by the Soviet Union) would be burdened with the task of countering China's nuclear force singlehandedly.

The NPT, like so many other aspects of American policy, is a reflection of an earlier and simpler period of a more unambiguous bi-polar order. It tries to shore up one crucial element of that order, the limited number of nuclear powers— which is to say, essentially, the nuclear preponderance of the United States and the Soviet Union. Though a nonproliferation treaty is probably a weak device for coping with the problems of the more pluralistic world that seems to be emerging, until the nature of that world is clarified in the next decade or so the significant arms control agreements will continue to reflect the special perspectives of the superpowers in a transitional period.

Another major proposal that grows out of these perspectives, though it does not suffer the onus of trying to order the rest of the world's military affairs, is an offensive and defensive strategic nuclear arms limitation.[49] The major purpose of such a limitation would be to stabilize the arms competition. The logic of seeking an agreement for this purpose is convincing if both superpowers want no more than assured-destruction capabilities and both are more interested in avoiding the expenditures of the new phase of arms competition that is latent in BMD and MIRV than in exploiting this phase to their advantage. But even if these conditions exist, there are formidable and probably insurmountable obstacles to a comprehensive arms agreement: the difficulty of formulating the terms of a mutually acceptable military ratio and the difficulty of verifying adherence to the agreement. The first difficulty arises from the number, complexity, and uncertain performance of the determinants of strategic offensive and defensive power and the asymmetry of American and Soviet requirements. It is not difficult to devise a treaty that would be to America's advantage, but it is hard to imagine one that both the United States and the Soviet Union would accept. The second difficulty arises from the inability of unilateral inspection to verify these components—particularly the quantity of warheads and the quality of decoys and penetration aids on missile launchers. It is not difficult to devise verifiable

49. In January, 1964, President Johnson proposed discussions with the Soviet Union to explore a verified freeze on the numbers and characteristics of offensive and defensive strategic nuclear delivery vehicles. The nonaligned states endorsed the proposal as a step toward disarmament and a concomitant of a nonproliferation treaty. The Soviet Union at first opposed the proposal, on the ground that it would entail unacceptable inspection without disarmament. The United States later stressed unilateral inspection. On March 2, 1967, President Johnson announced that Premier Kosygin had agreed to bilateral discussions on means of limiting the arms race in offensive and defensive nuclear missiles. On July 2, 1968, *Pravda* announced Soviet willingness to discuss the agreement, but the Soviet intervention in Czechoslovakia later that month delayed the expected talks.

limitations on strategic arms, but it is very difficult to devise verifiable limitations that will also achieve significant and stable restrictions.[50]

The achievement of useful strategic arms limitations, therefore, will depend much less on a treaty than on reciprocal unilateral limitations, motivated principally by domestic economic and political constraints, and sustained by mutual assurance that neither side intends major extensions of its control and influence to the disadvantage of the other. Bilateral discussions aimed toward an agreement, however, could provide a useful context for achieving such limitations. In this respect proposals for formal arms freezes and reductions will continue to have an important place in the international dialogue on military questions, since they will continue to represent objectives and aspirations having a wide appeal and to dramatize man's halting efforts to regulate military competition.

50. Both of these difficulties might conceivably be surmounted if each side wanted only a minimal second-strike capability and both were confident that within a large margin of inferiority in relative striking power an adequate second-strike capability would not be jeopardized. An agreement would also be facilitated if the restriction on offensive weapons were fixed at a high level. The verification problem could be minimized if the limitations applied only to the number of fixed land-based offensive and defensive missile launchers and to the flight-testing of MIRVs while mobile surface missiles were prohibited. But there is no assurance that such limitations would stabilize the nuclear balance or restrict arms expenditures, and it is unlikely that the United States and the Soviet Union could agree on these terms.

6

THE ECONOMIC CONSTRAINTS

Isaiah Frank

Jacob Viner, the distinguished Princeton economist, once defined a period of transition as a time that falls between two periods of transition. Ever since he uttered those words, I have suffered the greatest resistance to describing any period as one of transition. Yet it is hard to escape the conclusion that, at least insofar as the economic aspects of American foreign policy are concerned, the present is such a time, that we have reached the end of a cycle, and are not quite sure where we go from here.

One aspect of the change is the widespread feeling, stemming in part from Vietnam, that the United States is "overcommitted" abroad. The notion of overcommitment may center primarily on the nature and scope of our foreign objectives or on the extent of the resources devoted to them. In the first sense, we would be overcommitted if we have set goals for ourselves abroad beyond our capacity to fulfill on the basis of the present allocation of resources. ("We can't police the world.") In the second sense, we would be overcommitted, not because our foreign objectives are necessarily out of line with the resources allocated to them, but rather because the present allocation itself is excessive in relation to competing domestic demands on the national product or the federal budget. ("We should be spending more of our public funds to fight poverty at home and less on overseas ventures.")

Both of these elements are present in varying degrees in the present feeling of overcommitment. There is one sense, however, in which the volume of resources currently directed to international programs can hardly be viewed as excessive. Compared to the budget for defense or foreign aid at times when we believed our security to be threatened, the present allocations are modest indeed. In World War II, the United States devoted 42 percent of its GNP to defense without seriously impairing the standard of living of its people. The present allocation to defense is less than 10 percent. When the communist threat to Western Europe seemed imminent, the United States provided aid through the Marshall Plan amounting at its peak to 2 percent of its GNP, as compared to less than one-half of 1 percent today, for all forms of official aid to less developed countries. The change in our willingness to devote resources to overseas purposes today reflects a massive shift in priorities, a shift compounded in part of new and politically effective demands on the domestic front and in part of the general relaxation of tensions in our relations with the Soviet Union.

1. U.S. Economic Policy and the Cold War

That we have entered a different and more complex period in international affairs is a theme sounded by Robert E. Osgood in his introductory essay. With the transformation of the Cold War, American foreign policy has lost its simple guiding principle and finds itself without a coherent and unifying frame of reference with which to confront a world of rapid change. Among the grand concepts of the past that "seem dead or at least drained of hopeful expectations," he mentions regionalism, European unity, Atlantic partnership, and the economic development of the Third World.

Beyond these unfulfilled designs, originating largely as responses to Cold War pressures, we seem also to be in process of altering some of the more basic underpinnings of the international economic system that have served us well for a period extending back even before the onset of the Cold War. The inherent contradictions of the gold-exchange standard have become so obtrusive as to lead to a consensus on the need for its improvement or replacement by a new system, the full significance of which cannot yet be perceived. The recent completion of the Kennedy Round of tariff negotiations has led to a general acknowledgment that future efforts to free the channels of world trade cannot simply be a replica of the past but will have to come to grips with problems never before seriously confronted on an international scale. And the internationalization of production through the instrument of the multinational corporation has called into question the very concept of the nation state as the relevant entity for shaping policy in the whole field of trade and investment.

There is a certain analogy between the international politics and the international economics of the postwar period. The attenuation of the Cold War calls for new approaches to international politics, but it does not signify that our past policies of containment were mistaken. On the contrary, the easing of East-West tensions may well be viewed as at least a partial validation of those policies. Similarly, in the economic field, the obsolescence of traditional approaches to international trade, payments, and investment does not signify the failure of those policies to achieve the goals that were conceived for them. In fact, a case can be made that it is precisely because of the success of our postwar policies in freeing trade and payments that one of the basic economic dilemmas of our time has arisen: how to maintain international equilibrium in a world of nation states committed to full employment and growth, but in which trade restrictions and exchange rate adjustments are ruled out as ready devices for correcting imbalances of payments.

This fundamental dilemma—essentially, the conflict between the fact of international economic interdependence and the desire for autonomy in pursing national goals—would be bedeviling us today, regardless of whether a Soviet threat had existed in the postwar world. The problem arises in part from the substantial fulfillment of policy designs laid down toward the end of World War II, when the Soviet Union was an American ally and when economic planning for the postwar period was universalist in its conception, encompassing the communist states of Eastern Europe as well as the market economies of the West.

The worldwide approach to restoring a multilateral system of trade and payments at the end of World War II was formally embodied in the Articles of Agreement of the International Monetary Fund (IMF) and in the General Agreement on Tariffs and Trade (GATT). Despite the inclusion in the GATT of special provisions for "state-trading enterprises," both GATT and the IMF were basically predicated on the dominance of the market mechanism and were hardly suited to ordering economic relations between market and centrally planned economies. Though the Soviet Union was invited to join both organizations, it refrained from doing so, a fact which did not significantly impair the effectiveness of either body in achieving its major goals. At the same time, despite the absence of the Soviet Union, neither organization became an instrument in the Cold War, and various states of Eastern Europe have over the years either joined or expressed an interest in becoming members.

While the need for a fresh approach to major elements of U.S. foreign economic policy would exist apart from any changes in U.S.-Soviet relations, there are at least three areas in which the abatement of the Cold War has been a principal reason for the widespread feeling that current policy is out of step with current realities. These policy areas are European integration, the economic development of the low-income countries, and East-West trade.

The United States became an ardent and at times even a crusading champion of European integration because it saw in unification a means of coping with several urgent problems: the need to contain

Germany within a broader Western political framework in order to prevent a recurrence of Franco-German conflict, which had led to two world wars in one generation; the need to accelerate the process of European recovery by widening the market for labor, capital, and products and by exposing highly protected internal economies to the pressures of competition; and the need to build a center of strength in Europe to deal with the growing Soviet political and military threat.

Of these various motivations, the first two take on a certain archaic quality today. The world is full of centers of tension, instability, and conflict, but the Franco-German relationship is not one of them, nor is it likely to be in the foreseeable future. As for the state of the European economy, the countries of the European Economic Community have been the envy of the United States, both in terms of growth rates and over-all payments positions during most of the postwar period.

We come now to the Soviet threat as the last of the major original impulses for U.S. support of European integration. So long as the disparity between Western European and Soviet military capabilities remains as great as it is today, some residual sense of menace will persist. But, for a number of compelling reasons, the Soviet threat no longer appears as the dominant consideration in ordering relations among the Western European states. Nuclear weaponry has produced a stalemate between the superpowers, and no matter how delicate the balance of terror, it does provide a protective umbrella for Western Europe. Today the Soviet Union's salient berator and antagonist is China, a power whose containment is a principal objective of both Soviet and American strategy. Within Europe itself, where spheres of influence are clearly marked and recognized, the Soviet Union's major preoccupation is not expansion to the West but the maintenance of its hold on the smaller states of Eastern Europe in the face of their yearning for independence and of new outcroppings among them of policy divergencies.

All these reasons for the abatement of the Soviet threat have to do with developments external to Western Europe. There is an additional reason, an internal one, which has made Europe virtually invulnerable to the principal weapon of communist aggression, namely, internal subversion. If the West had been incapable of preventing the kind of unemployment and stagnation which had afflicted its societies in the thirties, Soviet penetration might well have succeeded, even without overt military aggression. With the communist parties commanding wide support in France and Italy, this was the specter that loomed in the immediate postwar period. Western Europe's success in taming the business cycle and in providing jobs for everyone was aided by the

Marshall Plan and by the establishment of the Common Market, but the major credit must go to the application of Keynesian principles to the management of internal demand within the Western European economies.

The Keynesian Revolution, which completely altered the economic performance and the prospects of the West, penetrated Western Europe well in advance of its acceptance in the United States. Against the backdrop of a striking lag in the U.S. economic growth rate, as compared to that of the major countries of Continental Europe, President Kennedy called attention in 1962 to the greater readiness of even conservative European governments to accept the fiscal implications of the "new economics":

How, in sum, can we make our free economy work at full capacity— that is, provide adequate profits for enterprise, adequate wages for labor, adequate utilization of plant, and adequate opportunity for all? These are the problems that . . . cannot be solved by incantations from the forgotten past. But the example of Western Europe shows that they are capable of solution—that governments, and many of them are conservative governments, prepared to face technical problems without ideological preconceptions, can coordinate the elements of a national economy to bring about growth and prosperity.[1]

At the same time that the EEC countries were achieving full employment and growth rates in GNP equal to more than twice their prewar average, the U.S.S.R. was experiencing a slowdown in growth and serious difficulties in the management of its agricultural and consumer sectors. The net result was a progressive diminution in the ideological appeal of communism as a way of improving the quality of life of the ordinary European citizen.

As the original impulses behind the movement toward European integration gradually lost their force, the interests of Western Europeans turned more and more inward. Lofty visions of political unification gave way to a preoccupation with the more mundane problems of managing prosperous economies and enjoying their material fruits. Completing and perfecting the customs union seemed a sensible thing to do, but, unlike earlier times, no crises confronted Europe in the mid-1960s which seemed to call for anything as far-reaching as the political fusion of national states.

In this setting there are still true believers on both sides of the At-

1. President Kennedy's commencement address at Yale University, June 11, 1962, *New York Times*, June 12, 1962.

lantic who cling to the concept of European unity, perceiving it as the solvent for new exigencies appearing on the international landscape. On the European side, a new rationale is the widening "technological gap" between Europe and the United States, a condition believed to be undermining Europe's independence and threatening to cast it into the backwash of American progress, much as the less developed countries find themselves in the role of hewers of wood and drawers of water for the industrial countries of the North.

Economists in general have difficulty in giving precision to the concept of the "technological gap." They see it as a case of a new label on an old package, and they doubt the dire consequences in material if not in psychological terms that purportedly flow from the gap. As a current rationale for European integration, however, the concept takes on added significance, since it implies a distinct shift in emphasis and perspective, from protection against the menace of Soviet aggression to protection against the threat to European independence posed by the American colossus.

On the American side too a new rationale has been constructed. As it has become increasingly apparent that U.S. economic and military strength cannot solve all the world's problems, there has arisen a longing for companionship, for a partner of similar outlook and comparable strength to share the responsibility of maintaining a viable world order. A politically fragmented Europe cannot muster the will to assume such a role nor dispose of the resources required to carry it out. Only a true coalescence of national states would be adequate to the needs of the day.

This particular appeal for unification is less persuasive now than it was when the grand design of U.S.-European partnership was originally launched by President Kennedy. Vietnam has produced in Europe a traumatic disenchantment with the activist role in international affairs, a fatalistic feeling that vast forces are at work in the world that even the superpowers are incapable of controlling. In addition, the massive shift in priorities toward the domestic problems of poverty, the cities, and mass education (a shift so familiar in America) has its counterpart in Western Europe.

More fundamental, however, is the growing recognition in Europe that the EEC model is not the only way; that progress toward a better world economic order can be achieved through a variety of special organizations with differing memberships and functions and with varying degrees of structural formality; and that this pragmatic approach may well serve the needs of the Six as effectively as some of the earlier designs predicated on the progressive extension of integration from the customs union to the ultimate fusion of sovereign political entities.

The second area in which the abatement of the Cold War has profoundly affected U.S. policy is the program of assistance to less developed countries. Today the aid program is in disarray—its purpose unclear, its appropriations drastically cut, and the morale of its personnel at low ebb.

Beginning in 1947, the various U.S. aid programs have been justified to the American people and the Congress primarily in terms of the Cold War. What came to be known as the Truman Doctrine was first proclaimed in a message to Congress in 1947, requesting aid for Greece and Turkey and enunciating "the policy of the United States to support free peoples who are resisting attempted subjugation by armed minorities or by outside pressures." Later that same year and as a logical outcome of the Truman Doctrine, the Marshall Plan was launched to counter the communist threat to Western Europe by aiding in its recovery and rehabilitation and by promoting European economic cooperation. In the four years from mid-1948 to mid-1952 the United States provided more than $12 billion under the Marshall Plan, mostly in the form of grants, with results that were spectacularly successful.

During the Korean War the center of Cold War attention shifted from Europe to Asia. From 1953 to 1957 the greatest part of U.S. economic assistance, as well as extensive military aid, went to countries proximate to the Soviet Union and Communist China, including Turkey, Iran, Pakistan, Korea, and Taiwan. At the same time, however, economic aid was extended in increasing amounts to other countries such as India and Ceylon, mostly newly independent states which were in principle neutral and whose overriding concern was not the Cold War but economic and social progress. Yet even in the case of these countries the official rationale for the aid program placed heavy emphasis on the threat of communist subversion to countries suffering appalling poverty and possessing political structures too new and too weak to cope alone with their enormous internal problems.

As a reaction to the Korean War, the prices of primary commodities soared in the early 1950s, giving a tremendous boost to Latin America's earnings from exports and providing the foreign exchange needed to support satisfactory growth rates. When the commodity boom petered out and prices tumbled, Latin America found itself in difficult straits and without the means to come to grips with its deep-seated social and economic tensions. At the same time the communist revolution in Cuba posed the threat of subversion in much of Latin America, feeding on widespread frustration and unrest. It was in response to these conditions that the United States signed the Act of Bogota in 1960 and joined the Latin American republics the next year in launching the program of social and economic development called the Alliance for Progress.

Although the communist threat provided the major impetus and principal public justification for economic assistance to less developed countries, the programs were in fact carried out day-to-day in response to a much more complex set of U.S. interests in the countries of the third world. Economic assistance became the principal instrument of U.S. foreign policy in virtually all countries receiving substantial amounts of aid. Depending on the country and the type of assistance, the mix of purposes for which aid was deployed included such diverse elements as short-run stabilization, long-run economic development, economic support for military programs beyond the capabilities of the country concerned, bargaining for military base rights, export promotion, support of regional integration, and the use of aid as a lever to damp down border disputes such as that between India and Pakistan.

The core of the argument for the aid programs remained, however: the political-security threat posed by communism to the poor and weak countries of the less developed world. Over time the argument shifted from the simple notion that poverty breeds communism to a more sophisticated doctrine. The latter version recognizes that the process of modernization itself involves profound political and social change which can be highly destabilizing in the short run; that such forces are already under way in much of the less developed world regardless of what the United States does; and that by assisting the development process and reducing the sacrifice required, the odds in favor of the evolution of stable, cohesive, and independent states will be increased and the risk of U.S. involvement in crises abroad thereby reduced.

Today the political argument for foreign aid is increasingly being called into question. Indonesia has cast off the communist threat without benefit of aid—military or economic—from the United States, and Nigeria is beset by civil war, although it had been the largest recipient of U.S. aid south of the Sahara. Outside of Vietnam, the principal threat to peace is in the Middle East, where the instrument of economic aid seems almost irrelevant to the issues that rouse such passion.

With the détente in U.S.-Soviet relations, there have come not only explicit agreements on the testing and proliferation of nuclear weapons but also a de facto mutual de-escalation of competitive assistance programs in the less developed world. Paralleling the drastic reductions in U.S. aid appropriations, there have been sharp cutbacks in nonmilitary aid commitments by the U.S.S.R. from an average of about $800 million per year in 1964–66 to an average of less than $200 million per year in 1967–68. Disenchantment with the political returns from large-scale assistance may well have set in on both sides in the Cold War.

As the political-security rationale for foreign aid has deteriorated, increasing emphasis has been placed on its humanitarian basis. Although this element was always present, it was projected into prominence in the stirring rhetoric of President Kennedy:

> To those peoples in the huts and cottages of half the globe struggling to break the bonds of mass misery, we pledge our best efforts to help them help themselves, for whatever period is required—not because the Communists may be doing it, not because we seek their votes, but because it is right.[2]

More recently the concept of America's moral responsibility to the Third World was stressed by a high State Department official in the following terms:

> A growing North-South division could not threaten America's power position; the developing countries are too weak to do us physical harm. But the moral values which are as much a part of our country as its physical resources could be eroded if we were content to accept the role of passive bystander in the face of deepening hostility and human misery abroad. Like the traditional rich landlord, we could wind up being corrupted by our isolation and alienation from those about us.[3]

There are even some who believe that from the beginning the traditional political-security justification for assistance in development was in its more sophisticated version an elaborate and not entirely conscious intellectual expedient designed to move a hardheaded Congress while masking the true humanitarian motives of its proponents.

The humanitarian appeal for foreign aid is coming to the fore at a time when its effectiveness in moving the Congress to appropriations is substantially diminished. Vietnam is part of the difficulty. One view, of which Senator Fulbright is the principal exponent, holds that economic aid inevitably carries with it the risk of military involvement

---

2. Inaugural Address, January 20, 1961.

3. Henry Owen, "Foreign Policy Premises for the Next Administration," *Foreign Affairs*, July, 1968.

and that assistance should therefore be carried out only through multi-lateral channels. At the same time, however, Congress has been re-luctant to step up U.S. contributions to multilateral programs, partly because of the budgetary and balance-of-payments stringencies brought on by $30 billion of annual expenditures for the war in Vietnam. But it is not really a question of whether we can "afford" larger contribu-tions. Rather, it is our diminishing capacity to muster the political will for larger aid appropriations for low-income countries at a time when so much of our political energy is devoted to resolving the profound internal conflicts and strains of an affluent, urban, biracial society.

The third area where changes in policy have failed to catch up with changes in the Cold War is East-West trade. Here we can be quite brief, since the lag has long been recognized by the Executive Branch. The trouble has been mainly in the Congress, which has shown strong emotional opposition to bringing our trade policy toward the European Soviet bloc into accord with political realities.[4]

U.S. policy on trade with communist countries still reflects in its basic elements the line adopted during the Korean War. At that time Congress revised the Trade Agreements Act, placing the Soviet bloc outside the reciprocal trade program and thereby denying it the benefits of tariff reductions negotiated with other countries. U.S. ex-port controls were also tightened, and the "Battle Act" was passed in 1951, conditioning American economic or military aid to foreign coun-tries on the latter's cooperation in a selective embargo on the export of strategic goods to the Soviet bloc. At the same time, an absolute prohibition was imposed on trade with Communist China and North Korea.

Over the years there has been some easing of these restrictive poli-cies. But the absolute prohibition on trade with Communist China and North Korea continues, and Cuba has been added to the embargo list. Imports from the Soviet Union and all Eastern European countries other than Poland and Yugoslavia are still denied most favored treat-ment. And our strategic export controls and export credit policies to-ward the Soviet bloc remain more restrictive than are those applied by the countries of Western Europe. Because of this divergence in policies, moreover, there is serious doubt as to the effectiveness of our additional restrictions.

4. A reversal of roles may be emerging under President Nixon, with Congress more ready to liberalize East-West trade than the administration. "Nixon Against Easing Curb on Trading with Red Bloc," *New York Times*, May 29, 1969.

The more basic question, however, relates to the long-run national purpose presumed to be served by the present structure of U.S. controls and discriminatory treatment. It seems especially difficult to reconcile with a policy of détente those restrictions on trade with European communist countries which clearly serve no strategic objective. Although elimination of the restrictions is unlikely to produce a dramatic increase in trade, it should at least lessen tensions and, by improving the general atmosphere, could even serve as a prelude to negotiations on broader political issues.

In the foregoing we have isolated three areas of foreign economic policy—European integration, aid to less developed countries, and East-West trade—in which traditional approaches have been called into question as a result of the détente in U.S.-Soviet relations. Because the theme of this volume is the impact of changes in the Cold War, it seemed appropriate to discuss those subjects briefly at the outset. As stated earlier, however, other profound changes have taken place, independently of the Cold War, which call for a more general reappraisal of U.S. foreign economic policy at the end of the decade of the 1960s. In what follows we will deal successively with developments in U.S. economic relations with each of three groups of countries: the noncommunist industrial countries, the developing world, and the communist countries.

2. Economic Relations
with the Noncommunist Industrial Countries

In economic terms the noncommunist industrial countries—broadly, the members of the Organization for Economic Cooperation and Development (OECD), including Western Europe, Canada, and Japan—are far more important to the United States than are either the countries of the less developed world or those of the communist bloc. Two-thirds of American trade is with the OECD countries, as is about the same percentage of U.S. direct private investment abroad. Moreover, these economic relations have grown in the past decade much more rapidly with the OECD countries than with other parts of the world. Though America's principal political and security problems have centered in recent years in the less developed world or in the Soviet bloc, in strictly economic terms it is the OECD countries which count.

There is a certain asymmetry, however, in America's economic relations with the rest of the industrial world, stemming from the overwhelming size of the U.S. economy. Canada exemplifies the problem in its most extreme form, since it is the single most important trading partner of the United States and the principal destination of U.S. foreign investment. Yet Canada's economic importance to the United States, great as it is, is only a fraction of the importance of the United States to Canada on any reasonable measure. To a lesser extent, the same asymmetry exists in U.S. relations with Japan and the individual countries of Western Europe. As a consequence, other countries are often extremely sensitive to changes in U.S. economic policy, regarding them as front-page news, while comparable policy shifts on their part command only limited and specialized concern in the United States.

Many of the current strains in American relations with Western Europe derive from the economic preponderance of the United States. Brain drain and technological gap reflect in part the ability of the United States to devote resources to research and development on a scale beyond the capacity of the individual European states. The enthronement of the dollar as the world's key currency for both international transactions and reserves, a condition so deeply resented by the French, is not the conscious work of man but simply a natural accommodation to the economic supremacy of the United States. And more basically, the discrepancy in size is at the root of the conflict between the desire of some Europeans for a more effective voice in the great political decisions of our time and the capacity of individual European states to assume responsibility in the world arena.

Actually, the U.S. role in the international economy is less overwhelming today than it was in the decade following World War II. We still account for more than 50 percent of total goods and services produced in the OECD area, but the proportion is less than it was prior to the phenomenal reconstruction and recovery of Western Europe and Japan. Though we are still the largest national market and trading nation, the European Economic Community as a unit accounts for a far greater proportion of world trade than does the United States. But the major change over the last decade has been the deterioration in our international reserve position as a result of large and persistent deficits in our balance of payments. Whereas formerly the United States could conduct its domestic and foreign affairs without anxiety about the impact on its international accounts, the latter has become today a pervasive constraint on policy both at home and abroad.

For the United States, the making of foreign economic policy was a lot easier in the earlier period, when its position in the world was so dominant. The main focus of the U.S.-European bilateral relationship was on how the United States could assist the process of reconstruction and recovery rather than on the resolution of issues in which competitive U.S.-European interests were at stake. And on the broader and longer-range question of restructuring the postwar system of trade and payments, the Americans were given a fairly free hand to take the lead on problems that seemed remote to the Europeans as compared to the crises preoccupying them in the aftermath of the war. In any case, the leverage implicit in Europe's position of dependence on America's military and economic resources was always in the background.

The problems we face in our economic relations with Europe are so perplexing for two reasons. First, the United States can no longer call the tune. The Kennedy Round will undoubtedly go down in history as the last time the Europeans were willing to fall into line and negotiate in accordance with policies and conditions laid down in U.S. domestic legislation rather than those agreed in advance. And second, the principles that shaped Atlantic economic relations more or less continuously in the postwar period are widely regarded as insufficient guides in coping with the complexities facing us today.

Two strands may be discerned in U.S. postwar foreign economic policy. The first is universalist, seeking to build a system of international economic relations for the world as a whole (or at least for the noncommunist world) based on nondiscrimination among foreign countries and a minimum of protection for the home market; the second is regional, seeking to promote closer ties among smaller groups of countries through a variety of arrangements whose common feature has been discrimination against nonmembers, including the United States.

The basic rationale for the universalist approach derives from classical trade theory. By following liberal and nondiscriminatory trade policies, incomes will be maximized as each country is induced to concentrate on producing those goods in which its comparative advantage is greatest. The appeal of this approach to the United States was bolstered by certain special considerations. It was widely believed that the highly protective U.S. tariff structure of the 1920s culminating in the Smoot-Hawley tariff of 1930 had had something to do with the Great Depression of the 1920s. And the United States had come to regard itself as one of the main victims of the quota restrictions and discriminatory trading arrangements that proliferated in the decade of depression.

Accordingly, the United States took the lead toward the end of World War II in building a framework of principles and institutions predicated on an open, multilateral trading system. Basic to this ap-

proach as incorporated in GATT and the IMF were several principles: (1) the outlawing of discrimination as among foreign countries;
(2) progressive tariff reduction; (3) the maintenance of fixed exchange
rates; and (4) the avoidance of quantitative restrictions or exchange
controls on current transactions. Underlying these principles was the
tacit assumption that countries would remain in equilibrium in their
over-all payments positions; otherwise recourse to quantitative and
exchange controls might be unavoidable, bringing with it the discrimination inherent in a system of controls.

In addition to embodying codes of international behavior, GATT
and the IMF provide facilities for administering the commitments and
for sanctioning exceptions on the basis of international consensus. In
the case of GATT, the principal mechanism has consisted of procedures for the settlement of trade disputes and for the grant of waivers
from GATT rules. In the case of the Fund, the main technique has
been its annual consultations, originally with members whose currencies were inconvertible, but more recently including members with
convertible currencies as well. Essentially, the two institutions have
served as guardians of a liberal international economic regime, with
GATT responsible for the trade side of international transactions and
the Fund responsible for the payments side.

Looking back over the period since the end of World War II, one
cannot but be impressed with the progress made under the set of
policies embodied in those two institutions. Starting from a situation
in which Western European trade and payments were constrained in
bilateral straitjackets, obstacle after obstacle was gradually lifted so
that goods move more freely now than at any time since World War I.
By 1958 full currency convertibility was achieved by the industrial
countries, quantitative restrictions on trade in manufactured products
were well on their way to being eliminated, and tariffs had been steadily reduced through a series of worldwide bargaining sessions under
the general aegis of GATT. The payoff on these policies has been the
rapid expansion of trade at an annual rate of almost 9 percent for the
industrial countries. Since the growth in trade has been twice as rapid
as the growth in output, it is apparent that a more integrated world
economy is emerging, conferring substantial benefits in the form of
a more efficient use of world resources.

In the semantics of international economic policy a distinction is
drawn between measures favoring domestic over foreign producers
and measures favoring one foreign producer over another. The former
is called "protection" and, when moderate, is accepted as consistent
with a multilateral world trading system; the latter, however, is called

"discrimination" and is generally viewed as incompatible with such a system. Nondiscrimination is the essence of the most-favored-nation policy which, in its unconditional form, has governed U.S. trade relations with most countries for almost fifty years and which has been endorsed by the principal trading nations of the world.

Running counter to the most-favored-nation principle, however, has been the second strand in postwar U.S. policy, the support of regional arrangements. Although this policy gathered momentum in the fifties as a way of building strength in Europe in the face of the Cold War, certain deviations from the principle of nondiscrimination were regarded as acceptable from the outset.

At the time that GATT was formulated in 1947, it permitted two major exceptions from the most-favored-nation rule. Certain existing preferences, such as those of the British Commonwealth, were allowed to continue, provided the margins of preference were not increased; and a specific exception was incorporated to permit the formation of customs unions or free trade areas. In order to qualify for the GATT customs-union exception, conditions are stipulated to ensure both that the potential benefits of the arrangement will in fact be realized and that the interests of outsiders will be protected.

The first requirement is that duties and other restrictions must be eliminated in respect to substantially all the trade between members. By insisting on a comprehensive and nonselective removal of internal barriers, customs unions and free trade areas are believed to offer advantages that are unlikely to flow from mere partial preferential arrangements: a greater likelihood that the beneficial trade-creating effects will take place, leading to a more economic distribution of resources and output within the area; greater security against the reimposition of internal restraints; and a greater probability that the arrangement will lead to desirable long-run political developments because of the need for the partners to coordinate more closely their domestic economic and financial policies and their external commercial policies.

The second GATT requirement is that duties or other restrictions applying to outside countries shall not on the whole be greater than the general incidence of the restrictions obtaining prior to the formation of the customs union or free trade area. Whereas the first provision is designed to maximize the trade-creating effects of the arrangement, this one is intended to minimize the undesirable trade-diverting effects. It does so by ensuring that whatever discrimination results from the establishment of a regional arrangement comes about through the elimination of internal barriers rather than through the raising of barriers against outsiders. Moreover, the external tariffs are subject to reduction through negotiation with outsiders so that the trade-diverting effects can be reduced over time. In short, a customs union or free-trade area conforming to the GATT criteria can be viewed as a contribution toward freer trade, world-wide, rather than simply as a discriminatory arrangement.

Years before the establishment of the European Common Market (EEC) and the European Free Trade Area (EFTA), however, the United States gave its blessing to a variety of discriminatory arrangements within Europe that clearly fell short of the criteria for regional groupings laid down in the GATT. Among such arrangements were the European Payments Union (EPU), the intra-European trade liberalization program, and the European Coal and Steel Community. But the first two were never regarded as more than transitional devices which, along with Marshall Plan assistance, would help Europe through its difficult period of reconstruction, so that it eventually would be able to face competition from the entire non-Soviet world without discrimination. Similarly, the European Coal and Steel Community was regarded as merely the first step toward a more far-reaching program of European integration which, in its economic aspects, would comprehend as a minimum the basic GATT conditions for a customs union. By the second half of the 1950s, these expectations were substantially vindicated as the EPU was dissolved, as dollar liberalization caught up with intra-European trade liberalization, and as the Coal and Steel Community was followed by the more encompassing European Common Market. And, as a reaction to the establishment of the EEC, the United Kingdom led six other countries of Europe in forming the EFTA, an arrangement more limited in scope and purpose than the EEC but conforming to the basic GATT conditions for regional groupings.

Compared to the ardor of its support for the EEC, the American attitude toward the formation of the EFTA was cool indeed. The difference can be explained in both political and economic terms. Politically, the EEC was viewed as the first stage in the progressive evolution of an "ever closer union among the European peoples,"[5] a goal that captivated American policy-makers, since it was an affirmative and forward-looking response to the political and security problems besetting Western Europe in the early 1950s. By contrast, the EFTA was regarded as a limited, defensive, and strictly commercial

5. Preamble to the Treaty of Rome, 1957.

reaction to the EEC, a move which, under British leadership, threatened to divide Western Europe into two opposing economic camps.

Because of the political significance of the EEC, the United States was more inclined to accept the commercial discrimination against outsiders inherent in it than in the EFTA. But the difference in the U.S. attitude also reflects a change in the economic climate. When the EEC was negotiated, the United States had been conditioned by many years of dollar shortage to welcome, or at least to take lightly, the discriminatory features of an arrangement which would improve the competitive position of the Europeans vis-à-vis the dollar area. By the time the EFTA was established, however, the U.S. external financial position had seriously deteriorated, and any new discriminatory arrangements became matters of major concern.

The establishment of the EFTA, however, marked only the beginning of the strains that developed as a consequence of the successful launching of the European Common Market. By the first year of the Kennedy Administration, a consensus was emerging in the U.S. government that a major effort would have to be made to reconcile support for integration with an increasingly urgent need to reduce the discrimination against U.S. exports inherent in the European arrangements. Among the main elements contributing to the consensus was the spectacular economic performance of the Six contrasted with the sluggish growth and massive balance of payments deficits of the United States, and the announcement by Prime Minister Macmillan in July, 1961, that Britain would seek membership in the Common Market, a step that would widen the discrimination against the United States.

The economic response within the Six to the establishment of the EEC demonstrated from the start the simplistic character of the orthodox view of customs unions as reflected in the GATT. According to the traditional doctrine, the effects of a customs union on its members and on the world as a whole depend on the balance between the trade-creating and trade-diverting effects of the tariff changes incident to the arrangement. But the Common Market experience showed that the main benefits flowed, not from the static reallocation of the existing resources of the Six in accordance with comparative advantage, but rather from the profound changes in method, scale, and organization of production that occurred in response to the expectation of enlarged market opportunities and more intensified competition. The principal gains were in the form of more rapid innovation, an increased flow of investment, both domestic and foreign, greater specialization, and a larger scale of operations. All this added up to more rapid growth internally, improved competitiveness externally, and balance-of-payments surpluses, which in the first three years of the Common Market's existence yielded additions of over $6 billion to the reserves of its members.

Contrasted to this performance was the sluggish growth in the United States, a condition that played a prominent part in the presidential campaign of 1960, when John F. Kennedy's battle-cry was, "Let's get this country moving again." Equally serious, however, was the adverse balance-of-payments situation. Though the United States had run moderate deficits in most years between 1950 and 1958, the earlier ones reflected a conscious effort to rectify the European dollar shortage and were in any case largely covered by increased foreign holdings of short-term dollar claims. What differentiated the U.S. payments position after the establishment of the EEC in 1958 were both the size of the deficits (averaging $3.7 billion annually in 1958–60) and the fact that they had to be settled to a substantial degree by an outflow of gold. At the beginning of 1958 the U.S. gold stock was just about the same as it had been seven years earlier; but in the three years 1958–60 the loss of gold amounted to almost $5 billion, bringing our gold reserves down below the total of foreign official and private dollar claims.

The initial U.S. reaction to these developments, at least in terms of trade policy, was quite conventional. The Dillon Round of tariff negotiations, which began toward the end of the Eisenhower administration and continued until early 1962, followed the traditional pattern. It accomplished only a modest reduction in discrimination against the United States by cutting the Community's common external tariff by about 10 percent. At those negotiations in which the Community was represented as a unit for the first time, little basis was conveyed for believing that the EEC would be much more outward-looking than the least common denominator of its most protectionist member. The Dillon Round confirmed, moreover, that if the Community's markets were really to be opened up, the U.S. negotiators would have to be equipped with more powerful bargaining levers than those provided in the traditional extensions of the U.S. Trade Agreements Act.

With the British decision in mid-1961 to seek accession to the Common Market, a new situation confronted the United States, providing the setting for more far-reaching initiatives. On the one hand, British accession would widen the area of preferential treatment to the disadvantage of the United States, a consequence that would be reinforced by the inevitable inclusion of a number of other EFTA members in the British wake. On the other hand, the United States warmly supported the British move as one that would repair the breach in the Western alliance. In addition, it was hoped that Britain would throw its weight in the Community on the side of the Dutch and the Germans, who were more favorable than other members to a liberal trade policy toward the outside world.

The vehicle for reconciling an enlarged Common Market with the need of outsiders for better access to the expanded trading area was the Trade Expansion Act of 1962 (TEA). Because this far-reaching piece of legislation represented a break with the past in so many respects, its supporters within the administration realized that the only way of gaining its acceptance was to lift it out of the conventional context in which tariff legislation was normally considered and to present it as the path to a brave new world. Here at last was the vehicle for carrying out the grand design of Atlantic partnership in a way that would lead the entire world to freer trade. "Led by the two great common markets of the Atlantic, trade barriers in all the industrial nations must be brought down.[6] By wrapping the new trade program in a broad appeal to America's leadership in world affairs, the administration succeeded in reducing to secondary importance much of the traditional bickering between protectionists and free traders.

The TEA provided the president with greater authority to negotiate reductions in tariffs than any president had received since the launching of the trade agreements program in 1934. In addition to the basic authority to cut tariffs by 50 percent and various more specialized tariff-cutting provisions, the Act authorized the complete elimination of tariffs on any category of products for which the United States and the EEC (including acceding members) together accounted for 80 percent of world exports. If the United Kingdom had acceded, the latter provision would have permitted a sweeping elimination of tariffs over a significant range of products. Without accession, the 80 percent provision was rendered ineffective, since it would apply to only a few products. But even if the British had acceded, it is questionable whether the members of the EEC would in fact have been able to agree among themselves to reciprocate by eliminating the tariff distinction between insiders and outsiders on an appreciable number of products. So far as is known, the administration had no

6. Speech of President Kennedy to the National Association of Manufacturers, December 6, 1961, quoted in the *New York Times*, December 7, 1961.

assurance on this score but was operating on the hope that somehow the EEC would get caught up in the momentum generated by the U.S. rhetoric at home.

Even without the 80 percent authority, the TEA was a powerful tariff-cutting tool, since it permitted the president to use a new technique in applying the basic authority to cut tariffs in half. Instead of the traditional method of item-by-item negotiation, the intention was to seek an agreement with the EEC to reduce substantially all tariffs across the board by 50 percent. Theoretically, the detailed negotiations would then be limited to exceptions, making possible a much fuller use of the authority than had been possible in previous negotiations.

In addition to tariff-negotiating authority, the TEA revamped in a radical way the existing approach to providing relief from injury resulting from reductions in trade barriers. Previously, an "escape clause" made it possible to raise tariffs in such cases, and, although used sparingly, it remained as a constant threat to the stability of negotiated tariff concessions. Although the TEA retained the escape clause as an ultimate recourse, it tightened the standards for using it, and it provided the alternative of adjustment assistance in the form of financial aid to help firms shift into new lines of production, as well as unemployment and retraining payments to affected workers.

The theory behind the provisions of the TEA for adjustment assistance is impeccable: instead of reacting negatively to intensified import competition by restoring barriers to trade, we could react affirmatively by facilitating precisely the type of improvements in efficiency and reallocations of resources that import competition is intended to induce. Unfortunately, however, in their zeal to tighten the escape clause, the free-traders outdid themselves by applying the same strict criteria to the alternative avenue of relief through adjustment assistance. In order for workers or firms to qualify for such assistance, it must be shown that tariff concessions are the *major* cause of increased import competition and that the increased imports are the *major* cause of injury. In no case presented to the Tariff Commission since the enactment of the TEA has any petitioner been able to qualify for assistance, not necessarily because there has been no injury, but because so many other factors affect competitiveness that tariff concessions could not be adjudged the major one. By making the standards so rigid, the principal safety valve for the trade liberation program has been rendered ineffective, thereby weakening the case against relief through protectionist measures enacted directly by the Congress.

The administration has recently sought to liberalize the criteria for adjustment assistance by loosening the links between tariff concessions, increased imports, and injury. A case can be made, however, for opening access to assistance even further by completely eliminating the link to tariff concessions. Why should it not be sufficient to demonstrate that increased imports have been a substantial cause of injury? The link to tariff concessions implies that there is something sacrosanct about the levels of protection established in the Smoot-Hawley Tariff of 1930 to which concessions relate.

Because of the urgency of the U.S. balance-of-payments problems, a great deal of emphasis was placed in the campaign for the TEA on the contribution that reciprocal tariff reductions would make to improving the U.S. payments position. But it was not easy to reconcile equal percentage reductions with the claim that the United States would gain a net payments advantage, and many of the arguments put forward were shaky indeed. Curiously, the most cogent reason of all was not even explicitly advanced in the congressional hearings. It derived from a basic asymmetry in U.S. negotiations with the EEC: a reduction in the U.S. tariff would simply remove some of the protection afforded domestic producers, but a reduction in the external tariff of the EEC would not only reduce the level of protection in each member country but would also forestall part of the preferential advantage each would otherwise enjoy in other members' markets.

Under the authority of the TEA, the Kennedy Round negotiations were pursued over a period of almost five years. It was a time of great tension within the Atlantic area, marked by the veto of the British bid for entry into the Common Market, the crisis in NATO, deep concern about the viability of the international financial system, and the more general strains related to the expanding war in Vietnam. On all these matters, the position of France was opposed to that of the United States, and it was inevitable that some of the sharp divergencies would carry over into the Kennedy Round negotiations, as indeed they did in the form of confrontations on such technical issues as tariff disparities. A mood of pessimism persisted throughout, and many feared that in the end de Gaulle would not allow the negotiation to succeed. Perhaps the most important factor inducing him to agree was the internal deal worked out in the EEC in which German acceptance of Community decisions on farm policy was linked to good behavior on the part of France in the Kennedy Round.

Under the circumstances, the results of the Kennedy Round were impressive. Average tariff reductions of about 35 percent were made by all major industrial countries, with about two-thirds of the cuts equal to 50 percent or more. The largest cuts were in the technologically advanced and rapidly changing industries characterized by a high degree of product differentiation such as machinery, transport equipment, and chemicals. In these industries a reduction of protection is more easily accommodated, because they are constantly adapting anyway to changes in processes, products, and markets. By contrast, only modest reductions were achieved in industries characterized by more standardized output and more stable technology, such as textiles and steel, in which protectionist pressures have been strongest.

In agriculture the United States failed to achieve its main objective of assured access to Community markets for products subject to the EEC variable levy system. The basic conflict between liberal trade policies and national support systems for domestic agriculture remained unresolved. Substantial tariff reductions were made, however, on many individual farm products, and agreement was reached on joint food aid for less developed countries. In addition, a start was made in the vast field of nontariff barriers: an agreement was reached on an antidumping code designed to limit some of the trade-restricting effects of national regulations; and, as part of a package deal, the United States agreed, subject to congressional action, to get rid of the highly objectionable American-selling-price method of valuation for certain chemicals in return for European action on road taxes that discriminate against American automobiles.

The long-run effects of the Kennedy Round are not easy to assess. In strictly static terms, the economic consequences of the reduction in tariffs are likely to be modest. One study[7] made before the completion of the Kennedy Round estimated that a 50 percent reduction across the board in duties on industrial products would lead to a 6 percent increase in the total trade of the advanced countries in these products. In relation to the GNP of the industrial countries, the expansion of trade would amount to only about 0.5 percent, and the welfare effects to a much smaller percentage. But these are estimates of the purely static effects. As noted earlier in the discussion of the effects of tariff dismantlement within the EEC, the main benefits of liberalization are the dynamic consequences flowing from more intense competition, greater specialization, economies of scale, and improved technology. Although estimates are not available, these effects are likely to be substantial, certainly overshadowing the projections based on static assumptions.

The completion of the Kennedy Round in 1967 marked a turning point in the long process of freeing the movement of goods among countries. Although significant tariffs remain on a number of products,

7. Bela Balassa and Mordecai Kreinin, "Trade Liberalization Under the Kennedy Round: The Static Effects," *The Review of Economics and Statistics*, May, 1967.

particularly as measured in terms of effective protection, average tariffs are now quite low by historical standards. In any case, there is a general consensus that, after six general rounds of tariff negotiation, new approaches to trade liberalization are needed today.

One problem is that, unless there is forward momentum, the gains of the past are unlikely to be maintained. Protectionist forces have gathered strength in the United States, and in the last several years more than the usual number of bills have been introduced in the Congress to apply new restrictions on imports or to intensify existing ones. The textile bill had sixty-eight sponsoring senators, and strong support was also evidenced for new restrictive measures in petroleum, steel, electronics, meat, and dairy products. Some of the efforts are being pursued through the extralegal route of so-called "voluntary" agreements. If even a portion of these moves to impose quantitative import restrictions is realized, we may be left, despite the Kennedy Round, with the form of a liberal trade regime but without its substance. The best way to contain the protectionist pressures is through new initiatives in tackling the remaining barriers to trade, combined with a basic liberalization of the present provisions for adjustment assistance.

Despite the success of the Kennedy Round in moderating the discrimination inherent in existing European regional arrangements, there is a growing feeling that the world has been moving away from nondiscrimination in international trade. A number of African countries not previously linked preferentially to the EEC have been exploring some form of association with the Common Market. Spain is seeking a form of preferential arrangement with the EEC similar to that already established by the Common Market with Greece and Turkey. An enlargement of the area of discrimination through some link between the EEC and EFTA gets revived periodically. And the developed countries as a group have responded to the urgings of the poor countries by agreeing to explore ways of granting tariff preferences to all less developed countries. If these various moves come to fruition, little will be left of the unconditional most-favored-nation treatment that has been the cornerstone of U.S. trade policy for almost half a century.

One suggestion for ridding the industrial world of discrimination is to agree on a firm target for free trade in nonagricultural products and on an automatic formula for reaching the target. By setting the date far enough in the future—perhaps twenty years—the advance to free trade would be so gradual as to make the adjustment problems negligible.

However laudable the objective of eliminating the discriminatory features of present European groupings, I doubt its realism. The EEC in particular seems hardly prepared at this stage to consider new and far-reaching tariff-cutting commitments that would have the effect of doing away with what is still the major distinction between membership and nonmembership in the Common Market. Anticipating this reaction from the Community, some people suggest that the United States enter into a free trade agreement with all countries ready to undertake the commitment, leaving the door open to others to join later. In the meantime, the benefits of the new tariff reductions would not accrue to nonparticipants: in other words, they would be discriminated against by the others. (Less developed countries might be given the benefits without reciprocity on their part.)

Who, however, would join the United States in such a move? Certainly not the EFTA countries. For them, trade with the Common Market is of far greater importance than is trade with the United States, and they could hardly be expected to invite the sort of retaliation from the Common Market that would inevitably follow. In any event, the United Kingdom and other members of the EFTA have set their main sights on entry into the Common Market, and they would certainly not take a step which could only serve to perpetuate their exclusion. It is even doubtful whether Canada or Japan would be interested.

If we set aside such grandiose but divisive ideas, there are still possibilities for moving toward freer trade along more modest lines. One approach worth exploring has been called "sectoral integration." It would consist in eliminating all tariffs and harmonizing other conditions of competition in certain industries over the course of a prescribed transition period.

In a sense, sectoral integration would be a natural evolution from the actual negotiating strategy adopted in the Kennedy Round. In that negotiation, when especially difficult problems existed in particular sectors—steel, chemicals, and textiles are examples—industry-by-industry discussions were held in an effort to achieve a certain balance in the results for each sector. Negotiations on steel, for example, were carried on against a background in which U.S. duties were generally lower than those of other countries. As a result of the Kennedy Round, a much closer harmonization of tariffs was achieved among the major steel-producing countries: almost all rates will be no higher than 15 percent, and most will be well below 10 percent. Drawing on this experience, Eric Wyndham White, the former Director General of GATT, put forward the idea of sectoral free trade in the following terms:

. . . there are certain sectors of industrial production—characterized by modern equipment, high technology and large-scale production, and by the international character of their operations and markets—where there are evident gains to all in arriving, within a defined period, at free trade.

The idea of free trade by sectors is not entirely new. After all, the European Economic Community was preceded by the Coal and Steel Community; and even the U.S.-Canadian automotive agreement might be cited as an example of sectoral free trade. What would be new, however, is the extension of the idea from a strictly regional to a global context.

One should not underestimate the problems that would attend a move toward free trade along sectoral lines. There may not be many industries in which the principal countries have both protected and exporting sectors so that self-balancing agreements can be negotiated. In order to achieve a balance of advantages, it may in practice be necessary to negotiate simultaneously with respect to more than one industry, thereby approaching the more standard type of tariff negotiation. It is doubtful, moreover, whether the negotiation could be limited to tariffs alone. As the EEC experience demonstrates, the elimination of duties is hardly feasible, unless other measures affecting the international competitiveness of particular industries are introduced. Quotas, taxes, subsidies, restrictive business practices, antitrust legislation—all these become relevant and add to the complexity of negotiating free trade along sectoral lines.

Nontariff barriers need not, however, be dealt with solely in the context of sectoral negotiations. A start in fact was made in the Kennedy Round. With duties on many products now quite low, the remaining nontariff barriers are assuming greater importance. There is much to be said, therefore, for placing their elimination high on the agenda of future general trade negotiations.

Negotiations on nontariff barriers will be difficult, prolonged and unspectacular. They will have none of the simplicity and appeal of a clarion call to get rid of all tariffs by a certain date. One problem is the sheer number and diversity of the restrictions—for example, outright quantitative limitations on imports, health and safety regulations, marketing and labeling rules, government buy-at-home practices, trademark and patent laws, border equalization taxes. Another problem is the fact that some of the practices, while protective in their effect, were originally adopted for the purpose of serving some perfectly legitimate public purpose. It will not always be easy to preserve the socially desirable effects while eliminating their incidental restrictiveness.

Perhaps the most difficult issues in the nontariff field relate to border-tax adjustments. Under GATT rules, countries are permitted to levy taxes on the import of products up to the level of taxes imposed on like domestic products. This equalization tax may be levied in addition to whatever duty is applied to the import. Furthermore, taxes levied on domestic products may be rebated when exported, and such rebates are not considered export subsidies. These adjustments at the border may not, however, be applied in the case of all taxes, but only to so-called "indirect taxes," which are essentially taxes on goods, such as excise, turnover, and value-added taxes. "Direct taxes"—that is, personal or corporate income taxes—do not qualify for adjustment. The rationale behind the distinction is that indirect taxes are shifted to the consumer in the form of higher prices, whereas direct taxes are not.

In the United States increasing concern is being expressed as to the equity of this system. As compared to most European countries, the United States relies only to a minor extent on indirect taxes qualifying for adjustment. Yet many economists question the validity of the underlying distinction between direct and indirect taxes, a common view being that the difference in shiftability is one of degree. In short, many American businessmen feel disadvantaged by a system under which their goods are taxed on entry into a European country, whereas European goods are not only free from a comparable tax in the United States but also enjoy tax rebates when exported.

It is a lot easier to pose the border-tax issue than to come up with a negotiable solution that makes economic sense. But a serious effort to deal with nontariff barriers should be made over the next few years.

A change may also be desirable in the GATT provisions regarding the type of temporary restriction that may be resorted to in order to defend the balance of payments. Under the existing rules, quotas may be used but tariffs may not, mainly because at the time GATT was negotiated quotas could generally be imposed quickly through administrative action. They were also viewed as less permanent measures than tariffs and as more certain in their short-run effects on the balance of payments. However, given the well-known advantages of tariffs which rely on the market, as compared to quantitative restrictions which require controls, various countries (for example, Canada and the United Kingdom) have in recent years sought and obtained GATT waivers to enable them to impose temporary import surcharges to defend their reserve positions. In a world of fixed exchange rates, there would appear to be merit in introducing some additional price flexibility into the balance-of-payments adjustment mechanism. However, whether this should be accomplished by legitimizing temporary uniform import surcharges (and export subsidies), presumably under carefully prescribed conditions, would depend on the broader approach that is taken to international monetary reform.

An awareness of what constitutes a well-functioning international monetary system is less general and certainly more recent than an appreciation of the advantages of a liberal international trading system. The latter has been widely accepted since the nineteenth-century classical economists began to expound the theory of comparative advantage; but it was not until the breakdown of the gold standard after World War I that serious attention was given to the question of the efficiency of the international monetary order. Yet the two are closely linked. Without a well-functioning international monetary system, balance-of-payments disequilibria would have to be rectified either by imposing barriers to international trade and capital movements or by adopting excessively sharp domestic deflationary or inflationary policies. Either alternative is inefficient in that it leads to a misallocation or waste of resources. Since the extreme deflationary or inflationary route is politically repugnant today, the risk is high that rectification of payments disequilibria will be pursued, at least in part, through trade and capital restrictions. In the case of the United States this has in fact happened: our foreign aid is tied to procurement in the United States, and mandatory limits are imposed on the outflow of capital.

The weaknesses of the present international monetary system have been sharply exposed in recent years by the persistence of large U.S. balance-of-payments deficits. But the two problems are not identical. Even if the United States achieves a sustained international payments equilibrium,[8] the need for monetary reform would remain. And no reform of the international monetary system would by itself obviate the need for the United States to bring its payments position into better balance.[9]

Of the two problems, the U.S. balance-of-payments position has generally been regarded as the more pressing. Although the United States had substantial annual surpluses in net exports of goods and services throughout almost all of the period 1958–67, the surpluses were inadequate to cover the net outflow of capital and government expenditures overseas for security purposes. Furthermore, the trade surplus deteriorated after 1965, while overseas military expenditures for the Vietnam War mounted. The net result was a succession of deficits so large as to lead to a shrinkage in our gold reserves over the decade

8. "Equilibrium" does not imply the elimination of the U.S. balance-of-payments deficit. Rather, it means that over time the deficits would be equal to the additional dollars that the rest of the world wishes to add to its private and official holdings at existing exchange rates and without the imposition of government controls on trade or capital movements.

9. The degree of automaticity by which the adjustment is achieved would, of course, be affected by the nature of the reform.

1957–67 from $24 billion to less than $11 billion, while our liquid liabilities to foreign central banks and governments increased from $9 billion to $16 billion.

Despite the virtual disappearance of the U.S. trade surplus in 1968, the over-all balance of payments improved markedly as a result of developments on the capital side. As measured on what is known as the liquidity basis, the U.S. position changed from a deficit of $3.6 billion in 1967 to a small surplus. On the so-called official settlements basis, the balance of payments improved from a deficit of over $3 billion in 1967 to a surplus of $2 billion in 1968.

There is some question as to the extent to which these favorable figures reflect a true strengthening of the U.S. external position. One offset to the reduced surplus on goods and services is partly cosmetic, consisting of shifts of foreign liquid dollar holdings into special medium-term U.S. government securities or in time deposits in U.S. banks having a maturity slightly longer than one year. Another influence has been the mandatory limitations on direct foreign investments by U.S. companies and the restrictions on bank lending imposed by presidential order at the beginning of 1968. Together, these factors account for well over $2 billion in the improvement over 1967.

More promising from the long-run point of view has been the dramatic and unexpected increase in foreign private investment in the United States, particularly in equity securities. It is difficult to tell how much of this was due to special circumstances in 1968, such as the disturbances in France in the spring and the Russian invasion of Czechoslovakia in August. Some of the increased flow undoubtedly reflects more fundamental reasons, such as the rapid growth in savings in other industrial countries and the expansion of U.S.-oriented mutual funds.

Balance-of-payments projections are notoriously subject to error, because they attempt to anticipate the relatively small residual between certain designated receipts and payments, and because they are heavily affected by policy changes abroad as well as at home. Early in 1969 the Council of Economic Advisers referred quite properly to "the uncertain prospects for the balance of payments." What is clear, however, is that the persistence over so many years of the adverse U.S. payments position has already taken its toll. It has led us to limit American foreign investment, tie foreign aid and government procurement, and slow the pace of economic growth. We have also been in the position of having to cajole European countries into taking various steps which they resist, and we are under constant pressure to reduce our troop levels abroad. Finally, the persistence of the U.S. payments disequilibrium has delayed and made more difficult the longer-run reform of the world monetary system.

For some years it has been recognized that monetary reform would have to address itself to three interrelated deficiencies of the gold-exchange standard: its failure to assure adequate international liquidity to keep pace with the desire of countries for increases in reserves as their trade increases and their economies expand; its susceptibility to crises resulting from disruptive shifts from one reserve asset to another, in particular from dollars to gold; and its lack of an adequate mechanism for adjusting payments disequilibria. The three deficiencies are commonly designated as the problems of liquidity, confidence, and adjustment.

The liquidity problem stems from the fact that our international monetary system has been based fundamentally on gold, and that the world's supply of gold has been increasing in recent years much less rapidly than the world's requirements for international reserves. Additions to monetary reserves in the form of gold averaged annually only 1½ percent for a number of years, and in recent years gold reserves have actually declined.[10] Reserves in the form of gold have been supplemented by additions to reserves in the form of foreign official holdings of dollars convertible into gold at $35 per ounce. But this source has also dried up because the system by which both gold and dollars form the basic reserves is open to a fundamental contradiction: the United States as the reserve-currency country can supply additional dollars only by running a continuous deficit; but by so doing the ratio between U.S. gold and U.S. dollar liabilities deteriorates, causing an unwillingness on the part of foreign governments to accumulate additional dollars as doubts arise as to the ability of the United States to convert them freely into gold at par.

Apart from this inherent weakness, the present system is opposed by Gaullists and others on political grounds. In their view the system frees the reserve-currency country from the financial constraints to which other countries are subject, because of the ability of the reserve-currency country to obtain automatic credit in the form of liquid liabilities to foreigners that are the counterpart of its balance-of-payments deficit. Thus, the French regard the system as having enabled the U.S. government to pursue the war in Vietnam, and U.S. businessmen to buy up firms in Europe without regard to the balance-of-payments consequence of these actions. Prior to their own financial crisis of 1968–69, the French demonstrated their distaste for the system by calling for

10. By way of comparison, annual increases in world trade have amounted to about 8 percent.

a return to the discipline of a true gold standard and by themselves converting into gold as large a proportion of their official dollar assets as possible.

In the face of a growing disenchantment with the reserve-currency system, various ad hoc arrangements, such as bilateral credits and currency swaps, have evolved to provide temporary access to additional means for settling payments imbalances. The most important general supplement to gold and dollars, however, has been drawing rights on the IMF. Over the years, the Fund's resources for this purpose have been periodically increased and will soon amount to about $30 billion. But the liquidity provided by the Fund is temporary—its advances must be repaid within three to five years—and except for limited amounts, conditional on policies acceptable to the Fund for correcting the payments disequilibrium.

Valuable as these supplements are, they do not meet the desire of countries for regular increases in their owned reserves which can be used unconditionally. Unless some new source of reserves is created, countries can increase their owned reserves only by shifting reserve assets from one another through forcing deficits on their trading partners.

It was to meet this problem that the member countries of the IMF, after four years of negotiation, agreed to the plan for the creation of Special Drawing Rights (SDRs), a new asset that can be added to reserves without drawing liquidity from others. The SDR arrangement constitutes a major advance in meeting the problem of world liquidity by making it possible to create international means of settlement by conscious, collective decisions, just as domestic money is created by conscious decision.

The amounts of SDRs to be created is subject to determination by an 85 percent vote of the IMF members, an arrangement which gives a veto power to either the United States or the EEC. In July, 1969, the principal financial nations agreed to support the activation of $9.5 billion of this new kind of international money over a three-year period, an amount representing an annual addition of almost 5 percent to world reserves. The allocation of SDRs will be in accordance with the individual countries' IMF quotas.

Among the questions debated in connection with SDRs is whether their distribution should be linked in some way to the provision of real resources to less developed countries. This idea has a great deal of theoretical appeal, but it is a subject more pertinent to the next section and will be taken up there.

The second major problem of the gold-exchange standard arises from the danger that a loss of confidence in a reserve currency will lead to a massive flight from that currency, precipitating demands for conversion into gold that cannot be met and thus bringing on a collapse of the system. The crisis of confidence in late 1967 arose because of the flight from sterling in anticipation of devaluation. In early 1968 the crisis arose because of shaken confidence in reserve currencies, both as a result of sterling devaluation and the serious weakness in the U.S. payments position. The consequence was a flight to gold in expectation of an increase in its price.

An important step in meeting the crisis of confidence was the decision of March, 1968, by the governments participating in the London gold pool to cease supporting in the free market the $35 price of gold. By agreeing not to sell gold on the private market (and also not to sell it to central banks that supply the private market), the participants plugged the major leak of gold out of official reserves. By agreeing at the same time not to buy gold in the private market, they accomplished a virtually complete separation of the private gold market, in which the price would fluctuate freely, and the official gold market, in which transactions between central banks would continue to take place at $35. In effect, the amount of gold in official reserves was frozen, and new gold production as well as gold held privately for speculation and hoarding was largely demonetized.[11] This action restored confidence in the reserve currencies by making more credible the commitment of the major countries not to raise the price of gold.

The present situation, however, is not stable. If the free market price of gold should rise substantially above the official price, central banks may not feel indefinitely bound by the agreement. Sales of South African gold on the free market may, however, substantially reduce this risk for some time. But the agreement as such would not prevent central banks from shifting from dollars to gold by requesting the United States for conversion in the event of a further serious deterioration in our balance-of-payments position.

Over the long run, the cleanest way of avoiding the disruptive effects of shifts in reserve assets would be through some process that would eliminate differences in the quality of such assets. This is the essence

11. The major qualification relates to the marketing of South African gold. Under an arrangement discussed at the annual meeting of the IMF in October, 1968, the IMF would buy gold from South Africa when two conditions are met: the purchase is necessary to prevent the price of gold in the private market from falling below $35; and South Africa needs to sell gold to meet current requirements for foreign exchange. Gold acquired in this way by the IMF could find its way into member country reserves if the IMF should sell the gold in order to acquire currencies of which it is in short supply.

of various plans for consolidating reserve assets put forward by Bernstein, Triffin, Machlup, and others. Although differing in detail, the essential idea is that central banks would deposit all or a major part of their reserves in the IMF. The Fund would credit each country with its share and would then simply carry out bookkeeping to reflect an individual country's deficits or surpluses. Since there would be no differentiation as to the type of asset, the plans would remove a major source of instability by bringing to an end the competitive race for gold whenever weakness develops in reserve currencies.[12]

Last, we come to the problem of adjustment or the mechanisms open to countries to reduce their payments deficits or surpluses. This problem is closely related to the problem of liquidity, since the purpose of international liquidity is to finance deficits that are in the process of being corrected. But it is far more complex than the liquidity problem, since it involves on a continuing basis highly sensitive issues of national policy, including the degree of unemployment, the rate of growth, the extent of protection for domestic industries, the freedom to invest abroad, and the scale of foreign commitments involving overseas expenditures.

The correction of balance-of-payments disequilibria is fundamentally a process of bringing domestic and international prices and costs into alignment. This process is accomplished automatically under the traditional gold standard or under a system of flexible exchange rates. Under the gold standard, the correction was brought about primarily through short-term capital movements induced by changes in British discount policy. Since the process often led to extremes of deflation and inflation, it is politically out of the question today, when high employment, price stability, and economic growth are universal and basic objectives of economic policy. At the same time, automatic adjustment through changes in exchange rates is ruled out, since the present system is predicated on fixed exchange rates.

The alternative to exchange-rate adjustments and internal monetary and fiscal measures is restrictions applying to external trade and capital movements. But certain types of restrictions can be highly disruptive to the international economic system, since they in effect transfer to other countries a large share of the burden of adjustment and may, if unilaterally adopted, lead to retaliation. In any case, they do not constitute true adjustment mechanisms in the sense of bringing

12. Among the open questions are whether foreign dollar holdings should be permitted to expand and whether the United States should be required to amortize or pay interest on dollars deposited in the reserve accounts.

about an international realignment of prices and costs, but they are more similar to liquidity in the sense of providing a breathing spell during which more basic adjustment can take place.

As a practical matter, what is needed under the present situation of managed national economies is a variety of mechanisms for correcting payments imbalances and a means of assuring a reasonable degree of consensus on their use through close consultation and cooperation among the major economic powers. Internationally agreed codes of good behavior for deficit and surplus countries may have their place, but they are no substitute for the kinds of discussion and consultation that have occurred in recent years in the OECD, the Group of Ten, the IMF, and the informal meetings centered around the Bank for International Settlements. Moreover, the problem of correcting imbalances is such that none of the weapons in the adjustment arsenal should be ruled out. What this means is that, in addition to the orthodox remedies of expansionary or restrictive domestic policies, a more recognized place should be found for temporary direct measures to cope with payments imbalances.

Among such direct measures are temporary uniform import surcharges and export subsidies, measures which we earlier indicated are preferable to quantitative restrictions, despite the GATT sanction of the use of the latter and not the former for balance-of-payments purposes. Such tax and subsidy measures should not, however, be adopted unilaterally. Better still would be the introduction into the present system of some modest degree of exchange-rate flexibility, either through the "crawling peg" or by permitting variations in rates beyond the present permissible margin of 1 percent on either side of par. The purpose would be to relieve internal policies of some of the burden of adjustment and to equalize the pressure on surplus and deficit countries, instead of allowing the pressure to fall, as at present, almost exclusively on the deficit countries.

Many of the problems that confront the Western world today arise out of the greater economic interdependence of national states. Trade, capital, and technology flow more freely now than ever before. With improvements in transport and communications, the reduction of tariffs and other artificial restrictions, and the emergence of the multinational corporation, national economies have become more open. They are much more affected by economic policy change in other countries and are in turn more limited in the effectiveness with which they can apply traditional national instruments, such as monetary policy (higher interest rates may be defeated by an inflow of funds from abroad). In order to cope with this evolving situation, a high degree of international consultation and cooperation has developed in recent years, both on an ad hoc and on an institutionalized basis. There is good reason to believe that even closer international cooperation will be necessary, as efforts are made to deal not only with the problems arising out of the economic relations among the developed countries but also those arising out of their relations with the countries of the less developed world.

3. Economic Relations with the Developing Countries

Earlier we indicated that the U.S. interest in the developing world has been compounded primarily of political-security and humanitarian elements, with a shift in recent years toward greater emphasis on the latter. In a speech on August 8, 1968, to the World Affairs Council of Los Angeles, Undersecretary of State Katzenbach addressed himself directly to the question: "Why . . . should their fate concern the United States," and he reiterated those same two components of U.S. interest, mentioning the humanitarian one first. What is of particular significance in this speech, however, is the absence of any mention of a U.S. economic self-interest in the less developed world.

The United States does of course maintain substantial trade and investment relations with the developing countries. Our exports to them in 1966 amounted to about $10 billion, or about one-third of our total exports; and our direct investments in the developing world were $21.5 billion, or almost 40 percent of the total of such U.S. investment abroad. But this economic stake can hardly serve as a major rationale for special U.S. programs to accelerate growth in the developing world. More rapid growth would certainly benefit us through increased trade and greater opportunities to invest, but the size of the benefits would not be such as to make a substantial difference to the material well-being of the American people as a whole.

Although the U.S. economic stake in the developing world is modest, the stake of the developing countries in U.S. economic policies is in many cases critical. The policies that are of particular concern to them pertain to foreign trade and international capital flows including both aid and private investment.

In order to accelerate their growth, the low-income countries seek greater access to the resources of the industrial countries through both more trade and more aid. The two are not, however, equivalent alternatives for acquiring additional resources. External capital adds to the total resources of a country, whereas, in the short run, increased trade merely permits the conversion of more domestic resources into foreign resources. It adds to the total resources only to the extent of the gains from the improved allocation of domestic resources. Over and above these "static" effects, however, foreign trade can have a substantial "dynamic" effect in increasing the productivity of a low-income country. It provides the access to the capital equipment and technology of advanced countries that is essential to the development process. And it acts as a spur to domestic investment, as a magnet for attracting foreign capital, and as an escape from the limitations imposed by small domestic markets on the possibilities of exploiting economies of scales.

Over the past decade it has come to be recognized that a major constraint on the growth process has been the inability of low-income countries to finance, through export earnings and capital inflows, the imports of machinery, equipment, and materials required to sustain their development. Of the two sources of foreign exchange, exports are by far the larger, accounting for almost four times the volume of foreign exchange accruing from aid and foreign investment combined. Although export earnings have been increasing steadily, the rate of increase for many developing countries has fallen substantially short of their growing requirements for foreign exchange to finance essential imports as well as a rising burden of foreign debt service.

The current attention to the need for export expansion represents a shift from the inward-looking approach that characterized the trade policies of the developing countries in the 1950s. Under the impact of ideas emanating from the Economic Commission for Latin America (ECLA), import substitution was widely regarded as the main path to development, and comparatively little attention was given to the need to stimulate exports. Two major advantages were claimed for a policy of subsidizing through high protection the domestic production of a wide range of manufactured goods that had been formerly imported. First, it would lead to "balanced growth" and industrialization as opposed to the natural tendency toward specialization in primary commodity production for export, a pattern that was widely regarded as synonymous with underdevelopment. And second, it appeared to be a good way of coping with the balance-of-payments pressures that inevitably accompany the effort to force the pace of development. Import substitution would, moreover, help to insulate the domestic economy from the hazards of unpredictable foreign-exchange earnings resulting from fluctuating world prices for primary commodity exports.

As a result of two developments in the latter half of the 1950s, the limitations of this approach became increasingly apparent. One was the realization that the strategy of industrialization through import substitution could be pushed only so far before running into a dead end.

Because of the small size of domestic markets, industrialization in "watertight compartments" meant high costs and inefficiencies, and the possibilities of development along these lines were quickly exhausted.

The second factor was the serious deterioration in the export performance of developing countries: the rate of increase of their export earnings declined from 4.2 percent annually in 1950–55 to 2.9 percent in 1955–60, with a concomitant sag in the growth of per capita income from 2.5 percent to 1.8 percent. These trends were the product of a sluggish growth in external demand for the primary products of developing countries combined with an adverse movement in their terms of trade. As the end of the 1950s drew near, it became clear that the principal trade need of the developing countries was not so much the encouragement of further import substitution as the stimulation of an increase in their exports in order to pay for the imports essential to development.

As their trade situation began to deteriorate in the mid-1950s, the developing countries became increasingly disillusioned with the underlying principles of the world trading system as laid out in the GATT under U.S. leadership. In the view of many leaders of the developing world, the GATT system nicely accommodated the requirements of those countries that had already achieved economic maturity, but it failed utterly to address itself to the need to make international trade a more effective instrument for promoting growth in the low-income countries.

The rules and practices of GATT as originally adopted after World War II were essentially a reflection of the classical doctrine that unhampered international trade tends to bring about an optimum allocation of resources within countries and therefore to maximize income. By following liberal and nondiscriminatory trade policies, each country would be induced to concentrate on producing those goods in which its comparative advantage is greatest. But in the eyes of many leaders of the developing countries, by treating all countries alike, these policies tend to perpetuate existing patterns of production in the world and therefore the existing inequities. In this line of thinking, the trouble with the classical theory is its static view of the world; it takes as given the existing distribution of resources among countries. Yet the whole point of the newly awakened drive for development is to alter the existing pattern and therefore to change the structure of comparative advantage. This means changed technologies, new industries, and altered consumption patterns in the less developed countries.

To be sure, a respectable place is found within the established system for the protection of infant industry, but as a mere exception to the basically static body of doctrine. And while in the classical system the structure of comparative advantage and therefore of trade can change in response to dynamic forces such as new investment, these changes are viewed as passive responses to outside factors. What is needed is an overhaul of the international trading system, so as not merely to permit an accommodation to autonomous forces of change but also so that trade principles and policies will themselves operate to induce economic development.

GATT's early approach to economic development was a reflection of the tendency until about the mid-1950s to think of development largely in terms of industrialization through import substitution. The prime concern of GATT in relation to the less developed countries was therefore to assure that the obligation to reduce trade barriers or to limit their use would not impede the freedom of low-income members of GATT to protect their infant industries. This was the rationale of the original Article 18 of GATT and of the subsequent revision adopted in 1955, which further loosened the constraints on developing countries against the imposition of import restrictions considered necessary to advance their growth.

As the idea began to penetrate that the need for export expansion was at least as important to the developing countries as the need for protection against imports, a number of radical departures from traditional GATT rules and principles were pressed by the developing countries and ultimately accepted by the United States and other major powers. Two in particular deserve mention here, because they reflect a basic evolution in the policy of the United States and other advanced countries away from ideological preconceptions and toward a greater willingness to accommodate on a pragmatic basis the trade needs of the developing countries.

The first principle was the reciprocity rule, which had traditionally governed the process of negotiating tariff reductions under the aegis of GATT. Even with respect to negotiation among advanced countries, the doctrine of reciprocity is open to serious conceptual as well as statistical ambiguities. Nevertheless, the principle has been retained, and a rough modus vivendi has been worked out. But in negotiations between advanced and less developed countries, the reciprocity principle combined with the "principal supplier" rule has often meant that products of specific interest to developing countries fell outside the scope of the negotiations.

Through the application of the most-favored-nation clause, the developing countries did become incidental beneficiaries of important tariff concessions negotiated among advanced countries. But they urged explicit recognition of the principle that they should be able to seek tariff concessions from the advanced countries without offering equivalent concessions which might entail sacrificing the protection of their infant industries. In support of this position, Dr. Prebisch put forward the argument in the early 1950s that unilateral tariff concessions by the advanced countries carried with them "built-in reciprocity," in the sense that poor countries could be depended on to buy more from the rich countries if they were enabled to sell more. Unlike the rich countries, they could not afford the luxury of accumulating export earnings in the form of excess foreign-exchange reserves. Whatever the reasons that ultimately swayed the United States and other advanced countries, the special position of the developing countries in tariff bargaining was acknowledged, and early in the 1960s the requirement of reciprocity from them was dropped.

The second principle that has been modified is that of nondiscrimination. In essence, the developing countries argued that the universal application of this principle[13] was unjust, in that it called for the equal treatment of unequals. In not recognizing their need for preferred rather than simply equal access to the markets of advanced countries, the traditional approach as reflected in GATT was regarded as equivalent to Anatole France's majestic equality of the law, which "forbids rich and poor alike to sleep under bridges."

At the first session of the U.N. Conference on Trade and Development (UNCTAD) in 1964, the United States emerged as one of the few countries to oppose tariff preferences in principle. As the pressure of the developing countries mounted and as the United States felt increasingly isolated, it gradually shifted its position from one of ideological opposition to preferences to a willingness to see if a practical way could be found to meet the demands of the developing countries. As expressed by President Johnson at the Punta del Este meeting in 1967: "We are ready to explore with other industrialized countries, and with our people, the possibilities of temporary preferential tariff advantages for all developing countries in the markets of all the industrialized countries."

Changes in ideology can help, but they cannot in themselves provide the answer to the developing countries' need for a more rapid growth in exports. In part, the problem is inherent in the heavy dependence

13. The main exception permitted under GATT is for customs unions and free trade areas.

of low-income countries on exports of primary products, the prospects of which are unlikely to be significantly improved either by changes in tariff bargaining techniques or by preferences.

Concentration on primary products inevitably means unstable foreign-exchange earnings for the less developed countries in the short run and, especially for exporters of agricultural raw materials, slow growth in world demand for their products over the longer run. These prospects reflect deep-seated forces that the less developed countries feel powerless to cope with on their own. In particular, they are unable, because of the very fact of their underdevelopment, to shift resources readily from products that are redundant to others with a more favorable market outlook. For some primary producers, a slowly growing demand combined with an inability to control increases in supply have led to declining terms of trade, in which the prices of their exports have fallen sharply relative to the prices of their imports.

The United States has attempted to help meet the commodity problem of the developing countries in a variety of ways. To help cope with the wide and destabilizing fluctuations in their export earnings, the United States supported the establishment of the compensatory financing facility of the IMF to provide assistance to countries experiencing severe export shortfalls arising from causes beyond their control. By the late 1950s, moreover, the United States had abandoned its previous opposition in principle to international commodity agreements and later even took the lead in the successful negotiation of the International Coffee Agreement. Despite many early frustrations and difficulties, the Agreement has succeeded in stabilizing world coffee prices and in increasing the export earnings of developing countries by perhaps half a billion dollars a year.

Recently an international sugar agreement was negotiated, and the outlook is favorable for agreements in cocoa and perhaps a few other commodities whose market characteristics lend themselves to such arrangements. Notwithstanding the French predilection for the "organization of markets," however, price-regulating agreements are not a panacea for the problem of primary commodities. What is needed in the long run is action to limit the output of those commodities whose market prospects are unfavorable and to encourage diversification into more promising lines of production. This is a slow process but one to which the United States has given active support, both in its bilateral aid programs and also through multilateral development institutions.

In theory, the long-run commodity outlook of the low-income countries can be improved not only by action to limit excess supply but also by steps to increase demand. Prominent among such measures would be greater access to the markets of advanced countries. Primary agricultural exports face a wide range of restrictions in those markets, including quotas, excise taxes, and discriminatory arrangements favoring particular low-income countries at the expense of others. Pledges to moderate or eliminate such restrictions were made by the advanced countries both at the UNCTAD conference and, more recently, in the new GATT article on trade and development. Despite high-sounding expressions of principle, little progress can be reported. The basic pattern of restrictions remains—either because of a fiscal interest in maintaining revenues, or, more commonly, because of the overriding desire of governments to protect competing domestic producers. Moreover, given the internal political pressures in advanced countries, it is probably unrealistic to expect any major dismantling of agricultural restrictions in the near future.

Diversification into manufacturing could lead to a more rapid expansion of exports from developing countries while moderating the sharp short-term swings to which primary commodity trade is peculiarly vulnerable. Even aside from foreign-exchange considerations, developing countries regard the growth of manufacturing as essential in the modernization process, because of its "linkage" effects in inducing investment in related sectors—that is, in industries supplying the inputs and using the outputs of the manufacturing sector.

Recent trends support the view that manufacturing is the most "dynamic" export sector of the low-income countries. Excluding processed metals, exports of manufactures to the developed countries increased 14 percent annually in 1960–65, outstripping even the growth rate of petroleum exports. But the absolute volume of exports of manufactures is still low and heavily concentrated in a small number of developing countries: Hong Kong, India, Mexico, Taiwan, and Pakistan.

Obstructing efforts to broaden and accelerate the expansion of the developing countries' exports of manufactures are two main roadblocks; restrictions imposed by the advanced countries, and questionable policies in the developing countries themselves. Thus far, most of the attention of the international agencies, including UNCTAD, has concentrated on the first set of barriers, though the obstacles erected by the developing countries themselves are at least equally important.

Some progress was made in the Kennedy Round in opening up the markets of the advanced countries to the products of the newly emerging manufacturing industries of developing countries. By and large, however, the concessions resulting from that negotiation will be of principal benefit to trade among the advanced countries themselves. Moreover, exports of cotton textiles, the most important manufactured product from developing countries, continue to be subject to the restrictive provisions of the Long-Term Cotton Textile Arrangement, which was renewed in 1967 in conjunction with the Kennedy Round.

As the UNCTAD has demonstrated, effective tariffs in the advanced countries on manufactured exports from low-income countries are still high. How should they be brought down? One need not be enthusiastic about the preferential approach in order to favor it as a practical expedient under present conditions. If improved access to the affluent markets is to be given for the manufactured products of developing countries, it may be academic to debate whether tariff preferences are the best way of providing it. There may be no alternative, since, so soon after the Kennedy Round, industrial countries, and particularly the EEC, may not be prepared to enter into another general negotiation of commitments to reduce tariffs on a most-favored-nation basis.

In the recent negotiations on preferences, all the major industrial countries tried to agree on a common set of principles. Though some progress was made, the discussions brought to the surface differences of view on such basic issues as product coverage, depth of tariff cut, the nature of safeguards against market disruption, and the disposition of existing systems of preferences, including reverse preferences, maintained by the EEC and the British Commonwealth.

If the resolution of these outstanding issues is regarded as a precondition for the adoption of generalized preferences, it may well be a long time before anything tangible gets accomplished. An internationally agreed preferential arrangement is bound to be more complicated than the Rio Agreement of 1967 on a new international monetary facility. Yet the latter took four years to negotiate and another couple of years to bring to the point of activation. In the case of the Rio Agreement, however, a consensus among the major financial powers was an absolute necessity, because of the inherent nature of the liquidity problem. The case of preferences is different. Arrangements do not rest fundamentally on mutual accommodation among the industrial countries, but simply entail the grant of trade concessions from those countries to less developed countries. If the United States believes preferences would help developing countries, why not extend them unilaterally, without waiting to resolve all the sticky issues that have been opened up in the effort to arrive at a common position with other industrial countries?

The main objection to the unilateral approach has been the burden-sharing argument: if the United States alone opens its markets preferentially, it will become the target for a flood of low-price exports, whereas, if all industrial countries move at the same time and on the same basis, the "burden" of accepting cheap imports would be spread more evenly. This argument is not persuasive. The United States, France, Germany, and the United Kingdom have already agreed that some provision for safeguarding against market disruption would have to be an integral part of any preferential scheme. A country would be protected, therefore, against having to assume an undue "burden" of imports by its right to invoke the safeguard.

Improved access to the markets of advanced countries, even on a preferential basis, is unlikely by itself to be a major stimulus to exports of manufactures from low-income countries. Crucial to the success of such measures are the trade and financial policies of the low-income countries themselves.

Policies of import substitution frequently operate at cross-purposes, with the avowed objective of promoting exports of manufactured products. Reliance on a highly protected domestic market tends to relieve an industry of the disciplines required for achieving international competitiveness. This is not to say that import substitution is undesirable. Newly established industries often do require some initial protection before they can stand on their own feet and compete on equal terms with foreign manufactures. And balance-of-payments considerations often impel developing countries to seek to save foreign exchange by producing at home manufactured goods that were formerly imported.

The issue today is not whether developing countries should pursue policies of protection or of free trade. After all, neither the United States nor continental Europe industrialized under conditions of free trade. For the developing countries, the issues are rather which industries to protect, by how much, and in what way to effect the transition from import substitution to export promotion. As the flow of aid to developing countries levels off, it becomes even more urgent that the UNCTAD and other international organizations should address themselves to these questions.

The falling off of U.S. foreign aid appropriations to the lowest level in two decades reflects in part a disenchantment with the program and in part a massive shift in American priorities in favor of concentrating budgetary resources on long-neglected domestic activities vital to a healthy society at home. In any case, after twenty years in the foreign aid business, the need for the United States to take a fresh look at the program is generally acknowledged.

Earlier we discussed the complex and shifting rationale underlying the U.S. interest in economic progress in the low-income countries.

Now we address in broad terms the questions as to how successful foreign aid has been as an instrument of development and how the program can be made more effective.

Conclusive evidence as to the contribution of foreign aid to development is hard to adduce, because of the difficulty of isolating the effects of this single factor from the multiplicity of external and internal forces that affect a process as complex as economic growth in the developing world. Yet such evidence as exists is strongly positive. Vast areas of the world that have stagnated economically for centuries have in recent years achieved over-all growth rates in GNP equal to those of the advanced countries of Europe and North America. Per capita growth rates have lagged, but this reflects the explosive increase of population in the less developed world. Even on a per-capita basis, however, the gains are equal to the long-term historical record of the West.

Aid makes a twofold contribution to development. The first is the margin of resources which it introduces into an economy. Here the main benefits arise, not through the simple addition of foreign capital, but through the way in which the foreign resources make possible a fuller utilization of domestic resources which would otherwise have remained idle or have been used less productively. According to a recent AID study, "because foreign assistance permitted the fuller use of domestic resources by relieving critical bottlenecks in equipment and other goods, there was a one-to-one relationship between the assistance dollars provided and the additional dollars of gross domestic product in the countries the United States was aiding."[14]

A second contribution of foreign assistance is the improvement of the over-all development strategy and policy brought about in the recipient country as a result of the influence brought to bear by the donor as part of the aid-giving relationship. This leverage function of aid is probably at least as important as its resource contribution. One reason is that aid from all external sources amounts to less than 25 percent of the total investment or the foreign-exchange availabilities in the developing countries as a whole. How the latter use the 75 percent or more that is internally generated is clearly as important as how they use the remainder that is provided through external assistance.

Another reason for the importance of leverage is the need to improve various policies affecting development performance in addition

14. Charles D. Hyson and Alan M. Strout, "Impact of Foreign Aid on U.S. Exports," *Harvard Business Review*, January-February, 1968, p. 67. The study covered thirty-three developing countries over the period 1960–65.

to those specifically bearing on the allocation of investment and foreign exchange. Much of the recent improvement in the growth rate in Pakistan, for example, has been ascribed to the import liberalization program which was adopted in agreement with the major aid donors. Among other policies which can profoundly affect development performance and prospects are fiscal and monetary policies, exchange-rate policies, population and education policies, and policies affecting the climate for private enterprise.

Per capita growth in GNP is the most commonly used measure of development performance but, even in strictly economic terms, it is an imperfect gauge. As a measure of the extent to which long-run objectives of a political and social nature are being achieved, it is even less reliable. Much more attention in assessing development performance needs to be given to the evolution of political systems within the countries of the Third World and to the extent of the efforts being made to improve the opportunities and welfare of the most deprived groups in those societies. The Alliance for Progress gave explicit expression to objectives of this sort, but they are for the most part ignored in the economists' conventional indices of development performance.

As an instrument for influencing development policy, bilateral aid as practiced by the United States and other major national donors suffers from certain deficiencies as compared to multilateral aid. A major limitation is the diversity of objectives, which inevitably tends to weaken the effectiveness of the bilateral aid-giving process in promoting development. In the case of the United States, for example, half of the aid resources are transfered in the form of Export-Import Bank loans and surplus agricultural commodities under P.L. 480. Yet the prime objective of the former is export promotion, and a principal consideration in the latter is the noninterference with U.S. commercial exports of farm products. Even the economic assistance funds appropriated to AID are administered subject to a variety of considerations that may be only remotely related to economic and social development. "Supporting assistance" has always been closely related to military operations in recipient countries and has in recent years been allocated largely to Vietnam. And from time to time AID development loans have been used in support of short-run political objectives, such as the consolidation of the position of new and friendly regimes in developing countries.

Because of the singleness of purpose of multilateral development institutions as contrasted with the diversity of relationships between national governments of donor and recipient countries, the multilateral institution may be in a better position to exert influence to induce improved development performance. Its advice may, moreover, be more acceptable because it is less likely to appear as an affront to national sovereignty. Multilateral agencies such as the World Bank represent both parties and therefore can more credibly convey a sense of participation by the developing countries themselves in the decision-making process. But the potential advanges of international institutions in exerting leverage can be realized only if they depart from their traditional banking function and assume much more active roles in development, including country programing, field missions, and a greater capability to engage in program lending.

As practiced by the United States, the aid-giving process has suffered another disadvantage, which, while not inherent in bilateralism, nevertheless contrasts with the prevailing situation of multilateral institutions. Congress has been willing to make multiyear commitments to international financial agencies such as the soft-loan windows of the World Bank or the Inter-American Development Bank, but it insists on keeping the U.S. aid agency on the short tether of annual appropriations. As a result AID has at times been under pressure to commit or disburse funds more hurriedly than was warranted by objective considerations of aid effectiveness.

The advantages, however, are not all with the international institutions. Some of the latter are excessively prone to allocate jobs according to nationality and to try to accommodate all their potential beneficiaries by a national rationing of resources with little regard to relative needs. Because agreement must be obtained from many member governments, multilateral agencies may also be less flexible and innovative. It should be recalled that it was the United States that pioneered in technical assistance, in soft lending, in nonproject assistance, in establishing a Peace Corps, in country programing, and in many other ways. There is much to be said, therefore, for preserving a separate U.S. aid program while moving toward a larger proportion of multilateral aid by channeling through international institutions the bulk of additions to U.S. aid.

More important than the issue of bilateral versus multilateral aid is the need for larger total capital flows to the developing countries. The World Bank estimated recently that the developing countries could effectively use an additional $3 billion to $4 billion of external capital over and above the approximately $11 billion provided from public and private sources in 1967. Other estimates of the external capital needs of low-income countries during the 1970s range between $15 billion and $20 billion. These projections, largely the work of U.N. bodies and academic sources, are based on a variety of assumptions, including certain target rates of growth in the developing countries.

The lower end of the range corresponds approximately to 1 percent of the national income of the industrial countries in the early 1970s, whereas the upper end corresponds to 1 percent of their GNP. The latter ratio was endorsed at the last UNCTAD Conference as a reasonable target for aid-giving on the part of the rich countries.

At a time when appropriations for aid have been moving downhill, it may seem utterly unrealistic to be talking about increases in capital flows to developing countries. Though the climate for foreign aid may improve after Vietnam, competing domestic claims on the budget will inevitably mount. It would seem, therefore, that the long-term solution to the adequate financing of development may lie in creating supplementary sources of funds more independent of the annual budgetary process than are conventional appropriations.

One such possibility is to set up a corporate development entity outside the federal budget, one that would be empowered to raise funds by the issuance on the U.S. capital market of securities guaranteed by the U.S. government. Both the World Bank and the Export-Import Bank raise the bulk of their funds by tapping the private capital market and as a result have been largely free from the uncertainties, operational disabilities, and domestic political involvements that inevitably attend the appropriations process.

A scheme of this sort can be self-contained, however, only if the relending to the developing countries takes place at rates of interest which fully cover the cost of borrowing as well as expenses for administration and reserves. Though many developing countries are in a position to assume such loans, some are not, particularly those countries with poor export prospects that are already saddled with heavy debt-service obligations. For them it would be necessary to add to the scheme some interest-subsidy mechanism that would make possible borrowing at concessional rates. However this is arranged, it would require additional foreign aid appropriations, but on a much more modest scale than if all the capital were provided by the government.

Multilateral financial institutions are also hard-pressed for soft money that can be loaned to developing countries on concessional terms. A case in point is the International Development Association (IDA) of the World Bank, which has relied mainly on appropriated funds of national governments and which has encountered great difficulty in replenishing its resources on an adequate scale. One possibility for overcoming this problem is to establish an additional source of multilaterally administered soft-loan funds by linking it to the creation of new international liquidity.

As explained earlier, the world has now devised a new means of creating international money through the agreement to set up Special

Drawing Rights. When the agreement is activated, $9.5 billion of new reserve assets will be created over a three-year period to be distributed to countries in proportion to their IMF quotas. Under this agreement about one-fourth of the SDRs will go to the developing countries.

Various proposals have been made for linking the creation of new international reserve assets to the financing of development. The essential idea would be for the rich countries to transfer real resources to the LDCs in return for their receipt of SDRs. A pool of development funds could be created by requiring the rich countries to "buy" their alloted SDRs from the IMF in exchange for their own currencies. In order to insure that the funds were allocated to developing countries in accordance with rational development criteria, an international institution such as the World Bank's IDA could serve as intermediary for distributing the funds to the developing countries, which would spend them in the advanced countries. No aid-giving country could suffer any net reserve loss as a result of the operation, since at worst it would simply lose the increment in reserves represented by the initial distribution of SDRs.

The central bankers responsible for negotiating the SDR agreement are opposed to linking development aid and liquidity. But after the SDRs have become an established asset, it may well be that some arrangement will become acceptable for distributing the purchasing power equivalent of new allocations of SDRs to developing countries, provided the amounts of SDRs created would be based solely on the need for liquidity.

Another possibility for generating a source of funds independent of the annual legislation process would be through a once-and-for-all earmarking of certain sources of taxation for international development. For example, if the advanced countries were to earmark for this purpose a 2 percent tax on imports of all commodities from all sources, it would yield over $3 billion, a sum equivalent to about half the present volume of official aid to less developed countries. Moreover, because the trade of advanced countries has been increasing by 9 percent annually in recent years, the yield of the tax would rise rapidly.

Alternatively, a tax could be levied on incomes in the advanced countries. This approach would have two advantages over an import tax. First, it would conform more closely to principles of equity, since income per capita is superior to imports per capita as an index of the capacity to contribute. And second, the income base is about ten times larger than the import base for DAC countries as a group, so that the same illustrative yield of $3 billion could be obtained with an income tax equivalent to only two-tenths of 1 percent. The lower the rate of taxation, the more politically acceptable it may be.

Any of the courses of action that have been described would of course require an expression of political will through the Congress. But the problem with foreign aid is not that the public is opposed to it. It is rather that foreign aid has no constituency, no vocal and effective group, that will defend the program against the constant pressure of competing claims upon the budget.

If official aid in its present form is to survive the current onslaught and ultimately to increase in accordance with the needs of the developing countries, something more than a generally favorable public opinion would be required. An organized constituency would have to be built, composed of a variety of interested groups drawn from church organizations, business, labor, citizen groups, and educational organizations. The major difficulty, however, is how to sustain this kind of constituency and maintain its fervor for a year-in and year-out effort in support of development, a process which inevitably will be long-term and accompanied by frustration and crisis. It is because of this difficulty that consideration should be given to suggestions for financing foreign aid in ways that would minimize the need for revalidating the program each year through the regular appropriation procedure.

4. Economic Relations with the Communist World

From the standpoint of economic relations, the U.S. policy toward the communist world has for the past twenty years been one of varying degrees of disengagement and discrimination. Partly as a result of this conscious policy, the United States is today a virtual nonparticipant in East-West trade. Exports to Eastern Europe from the rest of the world have increased in recent years to about $7 billion, but U.S. exports to those countries remain at less than $200 million. Whereas the United States ships about 16 percent of total world exports, we account for only about three-tenths of 1 percent of exports to Eastern Europe.

While the United States has sat on the sidelines, the trade of the noncommunist world as a whole with Eastern Europe has more than doubled over the past ten years. It has in fact grown faster than trade either within the Soviet bloc or among the Western countries themselves. Today Eastern Europeans are increasingly looking to Western Europe for capital equipment and other sophisticated products, and even for partners in expanding their industries. At the same time West European manufacturers are actively exploring what some believe may become greatly expanded and highly profitable markets in the East.

The recent trends should be placed in perspective, however. For the European communist countries, East-West trade is clearly important, comprising over 20 percent of their total trade. For the European NATO countries, however, this trade, while far more important than for the United States, still constitutes only a small fraction (about 5 percent) of their total trade.

The low level of American trade with the Soviet bloc is partly a result of discriminatory policies in the United States. Although export controls have been liberalized in recent years, U.S. strategic controls remain a good deal more restrictive than those of Western Europe. This is as much a matter of administration as of legislation. Under our export control regulations, we not only require validated export licenses for many goods that can be freely shipped from Western Europe, but also subject our exporters to bureaucratic procedures and delays which discourage the investment of time, effort, and money in seeking trading opportunities in the East.

U.S. policy on export credits is also more restrictive. The Export-Import Bank does not extend direct loans to any communist countries, although until recently it guaranteed normal commercial credits on industrial exports to most countries of Eastern Europe other than the Soviet Union. Since March, 1968, however, a new congressional restriction has prevented the Bank's support of exports to any communist country other than Yugoslavia. While our export credit guarantee policies have become more restrictive, the governments of Western Europe and Japan have become more active than ever in using this technique of promoting their trade with the East.

The time is ripe for the U.S. government to re-examine all its policies on exports to communist countries—both its strategic controls and its export credit restrictions—so that it does not simply deny trading opportunities to American businessmen when the goods are going to be supplied anyway from other Western countries.

The United States is also more restrictive than its Western European allies in its import policy toward the communist countries. Whereas most-favored-nation treatment is generally accorded by the Western European countries, the United States extends this policy only to Poland and Yugoslavia among the communist countries. Imports from other countries of Eastern Europe are subject to the generally higher duties in the U.S. Tariff Act of 1930. There was much merit in President Johnson's request to Congress in 1966 for authority to extend nondiscriminatory tariff treatment to any country in Eastern Europe in the context of commercial agreements with it. The president would then have the flexibility to use most-favored-nation treatment as a bargaining counter for economic and perhaps other concessions from the East.

It would be wrong, however, to look entirely to American discriminatory policies as a reason for the low level of trade with communist countries. The major restraint, not only to greater U.S. trade with the East, but to greater Western trade generally, is a shortage of products in the communist countries for which they can find Western buyers. More than three-fifths of Eastern sales today consist of food, raw materials, and fuel, a pattern of exports that approximates that of the less developed countries. In general, demand for these products in the West grows only slowly, and, particularly in the United States, such basic products as food and fuels encounter a high degree of self-sufficiency.

A substantial increase in East-West trade will probably depend on progress in the East in developing exports of manufactured consumer goods, the demand for which is growing much more rapidly than that for primary products. But quick results should not be expected, because of factors inherent in the centrally planned economies. Traditionally, their capital-goods sectors have been given priority. In addition, their domestic market for consumer goods has remained undeveloped, because the whole concept of marketing as practiced in the West is alien to the controlled economies. Producers produce for the plan, and only indirectly meet consumer demand. This means that the marketing skills characteristic of the West are almost unknown in the East. The lack of sophistication in selling at home is carried over into the international field, where marketing is commonly viewed as a one-shot booking of an order, rather than as a long-term process of building up a stable trade based on market research, product development, adequate publicity, and continuity of quality and supply.

More fundamentally, a tightly centralized economy places a great premium upon the ability to predict, or at least control, situations so that they will conform to the long-term plan. Prediction and control are fairly attainable goals in the domestic sector, since the planner can exercise his political authority to make the predictions come true. This is in marked contrast to the international sector, which is not only less certain, but also beyond the political authority of the planner. For the centrally planned economy, therefore, the gains from freer trade must be offset against the loss of predictability and control.

Until the invasion of Czechoslovakia in 1968, trends in the Eastern countries were in the right direction. Though far from true market systems, they had been moving away from rigid, highly centralized plans. How serious a blow has been dealt to those economic trends remains to be seen. To the extent that the Eastern countries can continue to adopt more decentralized, market-oriented systems, such as those in Yugoslavia, the possibilities of responding to selling opportunities in the West will be increased.

If the scope for East-West trade is increased, it will become all the more important to negotiate understandings on a host of problems peculiar to this trade. What sort of reciprocal commitments can the communist countries give in return for most-favored-nation treatment? Where prices do not necessarily reflect costs, how can assurances be given against dumping? What are the possibilities of the communist countries' moving away from the present practice of bilateral balancing in trade with the West? How can Western sellers be given greater access to end-users in the East, as opposed to dealing with centralized purchasing authorities? To these and other questions there may be no simple answers. But joint discussion and some experimentation will help to resolve them over the coming years.

Two courses of action would serve to move present U.S. policy in this field along constructive lines. The first is to liberalize current export and import restrictions applying to the states of Eastern Europe. By discriminating against those countries, we not only increase tensions but also place our own businessmen at a disadvantage, without achieving any offsetting political or security gains for the United States as a whole. And second, we should propose the convening of an East-West conference which, after careful preparation, would seek to overcome some of the inherent and longer-run difficulties that stand in the way of an expansion of trade with the communist world. Increased trade will not insure peace, but in a still divided world it can help to build badly needed bridges.

As the decade of the 1970s approaches, it appears that we have come a long way from the conception of world economic order that shaped international policy in the period immediately following World War II. That conception was predicted upon the traditional view of foreign trade as based upon broad national differences in natural-resource endowments and relative supplies of labor and capital. Because resources were regarded as basically imobile internationally, foreign trade was clearly distinguishable from domestic trade. Institutionally, trade, finance, and development were sharply separated, and certain simple and sweeping rules of behavior were adopted to guide the relations among nation states in these various fields.

With the emergence of the multinational corporation and the adoption of major programs of financial and technical assistance to developing countries, the orthodox assumptions have become increasingly out of tune with the real world. Capital, technology, and highly skilled labor are today extremely mobile internationally, drastically altering traditional economic relations among politically independent countries. This change is reflected in the fact that, whereas U.S. exports currently amount to only about $35 billion, sales of U.S. foreign subsidiaries have grown to somewhere in the order of $200 billion annually. What the longer-run effect of the ready international movement of factors of production will be on trade patterns, payments positions, growth, and welfare is currently the subject of active study and debate among economists and men of affairs.

What is much less a matter of debate, however, is the proposition that the world has become too complex for the simple guiding principles that were sanctified in the charters of international economic institutions erected in the aftermath of the war. The orthodox ideology of GATT, the IMF, and the original IBRD is gradually giving way, not to new sets of universal rules, but rather to an evolving pragmatism that attempts to cope with problems in whatever way seems most effective at the time. The GATT principle of nondiscrimination yields to the urgings of the developing countries for preferential market access in the industrial countries; alternatives to the IMF doctrine of fixed exchange rates are the subject of systematic review in the 1969 Annual Report of the U.S. Council of Economic Advisers (whereas a few years ago official consideration of greater flexibility of exchange rates could not even be publicly acknowledged); and the World Bank has recently been considering whether it should enlarge its traditional function of project-lending and play a broader role in stabilizing and improving the markets for primary commodities exported by the developing countries. Even U.S. trade with the communist countries is likely before long to be lifted out of the straightjacket of the Cold War in which it has been constrained for the last twenty years.

As a concomitant of the emerging pragmatism, it is becoming increasingly apparent that the compartmentalization of international economic policy into trade, finance, and investment no longer accords with current realities. These elements of policy are inseparable, not only in relations among the industrial countries but equally in the latter's relations individually and as a group with the countries of the less developed world. The traditional fragmentation of economic policy among different ministries within governments and among different international bodies will have to be replaced by much closer cooperation and coordination.

Last, as the familiar Cold War recedes, considerations other than security have come to the fore to modify the criteria that fall within the normal purview of economists. "Equity" and "sovereignty" have become important constraints on economic policy affecting other nations, and they cannot always be subordinated to the criteria of growth and allocative efficiency.

Part 3

THE ARENAS

7

EUROPE

Laurence W. Martin

1. Introduction

There is a wearisome familiarity about discussions of American policy toward Europe. The center of immediate attention of American foreign policy may shift about the world with the incidence of crisis or the whim of intellectual fashion, but over the years Europe reasserts itself as the most important and most debated aspect of postwar foreign policy. Europe is the home of the Cold War, and events in Europe largely defined that dominating conflict. So long have the patterns set in the early years of the Cold War endured that it is difficult not to believe that they must soon shatter under the pressure of changed circumstances. Yet it has become a commonplace that, general though a premonition of change is, no one can perceive the future shape of Europe. Those who boldly sketch a new design do so only at the price of departing from plausibility in prediction or from wisdom in prescription.

Europe is a dangerous place, and America has shared its perils throughout this century. It was Europe that dragged the United States, protesting, out of its isolation and into the balance of power. The dominance of Europe in American concerns is less surprising if we reflect that until a very few years ago the European balance was virtually the world balance. A European orientation is not unnatural for the United States, given its historic and constitutional beginnings, the origin of most of its people, and its most substantial economic ties. In 1945, it was only in Europe that any serious and immediately potential foe survived. Admittedly there were also problems in Asia, but the more important prizes were in Europe. Until the advent of the long-range missile, it was only across Europe and the Atlantic that the two adversaries could readily threaten the heart of each other's power.

One can depict Europe as both the greatest success and the most serious failure of postwar American diplomacy. The failure is the inability to reach an agreed settlement for the issues resulting from World War II. The fact that the absence of agreement has resulted in de facto boundaries quite possibly more firm than negotiations could

291

have achieved is no substitute for a solution to the problems engendered by the repeated collapse of the European political system in this century. We face the dilemma of a seemingly stable arrangement that is found tolerable only so long as it is regarded as makeshift.

The postwar arrangements that emerged in Europe were clearly a second-best substitute for American preferences. Whether one believes that President Roosevelt had a naive faith in potential Russian benevolence or that, more realistically, he was resigned to conceding Russia a substantial sphere of influence in Eastern Europe, however repugnant her political practices, it was certainly his hope that an explicit agreement on a regime for Germany would inaugurate a great power concert within a universalistic system of world order. This would permit America to withdraw from what was still thought to be an unnatural presence in Europe, where, as Roosevelt told Stalin, American military power would not be a permanent feature.

These hopes were part of a more general American attitude to foreign policy. America was dragged from isolation into world politics; its persistent hope, first crystallized by Woodrow Wilson, was to escape by transforming the nature of international affairs by a kind of universalistic constitutionalism. In this line of thought Europe again played a special part, for it was European dangers and a predominantly European system against which American leaders rebelled. Revulsion from European vices has a long and respected history in America. It had no small influence on the feelings that gave birth to the United States. In our own age these venerable suspicions were echoed in Roosevelt's disapproval of his French and British colonialist allies. They may well have warmed a sense of fellow-feeling with Russia as the other outsider, repeatedly troubled by the pests of Europe proper. Had the Soviet-American conflict not arisen, it is possible to imagine that the major postwar tension would have been between America and the colonial powers, particularly Britain.

Stalin saved the British from such a fate. Revisionist historians today suggest that the threat of Soviet expansionism was illusory and that a greater readiness to concede legitimate Russian security requirements would have made a tolerable agreed peace settlement possible. Such suggestions do not carry conviction. In particular they take a mechanical view of affairs and concede too little to the sociological distinction between East and West which makes it most unreasonable to equate the extension of Russian influence with that of other powers. The nature of the two societies was the more important because the prostration of Europe compelled the victorious powers to undertake the reconstruction and day-to-day management of occupied territory. This in turn required the establishment of some degree of political confidence. Rightly or wrongly, the peoples of Europe who remained outside the bounds of Russian influence—an influence that daily proved more intrusive and oppressive—were unnerved by the proximity and grim appearance of Soviet power. By entering the war America had taken up the traditional British task of redressing the overturned balance of European power. Now the United States was compelled to continue the work in peacetime. It is because the balance has yet to be restored indigenously that America remains in Europe to this day and that varied recipes for disengagement appear impracticable.

Fundamentally, the decisions made in that early period of ad hoc reconstruction still determine the pattern of European affairs. The major one was to proceed with reconstruction without Russian participation, at the heart of which was the decision to abandon hope of an agreed order for Germany and to create a distinct West German state. This meant giving the short run priority over the long. Much of the subsequent controversy over policy toward Europe has entailed second thoughts about this momentous step. The creation of West Germany entailed the division of Europe, and the erection of a framework of security that had to embrace this new creation led to German remilitarization.[1]

Theoretically these decisions represented the postponement rather than the abandonment of hopes for an agreed European order. In theory the West was retiring to build up its strength in order to negotiate more successfully later on. The practical result has been the emergence of a de facto settlement based on division and confrontation. The German problem has been solved by the destruction and division of Germany into four parts—West Germany, East Germany, Austria, and the Lost Territories—more effectively than any agreed Morgenthau Plan could do. Just as decisively for our present problems, the decision left Russia with the ungrateful task of making something out of East Germany on the basis of a bankrupt political and economic system. Her failure to do this to her own satisfaction, at least up to the present, is one of the main reasons why the superpowers cannot legitimize their short-run achievement and leave Europe more to its own devices.

The era of reconstruction—of the Marshall Plan, the Brussels Treaty, the Vandenburg Resolution, and NATO—also did much to predetermine relations within the West itself and to form molds which may only now be breaking. It was very much an era of improvization, so

---

1. J. L. Richardson, *Germany and the Atlantic Alliance* (Cambridge, Mass.: Harvard University Press, 1966) is one of the best treatments of this subject.

short was the time to achieve so much. From VE day to the appointment of the first SACEUR was little more than five years. As a result, much of what was done was strongly influenced by the recent past, and particularly by the precedents of the Anglo-Saxon powers' joint war effort. The military institutions of NATO looked very much like the allied commands of the war, and many of the headquarters were established on wartime sites. More importantly, the strategy also was that of the previous war. For the North Atlantic Treaty was essentially a guarantee, in the form of a promise, that if Western Europe were again attacked, America would once more mobilize to repel the aggressor, but this time without the delay that occurred on the previous two occasions.

Precedent was followed in other ways. Britain took up its role of junior but foremost partner. This was natural for the only undefeated European ally, one still disposing of considerable military power. It was symbolic that the RAF carried a third of the tonnage in the Berlin airlift. Once again, a relationship was created that was to run like a thread, sometimes helpful, sometimes obstructive, through subsequent American policy. This partnership is only now undergoing what may be a final reassessment.[2]

The improvizations of the late 1940s also had their determining effects on other future allies. Germany under Adenauer gave precedence to recovery and rehabilitation of a truncated state, thereby leaving its ultimate future obscure, as was implied by the provisional nature of its constitution. France, which showed some early signs of a return to its own precedents by establishing a special balancing relationship with Russia, was drawn into the Western bloc by its need for the Marshall Plan. Russia's rejection of the plan and the parallel departure of the communists from French coalitions cleared the way for France to throw in its lot with Western schemes. Today this French policy is also undergoing a latterday reappraisal. Even on the flanks of NATO the 1940s foreshadowed the 1970s. In the north the tentativeness of Norwegian adherence lives on in thoughts of Scandinavian neutralism and the contraction of the alliance. In the south, it was over Greece and Turkey that America most explicitly took up British burdens. Yet the initial exclusion of those countries from the pact suggests that, however difficult it is for those concerned with Western

2. For a sceptical treatment of the Anglo-American relationship, see Coral Bell, *The Debatable Alliance* (London: Oxford University Press, 1964). A thoughtful account of early postwar British attitudes to joining Europe is in the first part of Nora Beloff, *The General Says No* (London: Penguin Books, 1963).

Europe to ignore the eastern Mediterranean, it is little easier to integrate it with a European or an Atlantic system.

By giving precedence to building up and consolidating the portion of Europe to which it had access, rather than to arriving at a settlement with Russia, the United States gratified a preference, apparent in many aspects of its foreign policy, for solving international problems by creating organizations and mounting operations rather than by maneuver and manipulation. The Russian rejection of a part in the Marshall Plan was a more or less superfluous reminder that ideological antipathy and divergent interests made cooperative working relations with the Soviet Union impossible. American statesmen consequently set about the erection of wholly Western structures. This architectural zeal flowed in two main directions: on the one hand, an Atlantic framework of defense, embodied in NATO; and, on the other, what was intended to be a European edifice of economic and political union. Today both enterprises, uncompleted, remain to absorb our energies.

In the field of Atlantic security one can distinguish, at least in theory, between the American guarantee, enshrined in the North Atlantic Treaty, and the standing organization established later to implement that guarantee at a time of unanticipated and early crisis.[3] This distinction has come to life again as many Americans search for a way to resume the process of disengagement interrupted in the late 1940s.

The guarantee was extracted in large part thanks to European, particularly British, diplomacy, which created in the Brussels Pact and the Dunkirk Treaty the appearance of a deserving but inadequate readiness of Europeans to help themselves. The ensuing North Atlantic Pact, a truly revolutionary passage of American diplomacy, opposed by only thirteen votes in the Senate, marked a triumph for the spirit of Clemenceau and Churchill, calling America into the European balance of power. At the beginning, however, it was a deterrent guarantee, somewhat furtively symbolized by the deployment of B-29s to England in the Berlin crisis of 1948, but not yet entailing a permanent and physical American presence. As occupation forces, the American troops in Europe marked the end of the previous war rather than a preparation for the next.

The Europeans could thus not yet be sure that the American guarantee was reliable. In deference to American constitutional scruples, the operative clause of the treaty was weak, as were the forces America

3. The standard historical work on NATO is Robert E. Osgood, *NATO, the Entangling Alliance* (Chicago: Chicago University Press, 1962).

possessed to make good its promises. Europe still needed to deepen the American entanglement, and the Korean War provided an opportunity by creating the appearance of an imminent Russian readiness to resort to force. Implementing in part the policies overoptimistically designed as a reaction to the Russian achievement of nuclear weapons, the Truman administration wove the institutional bonds that make up NATO. In today's mood of reappraisal it is an important question whether these later entanglements are essential to or separable from the fundamental American guarantee.

The flurry of activity that followed the Korean crisis created expectations about European defense that have subsequently been neither realized nor abandoned. President Truman, again on the wartime precedent, gave explicit priority to Europe over Asia. A program of military assistance was set on foot in an effort to assure that Europe would enjoy a defense, and not merely liberation or revenge, if deterrence failed. The distinction between defense on the ground and deterrence could not, in fact, be sharply drawn at that time, when nuclear weapons were still scarce and of limited power. To give the Europeans sufficient confidence to undertake rearmament—which they undertook on a considerable if dwindling scale—the United States conferred an American officer on the alliance as Supreme Commander. Henceforth SACEUR was to be an important element in strategic debate, attaining almost viceregal status in General Norstad and acquiring a viceregal capacity to see questions in a different perspective from that of the authorities at home. NATO was on the way to acquiring the bureaucratic structure and independent momentum that became an important factor in strategic debate. At the same time the United States reinforced its troops in Europe, transforming them from an aftermath of war to a standing support of peace, and setting off the great domestic debate on the course of American policy.[4]

Providing Europe with a conventional defense, doubly necessary if Russia now seemed militarily adventurous and was about to acquire a nuclear arsenal, called for far more troops than were available. The provision of the Mutual Defense Assistance Program that aid would begin only when the European allies agreed upon a strategy began the long and still persisting series of American efforts to goad

4. U.S., Congress, Senate, Armed Services and Foreign Relations Committees, *Assignment of Ground Forces of the United States to Duty in the European Area*, 82d Cong., 1st Sess.; see also Laurence W. Martin, "The American Decision to Rearm Germany," in H. Stein (ed.), *American Civil-Military Decisions* (Birmingham, Ala.: Twentieth Century Fund, 1963).

the Europeans into greater military activity. The same necessities stimulated a complicated calculation leading to German rearmament and the ultimate admission of Germany to NATO—steps which more decisively than any others cemented the division of Europe and confirmed the precedence of constructing the Western framework over the achievement of an agreed pan-European settlement. For the prospect of a defense on the ground both created a demand for German manpower, the only untapped source of men supposedly apt at warfare, and also prompted anxious inquiry as to where the defense was to be mounted. Thus was engendered the demand that plans for defense should be for "forward" defense. Unfortunately, ever since the Russians took up their present forward positions, a defense far enough forward to preserve the bulk of West Germany would be something of a strategic miracle. An underlying scepticism about defense and a preference for deterrence arose among the European allies. This still persists with an intensity roughly proportional to each country's proximity to the Russian starting line. Such doubts could be partially suppressed at the outset of a program of rearmament that might yet be fulfilled. But the wave of enthusiasm for rearmament had been the product of the Korean emergency, and with its subsidence the wave not unnaturally receded.[5]

At the same time as the United States was participating in these military ventures on an Atlantic scale, it also set afoot its parallel policy of sponsoring economic and political unification for the Europeans. This element in American policy for Europe became so prominent in the next decade that it is easy to regard it as the necessary and inevitable form of European recovery. Such an assumption is commonly supported by reference to the requirement for cooperation laid down in the European Recovery Program. There is, however, a considerable difference between such a commonsense demand for a joint attack on common problems—which could be satisfied by cooperation across national frontiers on lines congenial to some Democratic proponents of free commerce—and the drive toward real integration. This more ambitious project followed later, under the leadership of some Europeans, typified by M. Monnet, and a group of Americans who came to dominate the Economic Cooperation Administration, typified by Mr. Paul Hoffman. Thus by the time the Economic Cooperation Act was

5. On early NATO strategy, see Roger Hilsman, "On Nato Strategy," in Arnold Wolfers (ed.), *Alliance Policy in the Cold War* (Baltimore: The Johns Hopkins Press, 1959).

amended in 1949 it was indeed declared to be explicit American policy to promote the unity of Europe.[6]

Here was another decisive stroke to divide Europe, another reversal of earlier American universalistic hopes—which had opposed regionalism—and another determination to pursue the short-term goal of Western institutions instead of solutions for Europe as a whole. Including West Germany in the scheme also reinforced partition as a solution to the German problem. As such it was a convenient device, for it made possible the reinvigoration of German economic—and, later, military—strength within a framework that provided some assurance against its misuse.

The federal blueprint left some ragged edges within the West as well as on its marches with the East. Britain in particular was to prove an anomaly. For the moment she remained aloof from the federal though not from the consultative structures, largely out of the belief that she acted on a wider stage than her continental opposites. This illusion was not surprising in view of Britain's very different experience in the war, her embryonic nuclear role, and her continuing imperial responsibilities. It was only in 1947 that Britain ceased to rule India. America shared the illusion to a great extent; indeed, it was not yet completely an illusion, and the special relationship provided the United States with a useful auxiliary in Afro-Asia, an interlocutor on foreign policy in general, and a loyal advocate in Europe. All of these virtues were later to become embarrassing to both parties.

The heyday of integrationist fervor endowed America with a breed of official dedicated to European unity and a set of fixed ideas about the desirability of such a goal. With the passage of years a good deal of the optimism about ultimate federalism has evaporated, although the remarkable achievement of the European Community is not to be underestimated. Indeed, the success of the integrationist movement by the end of the 1950s made it necessary to ask what the relations between America and its foster child were to be. It then became apparent that this question had been little considered at the outset. Rather it was taken for granted that an enterprise that promised efficiency, solved the Franco-German problem, and flattered American constitutional history must accord with American interests.

One source of complacency on this account was the difficulty of imagining Europe in its weakened and fragmented state as a serious potential rival to America. Another may well have been the hope, that

6. See Max Beloff, *The United States and the Unity of Europe* (London: Faber, 1963).

still running through much of American policy, that building up Western European power might yet enable the United States to disengage
from its European entanglement. Building Western Europe into an
Atlantic alliance marked a postponement of hopes for a more fundamental settlement but not their complete abandonment. The strength
that was being created was, after all, alleged to be strength from which
to negotiate. Containment also, though a long-term policy, was a policy
of waiting for Russia to become the kind of state with which one could
do business. American policy was to make the best of a bad job and
adopt a Micawberish hope that something would turn up. Such attitudes make for uneasiness in a household, and there hung over America's European policy, for all its structures, an air of temporariness
that never ceased to unsettle America's European allies and returned
with a vengeance in the 1960s.

Such an air of contingency was not unjustified. However stable from
year to year, it is hard to regard the arbitrary layout of Central Europe,
epitomized in Berlin, as permanent. It was even more difficult before
we had twenty-five years' experience to foster confidence that the
arrangement might yet last a little longer.

Thus there was and is something tentative about American commitment to Europe. It is a commitment, one European writer has said,
that has to be renewed by each president to carry conviction.[7] This
may be an extreme view, but certainly the spate of questions and
assurances upon the accession of President Nixon suggest that many
believe it to be true.

The most entangling of America's early commitments were the
North Atlantic Treaty and its subsequent extrapolation into a standing
military organization with an American commander and a contingent
of American troops. At American insistence the treaty was for twenty
years, whereas the preceding agreements among the Europeans had
been for fifty. Sending the American troops and appointing the commander set off a great debate in which the prospective commander
himself joined to suggest the temporary nature of the arrangement.
"General Eisenhower's contention here," his deputy assured the Senate,
"is that Western Europe must be able to defend itself."[8]

This temporary arrangement has lasted to the present. Indeed, the
recent demands by Senators Mansfield and Symington that American
troops be recalled from Europe are reminiscent in the most detailed
way of the critics' position in the earlier debate of 1951. In neither

7. Bell, *Debatable Alliance*, p. 6.
8. Quoted by Max Beloff, *The United States*, p. 78.

debate did serious participants question an American interest in European security. They did and do object to the way in which it is upheld, to the investment made in European defense, and to the failure of the Europeans to protect themselves. Senator Mansfield's resolution demanding "a substantial reduction in U.S. forces permanently stationed in Europe" is intended to leave the over-all American guarantee intact. In just the same way, on January 5, 1951, Senator Taft declared that he did not "agree with those who think we can completely abandon the rest of the world and rely solely upon the defense of this continent.... What I object to is undertaking that battle primarily on the vast land areas of the continent of Asia or on the continent of Europe where we are at the greatest possible disadvantage with Russia."[9]

In the face of Russian intransigence and the complexity of European problems, America had created a structure of defense within which it began to build a new Western Europe divided from the East. The strategy rested upon an unprecedented projection of American power into the European balance. But from the beginning the commitment was reluctant and resented, and the United States has never abandoned hope of ultimate release.

There were two possible ways to achieve this escape. Either the Europeans might one day at last be ready to shoulder the task of maintaining the security of their truncated continent by themselves, fulfilling the original purpose of the assistance programs, or America might once again return in happier circumstances to the earlier postwar hope of an agreement with Russia to dispose of European affairs amicably.[10]

2. From Division to Détente

Neither way has yet proved open. Nor has a satisfactory combination of the two been devised. The problems we face for the 1970s are still very much those of the postwar years, transformed and complicated but still recognizable under changed circumstances. Questions of détente, of East-West settlement, German Ostpolitik, and a proposed European security system reflect, as it were, the frustrated spirit

9. Senator Mansfield's original resolution was S. Res. 300, August 31, 1966; see also his speech, *Congressional Record*, January 19, 1967, and *The Washington Post*, November 26, 1968; and Senator Taft's speech, *Congressional Record*, January 5, 1951.

10. A fine exposition of the tentativeness of American policy is Charles Burton Marshall, "Détente: Effects on the Alliance," in Arnold Wolfers (ed.), *Changing East-West Relations and the Unity of the West* (Baltimore: The Johns Hopkins Press, 1964).

of 1945: the ambition to resolve the fundamental conflict between Russia and the Western democracies and to break through into a harmonious era in which the wearing task of maintaining a balance of power of pure antagonism can be relinquished. The short-term compulsions of building up a framework of Western strength have continually compelled postponement of efforts to pursue this alternative wholeheartedly, and Soviet conduct has repeatedly dashed what hopes have arisen. But the task of maintaining a gladiatorial posture for years on end is so uncongenial and distasteful to a democracy that the hope of détente has never wholly perished, while the search for accommodation is continually stimulated by the day-to-day practical inconvenience of division in Central Europe.

In the interim, the imperatives of containment and alliance-building survive. Questions of alliance strategy, nuclear control, diplomatic coordination, and the shifting balance between American and European roles within the coalition still perpetuate the ambiguities of 1950, when the United States committed its military power to Europe while consoling itself with hope of an early release following the intended revival of its European allies.

The themes of détente with Russia and of Europe shouldering its own defense can be complementary. As the tension with Russia seems to relax, some Europeans are more inclined to fancy themselves equal to conducting an independent policy, just as some Americans are tempted to minimize the risk of reducing the American role. So far, however, neither avenue of escape for the United States has actually opened up. Meanwhile the entanglement continues. But, as the long haul has dragged toward the end of the first quarter-century, the search for some means of release has understandably become more energetic, the more so as America's Asian troubles have grown.

In the 1960s, while the progress of Europe toward creating an independent center of countervailing power has been much slower than many American advocates of the "Grand Design" expected, the pervasive atmosphere and language of détente has made escape by reconciliation seem closer at hand. The belief that Russian pressure is weakening has created a widespread expectation of impending change and a certain embarrassment with the established policies and outlooks of the Cold War. Merely to ask whether it is time to take up once more the resolution of East-West differences compels evolution within the Atlantic alliance. For, if the answer is favorable, the basis of alliance is eroded as the danger seems to recede. If the answer is unfavorable, many of the hopes of quick success with which the alliance was founded appear more remote than ever, and it becomes necessary to ask whether the commitments that were made for the relatively short run can be tolerable for the long.[11]

The single most enervating influence upon the alliance has been the rising sense of security from attack. The prime sources of this confidence have been the supposed establishment of stable nuclear deterrence, the renewed self-assurance of a politically and economically reconstructed Europe, and the apparent modification of Soviet policy.

Each of these factors needs closer attention. There are also, however, less substantial influences that deserve mention for the way they condition the effects of more conventional diplomatic factors. The dominance of Asian problems over American policy in the last few years has naturally diverted intellectual as well as material resources from Europe. It has also resulted in a marked divergence between American and European perceptions of the diplomatic world. During the period of decolonization, a great deal of Europe's own energy was directed toward Afro-Asia. Since decolonization has become virtually complete, however, there has been a rapidly growing conviction in Europe that the so-called Third World has relatively little to offer or to threaten. The continued and indeed intensified American involvement in Asian wars has consequently been commonly depicted in Europe as an outdated enterprise imperiling hopes of improved relations with the communists in Europe. To many Americans, on the other hand, their European allies have seemed singularly unhelpful in meeting a serious common danger.

At the same time, the widely discerned shift in public attention within Western societies from foreign to domestic affairs has accelerated the decline in concern about European security both in the United States and in Western Europe itself. Indeed, the belief that the scoreboard of international power is no longer a primary concern has possibly proceeded further in Europe than in America, where it is encouraged by an appreciation of the rapid reduction of the greatest European nations to secondary status. The phenomenon is also undoubtedly associated with the change of generations. Many voters, both American and European, have not the faintest recollection of the formative years in which the issues of the Cold War were defined and a vocabulary coined to describe them. Much of the language in which diplomatic analysis is carried on, the notions of Cold War, Iron Curtain, containment, and even of the West itself, appear anachronistic. The concept of totalitarianism has little menace for those who have

11. For one of the earliest and most widely read negative answers, see Ronald Steel, *The End of Alliance* (New York: The Viking Press, Inc., 1964).

not only never experienced its rule but never even lived in an age or on a continent where it seemed to have any real prospect of success. It remains to be seen whether even the invasion of Czechoslovakia breathes any sustained new life into the old fears.

Changed perceptions of foreign affairs affect all aspects of American foreign policy, but they have a special relevance to Europe where the categories of the Cold War were first established and where the most elaborate international structure was created for the pursuit of containment. The Atlantic alliance was created to contain the Soviet military and political threat. It could not survive the spread of the belief that the interests once thought to be at stake have somehow become irrelevant to modern society or that military power is ineffective as an instrument of policy in today's technological and political circumstances. The eagerness with which many commentators seized upon such relative success as Czech passive resistance achieved in 1968 suggests a deep desire to take this optimistic view of power relations today.

Real though this "civilianization" of substantial sections of opinion is, and however much changes in conceptions of political interest may do to create a receptive climate for an optimistic analysis of the European situation, it is supposed changes in Russian policy that do most to support the common assumption that danger has subsided. The reasons for believing that Russia is now in a more amenable mood can be crudely summarized under three heads. First is the belief that the Soviet Union, which has always found it strenuous to compete with so rich an adversary as the United States, is under increasing pressures from within its own society to devote more resources to welfare and fewer to the apparatus of external power. The same trend is thought to encourage the rise of rational, economizing, tractable leaders. Second is the belief that, partly because of these social trends and partly because of the recalcitrance of China, the Soviet Union is compelled to concede greater economic and diplomatic latitude to the countries of Eastern Europe. Third is the conviction that Russia, perceiving the rise of Western military power and appreciating the implications of nuclear strategy, has come to recognize the hopelessness of making any gains in Europe by armed aggression and to see the danger of a disastrous encounter if confrontation continues unmoderated in Central Europe.

The combination of these influences has been thought by many to have inspired a new Russian readiness to ameliorate the situation in Europe and to make agreed reductions of military forces. Such a program might have its intrinsic attractions for Russia. It would reduce the considerable financial costs involved in maintaining in Eastern Europe large, balanced armed forces, which are costly in both men and money. Russia might also see such an agreed reduction as a step toward achieving its long-declared goal of getting American troops out of Europe. If troop reductions went hand in hand with political agreements, they might contribute to putting Russian influence in Eastern Europe on a more substantial basis of consent, one less irritating to the local inhabitants and consequently more stable. In all these respects the proposal for an East-West agreement to stabilize the European military balance harks back in spirit if not in detail to the disengagement proposals of the 1950s. Some of the less optimistic plans envisage merely tacitly agreed parallel force reductions; others more ambitiously suggest an openly negotiated arrangement, perhaps accompanied by the construction of some joint machinery or forum for discussing common security problems and managing crises. Hopes of attaining some such arrangement have been strongly supported on the Western side, of course, by the independent pressures for a reduction of forces working within NATO countries.[12]

Such hopes rode high in the West in the year or two preceding the invasion of Czechoslovakia in 1968, when polycentrist self-assertion seemed to be proceeding relatively unchecked in the East. There was considerable criticism of Western policy, indeed, on the ground that more flexible policies would have allowed much earlier progress toward both arms control and political settlement. Hopes of such progress may be traced back almost to the end of the Korean War, when the armistice there and the death of Stalin produced at least a more flexible style of Soviet policy. For domestic political reasons, President Eisenhower enjoyed greater latitude in dealing with Russia than did President Truman, who also had to give priority to founding the Western coalition.

It is indeed possible that Russia would have been willing to pay some price in terms of German reunification on a neutralized basis in order to ward off German rearmament. The West, it has been suggested, failed to recognize that this was the moment of greatest relative strength from which to negotiate.[13] Rightly or wrongly, the oppor-

12. See such studies as George Bluhm, *Détente and Military Relaxation in Europe: A German View* (Adelphi Papers, No. 40; London: Institute of Strategic Studies, 1967); and Pierre Hassner's masterfully complicated *Change and Security in Europe* (Adelphi Papers, Nos. 45 and 49; London: Institute of Strategic Studies, 1968).

13. See Coral Bell, *Negotiation from Strength* (New York: Alfred A. Knopf, Inc., 1963).

tunity, if such it was, was not taken. American policy had elected to give priority to building up the West and had tied itself to Chancellor Adenauer and the Christian Democrats, who would not have accepted any steps toward unification that precluded a free hand for future German policy. In any case, the sincerity of Russian intentions was highly suspect and the rapid reverse of Russian concessions toward free elections, which seemed to have been made at the Geneva conference of 1954, reinforced Western misgivings. Not for the first time, and perhaps not for the last, contradictions appeared between the aims of Western solidarity and of agreement with Russia.

As further possibilities of modifying the situation in Germany came under discussion later in the 1950s, and as Adenauer's Germany took a cautious and conservative line on moves toward rapprochement with the East, it became apparent that, by creating West Germany, the United States had conceded it a virtual veto over future resolutions of the fundamental issues in Central Europe. This, indeed, was symptomatic of the way in which Europe as a whole was ceasing to be a mere object of great power diplomacy, especially as far as a European settlement was concerned. Merely by being the prime parties—the owners, as it were—of the main issues in dispute, the Western Europeans possess an inherent capacity to influence and frustrate any American policy toward Europe that falls short of complete abdication.

Although this remains true, initiative on the German question has shifted from the West. From 1958 to 1962 Western hopes of improving the situation in Central Europe faded in the face of Khrushchev's Berlin offensive. While, by suggesting the status of a free city for Berlin, the Russian leader produced a solution that may yet come to receive more serious attention, he did so as part of a campaign clearly designed to win considerable gains for the East. Apparently he was encouraged by a supposed or pretended strategic nuclear superiority that Russia derived from the missile gap. Yet, as the Berlin Wall demonstrates, Russia's position also was, and is, one of great weakness deriving from the instability of the East German state. Later events suggest that this alone would have precluded any reasonable bargain tolerable to the West.

The termination of Khrushchev's offensive, as a result of the Cuban crisis and the exposure of Russia's real strategic inferiority, ushered in, with the renewed atmosphere of détente, fresh hopes of a relaxation of tensions in Europe. This time, however, the retirement of Adenauer and the rise of the German Social Democrats set Germany on a new course. It took the lead in a policy of movement aimed at freer East-West contacts and an ultimate growing together of the two

Germanies. The entry of the Social Democratic Party (SPD) into a coalition with the Christian Democratic Union (CDU) in 1966 opened a new and more energetic phase in this Ostpolitik. The extreme ambition was that, by reassuring the Warsaw Pact nations of German harmlessness, by closer and economically useful ties with Eastern Europe, and by moving toward reduction of forces, including a contraction of the Bundeswehr, Russia's grip on the European satellites would be loosened, and liberalization would take place at last in the East German regime. The Johnson administration encouraged, and took no little credit for having inspired, these initiatives.[14]

By 1968 these fine hopes were greatly depressed, and the invasion of Czechoslovakia dealt them a devastating blow. The Eastern Europeans had risen to the bait and embraced the economic opportunities. Abetted by General de Gaulle's encouragement of Eastern European nationalism, Germany made real headway in penetrating the Soviet sphere. But these successes apparently served only to alarm some of the rickety Eastern European regimes and to incense the Soviet Union. In East Germany, not the regime alone but also the very existence of the state was ultimately at stake. The drastic action Russia took when the Czechoslovak government seemed about to follow the dictates of Czech popular opinion demonstrated at one and the same time the weakness of the communist political position in Eastern Europe, the importance Russia placed upon her continued unquestioned dominance in the area, and the capacity of the Red Army to trump any political card.

In any case, the latterday policy of movement represented in itself a sharp contraction of ambition from the early days of Western resistance to communist expansion. The original policies of containment or of negotiation from strength looked to the entry of the Eastern European countries, and particularly of East Germany, into the European system as liberal democratic states. It was perhaps an overly ambitious aim, especially as most of the nations in question had never succeeded in sustaining democracy in the past. Be that as it may, the policy of rapprochement with the existing regimes of the East, albeit in the belief that they were themselves becoming more progressive, implied resignation to a considerably longer time before the emergence of free societies. Above all, in the German context, that policy clearly tended toward the recognition and preservation of East Germany rather than toward its dissolution. This implied a very different con-

14. One statement of this is Zbigniew Brzezinski, "The Framework of East-West Reconciliation," *Foreign Affairs*, January, 1968.

cept of reunification from the triumph of democracy by free election throughout Germany, to which hopes had been directed under Adenauer.

The vicious reaction of the Soviet Union in 1968, abetted by several of the satellite regimes, suggests that even this modified policy was more than the communists could tolerate. Indeed, it indicates that, whatever the intention behind the policy, the reality was not moderate at all. For, given the unsoundness of the East European regimes, and above all of East Germany, the relaxation of Russian control looked for in Western efforts to establish closer relations with the Eastern countries would undermine the entire basis of Soviet dominance. As articulated by some Western statesmen the policy of movement is, of course, overtly subversive of Russian influence. Thus on his Polish journey of 1967 de Gaulle encouraged his hosts to follow his own example of breaking free from the bloc leader. "If you look far and wide, there are obstacles which today seem insurmountable, but which without doubt you will overcome. We French are in the course of doing as much." And Franz-Joseph Strauss wrote in his *The Grand Design*: "We must be careful not to assist the Communist regimes to consolidate their power or to overcome too readily the weaknesses and deficiencies of their system. . . . We must support the process of the slow dismantling of these Communist regimes."[15]

Despite the undoubted gradual emergence of a sense of separate East German identity, the Eastern regime cannot yet trust its fate in anything approaching open political competition. Indeed, it seems debatable whether the East German government would even welcome recognition if it came at the price of a further opening to the West and a dilution of Russian support.

The stumbling block to a Western policy of movement is thus, paradoxically, Eastern weakness. There are therefore very narrow limits on the extent to which Russia could permit the development of détente in Europe, even if she wanted a controlled progress in that direction. There can of course be no firm assurance that it is only fear of losing everything that inhibits Russian acceptance of reform. A policy of relaxation could serve Russian interests by reducing the high political and economic cost of her present posture, but there are indications that a harder and more aggressive approach still has its advocates. As a recent Western European study has remarked: "It would be a mistake to believe that the Soviet leaders would be nicely

15. Franz-Joseph Strauss, *The Grand Design* (New York: Frederick A. Praeger, 1966).

weighing the advantages and disadvantages of this or that pattern of forces in Western Europe. Their attitude would continue to be governed by the notion that their country was in a state of permanent competition with Western capitalism—the continuance as *Pravda* has recently expressed it 'of an era of irreconcilable ideological struggle between the two opposing systems.' "[16]

In such political circumstances it is also difficult to believe that much progress can safely be made in adjusting the military balance by an agreement resulting in lower levels of Russian forces in Eastern Europe. For the political situation ensures that the size of Russian forces is not simply reciprocal to that of the West, but depends also upon the requirements of policing the East, preferably by a preponderance so great that it is never challenged. If anything, the Czechoslovak affair must have made it appear a serious mistake to withdraw forces in the first place or to allow Russian readiness to take military action ever to fall into question. The less popular Eastern European regimes must welcome the demonstration of this readiness as a discouragement to revolutionary elements within their own populations.

At the same time, Soviet strategy toward the West remains, as it has long been, designed to roll up NATO resistance as quickly as possible in the event of hostilities. This goes without saying if the image is one of total war. If, as some believe, Russia is now more prepared to envisage limited war in Europe, an overwhelming conventional superiority gives her the option of seizing Western territory and placing the onus of escalation on NATO. Such an operation is unlikely to recommend itself, but there is little doubt that Soviet forces could execute it if they dared. There remain twenty Russian divisions in East Germany alone, ten of them tank divisions, which the Russians have assiduously improved and kept up to strength. With these and the substantial forces further east, Russia preserves her traditional capacity to hold Western Europe hostage for American good behavior and to dominate any crisis that may occur in Central Europe.[17]

It is in this respect that the two elements in Soviet strategy with regard to Western Europe merge. A frontal attack by NATO must appear highly unlikely to Soviet planners, however useful the possibility may be as an instrument of propaganda. But instability in Eastern Europe in which Western forces might become entangled must seem a very real danger to the Russians. Indeed, the more suc-

---

16. *Pravda*, May 19, 1968.
17. See among many studies T. Wolfe, *The Evolution of Soviet Military Policy*, RAND Paper P3773, 1968.

cessful the Western policy of movement is, the more imminent a military danger of this kind appears. Moreover, it is not fanciful to imagine such upheavals spreading to the dissident nationalities within Russia itself. At the very least, unrest in Eastern Europe must be doubly distasteful as a bad example for the Soviet population. Furthermore, the assurance of control over the territory and armed forces of the Eastern European states must weigh heavily with Russian strategists in estimating the speed and decisiveness with which they could establish supremacy in any trouble spot.

If this is indeed the Soviet strategic outlook, it seems highly unlikely that much progress can be made in encouraging Russia to reduce its forces, for the Russian conception of security depends precisely upon great superiority. The Russian leadership that has succeeded Khrushchev appears not to share his euphoric faith in the adequacy of a moderate strategic nuclear force to serve all purposes. It takes the conservative and cautious line of maintaining strong, balanced forces. Since 1964 the strength of Russian ground forces has risen slightly, despite other greatly increased military expenditures, and the next five years are demographically very favorable for the supply of Soviet manpower. Nor do the well-known autonomous pressures within NATO making for a reduction of its military effort give Russia much incentive to offer reduction of forces as a bargaining concession. Any Russian effort to economize on armament by agreement seems far more likely to be directed toward the strategic nuclear field than toward the conventional balance in Europe.

It might be going too far to join those who declare that Russian anxiety to stabilize central Europe would make the Soviet Union reluctant to do anything to reduce American dominance over Western Europe, and especially over Germany. Admittedly, Russia has reasons to prefer the system of blocs to one of fluidity in Europe. Her purported enthusiasm for the liquidation of alliances, as in the declaration of Karlovy Vary in April, 1967, was noticeably muted by 1969 as her confidence in bilateral and party relations waned. Yet the prizes to be won by a mutual withdrawal of American and Russian forces, given the respective geopolitical relationships of the two countries to Europe, might well prove irresistible, despite the probability that an early and presumably risky reinjection of Russian power would be made necessary by the political magnetism of Western Europe for the East. Failing such an enticing prospect as complete American withdrawal, however, the present Russian policy of a massive military presence in Eastern Europe seems likely to persist.

If this interpretation is correct, it has important implications for any

American policy toward Europe that falls short of complete abdication, for it becomes apparent that, whatever changes may have taken place since the 1940s, Western Europe would still be highly insecure unless it constituted, alone or in alliance, a powerful military counterweight to Russia. To a large extent this would be so even if Russia appeared to have abandoned ideological and expansionist pretensions, for, if the more distant of the two external powers that intervened to restore the collapsed European balance in 1945 withdrew before a new indigenous center of power had been created, the other would inevitably become a brooding shadow across the whole continent. Political instability in eastern and southern Europe—which promises to become more rather than less pronounced in the coming decade—would offer many occasions for the exercise of such predominant power. Merely by carrying on their normal way of life, the Western Europeans cannot help threatening the integrity of the Soviet sphere in ways that Russia has already displayed a readiness to denounce as aggressive. By its very existence, unchecked Russian military force would oppress life and dictate policy in Western Europe even if it were never used.

Thus, if the Western policy of eroding the Soviet sphere by example is proving successful, the resulting situation may well initiate a decade more dangerous than the 1960s. Of the three sources of Soviet restraint, the military balance appears the most reliable and the only one under reasonably direct Western control. The internal pressures on Soviet policy have proven capable, as we might have expected, of producing assertive as well as restrained external action. A framework of Western solidarity appears as necessary as ever.

3. Military Diplomacy in the West

The continued need for a sturdy framework of military security in Western Europe does not of itself determine what form it should take or what the proportion of American contributions should be to those made by the Europeans. More than ever since the Czech invasion, most Europeans are eager to retain as intimate an American connection as possible. Even General de Gaulle recognized that in the event of a major war France and America would probably find themselves fighting side by side, and it is this assurance that gave him the confidence to pursue his uncooperative ways in day to day affairs.[18] Yet this is not to say that confidence in the American guarantee is complete. The enduring American hankering after release from entangle-

18. See General de Gaulle's press conference of July 30, 1963.

ment is well recognized in Europe. There is perhaps little fear that America would stand idly by if Europe were the victim of all-out, overt, and unprovoked aggression and conquest, though talk of "parity" gives some occasion for even such extreme anxieties. What is increasingly doubted is whether America would react as sharply as Europeans might like to limited infringements of their interests or whether the American reaction would be in a form compatible with European interests. The extreme version of this anxiety is the fear, expressed by de Gaulle among others, that the two superpowers might wage a nuclear war in Europe while sparing their own homelands. American doctrines of controlled and flexible response, enunciated during the reign of McNamara to meet changing technological circumstances, have done much to keep such fears alive.[19]

The Gaullist answer to the problem of American unreliability was to take the essence of the guarantee for granted, on the assumption that it is dictated by American self-interest, and at the same time to develop as much independent capacity as possible for Europeans to defend themselves and influence the course of events. Underlying this policy is usually a confident assumption that an actual military conflict in Europe is highly unlikely. The difficulties of giving real substance and credibility to independent national military forces in Europe consequently detract very little from the appeal of the policy of independence. Most of America's European allies, including not a few French soldiers, take the threat more seriously, however. They therefore prefer efforts to retain the American guarantee and to influence its application by being cooperative, thus deepening the American entanglement in the problems of European security.

Security is the firmest basis of the Atlantic relationship. For political and economic purposes, other and very often more appropriate frameworks exist. It is no coincidence that NATO, a military alliance, is the most highly developed and virtually the only serious Atlantic institution. The hollowness of repeated exhortations to develop the "political" and cultural aspects of the North Atlantic Treaty is itself a testimony to the fact that the essence of the European-American connection is security. It is therefore no more than to be expected that the soundness of common security arrangements should be under constant scrutiny. The fundamental and persistent difficulty is that the strategic as-

19. An earlier expression of alarm by General de Gaulle: "Who can say that if occasion arises the two, while each deciding not to launch its missiles at the main enemy so that it should itself be spared, will not crush the others?" Quoted by Osgood, *NATO*, p. 258. See also André Beaufre, *Deterrence and Strategy* (London: Faber, 1966).

sumptions upon which NATO was founded have been eroded by the passage of time and that the original military goals of the alliance have been neither realized nor replaced. In 1949, although American nuclear weapons were a useful underpinning, the American guarantee rested most firmly on the threat to conduct a third European war of expeditionary forces and attrition. The American motive for issuing such a guarantee was also reminiscent of earlier twentieth-century history, resting as it did on the assumption that if Europe fell into hostile hands it would constitute an intolerable military danger to the United States. Thus the United States assumed the traditional British concern for keeping adjacent shores in friendly hands. The measures that NATO took after the outbreak of the Korean War, culminating in the adoption of the Lisbon goals of large, ready, conventional armed forces, backed up by substantial reserves, represented an effort to meet the requirements of such a threat.

If the force levels of 1952 were never achieved, they at least served as a goal. After 1953, the apparently diminishing danger from the East, the subtler tactics of Stalin's successors, and the discovery of the supposed budgetary advantages of nuclear weapons, led to a relaxation of conventional military efforts. The strategy of massive retaliation was soon supplemented by the hope that tactical nuclear weapons might compensate for conventional inferiority on the ground. This was a crucial watershed from which today's virtually interminable strategic debates flow. For the alliance had gone from a strategic calculation that, if difficult and depressing, was material—the relative orders of battle—to one that was essentially psychological—the deterrence of the enemy. The alliance had therefore committed itself to debating an almost infinite range of options, ranging from the most slender of tripwires to a substantial and prolonged conventional pause.

NATO's achievements in the 1950s were impressive and are all too often underestimated. If the forces erected were inadequate, they represented a great advance on the almost defenseless condition of 1949. Particular progress was made in building up the logistical infrastructure which, valuable in itself, also contributed to an appearance of solidarity and determination. SACEUR, always American, came to dominate the affairs of the alliance, not infrequently regarding them from a very different perspective than did Washington, and thereby doing something to reassure the Europeans that their point of view always had an advocate in American military circles. The characteristic voice of Supreme Headquarters Allied Powers Europe (SHAPE) became a constant factor in strategic discussion.

SACEUR never succeeded, however, in acquiring the forces he

needed. It hardly ever looked as if he would. Economic constraint, a reluctance to consume manpower, and the extra-European military preoccupations of Britain and France—all these impeded efforts to achieve the strength thought necessary to hold back Russia in sustained conventional combat. Inexorably, the apparently cheaper and more convenient alternative of dependence on nuclear weapons eroded military effort, even though none of the new strategic doctrines evolved was without much-debated logical shortcomings. As the basis of European security became progressively, though not always admittedly, more nuclear, Europe became increasingly dependent on the United States, which had a virtual monopoly of tactical nuclear weapons and the only fully credible strategic nuclear force. This increased military dependence arose just as Europe was becoming economically vigorous and politically more confident. The United States held the nuclear umbrella, American ground forces were projected into Europe, but Europe made no corresponding contribution to the direct defense of the American homeland, although Britain and, to a much lesser extent, France did undertake a declining number of military enterprises in Afro-Asia of which the United States approved.

The development of nuclear weapons and their proliferation, both vertical and horizontal, could not have failed to play an important role in strategy in Europe, which was the world's most valuable stake of military action. But the diminishing role of conventional forces, to which Europe's contribution was initially intended to be pre-eminent, naturally shook the balance of mutual confidence within the alliance. At the same time, the price the United States paid for extending its guarantee rose, for the ICBM laid the United States open as never before to inescapable destruction if general war broke out. More than that, the ICBM altered the American motive for incurring such a risk. For when the United States first committed itself to defend Europe, a future war was expected to be not unlike the previous two world wars. American interest in preserving Europe from hostile occupation was thus defensible on the familiar grounds of denying the enemy a base of operations, depriving him of resources valuable in a war of attrition, and securing the foothold in Eurasia without which the United States could not hope to deliver its own knockout blow. The advent of the ICBM demolished this reasoning. Not only could Russia now destroy America without conquering Europe but, equally important, the United States could now deter Russia by the threat of nuclear devastation launched from the American homeland or from the high seas.

For a brief period Europe acquired a new value as a base for intermediate-range missiles and for the aircraft that compensated for the temporary dearth of longer-range rockets. This interlude was not without significance in European-American relations, for it encouraged the extension of nuclear assistance to Britain and inspired schemes for European missile forces. But it was easily recognized as a passing phase and the foreseeable American ability to dispense with European bases began to inspire the doubts that still unsettle the alliance. Yet another link in the Atlantic relationship had become less concrete and more psychological. The balance of contributions seemed more heavily weighted toward the United States. Europeans became even more anxious for reassurance that the American guarantee was both reliable and seen to be so by Russia.

European anxieties are compounded today by recognition of the mutual interest of Russia and America in avoiding reciprocal destruction. This interest might, it is thought, be pursued in ways inimical to European security and peace of mind. The most recent manifestations of this nervousness have concerned American handling of the nuclear nonproliferation treaty (NPT). The United States pursued the treaty to the final stages of negotiation with minimal consultation of her NATO allies, and she progressively abandoned any specific provision for a possible European nuclear force. In Germany the treaty was particularly ill-received, partly because of fears of commercial discrimination, but more fundamentally because the overriding Russian purpose served by the treaty is discrimination against West Germany.

The NPT was not an isolated issue. The American decision to construct a ballistic missile defense system, which agitated European opinion, was announced without consultation in 1967 and was radically modified in 1969 with little more consideration. In 1968 the conspicuously mild American reaction to the invasion of Czechoslovakia was widely attributed to anxiety not to foreclose the possibility of negotiating limitations on strategic weapons with Russia.

The prospect of mutual Soviet-American reassurance on strategic questions began to emerge much earlier than this, however, when discussion of a test-ban treaty began in the late 1950s. As usual, the Europeans were ambivalent. For the most part, neither did they then nor do they now deplore the prospect of a safer strategic environment; but they also perceive that too great a degree of assurance on the part of Russia that the danger of nuclear war is remote could undermine the deterrence upon which the protection of Europe increasingly depends. The persistent Berlin crisis that accompanied the introduction of the first Russian ICBMs revealed a reassuring degree of American firmness, although Europeans found something to criticize in certain aspects of American diplomacy, such as the toying with a new access agreement. At the same time, however, the Russian offensive made the need for protection seem real, as it was to do again upon the invasion of Czechoslovakia. Debate about the reliability of the American guarantee therefore took on some urgency, compounded by the skeptical and independent policies of General de Gaulle.

The American response to European misgivings, formulated chiefly during the brief regime of President Kennedy, took two distinguishable forms. One was an attempt to associate the Europeans more closely with nuclear planning. The most grandiose effort in this direction, the multilateral nuclear force (MLF), embraced a number of not always complementary purposes. Some of its advocates intended it not merely to alleviate German dissatisfaction with their remoteness from nuclear control and information, but also to kill off the British and French independent national forces. Other American spokesmen hinted that the United States might help the MLF become an independent European force. The two aims were perhaps not literally contradictory, but their advocates frequently had very different ends in view. This ambivalence in American policy toward the European nuclear forces still persists.[20]

With the collapse of the MLF proposal, the United States turned to the more modest notion of a nuclear planning group to inform and consult the European allies. This project has been realized. Views of its efficacy vary, but it has certainly enabled Germany, for instance, to acquire some basic information about American capabilities and intentions of which its statesmen had previously no official inkling. Agitation about nuclear control has largely subsided in recent years. To some extent this is a tribute to better consultations and to a rather more sophisticated European understanding of the mechanism of deterrence. It must be suspected, however, that the lull is chiefly owing to the atmosphere of détente, which has made all kinds of military contingencies appear remote in the late 1960s. If this is so, then a new era of tension could well reopen the old questions.[21]

The other approach to European security comprises the various forms of controlled and flexible response, dating particularly from Mr. McNamara's speech at Ann Arbor in 1962.[22] This effort to reinvigorate

20. See Robert E. Osgood, *The Case for the MLF: A Critical Evaluation* (Washington: The Washington Center of Foreign Policy Research, 1964); Alastair Buchan, *The Multilateral Force: An Historical Perspective* (Adelphi Papers, No. 13; London: Institute of Strategic Studies).

21. See Alastair Buchan, *The Future of NATO* (New York: Cambridge Endowment, 1967).

22. Mr. McNamara's speech can be found in *Survival*, September-October, 1962.

the construction of at least enough conventional forces to obviate the early use of nuclear weapons had the double purpose of making the Europeans feel protected and—by offering some prospect of an option that would not, at least initially, be suicidal for America—increasing the credibility of an American response to Russian aggression. The implication was that, once entangled in conventional hostilities, the United States would either frighten Russia into retreat or have passed beyond the point at which it could abandon its allies.

In theory, the strategy had much to recommend it, but it won a less than enthusiastic response in Europe. To make an increase of forces seem worthwhile, it was necessary to put a hopeful estimate on what already existed—a maneuver that encouraged the economy-minded to do little more, if the calculations were believed, or made the plan seem fraudulent if, as was commoner, the American figures were disbelieved. Even in 1968, when NATO, freed at last of French obstructionism, which had long prevented formal revision of the strategy of 1957, finally adopted flexible response as the official strategy of the alliance, the optimistic calculations of relative military capability assiduously propagated by American spokesmen were still being openly derided by European officials.[23]

The chief source of European scepticism, however, was the fear that flexibility and a pledge to delay nuclear action might well encourage rather than deter aggression, while at the same time ensuring that the resulting initial stages of combat were highly destructive to large areas of Europe. From its inception NATO has had to maintain at least the pretense of a forward strategy that would protect rather than fight over the more exposed members. None of the doctrines of flexibility formulated so far has passed this test to everyone's satisfaction. This being so there is an underlying preference in Europe for deterrence rather than defense.

Europe's dilemma is a real one. With the capability for any sustained defense lacking, let alone a forward one, her security must depend either on Russian forbearance, an uneasy basis indeed, or on American willingness to carry out a suicidal nuclear threat. So far as a Russian conventional attack is concerned, the United States has come closer and closer to disavowing any such intentions. In his later utterances, designed to encourage European military efforts, Mr. McNamara appeared to restrict the role of strategic nuclear weapons to deterring

23. One statement of the optimistic American thesis can be found in Robert S. McNamara, *Statement on the Fiscal Year 1969–73 Defense Program and the 1969 Defense Budget*, January 22, 1968, pp. 80–81.

nuclear attack on the United States or its allies.[24] Even if the allies can remain assured that they will be included in this category, a considerable hole is left in their defenses. In practice, this is less than desperate, both because Russian conduct is not utterly unrestrained and because no aggressor can utterly discount the possibility that America might react more violently in the actual event of an incursion into Western Europe. There is thus a deterrence of uncertainty that retains considerable force in such a vital and neatly partitioned area as Europe. Yet the situation is far from satisfactory, not least for the United States, involved in a confrontation in which success depends on the possibility of her doing something that by rational calculation would be highly unwise. Europe, of course, has always lived dangerously and displays a great capacity to continue to do so. Such a situation, however, perpetuates an uneasy suspicion that some better arrangement ought to be possible.

4. The Rise and Fall of the Grand Design

The possible unreliability of the American guarantee, the political inferiority implied by it, and the heavy material and psychological price exacted from the United States, all combine to prompt both Europeans and Americans to ask whether the rising economic prosperity and political self-confidence of Europe have not at last brought the day when the hopes of 1950 can be realized and Europe assume its own defense. However much conventional military force the Europeans were to produce, the nuclear strength of Russia now requires that a truly self-reliant Europe, which could completely release America from its dangerous guarantee, be nuclear itself. In recent years many voices in both Europe and America have been ready to welcome such a prospect.

From America the notion of a European nuclear force was envisaged in some versions of the MLF and in many of the conceptions of Atlantic partnership. Thus at Copenhagen in 1962, Mr. McGeorge Bundy declared that "we ourselves cannot usurp from the new Europe the responsibility for deciding in its own way the level of effort and of investment which it wishes to make in these great matters."[25] In Europe, the French *force de frappe* and the less vaunted but, for the moment, more substantial British deterrent keep the nuclear option open. Such European leaders as Franz-Joseph Strauss and Edward

24. *Ibid.*, pp. 47, 49.
25. Cited in Laurence W. Martin, "The Future of the Alliance," in Wolfers (ed.), *Changing East-West Relations*, p. 229.

Heath look forward to a united and nuclear Europe. For some, the prospect of greater military independence is a motive for unification; for others, military and therefore nuclear independence appear the inevitable consequence of unity.

A militarily self-reliant Europe would raise serious questions about its relation to the United States. The thought apparently underlying the notion of Atlantic partnership and of the "Two Pillars," advanced during the administration of President Kennedy, was that such a European center of power would not only be beneficial but in fact essential to good European-American relations. As President Kennedy himself put it, Europe should be "a world power capable of meeting world problems as a full and equal partner . . . with only such a Europe can we have full give and take between equals and an equal sharing of responsibilities and an equal level of sacrifice."[26] Mr. Dean Rusk's encouragement of a European "caucus" in 1968 was widely taken to represent the survival of these ideas in a more modest form.

On the other hand, some have feared that in world politics a partnership between equals is impossible and that irresistible centrifugal forces would develop. This fear accords with the belief that the impetus necessary for creating a united Europe would be a form of chauvinism. The European-American relationship might therefore be one of rivalry rather than cooperation.[27] Even this might prove better than the present relationship of dependence, so far as American burdens are concerned, but it is not what the architects of the Grand Design intended. Because Europe would inevitably be the weaker of the two, there is the further possibility that America might acquire a partner strong enough to be willful and uncontrollable, yet weak enough to get into trouble. To those who fear this, the precedents of Germany and Austria-Hungary or of Russia and China are alarming.

As an aim for early achievement, a Grand Design of equal political and military partnership was and remains an illusion. The material resources of NATO Europe would certainly support a world power of the first rank. European manpower of military age outnumbers that of America and the number actually under arms is well over ten million. Europe's combined military expenditure is more than half Russia's and its annual product is greater. What is lacking is political unity and the effective will to be a single great power. To do this in the nuclear age requires a particularly robust political structure in

26. See his "Declaration of Interdependence," *New York Times*, July 5, 1962.
27. This seems to be the view of H. van B. Cleveland in *The Atlantic Idea and Its European Rivals* (New York: Council on Foreign Relations, 1966).

order to preserve credibility and determination in crisis. Both existing superpowers happen to have highly centralized, almost personalized, systems of government so far as foreign policy and security are concerned. When there can be misgivings in Britain as to whether the Cabinet system is not too collective to exercise nuclear power effectively, the road to a sufficient degree of unity for Western Europe as a whole is bound to be steep.

The European pillar of the partnership is consequently far from realization. Less frequently appreciated is the effective absence of the American pillar. The existence of a potent American center of power and of decision is not in doubt. It is equally clear, however, that the United States cannot confine itself to a purely Atlantic role and that the Europeans have no present intention of sharing fully in American responsibilities around the world. Even the architects of the Grand Design betrayed some anxiety on this score by their exhortations that the new Europe should be "outward looking." While this anxiety partly reflected fears that the European Economic Community (EEC) might practice protectionism, it was also a plea for assistance to America in its role as global policeman. Today Europe shows little eagerness to share these duties either diplomatically or militarily. The only incentive capable of inspiring such efforts may be an outburst of self-assertiveness that would not go easily with partnership.

That building a federal Europe remains almost entirely a task for the future belies the fonder hopes of those who set out on the road to unity more than a decade ago, though it should surprise no one with a reasonable historical perspective. Much original enthusiasm has evaporated in the last few years, and a number of stubborn obstacles have been unearthed. The years since President de Gaulle's first rejection of the British bid for entry to the EEC have been particularly dispiriting. While Europe's own momentum toward unity has diminished, the United States has displayed increasing indifference toward the outcome. Distracted by domestic turmoil and above all by Vietnam, America had in President Johnson and Mr. Rusk two leaders who showed little concern or feeling for European questions. Puzzled by the confusion in Europe itself and justifiably unwilling to share the uncritical hopes of the Kennedy era, the Johnson administration substituted neglect for design.

In the years of suspended animation imposed by the stubborn refusal of President de Gaulle to countenance any Europe not made in his image, political currents in Europe became both sluggish and confused. Britain, once uncooperative, has been beaten into submission by economic adversity. The nation has decided without much dissent to contract its outward ambitions, and, with rather less conviction, the leaders of all major parties are committed to entering the EEC whenever they are allowed to do so.[28]

Having taken the psychological plunge, at least in anticipation, British leaders have sought to prove their good faith by demonstrating enthusiasm for rapid progress toward political unity in Europe. They have, for example, endorsed the idea of early direct popular election of a European assembly. To a large extent, however, this eagerness put the British once again out of step with their prospective associates. The Gaullist insistence that national institutions remain preeminent is well known. Less ostentatious but no less real is the decline in devotion to European unity as an ideal among large sections of the population, not least perhaps among youth, whose attention has turned toward domestic aspects of social order. The workings of the Community's customs union have become a fact of life rather than an object of enthusiasm.

One source of apathy has been success. Among the original objectives of integration was prosperity. The steady and often spectacular economic growth in Western Europe in the past decade—partly, but only partly, thanks to the EEC—has shown that affluence can be attained without traveling the further distance to full integration. Another motive of integration was to gain security from both the threat from without, and renewed armed conflict among, the nations of Western Europe. Once again, most people regard these goals as substantially realized, and they recognize, if only dimly, that the result arises more from nuclear weapons and the changed scale of the balance of power than from the framework of integration.

The sense of urgency about integration has thus been very largely lost, while a number of its shortcomings have had time to become apparent. The EEC itself has proved far from flawless. It has created a customs union, which remains the chief and almost the only effective cement binding the Six. The EEC's inflated and disastrous agricultural policy is now undergoing desperate but not particularly promising modification. Little has yet been achieved by way of community-wide industrial reorganization, or in the legal, fiscal, and social conformity required for a truly integrated economy. It has been left to American

28. See *inter alia* Miriam Camps, *European Unification in the Sixties* (London: Oxford University Press, 1967); and her "Is Europe Obsolete?," *International Affairs*, July, 1968.

companies to exploit the full opportunities opened up by the customs union.

While General de Gaulle was president of France it was a real question whether the spirit of life could survive in a community originally conceived as a movement toward goals now persistently blocked. It was also uncertain how long Britain could keep alive an application twice denied and without much prospect of early acceptance. Ironically, the British applications served chiefly to inhibit development within the EEC, for French intransigence angered the other partners and made them reluctant to undertake any further evolution that might make ultimate British entry even more difficult. Germany was torn in several directions. Dependent on the United States, on Western solidarity, and even on Britain as a legal guardian of Berlin, she has felt obliged to support British entry and the further integration of Europe. Yet for geographic and historical reasons Germany needs harmony with France, which, under de Gaulle, quarrelled with America, bullied Germany, and frequently displayed a disturbing tendency to see the German question in Russian terms. Caught in this trap, Germany supported British entry, but without vigor, and dragged her feet on all alternative approaches to further integration.

President de Gaulle was such a commanding obstacle to political progress in Western Europe that his removal inevitably opens up prospects of advance. If progress were once to resume, it could conceivably be rapid. Though Europe has been becalmed, some powerful currents have continued to flow beneath the surface. The European Commission has been preparing the way for advance on several fronts, such as transport and energy, monetary affairs, and technological cooperation. If the new French government proves cooperative and new members enter the Community, a fresh sense of purpose might carry Europe forward to a higher form of unity.

One can only surmise how far such hopes will be realized. Progress is certainly not assured. During General de Gaulle's incumbency it was frequently said that his style was personal but that his policies reflected fundamental French attitudes and interests. His political heirs retained a good deal of cohesion in the early weeks of the new regime, and their pronouncements on such issues as British entry were at most ambiguous. Because of Germany's artificial inhibitions, France has enjoyed an unnatural predominance among the Six. Britain would prove a formidable rival. Rivalry has indeed been the historic Anglo-French relationship, and British entry to the EEC might well mark the resumption of this competition in a new arena. Moreover, a more reasonable French government might win a readier hearing in Bonn for its genuine objections to British entry than was accorded a French president with a reputation for willfulness.

General de Gaulle's intransigence has obscured the many real difficulties attending the British application. Economically the process of adjustment will be painful for Britain, and Britain is at present ill-equipped to undergo the experience. The impasse in the agricultural system is particularly unfortunate, as this is one of the community policies that gives the British and their associate applicants most difficulty. If Britain is relieved of the problem of keeping up the momentum of her application in face of an indefinite veto, it may be replaced by doubt whether she can survive the transition to membership. For all these reasons, the transitional period may well be prolonged and this alone may prevent realization of some of the hopes for spectacular progress aroused by President de Gaulle's retirement.

De Gaulle's unreasonable tone should also not deceive us into believing that his political objections to Britain's EEC membership were baseless. British entry would probably be accompanied by that of several other countries, and the possibility that this would dilute the cohesion of the community and obstruct the evolution of a united political will among its members can certainly not be dismissed. Moreover, even if the will existed, the processes of achieving political unity have not been well defined. The domestic political stability of France, Germany, and Italy can by no means be taken for granted over the next few years. Germany has the special problem of reconciling closer political integration in the West with some conception of ultimate national reunification.

Thus the way forward is neither easy nor well marked. The original conceptions of the Treaty of Rome cannot simply be taken up, adding new members. The existing EEC is a design of the 1950s for the societies and economics of the 1950s. Economic, social, and political facts and conceptions have moved on since then. New patterns for handling European affairs in common will have to be evolved for the 1980s. The genuine need for evolution, however, at least undermines the argument that new members would serve merely to disrupt a going concern that otherwise requires no tinkering.

5. The Military Future of Western Europe

During the period of Gaullist suspension, some of those most eager to keep up the momentum toward European integration proposed various ways to bypass the blocked communities. Among such schemes was the idea of close consultation between Britain and the Six, with or without France, on questions of defense. The obvious framework for such consultation was WEU, but the resentment of France at what she regarded as illegal efforts to smuggle Britain in by the back door seemed more likely to produce disastrous wrangles than effective cooperation. But if the departure of de Gaulle should usher in an era of less rigid French exclusiveness, some of the schemes concocted in the last few years might well prove useful as transitional stages toward a fuller unity.

There are many pressing practical motives for increased military cooperation in Western Europe that would have to be recognized even in the absence of a broader movement toward political integration. By 1969 Great Britain had become the most energetic advocate of such schemes.[29] In part her enthusiasm can be accounted for by her eagerness to win a way into Europe, but it is only fair to recall that in 1948 and again in 1954 Britain took the lead in making military commitments to consolidate common defensive efforts in Europe. Moreover, withdrawal from east of Suez allows Britain to concentrate its military resources and attention on Europe as never before. Britain is also the European leader in defense technology—not, of course, in all aspects of it—and is probably even more in advance with modern techniques of defense analysis and planning. She is therefore well placed to perceive the imperatives that are arising from the strategic situation and the problems that Europe faces if it is to maintain a modern defense industry. As a committed ally of America increasingly compelled to move toward Europe, Britain is also exceedingly eager that the inevitable evolution of European military affairs is as compatible as possible with the retention of American guarantees and cooperation.

The chief compulsion for the Europeans to collaborate in defense is economic: only by some pooling of effort can the European countries hope to maintain sophisticated armed forces at tolerable cost. But there are also other incentives. The effort to construct a new European Defense Community is certainly not intended by most of its proponents as a way to get rid of the United States, although presentations designed to win support from the French, for example, not unnaturally stress the potential for independence that a broader military base would afford. Yet, given the increasingly vocal American desire to reduce its military effort in Europe, the Europeans must give some thought to what strategies would be possible if American force

29. See the annual *Statement on Defense Policy*, 1969.

levels were substantially lowered. Most Europeans see the answer in a greater degree of interdependence among the Europeans. Even in France, the extreme form of national self-reliance epitomized in the strategy of nuclear defense against all comers (*tous azimuts*) had been officially recanted even before the fall of President de Gaulle. An added motive for greater interdependence in the face of an American tendency to withdraw is the need to provide a framework within which German military power can be embraced if the Atlantic structure should loosen.

Militarily, geopolitics compels Western Europe to compete in the top league. With the possible exception of range of aircraft, the requirements of the European battlefield, if Russia is the enemy, dictate the highest standards of equipment. Such equipment is growing notoriously more expensive, and fewer and fewer units are produced for a given cost. Defense equipment is not unique in this respect, but it represents a very large sector of economic activity that is closely and entirely under government control. The opportunity to suspect mismanagement is consequently great, the leakage of expenditure to foreign manufacturers is peculiarly resented, and the belief that this sphere of economic activity must be susceptible of reform by fiat is particularly strong.

When the Western alliance began, there was considerable hope of national specialization in military functions. The scope for this has proved limited, largely because military forces serve political functions. Continental Europeans are not happy to provide cannon or missile fodder while America and Britain pursue maritime and air strategies involving more exciting technology. Nor can the offshore members of the alliance cut their land forces in the center without arousing suspicions about the degree of their commitment to the common cause. Hopes of rationalization in the design and production of military equipment—which constitute a rising proportion of all defense expenditure—avoid some of the problems besetting operational specialization. Such rationalization would moreover have real operational advantages if it made possible or, indeed, imposed a common logistical structure. But standardization of equipment is a venture in which NATO has been remarkably unsuccessful, chiefly because each member has pursued his own short-term economic advantage, but also because of real differences in strategic doctrine.

The alternative way to obtain defense equipment efficiently in terms of cost is for Europe to buy American weapons. Many proposed European weapon systems, especially the large, complex, and capital-intensive ones such as aircraft, are rendered uneconomic by one of the two or three major prospective buyers opting for the escape route of an American alternative. Apart from the foreign exchange costs, some of which can be justified as an inducement for the United States to sustain the expense of maintaining forces in Europe, the Europeans are understandably reluctant to abandon all participation in modern defense technology. Rightly or wrongly, there is a deeply implanted belief that the sophisticated defense industries lead technological growth in general, and in particular stimulate the advanced technology vital for continued competitiveness in the world trade of today and tomorrow. This belief operates with special force in Britain, where the chronic difficulties in balance of payments are widely attributed (almost certainly excessively) to a lag in advanced applied technology, which contrasts oddly with Britain's undoubted predominance in Europe so far as science and research are concerned.[30]

European fears of American technological domination and of European industry's becoming a voiceless adjunct to American enterprises have been well publicized. In absolute terms the scale of American investment in Europe is not large, but it is disproportionately intrusive in some of the advanced technologies believed most important for the future. In itself this is powerful evidence of the benefit Europe derives from the investment, which takes the directions it does precisely because of Europe's need for the fruits of advanced research and for managerial skill in the newer areas of technology. This is increasingly well realized, and the cruder defensive reactions against the American challenge find less favor today. Moreover the danger that American management might be inimical to European interests—in times of recession, for instance, or in policy regarding exports to third markets—loses some force as it comes to be appreciated that the great international enterprises may themselves be ceasing to take an exclusively American view of the world.

But defense is a special case. National control of the production of weapons is very closely associated with a sense of autonomy in foreign policy. Nationalization and close government control of the arms industry have been typical in modern times. It is virtually unthinkable for the Europeans to let their long-established and still competent arms industries die without a struggle. If there is an answer, it lies in international collaboration. This seems much more natural and practical within Europe, where there is at least the possibility of developing economic and political union, than across the Atlantic, where the

30. See the ISS Series, *Defense Technology and the Western Alliance*. London, 1967.

Europeans would feel dwarfed and where the operational requirements of an affluent global power must frequently diverge from those of a probably increasingly parochial Europe.

There is already a great deal of cooperation in arms development and procurement in Europe. In 1968 there were more than sixty joint Anglo-French ventures under way. Some projects, like the Jaguar strike aircraft, are impressive in scale. Germany, Britain, Italy, and perhaps Holland, may well succeed in producing a multiple-role combat aircraft to succeed the F-104. But such ventures are ad hoc, usually bilateral, and almost always executed on the basis of fair shares for all, rather than by producing the best weapon where it can best be made. By ensuring that part or some of the weapons are made at home, the partners may save foreign exchange; by increasing the production run, they may reduce unit cost; but by blending national preferences in design and accepting all the complications of joint effort, the total cost is usually raised again well beyond the level at which a national program could have produced the same number of weapons. Such schemes may, therefore, merely multiply all the vices of military procurement so well known to treasury officials.

The answer, many Europeans think, is a "community" approach, by creating a European defense authority or commission with a budget to execute projects where they could most effectively be conducted, without regard to the project-by-project effect on national economies, industries, or prestige. It might be possible to construct such a community outside the framework of a general economic community and without an over-all federal political structure, but it would obviously be difficult. Very real national sacrifices would be called for, at least in the short run. The more economic affairs are thought of in national terms, the more difficult it must be to take the necessary long-term view of mutual advantage. Nevertheless, the existing Coal and Steel Community did something not dissimilar in an area of the economy once thought fundamental to national welfare.

To do the work satisfactorily would require a coordination of research and development, both to save money directly and to obviate the present system, in which each nation thinks of an operational requirement, then of a weapon, and only later, when a joint project is suggested, begins the task of reconciling what may be scarcely compatible designs. Some suggest that joint research is easier than joint production, involving as it does (usually) less money and less employment. But research of the kind required for the more elaborate weapons lies at the heart of industrial competitiveness. Again full mutual confidence may require a high degree of common political identification. Always there will be the possibility of some American alternative. Several European countries, in particular Britain, already have close links with American military research, which might be jeopardized by closer involvement with Europe. The British are also inhibited in far more fields of activity than is generally realized, because of the nuclear knowledge they have received from America and are pledged not to reveal to others. This can affect the design of weapons that at first sight seem remote from nuclear matters.

When renewed enthusiasm for joint arms procurement became apparent in Europe three or four years ago, there was a widespread impression that this down-to-earth approach represented an easier way to unity and cooperation than a direct advance toward common political and strategic institutions. Considerable progress on specific projects may be made. But the more one considers the degree of cooperation required to make Europe a real rival to America in arms production, the more political will seems to be a prerequisite rather than a result. For until competitiveness is achieved, it will be necessary to accept an interim period of national self-denial on particular projects and very possibly to pay higher costs than buying American would entail.

Insofar as such a Europe would deprive America of potential markets and be a more potent competitor elsewhere, the United States may view the obstacles Europe faces with equanimity. Yet European failure in this respect is not without its risks for America. The existing European arms industries will be a long time dying, and the process may generate considerable interallied friction, much of it directed against America. The Europeans may be driven even more than now to extend their production runs by pushing sales in the developing countries. Successful European cooperation in procurement might accelerate French re-entry into the common fold. She has much to contribute and much to lose, while her philosophy of armament is far more akin to that of Britain, which is outside the existing Community, than to that of Germany, whose partnership she already enjoys.

A really vigorous European arms industry might have the self-confidence to welcome the participation of American industry in joint ventures. Most of the schemes put forward for European cooperation have recommended an open attitude to the United States in this respect, not least because retaining American alternatives may be the best way to compel efficiency in what otherwise would be a closed market.

The idea of joint research and development and of common specifications for weapons immediately creates a requirement for common strategic conceptions. Achievement of a common view on strategic matters is, indeed, the other main aim of those who advocate a European defense organization of some kind. It may well be the sine qua non for success in what at first sight appears to be the easier problem of joint procurement.

It is a remarkable fact that there still exists nothing like a consensus on even the most fundamental aspects of strategy among America's NATO allies. This is in part the result of the very different geographical situations of the European allies. The flanks are obviously a special problem. Italy has a preoccupation with the Mediterranean and Adriatic that France and Britain share to some extent, but Germany hardly at all. Germany is uniquely exposed geographically, legally, and politically, and needs the most forward of strategies. France and Britain have very recent traditions of extra-European military activity, which has absorbed the major part of their martial energy since 1945.

A full identity of strategic views and a unified operational command structure for Europe that could form a single partner for America within NATO or some successor organization almost certainly requires political unity. In the meantime, however, there is considerable interest in developing some common planning machinery to evolve a European view on strategic questions prior to discussion with the United States. Mr. Dean Rusk's statement that America would welcome a European "caucus" within NATO has been taken as an indication of approval for such schemes. A European consensus on strategy would simplify American alliance diplomacy, and if occasionally it resulted in a firmer resistance to American notions, this might well be preferable to the resentment and suspicion that bilateral relations between America and the separate allies frequently arouse within the coalition.

While General de Gaulle was president of France, it was not easy to devise a framework for such common consultation or to arouse the will to make it work. Although his successors are unlikely to contemplate renewed full cooperation with NATO, they may well prove more ready for military cooperation within Europe, which would in many ways serve the supposed Gaullist aim of increased independence from America better than the former policy of aloofness. Once again, however, de Gaulle's obstruction obscured some difficulties that progress would bring to the fore. In particular, the closer the countries on the central front move toward a common identity, the more anomalous the position of the flanks may become. There is a gross incongruity between NATO Europe and the Europe of which real integration might be anticipated.

To this problem there are, however, conceivable answers. The interest of several Western European countries in the flanks may rise if

Russia maintains its naval challenge or if the Balkans become turbulent. A Western European group within NATO might be the vehicle for developing and implementing this concern. Britain and Italy—associated with France if possible—might draw Germany into interests beyond her immediate frontier—surely a healthy trend—rather than the opposite. To avoid prematurely splitting the alliance at a time when the strategic problems of the European theatre are becoming more closely interlocked, it would be desirable if, in the earlier stages at least, the image of the "caucus" were literally fulfilled: any closer planning group of the Western European powers could be regarded as a working party on problems of special common concern. This would not preclude broader but still selective discussions with other members of the alliance especially involved in particular issues, and would by no means usurp the debates of the alliance as a whole. There is an analogy for this in the European group within the OECD.

There are pressures, however, that may soon impel the central core of European powers toward fuller integration and the more deliberate development of a common nuclear capability. The most articulate exponent of this prospect is Franz-Joseph Strauss, who has also expressed disquiet at the Mediterranean becoming the arena for a Russo-American competition in which the nearby Europeans carry little weight. Many Europeans relate their prospects as a military power to the apparent American tendency to reduce its commitments in Europe and to Soviet appreciation of the forces moving America to retrenchment. If progress toward unity is resumed in Europe, defense will necessarily be involved. Once involved, it may impose a logic of its own, leading beyond the modest schemes that appear practicable today.

6. The Political Future of Europe

Even after the departure of President de Gaulle, the future holds little prospect that Europe will quickly achieve the coherence necessary to preserve the European balance without American help. Nor does the recent past, realistically regarded, encourage hopes of a rapprochement with the Soviet Union sufficiently fundamental to permit reliance on the innocence of Russian intentions. Even if the Czech crisis of 1968 were, as M. Debré allegedly remarked, no more than a road accident on the route to détente, it served to confirm the wisdom of providing a secure guardrail.[31]

31. Quoted by James E. King, "NATO after Prague," IDA, November, 1968.

It would consequently be quite irresponsible for the United States to withdraw its countervailing power from Europe. The cultural and economic value of Europe to America is great. If its immediate strategic value has declined, its symbolic importance as a gauge of determination and success in the duel of the superpowers remains immense. Europe is probably the one area of the world where the issues, contained and stabilized though they appear to be for the moment, are weighty enough to be plausible potential causes of general war. Inconveniently at the center of these issues is the legal, political, and moral American commitment to Berlin. There, if anywhere outside the United States, American credibility is at stake. Any precipitate disengagement from an area of such significance would entail a grave risk that the United States would have to rejoin the balance at a more dangerous juncture when some later development had, on the Korean precedent, proved unexpectedly intolerable. An intimate American involvement in European affairs, both military and otherwise, will remain essential for some years to come.

It is not so easy to be confident about the form this involvement should take. Much will depend on the shape of Europe itself in the next few years. The various assurances and exhortations that accompanied President Nixon's first progress through Europe suggested that the approved official goal was still horizontal and vertical extension of the European Community: taking in new members and advancing toward full federalism. But the new administration displayed a welcome caution as to when and how progress toward this goal might come and a less doctrinaire inclination to urge American conceptions on the Europeans.

The disappointments of the past few years have done much to encourage a belief that the future of Europe may not lie in the federal direction at all, but may rather fall into a variety of functional cooperative relationships. It seems certain that, barring a wholly unlooked-for acceleration in the pace of political events, the individual states of Europe will remain the chief centers of decision-making for years to come. They may, however, increasingly surrender their freedom of maneuver in specific fields to transnational agencies. Already the interrelated nature of modern economic life is well on the way to imposing a great deal of such interdependence on all advanced nations, without their having any particular enthusiasm for political unity. The states of Western Europe have partially translated these intertwining forces into institutional relationships. But the very interdependence that affords them this opportunity may also preclude its realization on an exclusively European basis. For many purposes Europe is no more the appropriate unit than is the Atlantic Community. Thus, while the Six and the applicants for entry may create some new and larger union, they are also likely to become involved in broader and not necessarily congruent associations dealing with particular aspects of economic life. Energy and monetary policies are examples of matters unlikely to fit the narrower framework.

It is possible that the variegated patterns found useful for particular economic purposes may obstruct the development of a coherent Western European economic, and ultimately political, entity. Such an outcome would not be without its advantages for American policy. Those who, in reaction against the Kennedy Grand Design of partnership, have expressed jealous fears that a United Europe might prove a dangerous companion, would have obvious reason for relief if the specter of such a monster receded. A looser Europe might also meet the desires of those who are eager for Europe to be "outward looking." Such an open-ended set of groupings would make it possible to build such limited links with Eastern European countries as the Soviet Union and the Eastern regimes dare permit. An open-ended Europe would also fit into global arrangements on monetary and other matters, with which advanced countries like Japan and Australia could be associated, without creating what might at times be a powerful counterweight to an otherwise dominating United States. A loose European structure would also prevent a sharp division with NATO between those European members that were and those that were not in an inner grouping. Moreover, the postponement of political unity for Western Europe would put off the day when the aim of literally reuniting Germany must be openly abandoned. There might also be an optimistic hope that such a network of functional relationships would moderate international conflicts just as multiple individual roles are held to do in civil society.

A Europe like this may well be all that can realistically be expected for some years to come. It would certainly be preferable to the alternative of a Europe wearied by the years of Gaullist obstruction, divided by national rivalries, dispirited by a sense of reduced importance in the world, and drifting apart into a fragmented, nationalistic pattern of irritable coexistence. But even a functionally cooperative Europe might not be stable over the long run. Russia and the United States will remain as a permanent exhibition of the prestige and power that attaches to size. Their existence will demonstrate that the imperatives of global economic life do not role out large political units. Some Europeans may develop the Swiss, Swedish complacency with the virtues of a prosperous, happy and relatively irresponsible smallness.

But the Western European memory of greatness is recent and most Western Europeans, unlike the Swiss or Swedes, are in the mainstream of politics and history. The goal of a real unity may be needed to give a sense of pride and purpose without which even functional harmony might degenerate.

The present era of disillusionment might then come to be seen as the period in which alternatives to unity were tried and found wanting. Germany may reconcile itself once more to giving practical possibilities in the West priority over aspirations to the East. The final disappearance of West Germany into Europe might be the only point at which the regime of East Germany could relax and contemplate a true European settlement.

It would be unwise to react against the excessive optimism of the Grand Design and the Two Pillars by making a dogma of the dangers of a united Europe. There is admittedly no assurance that a Europe powerful enough to be more independent of the United States would remain an amenable partner. But there is equally no need to assume that it would inevitably be hostile or uncooperative. Much of the reasoning built upon this assumption makes too much use of mechanical analogies and concedes too little to elements of political nature and will. The inner political nature of Western Europe offers an appreciable assurance against its adopting an adversary relationship to the United States akin to that supported by the ideological ambitiousness of Russia and China. Admittedly, the political stability of several of the components of Europe—France, Italy, and not least Germany—is not all one might desire, but there is force in the argument that their embodiment in a larger grouping might have salutary influence.

The most persuasive reason, however, why the United States should not oppose the emergence of a larger state in Western Europe is that this is the only plausible way that the United States will ever be able to reduce its involvement in the European balance. For the next several years at least, this entanglement appears essential, and the mere twenty-five years it has endured would scarcely seem long on the Roman or British scale of imperial history. Yet it is difficult to imagine that the garrisoning of Europe could gain acceptance by the American democracy as the natural and perpetual order of affairs. If a weaker and fragmented Europe has its advantages for American dominance, this ascendancy, like all imperial power, is also an enslavement to European necessities. The goal of ultimate European independence may be necessary to permit a healthy relationship between Europe and America in the interim.

For the immediate future, however, the pattern of European organization must remain a mixed one. Partly as a result of this, the Atlantic framework must also be variegated and flexible. This is so not merely because Europe is lacking, but because American horizons are much wider than the Atlantic. Rather than a neat structure we must therefore anticipate a network of functional systems, some military, some economic, some tight and some loose, not as second-best but as the pattern least prejudicial to the shape of the future and most suited to the complexity of modern strategic and economic affairs. As part of this world there will probably be "a relationship among the highly-industrialized countries which is marked by great freedom of movement for goods, capital and people; fairly strict codes of conduct restraining enterprises and states from distorting competition or acquiring unfair advantages; and close coordination of fiscal and monetary policies.";[32] a framework in which the Atlantic nations work intimately with Canada, Australia, Japan and other more highly industrialized nations.

The organization of European security, however, requires a sharper framework, and in this the United States will inevitably have a dominant role for several years to come. Security is and always has been the essence of the Atlantic relationship, and it is in this respect that the Atlantic framework best suits the business at hand. Anxiety about the reliability of American support for Western Europe has been endemic in the alliance, just as the United States has been persistently dissatisfied with the level of European military effort. In the late 1960s, intensified American preoccupation with Asia and the increasing vehemence of demands for a reduction in the American military contribution to European defense—demands made by hitherto ardent proponents of the Atlantic alliance—have made European misgivings appear better founded. The chief source of anxiety, and to some extent the precondition for these other trends, has been American eagerness to achieve a détente with Russia. Europe is incorrigibly ambivalent on this topic, wanting to have its cake and eat it too. Most Europeans are themselves eager for a détente and are quick to criticize any signs of American intransigence; yet they watch with equal sharpness to see if American ideas of détente imply any weakness in upholding the interests of the European allies.[33]

In the last few years, the eagerness with which American administrations have pursued the idea of a deal with Russia has combined

32. Camps, "Is Europe Obsolete?," p. 441.
33. An excellent exploration of this problem is Curt Gasteyger, *The American Dilemma: Bipolarity or Alliance Cohesion* (Adelphi Papers, No. 24; London: Institute of Strategic Studies).

with American expressions of weariness with the European commitment, to encourage the impression that the United States is backing
away from Europe. This idea is the more disturbing since the Czech
affair, which, whatever interpretation one puts on it, can scarcely be
regarded as a reciprocal Russian gesture of disinterest. The Europeans
appreciate the desirability of stabilizing the strategic nuclear balance
and avoiding inadvertent war. They are well aware, however, though
they commonly choose not to dwell upon the fact, that their own
security depends on a degree of instability at the strategic nuclear
level, so long as the conventional defenses are weak and American
strategists increasingly imply that the use of nuclear weapons would
be justifiable only against nuclear attack.

It is an inescapable feature of an alliance between sovereign states
that there cannot be complete congruity of interests within it. The
United States cannot be expected to subordinate its own vital interests
entirely to those of even its most important allies. A more secure and
economical strategic balance is worth pursuing, even at the cost of
some friction within the Western alliance. The existence of a sturdy
framework of coordinated diplomatic and military policy within the
West is no small contribution in itself to strategic stability. How far
efforts to strike a stable strategic balance between the superpowers
prove compatible with continued solidarity and mutual confidence in
the Western alliance will depend very much upon how satisfactory are
the dispositions for maintaining the local balance in Europe. The strains
within the Soviet bloc may, as we have already seen, give rise to inci-
dents that will at the very least subject the adequacy of Western prepa-
rations to anxious scrutiny.

In such a context, the prospect of a radical reduction in American
forces stationed in Europe raises serious problems. The symbolic role
of American forces in Europe, particularly ground forces, as a hostage
and as an earnest of American commitment, is well known. More important, perhaps, is the way in which forces on the spot inevitably
involve the United States in European crises from the very beginning
and thereby confer legitimacy and credibility on the United States as a
party to crisis management. In these respects the prospect of reinforcement by air, upon political warning, is not a satisfactory substitute, for
the interpretation of warning is at American discretion. Forces inextricably on the spot introduce an element of deterrent rigidity into the
American posture. It may, of course, be in the American interest to retain as much flexibility as possible, whatever the Europeans may think.
But this will be so only if the flexibility does not encourage Russian adventures and leads to a more expensive and perhaps provocative and
dangerous American response later.

Nor can one treat American forces as if they were merely symbolic, for they have a place in a practical military strategy. At present NATO purports to maintain a thin line of conventional response to communist incursions, thus imposing a pause before a nuclear decision. The line is already painfully thin and the pause correspondingly brief. A diminution of the American contingent, which is among the most efficient and best-armed of all the allies, would make this strategy even less convincing than it is, particularly as the Czech invasion has strengthened the Russians on the American sector of the front. The solution preferred by the Americans is for the Europeans to do correspondingly more. Indeed they should, although, if the proportion of United States forces were to fall sharply, the position of SACEUR might become anomalous. The presence of an American commander is a valuable pledge of American involvement; but an American commander of a predominantly European force might have an unpleasantly imperial appearance.

Yet if logic calls for a more powerful European contribution to conventional forces, precedent does not suggest that the Europeans are likely to make one. American reductions would more probably be taken as an indication of receding danger than as a stimulus to action. Despite her ambition to enter the European Community, Britain, like America, is geographically and financially tempted toward an offshore role. The Germans and many others would be uneasy if their contribution to NATO forces became large enough to give plausibility to allegations that the whole affair was becoming a German-dominated threat to the East. Germany, has, in any case, its own budgetary motives for reducing its defense effort.

If more than two or three divisions were subtracted from the current effective total of NATO ground forces in Europe, or if the already inadequate air support were reduced, it is extremely doubtful whether even a pretense of a forward, continuous line of battle could be maintained. Forwardness being such a vital political feature of NATO strategy, it is possible that in such an event NATO would do better to adopt a wholly new strategic concept. Some Europeans see attractions in reverting to the idea of a "barrier" defense along the demarcation lines in Europe. Local forces, very largely made up of reservists, would be designed to fight a delaying action against communist forces. They would be aided in doing so by developments in modern military technology such as light antitank and antiaircraft missiles, which, it is claimed, greatly enhance the delaying potential of static forces. The remaining active NATO forces, organized in highly mobile armored and airmobile units, would provide a capability for reinforcement and counterattack.

Such forces could not long resist a determined Soviet attack. Their role would be crisis control and the containment of incursions probably arising out of conflict in the East. The purpose would be to ensure that no surprisingly easy advances should tempt the Russians to probe further. Against deliberate aggression, the West would have to rely on deterrence. If, nevertheless, the Soviet Union pressed home an attack, the Western response would quickly have to become nuclear. This, however, is virtually the case at present. There is much to be said for the view that the situation would be safer if this were more openly admitted and prepared for. A frank limitation of conventional efforts on the central front might also permit some Western European members of NATO to devote more attention to the flanks of NATO, particularly the southern one, which is likely to feel the fullest effects of turbulence in the communist Balkans. Britain, if not compelled to concentrate all its resources on the central front, may well be able to make a substantial contribution toward relieving America of what are now largely bilateral American obligations to the Mediterranean members of the alliance. A more cooperative France may also resume its traditional role in the Mediterranean—by no means wholly abandoned under de Gaulle but inadequately coordinated with NATO—and once more make it possible to rely upon reinforcing southern Europe directly from Germany.

If the potential for conventional resistance in central Europe falls further, whether by simple default or mitigated by enunciation of a new strategy, the dependence of Europe on nuclear weapons for its basic security will become even more apparent. As matters stand, this means even greater dependence upon and subordination to the United States. This must do much to keep the issue of Europe's own nuclear power alive. The United States will have to decide whether to maintain the hostility toward the European nuclear forces that has increasingly dominated American policy in recent years or to help the Europeans stand more on their own feet in this respect.

Europe already possesses more than a negligible nuclear capacity. The strategic forces already programed by France and Britain should produce a combined force of bombers, land-based missiles, and submarine-launched missiles of some three hundred delivery units. If the two countries could cooperate, their facilities would be to a considerable extent complementary. How far they could sustain a technological competition with Russia to maintain their capacity to penetrate Russian defenses is arguable, but the task is not necessarily beyond them. Given American assistance, their prospects would be much brighter.

Europe as a united nuclear power is only a distant prospect for the reasons rehearsed earlier. France is certainly not available as a nuclear partner for anyone until the Gaullist philosophy is decisively modified. Later, however, cooperation may become possible, although the removal of de Gaulle's drive may aggrevate the budgetary problems of the French nuclear establishment. Germany presents a serious problem, but there is something to the argument that a Germany participating (initially under safeguards) in a European nuclear force may be safer than one exposed and permanently discriminated against. This, however, is again something for the future. More immediately, there would be considerable attraction for the Western Europeans in a coordinated nuclear effort, designed in part to put tactical nuclear weapons in European hands free of American veto, and related to common interests by a European equivalent of the nuclear planning group. These attractions may grow if, in an age of strategic stalemate between Russia and America, the Europeans come to fear even more that superpower strategy would embrace a controlled nuclear response executed in Europe. A European force intended to preclude such strategies might be organized on a basis of no first use, with retaliation only for nuclear action on Western European soil. Such a strategy, being wholly reactive to nuclear aggression, would considerably ease problems both of control and of credibility.

Accepted wisdom is that such an option for the Europeans to break the rules set by the superpowers would not be in America's best interest. The complete retention of nuclear control in American hands certainly appears at first sight to be best for the United States. Yet one cannot utterly dismiss the argument of some European strategists that a plurality of control—or, more precisely in this case, a European center of control—may enhance the deterrence of aggression, which is the safest foundation of common security. A European force of the kind described would be intended not to invoke a nuclear war among the superpowers—which would inevitably destroy Europe—but to avert one by creating an additional mechanism of deterrence.

There seems no reason why such a force could not be associated with American planning and be as subject to American advice as the British force has been hitherto. If such a force is to exist—and European rather than American decisions will determine that—there is a case for the United States helping it to be technically stable and to constitute no greater diversion of energy from conventional forces than absolutely necessary. Given the technological nature of the existing European nuclear forces, the important decisions about their future will have to be taken in the early 1970s.

Opinions will differ sharply on the nuclear question. There are nevertheless one or two fundamental propositions that it is hard to avoid. So long as world order rests on a balance of power in which nuclear weapons play a dominant part, Europe, as one of the most valuable prizes in world politics, will remain an area where security rests openly on a nuclear stalemate. The resources of Europe, its technological capability, and its sense of its own importance will inevitably keep alive the possibility of Europe's providing some or all of the nuclear force upon which its security rests. Consequently, if America is to have even a distant prospect of release from the burden of defending Europe, it will be unrealistic to insist upon a perpetual state of European nuclear defenselessness.

7. America's Future Contribution to European Security

No one seriously suggests that the United States can wash its hands of Europe. American involvement in European security, once regarded as part of a brief postwar era, and later attributed to a supposedly passing Cold War, is now more clearly seen to be the lot of the United States as a great power in the nuclear age. The "long haul" for which President Eisenhower adjusted American foreign policy is consequently going to be even longer than then seemed possible. For most purposes it can be regarded as permanent.

Where policy toward Europe is concerned, any kind of grand design is out of favor, both because of shortcomings in the original design and because of general weariness. Insofar as it signifies abandonment of a doctrinaire and didactic tone of policy, this latter-day modesty of purpose is to be welcomed. We should certainly avoid the delusion that the future of great European nations will fall neatly into American-made patterns. However much we may analyze foreign affairs, the degree to which their course is subject to control is limited. Yet it would be a mistake to replace overconfidence with apathy. The United States alone has the power to take the initiative on many issues. Furthermore, the record of American policy in Europe is surely good rather than bad. If some schemes have gone awry, a remarkable number have come to fruition. Europe is promising material, and it would be a tragic mistake to transfer to Europe the disillusionments arising from Asia, or to allow the disappointments of the Gaullist era to breed a mood of indifference. The future internal organization of Europe will clearly be determined when and as the Europeans see fit. Nevertheless, America is entitled to its preferences and is by no means incapable of advancing them.

In matters of security and in dealings with the Soviet Union, the primary responsibility of America is inescapable. Yet on matters that concern Europe, and they include many aspects even of the strategic balance, Western Europe has not only a close and legitimate interest, but also considerable power to thwart American policy. It would therefore be wise as well as generous to bring the European allies into the preparation of East-West arrangements, and not merely, as too often in the Kennedy-Johnson era, to present them with a *fait accompli.*

Consultation with the European members of NATO will be some guarantee against disruption within the alliance. But consultative arrangements, though valuable, are bound to be something of a sham between a superpower and allies that are smaller and divided. In the last analysis it will be the substance of American policy, and not the trappings of consultative machinery, that determines the health of the alliance.

Probably the most important element in American policy is the level of American forces in Europe. Failing some radical reduction in Russian military pressure from the East, which may be unattainable in principle and must in any case take some time to materialize, the wiser course would be to make no substantial reductions in the permanent American contribution to NATO, although the concept of mobility and reinforcement might be acceptable for a portion of the air contingent. The virtues of sustaining this level of force for several more years are clear enough from the viewpoint of foreign policy. Such a sustained effort is best calculated to extract concessions from the Soviet Union on a European security arrangement and to retain the confidence of Europeans in American leadership while negotiations proceed on that and other matters. It also offers the best available assurance against military outbreaks in central Europe and the best prospect of containing them safely if they do occur. Every president since World War II, however reluctantly, has felt obliged to maintain a posture of this kind in Europe.

American domestic considerations, combined with the requirements of policy elsewhere in the world, may be allowed to dictate a different course. If this transpires and if severe cuts in the American military effort are made over the next two or three years, much could be said for attacking the problem frontally, and for making an early decision as to what level of American contribution is sustainable for the coming years. A coherent new policy could be founded on such a basis. The constant uncertainty about American intentions and the daily expectation of troop withdrawals that has persisted over the past several years, is probably the most demoralizing tactic that the United States can pursue. Decisions on force levels should, of course, be made after full discussion with the European allies and related so far as possible to the military intentions of the Europeans themselves, the whole related if necessary to a new strategy.

Although this is a counsel of perfection, it is at least worth discovering whether a sympathetic American approach that combined a new force structure for crisis management, a revised tactical nuclear doctrine, possible assistance to European nuclear programs, and cooperation with European efforts to preserve an arms industry could turn American retrenchment into a stimulus for European efforts.

The only conceivable basis for European success in such an endeavor is joint action. For practical, economic, and geographic reasons it is also essential that France be included. Good trans-Atlantic relations on military matters, particularly nuclear, require harmony within Western Europe and especially among France, Britain, and Germany. A France reassessing its position and counting the costs of self-assertion after de Gaulle may well be receptive to a cooperative venture if it held out the genuine hope of an increase in European self-reliance, albeit in harmony with America. This, then, may be another reason for postponing radical reductions in American forces for a few years, for a constructive package deal would have much more chance of success if proffered in some three or four years time when Europe may have adjusted to the sudden disappearance of the General. By that time the course of events in the East should also be much clearer.

8. America and Europe: Conclusion

American foreign policy has remarkable achievements to display in contemporary Europe. In some respects American dealings with Western Europe as a whole are reminiscent of the so-called special relationship with Great Britain. In its classic form the Anglo-American special relationship is, by common consent, a thing of the past. In some respects, however, it is indestructible and lives on in ways that are useful and may well be extensible.

For all the cultural affinity, the Anglo-American relationship has rested on a basis of common interest. The United Kingdom earned its special status by the global role it played as leading auxiliary to American policy. While there is no reason to believe that Europe, fragmented or united, would be eager to become a world power once more in the old military style, there are other respects in which its influence will remain considerable. Even militarily it is not impossible that Europe will remain a factor, and perhaps a growing one, in the Mediterranean and in Africa. As a political and economic power of the first magnitude, Europe will continue to carry great weight throughout the world. Frequently Europe is more acceptable and successful as a representative of the democratic world than the United States. Not the least value of such an active Europe would be as an interlocutor for the United States, capable from experience of bringing balance to America's sometimes excessively introspective debates.

The second sense in which a special relationship may persist is in the ease of communication and the mutual confidence arising from cultural and political affinities. For all the enthusiasm for détente, bridge-building, and the betterment of East-West relations, we should not forget that it is no mere accident that Western Europe and America have found themselves on the same side in the Cold War. A sense of being somewhat less than foreign has pervaded the Anglo-American relationship and, to a lesser but nonetheless perceptible degree, that between America and Western Europe at large. This rests on real foundations. Even though America is now inescapably a world power, the claims of Europe to pride of place in American interests cannot be easily overridden.

8

THE THIRD WORLD

George Liska

1. Administrations and Doctrines:
Differences and Continuities

A quarter century after the end of World War II and twenty years after the beginning of decolonization, the perspectives and requirements of the undeveloped world and the industrialized world are as divergent as ever. The key role in reconciling them still belongs to the United States. If the United States were to abdicate its leadership role, the task of reconciliation would go by default to other powers. Whether this occurs or not depends on the answer to a critical question: Has there developed, along the uncertain course demarcated by the Truman, the Eisenhower, and the Johnson Doctrines—which were aimed at "international communism" and its allies—a stable nucleus of state policy that can be identified with an emergent national tradition?

If the answer is yes, this tradition can be expected to restrict the options relative to what they were just before and after World War II. The specific present bearing of the question is whether a hard-core policy tradition would (1) limit the possibility of drastic retrenchments and (2) also point in any particular positive direction. More concretely, the issue is whether, after a short-lived United Nations-centered one-worldism and a gravitation of conflict from Eastern Europe to the Middle East and on to Asia during the Cold War, the main thrust of future U.S. policy will be toward something akin to uniregionalism (comprising the Western Hemisphere and Western Europe) or toward multiregional globalism. Should it be the latter, a U.S.-promoted world order could have three possible patterns: a loose, fitfully contained polycentric order that would verge on anarchy; a bipolar structure based on co-responsibility with the Soviet Union; and an imperial order, based on the pre-eminent responsibility of the United States. Each of these patterns implies some devolution of role for a United States that was indisputably salient in the period between the Cuban missile crisis (1962) and the Tet offensive in Vietnam (1968)—a period of political pre-eminence corresponding to an earlier period of nuclear-technological primacy between 1952 and 1957.

In the expansion of the American role, the prime events were two military interventions, in Lebanon and Vietnam, comparable in significance if not in scale. The war in Korea created many of the strategic and psychopolitical conditions that bore heavily on the war in Vietnam. But it was less significant for the definition of America's global role because of the overt nature of the military attack, the presumed responsibility of the Soviet Union for the event (which had European implications), and the ostensible association of American action with the United Nations. After discharging its duties under the Charter as a member-state and as a superpower under the doctrine of containment, the United States could still pretend to the status of just another major power without special responsibilities in ambiguous local disorders whose bearing on national security seemed remote. In contrast to Korea, Vietnam represented a barely disguised unilateral initiative to assert authority and to reserve access in a complex situation that combined civil- and international-war features.

Compared with Vietnam, the other key issue of the 1960s, the crisis in the Congo was a minor affair. The American approach to it tended to shift to the United Nations pole as the Soviet and, secondarily, Chinese bids faded in the Congo and in Africa generally. With the exceptions of U.S. interventions in 1964 and 1967—which, while notable, did not suffice to invalidate the disposition—the United States left the Congo and Africa as much as possible to their respective internal dynamics and to the residual responsibilities and solicitudes of the former colonial powers. For this reason, the African interlude in America's ascension to "globalism" was relatively insignificant in comparison with either the Middle Eastern or the Asian set of events. Only future historians will be able to say whether the self-limitation displayed in Africa was either an early portent of American global retrenchment and disengagement regardless of local consequences or a harbinger of deliberate devolution of responsibility by a United States eager to withdraw into the wings wherever regional powers appeared willing and able to act their parts in ways conducive to national development, regional system-formation, and global stability.

In terms of U.S. priorities, Latin America's significance has been so far closer to Africa's than to Asia's. The Cuban crisis was one of intersuperpower relations and of national security strictly defined; the Guatemalan and the Dominican interventions in the 1950s and 1960s, on the other hand, though they aroused domestic and hemispheric concern, did not go beyond the pre-globalist traditions that guided American statecraft in periods of exploitable unrest in Latin America. More generally, U.S. official concern for Latin America tended to fluctuate inversely with global involvement. The latest increase of concern, initiated in the early 1960s, sought to counterbalance resentments caused by U.S. global activism with propitiatory acts of good will and self-protection near home. This did not mean, however, that undertakings intended to secure a safe regional base could not be transformed into regional substitutes for global activities.

The course of America's rise to a global role, and the policies that delineate it, has been the subject of considerable debate, much of it acrimonious. Some observers perceive a steady moral and practical deterioration from the postwar political and economic policies—first those toward Europe and later those toward the Third World—to an increased emphasis on military aid and military solutions to political problems. This progressive deterioration has been highlighted, it is argued, by the relatively sudden demonstration that containment policies developed in the late 1940s and in the 1950s are irrelevant for the Third World at large and Asia in particular.

The critical theses are themselves not beyond criticism, however. The first thesis (of progressive militarization) has tended to discount the interdependence of political and economic approaches with military undergirding in an "age of crisis." The second thesis (of sudden irrelevance) has tended to discount the alterations in technique and application which the general concept of containment underwent when transferred from Soviet Russia to China. To a debatable but real extent, these changes have fitted the differences in the critical conditions, including the key difference between a weary Soviet Union of the late 1940s facing U.S. nuclear monopoly (however meagerly supplied with bombs) and a politically and militarily resurgent Soviet Union, and later China, acting or stimulating action in areas unsuited to nuclear deterrence. That difference, when admitted, has created a growing and valid need for conventional and nonconventional military complements to approaches modelled on the Marshall Plan, such as the "Johnson Plan" for Southeast Asia, which offered help to develop the Mekong River area as part of a peacemaking with North Vietnam.

The repeated calls for a "Marshall Plan" for the several Third World regions stressed the size of U.S. economic aid. They were less explicit about the distinctive political style requisite for useful economic activities in the Third World and about the interdependence between economic aid, military aid, and occasional military action. Amidst both plaudits for the success of the early involvements in Western Europe and criticisms of the alleged failures of later involvements in the Third World, one aspect tended to be forgotten: that the earlier activities in foreign policy were relatively unproblematical in their external dimension, having to do with politically dispirited friendly countries and an adversary faced by the nature of the terrain with the choice between all-out assault and a psychological warfare that was largely verbal. Even the intrinsically more difficult aspect of the task—that of "selling" postwar internationalism to the American public at home—was greatly facilitated by the continuing sense of insecurity owing to isolation.

By contrast, the foreign policy involvements in the Third World moved toward the military-political pole in decreasingly favorable international and internal milieux. What had to be dealt with now were problems deriving from cultures ill adapted to the familiar techniques of organization and economic management or to determinate political inducements and sanctions that had been applied with some success to Western Europe. A new and unwonted statecraft now had to be practiced before a domestic public that was increasingly reacquiring a sense of security, while becoming ever less prepared to accept the connection between this security and the aggregate effect of variably successful official efforts. Thus, while the foreign policy tasks of the government became progressively politicized as an expanding range of considerations and instruments had to be coordinated in increasingly complex confrontations, the public was becoming increasingly depoliticized. And the public was not only losing confidence in the relationship between national effort and international security, it was shifting its capacity for apprehending specific dangers and for anticipating positive achievement from the foreign to the domestic arena.

Thus almost simultaneously there occurred an erosion of the two pillars of the active post-World War II foreign policy. This followed upon a domestic New Deal that had been buttressed and then terminated by the war economy. These pillars were, first, fear of the consequences of military-political inaction, and, second, belief in the benign consequences of politico-economic activism abroad. On balance, the United States was learning the techniques of international involvement in semicritical conditions, across a wide range of alternating and variously related particular challenges. But by the end of the 1960s the United States was in the throes of a more crucial single challenge: how to consolidate the psychological disposition to a sustained and wide-ranging involvement anchored in what were no more than hypothetical dangers and were at best long-range accomplishments. As a result, the foreign policy problem, which until then had rested chiefly on the performance of upper- and middle-level political and expert elites, now engaged the extremes of the political pyramid: the uppermost political leadership and the broadest popular base. The question was whether the highest leadership could secure from the public a minimum of toleration for the operations of the foreign policy (including military) elites who, at least temporarily, had lost the relatively safeguarded position previously conferred by popular anxiety, indifference, or blind trust.

The conditions confronting the incoming Nixon administration have thus not been conspicuously propitious. The U.S. interest in the Third World has had to do with political aspirations deemed valuable in general, and it has been concerned with strategic assets even more than with economic assets—including raw materials. The strategic assets were deemed valuable for the contest with the Soviet Union in an arena supposed to be decisive politically because it was militarily less explosive. These foundations of U.S. interest in the Third World have been weakening in terms of readily ascertainable facts, including technological ones, concrete future prospects, and, not least, an intuitive credence in the timeless validity of the precautionary bias traditional to international statecraft. And yet, though the need has grown, there has been no discernible movement toward reformulating U.S. grand strategy. The need now relates the containment of both communist and noncommunist sources of radical disorder and the promotion of an elementary international system and order in the Third World.

Despite the New Frontier's peculiar fashion of talking (even more than thinking) of Third World policies, there has been little substantive difference between the Eisenhower, Kennedy, and Johnson administrations, once they had retreated from the greater rigor of the Dulles policy vis-à-vis the communist powers and their allies. The Eisenhower administration had adumbrated many of the Kennedy administration's policies, from Cuba to the Alliance for Progress in Latin America and from military commitment in Vietnam to the decision for a political solution in Laos. The difference between the Kennedy and the Johnson administrations was greatest in what each inherited in both the resources and the degree of commitment for intervention in Vietnam, and at home in the degree of toleration the predecessors of each showed for the plight of the incumbent. In comparison, the difference in personal style and in public relations and the difference in actual goals and the methods employed were substantial only in the light of an unflattering contrast between the unfolding predicament of the Johnson administration and the idealized retrospective image of the Kennedy.

The basic U.S. strategies in the Third World were initiated under the Truman administration. One reason they persisted was the difficulty of translating into a coherent new set of policies the perception of the narrowing disparity between U.S. and Soviet involvements, instruments, and even intentions in the Third World. Another reason was the difficulty of spanning the widening gap between the nuclear perspective of the United States and the prenuclear and preindustrial perspectives and requirements of the Third World. While the American perspective favored stability, prudence, and an organized evolution, almost any political or economic development in the Third World had to reconcile its own potential for turbulent change with the resources and restraints introduced from without. In the consideration of any new policy on the part of the United States, the growing pains of the Third World and those of American policy in that world must be assessed first.

2. The Postcolonial Revolution:
The Rise and Decline of the Third World

The so-called Third World (in reality the non-European world) existed as a geographic fact before it became a political phenomenon of our time. Between the 1930s and the 1960s it experienced a dramatic development, comprising the waning colonial system and what grew out of it.

In the 1930s the principal actors were the European colonial empires (of France, Britain, the Netherlands, Belgium, and Portugal) and the would-be imperial Asian state, Japan, while Kuomintang China occupied the ambiguous position of being the target of imperialism and also its potential exponent. The imperial powers knew what they wanted: a peaceful order—chiefly for material advantage—and they knew how to get it by administrative and judicial sanctions and by the solace of some economic and educational development. Any indigenous access to political activity was limited, in the case of Britain (practicing indirect rule by traditional authority), or of France (deflecting politics to the metropole), and Japan (distorting self-rule into the caricature of itself). Sooner or later the empires failed when they tried too much: for example, France in seeking to combine cultural and political assimilation, Great Britain in seeking to expand self-government and retain control, and Japan in seeking to expand both to the north and to the south; and also when they tried too little, as did the Dutch and especially the Belgians in the area of education. To an uneven degree, the concern of those primarily involved with the colonial dependencies was to depoliticize colonial administration, not least by segregating it from the domestic politics of the metropoles. The result was a situation of relatively limited relations, that were either stable or at least calculable—including the relations between the satisfied imperial centers and their aspiring have-not surrogates.

Remotely and at first ineffectually encircling the key actors were the ideological anticolonialists in the metropoles, chiefly in Great Britain, and (in a crescendo of intensity as time went on) in the United States and the Soviet Union. They depended on extreme, mostly economic interpretations of imperialism to inspire their campaign against it, a campaign which they fought in alliance with only a few moderately ambitious local nationalists. In the end, though, it was not the liberal-nationalist alliance that was the determining factor in the end of old-style colonialism, but the National Socialists of Germany, who started out by using the colonial issue as a bargaining counter, while concentrating on the means for colonizing Europe's colonizers themselves. The ferocity of late-coming Japanese imperialism and the bathos of the Italian—like the combined impact of both in Germany's larger enterprises—only expressed the obsolescence of a drive running counter to the historical trend.

Who were the principal actors in the 1960s? They were the newly independent states, which included a small number of ambitious unifiers, who vented their ambitions and frustrations against the background set by the two powers who were formally anticolonial but potentially imperial (the United States and the Soviet Union) and by the excolonial powers themselves. Whereas the colonial powers had depended on authority to implement the sovereignty of economics, their successors practiced a hypertrophy of politics to defy or conquer economic theory. Authority was either charismatic or symbolic, rather than effective or creative. Its tendency was to extend some kind of a claim or appeal beyond the limit of feasible performance. The new governors also knew what they wanted: power on a national basis and therefore status and influence that would be internationally acknowledged. They knew how to get, or move toward getting, both. The first means was to limit competitive political activities at home by one-party systems and mass organizations, while expanding them abroad by manipulating two or more opposed powers and by exercising membership in many international organizations. From the vantage point of the later 1960s, they seemed to fail when they tried either too little or too much—too little, when Sukarno tried to foster nationalism in Indonesia while neglecting economics, or when Nehru's India made the mistake in reverse. Too much, when superficial forms of representative government or multistate unions were superimposed on inadequate remnants of colonial administrations or immature postcolonial politics. The lack of mature constitutional or otherwise constructive politics did not mean, however, a lack of politicization of either the anticolonial drive or the postcolonial foreign policies. Both of these were closely linked to the domestic politics of, first, the metropolitan country and, subsequently, the newly independent states themselves. As a result, the new leadership first gained power, then leeway, and, toward the end, reprieve from its pledged achievements.

The tendency by and large was toward hyperactive but unstable relations, and toward for the most part shrewdly calculated but externally incalculable responses. The reasons for this situation included (1) the absence of specific external interests of the new countries once the anticolonial platform proved insufficient; (2) the primacy of domestic politics and the survival of the regime, implying a wide range of possible tactical policy linkages between internal need and presumed international remedy; (3) the penchant for ideologies, largely carried over from the era of preindependence, upgrading political myths and downgrading diplomatic methods; and (4) the deficiency of workable international sanctions to penalize the less developed countries for encroachments on such principles as political reciprocity and economic accountability.

Instead of being subject to the constraints of a healthy respect for risks, too many of the new leaders felt immunized by a unique combination of magical charms. They could invoke the evils of colonialism and the merit of having defeated it locally. They could claim infallibility and its corollary, political invulnerability, on the grounds (firmly held until a military regime proved them untenable) that beyond first-generation leadership there was either nothing or worse. And they could shield behind highly propitious power structures within the countries of the Third World and between them and other states.

Rightly, for the most part, the internal power structure was held to be too amorphous or too resilient for effective punitive sanction from the outside. However "penetrated" by external influences they may have been, the new countries proved relatively immune to external control. The primacy of domestic politics was confirmed when the only effective sanction for mismanagement (often attended by internationally disturbing behavior) required the leader's overthrow from within. The unpredictable timing of the sanction (intended to express cumulative disaffection rather than to penalize specific dereliction) only contributed to the uncertainty. As the "what" to follow charismatic leadership became virtually certain, the "when" became much less so. By contrast, the structure of international power was almost too sharply defined, and, in the view of the major powers, it was too delicate a structure to warrant their assuming the risks of penalizing concrete misbehavior for the sake of the hypothetical advantage of establishing a rule.

Other forces stood in the background. First came the superpowers, wavering (somewhat as Germany did in decades past) between Europe and the extra-European regions as constituting the principal or the preliminary stakes in a global contest. They were all the more attracted toward the seeming vacuum of the Third World the more Europe appeared to be replete with superpower crises or renascent indigenous drives. Second came the former colonial metropoles who, like the nationalist leaders before independence, counted on the conflicts of others to help them retain or resume a part of their former influence. And finally, the third or outer zone was taken up by the proponents of some perversion of earlier attitudes. One trend tended to convert imperialism into isolationism by asserting its disinterest in the Third World when the latter could no longer be ruled absolutely. This new isolationism (called Cartierism in France but differently elsewhere) turned economics as well as concern for national power and prestige into so many weapons against postcolonial involvement, and thus against those who had effectively used similar weapons against colonialism before. Another tendency (for example, Maoism in China) would perpetuate earlier deformations of the colonial ethos and reinvigorate the dying gasps of authentic anticolonialism by impregnating it with racist features.

Colonial pomp gave way to strident pretense. The postcolonial leaders were uncertain whether they represented a rising force or merely a revised format for an ongoing relationship between the periphery and the center (or centers) of activity. They seemed to have arrived on the world stage too soon in terms of their readiness and too late in terms of the disposition of the industrial societies to view the yet undeveloped areas as important potential additions to the power they could more effectively generate internally.

Besides the contrasts between the colonial and postcolonial eras, there were continuities. These were reducible to two givens: (1) the secondary character of the Third World as compared with the old world or the new; and (2) the continued effective primacy of the political factor backed by military power as compared with the economic factor, ultimately determinant or not. The colonial powers lost their colonies when they did because they had been weakened by their military struggle with their German and Japanese rivals and had lost their political bid for assimilating their colonial subjects. Nehru, Sukarno, and Nkrumah in their turn lost prestige or power because they failed in military containment, confrontation, or subversion, undertaken as part of forging the political frameworks of nation or empire. Their economic mismanagement did not in itself condemn any of them, although it was used to rationalize their decline or fall. Similarly, their good economic management was insufficient to save the colonial powers, nor did their economic "exploitation" destroy them, though the first was to be used for the posthumous apotheosis of colonialism, while the second had long provided the text for its condemnation.

In a panoramic view, the specific differences and continuities of colonialism and postcolonial events lose their sharpness. Then colonialism converges with postcolonial politics as two phases in the integration of the blank areas on the political map into an incipient global international system. Colonialism (often arbitrarily) had outlined the territorial units. This most traduced feature of colonialism became its most cherished bequest in the eyes of postcolonial beneficiaries. Colonialism had furthermore supplied the vital need of a first adversary and scapegoat, which was manageable because it was at once tangible and yielding. The postcolonial era imposed a more difficult problem: that of imparting positive identities to the geographic frameworks, making them internally viable and externally compatible. Only then would they fit into some kind of regional equilibria without any fatal detriment to the new hierarchy of world power.

The time between the high noon of colonial empire in the late 1930s and the relatively low estate of the Third World in the late 1960s has seen a fitful assertion and then a decline of the colonial empires, the expectations from decolonization, and the authority of those seeking control of the postcolonial Third World, namely, the United Nations and the two superpowers.

The decline of empires could not but condition deeply the first phase of postcolonial independence. The Japanese empire collapsed outright in a military defeat that could not be immediately offset by last-minute grants of "independence" in provisionally controlled countries such as Indochina and Indonesia. The fall of the colonial empires of the European nations was less immediately linked with the latter's setbacks in World War II. The effects on decolonization were both more delayed and longer lasting. The European empires lost face with colonial dependents; they experienced the shrinkage of material resources and of internal political support for their authority and prestige; and then they faced a change in the international atmosphere that was no longer favorable to political dominance of any—and most of all direct—kind. In the different metropoles, there was an unequally paced but, in the last resort, decisive and sudden collapse of nineteenth-century intellectual support for colonialism. More often than not, the colonial powers had managed to coordinate colonization by ad hoc deals and congresses. Yet, except for an ineffectual rearguard action in the United Nations and a rare coincidence of interests (such as that over Suez in 1956), they failed almost completely to coordinate de-colonization. The initiative passed to the other side.

Accompanying the assets of succession were the more enduring, built-in liabilities of the non-European world. Colonialism finally ceased to pay when it had to be supported, either by expensive wars or by police action, such as that of the Netherlands in Indonesia, France in Indochina, or Britain in Malaya. Fluctuations in the public mood in the West and the diminishing propensity in the West to in-vest beyond the seas its resources of enthusiasm, treasure, and blood had helped dismantle the empires. But the same propensities were to haunt the successors to these empires as soon as the heady spell of decolonization and postcolonial self-assertion had passed.

The dramatic decline of the colonial empires was important for the postcolonial scene mainly for what it revealed to the West about the place of the Third World in its scale of priorities. The place was tra-ditionally highest for powers that, rightly or wrongly, regard Third World assets as crucial weights in contesting or rivaling another major power. Thus France held stubbornly to her holdings and her policy of assimilation as part of a historically conditioned reflex effort to equal ascendant Germany or surpass temporarily reduced Germany (an effort that France transferred to nuclear weaponry the moment the colonial burden was lifted from her). The British and the Dutch were animated by economic concerns that were competitive in a differ-ent sense. Hence they yielded more readily to the imperatives of the balanced budget, international payments, foreign (American) aid or sanction, and to prospects of expanded postcolonial trade. In the following phase the United States, like France, was to fight stubbornly over positions in the Third World as long as these positions appeared to be vital to the strategic balance with the Soviet Union, and, sub-sequently, with China. The validity of this policy would be questioned only when the costs of the war in Vietnam began to impinge on U.S. domestic stability and international monetary standing.

The crucial importance of public opinion in regard to an area no longer vitally linked to the national security of Western industrial states then became apparent. Enthusiastic support alternating with disillusioned rejection had marked colonial experience since the age of the great discoveries and left a stamp on the postcolonial period.

This unstable psychological climate was kept in check by the climactic events of the Cold War. As the Cold War psychosis became more pragmatic, however, public opinion began to tell against the post-colonial successors—or, as in many instances, the successors to the successors—of the imperial statesmen and colonial proconsuls.

These impressions took time to form. But if decolonization revealed some things about the non-European world, it also conditioned the subsequent bid of the postcolonial politicians for pre-eminence in the international system—a phenomenon that in its rise and even more its decline displayed marked similarities to decolonization. The most burdensome bequest of decolonization lay in the very facility with which it could take place. The free grant of independence to India (1947) initiated a momentum that soon made decolonization appear necessary and (to salve imperial self-esteem) long foreseen and intended. With some exceptions, mostly to do with France (in Indochina and Algeria especially) and only secondarily with Holland (in Indonesia) and Britain (in Kenya, controversially), the independence of the former colonies seemed to transpire more easily the less qualified for independence the country in question was. What began in India with a stately calm (however drastic the immediate consequences were) ended in an almost unseemly haste on the part of the British to divest themselves of positions in the area of the Red Sea and the Persian Gulf in the late 1960s; in the middle period of decolonization less-qualified Tanganyika preceded Uganda and Kenya into independence in Africa.

Conciliation alone worked no better in decolonization than in the postcolonial phase. Overcompensatory reactions to the ease of establishing independence were responsible for the fact that Britain's postcolonial relations with Ghana, for example, were less close (if therefore less turbulent) than were those of France with Algeria or with one or another state in the former Indochina. The "peace of the brave"—covering up a de facto victory of the metropolitan power (as in Algeria) or its near defeat (as in Indochina)—seemed to create a mutual reappraisal approaching respect, whereas a "peaceful disengagement" had no such effect. The proof of recovered manhood implicit in material destruction seemed to matter more than parliamentary trappings, military drills, or even an ample treasury amassed by a thrifty rule—an incitement to folly in twentieth-century Pakistan or Ghana no less than in eighteenth-century Prussia.

With the few exceptions, the prevailing ease of decolonization made for the ensuing tendency in the new countries and in the Third World as a whole to overreach themselves. There arose the idea that achievement—such as military performance demonstrates particularly—somehow did not matter in the scale of importance among nations; that to win militarily (in Indochina) or to lose (in Indonesia, Algeria, or the Suez Canal Zone) meant equally that the Third World forces would still in the end carry the day in the courts of opinion and diplomacy. This conception of international relations, invigorated by decolonization, was further reinforced by the idea that had originally argued for colonialism: that in political, strategic, or economic terms the non-European world was the key to the world balance of power. Whoever controlled the peripheries of the European world, it was thought, would dominate, if no longer economically or militarily, then at least politically and psychologically. The decolonized nations, feeling exempt from the censorship of performance and relying on the strategic convenience of the United States or the pangs of conscience of the former colonial powers, were ready to bid for political and moral hegemony in the postcolonial world.

At one point in the late 1950s that bid seemed almost to supplant the superior drive of the communist powers. At other times it seemed merely to supplement that drive—though it was nearly subverted by China in its last phase. As is usual with this type of challenge, the objective of the bid was a form of influence that would strengthen an already propitious position in the configuration of power, one deriving from the competitive and apparently highly exploitable relations between the two superpowers. Moreover, in this case too, an ideology was expected to minimize opposition and disarm resistance. This ideology of anticolonialism reached its zenith when the target ceased to be colonialism and became neocolonialism. The shift occurred when the need arose to refuel a faltering drive (authentic colonialism having been defeated) and to compensate for a progressively worsening international context as the competition between the United States and the Soviet Union subsided owing to the intrusion of China.[1]

The Third World joined the Western and the communist powers as one of three main forces in world affairs. Its bid sought at least a moral pre-eminence over the "old" powers debilitated by conflict and compromised by the past. The bid was the child of negation feeding upon anticipations. As such it was unreal and doomed from birth.

The negation was primarily addressed to colonialism. It began with the independence of India and was soon followed by that of Burma

1. In the process the kernel of truth in all ideology (for example, the economic force of the Union Minière in the Katanga province of the Congo) was blown up into a total explanation of the supreme threat—the disintegration through secession of the postcolonial successor states.

and Ceylon. It rallied support with the struggle of Indonesia for independence in the first Asian phase and of Algeria in the second African phase, and thus it became an Afro-Asian movement. The second target of negation was any superpower conflict other than an exploitable competition. An acute conflict between the superpowers might endanger not only the decolonized and the decolonization process, but also aid in their development. Accordingly the Korean War supplied the first opportunity, while the United Nations supplied the stage, for an exercise in mediation by the yet small group of newly independent nations. Though repeated in later years, the intercession of the Afro-Asians was never again to look so disinterested or effective either to the United States, facing the Chinese on the military battlefield, or to the Soviet Union, discovering in the unsuspectedly "independent" new group a new political battlefield it had spurned hitherto. A decade later, even the more active involvement of the enlarged Third World in the U.N. operation in the Congo fell short of its involvement in Korea. The first instance proved to be the finest and the early promise outshone the subsequent performance.

Opposition to the two evils of colonialism and the armaments race of the superpowers was an easier common denominator than the challenge of economic development—the third and least solid plank in Afro-Asia's common platform. In an India-centered view, the high watermark of Third World unity and prestige was in 1958, when in the United Nations seventy-seven states endorsed four of Nehru's broad principles of postcolonial coexistence, which characteristically veiled in generalities the incipient quarrels between India and China.[2] Insofar as the U.N. resolution was platonic, its principles reflecting an unavowable specific interest, while the consummation was referred to the future, the climax was also an omen. The psychological strength of the Third World lay in the past (colonialism and its real or pretended misdeeds), while its political strength—if it was to have any—had to relate significantly to the future constructive deeds to be accomplished by the Third World countries in the international arena as well as within their own borders.

The anticipations upon which rested the international credit of the Third World were partly contradictory. The first was that of performance. It collapsed in the wake of failure by the new countries to move

2. The following decade from 1958 to 1968 was already one of decline, well under way by 1961. These were its main events: the Cairo and Belgrade conferences; the ebb of friendship between nonaligned and communist countries; the Sino-Soviet split; China's territorial penetrations on the Indian frontier. See G. H. Jansen, *Afro-Asia and Non-Alignment* (London: Faber, 1966), p. 279.

resolutely and on a broad front toward economic and political stability by means congenial to one or the other superpower. Moreover, the Third World countries tended to forfeit even their role as mediators and moderators when the virtual end of decolonization coincided with the initial depolarization in superpower relations in the late 1950s and early 1960s. The second anticipation bore on gains possible for either of the superpowers. Solid advantage was expected to result from success in competition over the less developed countries or from compliance with their visions of vital interests. This prospect also failed to materialize, or at least to materialize enough to keep the superpowers steadily involved in the affairs of the newest of states.

Seen in retrospect, it was hardly possible for the first wave of independence leaders to forestall this development. To do so, they would have had to fend off collective decline by separately enduring at a still hopeful early stage one or both of the evils they most feared: (1) to confine themselves to the intellectually and socially uncongenial sphere of domestic economics, in the hope that quick results would eventually revitalize a temporarily deactivated role in international leadership; (2) to concede substantial gains to one or another superpower so that such gains would be sufficient to maintain that power's interest while remaining potentially reversible so as to safeguard independence.

Many Third World leaders tried to walk the tricky tightrope of high policy in preference to the pedestrian approach of intractable economics. Most prominent among these were Nasser, Nkrumah, and Sukarno. Others, notably those of French-speaking Africa, settled for keeping the metropole interested in return for a somewhat nominal independence that earned them vocal opprobrium in postcolonial councils. While a man like Sukarno explicitly rejected the economic course, even Nehru could not travel it with any consistency or real hope of success. A few leaders in countries like Pakistan, Nigeria (before the military coups), Tunisia, Kenya, and the Ivory Coast, gambled on political sobriety and economic self-discipline, but their persistence was uneven and so were their rewards. The dilemma was a real one. Each Third World leader had to evolve his own peculiar palliative for it, showing himself more or less conservative or radical, passive or active, at home and abroad. For these and more specific local reasons, the third and crucial anticipation of the postcolonial drive—unity among the progressively decolonized countries—was no more realized than were the anticipations of small-state performance and superpower profit. A succession of more or less broadly supported initiatives in favor of conferences and organizations (on an intercontinental basis encompassing Afro-Asia, both within and without the United Nations) reflected a steady drive for unity less than they did the oscillating fortunes and enthusiasms of the Third World leaders themselves.

The slender psychopolitical basis of Third World politics is characteristic of both colonialism and its postcolonial sequels. The importance of prestige (personal for the independence leader and national for the colonial bureaucrat) came not only or even chiefly from the Oriental's alleged concern for face. It was also an expression of the fact that the decisive tests of power that normally regulate prestige lay outside the colonial sphere. For some time now the outcomes of crises in the Euro-Atlantic area have been merely projected onto the Afro-Asian stage in a later phase of contest. This was true of Japan's conquests following upon Germany's, of the anticolonial struggles or campaigns for emancipation in the post-World War II decade, and of the globalized phase of the Cold War in the post-Stalin era, beginning with the mid-1950s. In the colonial period, the primacy of prestige was manifest in the smallness of the largely indigenous military force the controlling power considered necessary. In the postcolonial period, it was manifest in Third World hierarchy being a matter of radical credentials of leaders rather than of a country's material potential.

Beyond similarities, there lay a difference. Prestige as a substitute for local power made sense for a colonial administration as long as it could readily draw on the power of the home country. The system made less sense for the postcolonial scene, in which leaders often could draw only on highly perishable assets of newness. Thus Nehru and Nkrumah headed countries among the first to win independence on a continent. Others, such as Nasser, Nkrumah, Sékou-Touré, and Ben Bella in their successive accessions to power or independence owed their ephemeral leadership to an anticolonialist radicalism that was purest and harshest as long as it was untested. Prestige was a stabilizing element in the colonial period. Then, once the charm was broken by defeats in Europe, it turned against its wielders. By contrast, prestige represented a destabilizing element in the postcolonial world because of the premium it placed on precipitancy and exaggeration.

The excessive importance ascribed to "pilot countries" was a feature common to the dynamics of decolonization and postcolonial international relations. To grant independence to one country in a given sector (To India in Asia, to Ghana in Africa, or to Tunisia in North Africa) actually meant conceding it to all the other countries in that sector and beyond. The British may have initially assumed that the distinction between those countries that were prepared for self-government and those unprepared would hold good and would regulate the tide. The French, on the other hand, held to a "domino theory" with some justice. Just as they had clung in the 1920s to the East European features of the Versailles settlement to forestall collapse on the Rhine, they clung to Indochina in Asia to protect North Africa in general and Algeria in particular. The regulatory British approach was implemented through delicately balanced, artful, regional federations in the West Indies and in Central and East Africa. Its main results were frustrations for the dwindling number of personnel in the colonial administration. The repressive French approach delayed the climactic expression of the frustrations of the French army and its political allies, while using up in less essential theaters popular tolerance for onerous resistance to decolonization. These approaches—repressive for France, regulatory for Britain—were not absolute, of course. When they faltered, they were exchanged for a simulacrum of the alternative approach. Thus the French tried the formula of "associated states" in Indochina, and the British toyed with repression in Southern Rhodesia. On balance, neither technique provided the noncolonial industrial powers with a reliable model for dealing with the postcolonial products of decolonization. Nor did either technique substantially affect the pattern that placed successive countries temporarily at the head of an expanding Third World community.

The pattern made more sense in one way than in another. It was easy and natural for recently liberated countries to capitalize on their independent status with respect to other movements yet struggling for independence. In this category was India vis-à-vis the Asian and later the African nations, Ghana vis-à-vis the African, and Tunisia and Morocco vis-à-vis the Algerian movements. What was less presumptive was the idea that each successive pilot country would be more internationally assertive and internally radical than the preceding one: that Indonesia would be more neutralist than India, Ghana more "revolutionary" than either Asian country or Nasser's U.A.R., and Guinea in some ways more than Ghana. The newcomers were overcompensating for their junior status, their less impressive domestic base as a nation or as continent, and their lesser merit in forcefully resisting or ejecting the imperial powers. The Algerians disposed of unassailable credentials in the last respect, and seemed anxious to escape the iron law of radicalization in the very first period of their independence and then again after the fall of Ben Bella, in part a result of his international activities. However, their independence came at a time of a gathering moderate reaction that exacerbated the radical tendency, first under Ben Bella's leadership on the global scale in relation to Cuba and China, later under the Boumedienne regime on the regional issue of Israel. Just as the easy grant of independence created a handicap that could be overcome only by militancy, so did the revolutionary fortitude displayed in war create a national capital that was difficult to forego in the absence of other assets.

Only a handful of leaders among the relatively late comers— Kenyatta of Kenya, for example—had sufficient personal prestige to allow them to behave with moderation without incurring the penalty of being ostracized by the waning but still tone-setting radicals. The moderate stance was consolidated in Kenya and elsewhere when the radical option was internally pre-empted by rival claimants to power too hard to outdo at a tolerable cost—as happened when the Sultan of Morocco pre-empted the "revolutionary" foreign policy of his radical internal rivals in the 1950s.

By 1961, when the conference of nonaligned countries met at Belgrade, the Africans, egged on by the Yugoslavs, found the Asians too tame indeed. The old-school-tie revolutionaries, à la Nehru, were yielding to younger revolutionaries in tunics of one sort or another. From the late 1940s on the several conferences—New Delhi, Bandung, Cairo, Accra, Belgrade, Algiers (as planned)—in their first or subsequent versions coincided with the apogees of successive leaders or with their attempts to regain lost ground. Like Napoleon III in an earlier age of revolution and reconstruction, the new leaders regarded the presidency of an international conference as a tangible, even a decisive, asset in promoting vague schemes. And, like the chieftains of contemporary superpowers or of the "new monarchies" of the European Middle Ages, they celebrated by summitry the emergence of their world into an excitingly fluid state—a state inviting attempts at personal management before proving amenable to gradual structural transformations only.

Up to the abortive Algiers meeting the period of the major conferences paralleled and overshadowed the more continuous parliamentary diplomacy in the United Nations. This diplomacy, too, reached its peak in the early 1960s in connection with the Congo operation. The Third World's stake in the United Nations found then its main ideologue in a non-Afro-Asian, Secretary-General Hammarskjöld. Both avenues to Third World unity differentiated between postcolonial processes and those of decolonization. Leadership in the latter could thrive on essentially formal or personal assets—timing of independence, the status of the leader, the verbalized ideology of the regime. By

contrast, leadership in postcolonial politics eventually proved inseparable from the development and exploitation of material assets.
Men like Nehru and Nasser seemed to perceive this fact while failing
to meet it, while men like Sukarno and Nkrumah rejected it as irrelevant. The last two could be regarded as less responsible, but they were
also more realistic about the time available for recasting political and
territorial givens and the ultimate cost of effecting even minor correc-
tions in a system of states whose formative period had been allowed
to slip by—a cost clearly shown in the contemporary experiences of
Germany and Japan. Yet this insight was invalidated by a second and
related difference. Pilot performance in decolonization tended to set
off a snowballing process, because the colonial powers were demoralized or eager to quit responsibility. By contrast, a bid for leadership
in postcolonial conditions tended to elicit a countervailing resistance.
This might come from the leaders of countries fearing the candidate
for leadership on local grounds (for example, U Nu or Ne Win of
Burma fearing India, or Olympio of Togo fearing Ghana), or from
those seeking leadership themselves, either by different means (Nuri-
as-Said versus Nasser, Houphouet-Boigny and Senghor versus Sékou-
Touré and Keita) or by similar means (Sukarno versus Nehru, Kassim or
the Baathist leaders versus Nasser, and Sékou-Touré versus Nkrumah).

Thus, with only a secondary assistance from forces outside its own
"system," the Third World tended to contain its collective drive by its
own internal dynamics. Its self-containment was largely facilitated by
the gross disproportion between its aim and its means, its affirmation
in words and its confirmation by deeds. To reach beyond its grasp
could only overstrain a conglomerate of nations whose innate strength
and cohesion fell short of even the Holy Roman Empire's—an earlier
successor to imperial order, one that also pretended to transcend local-
ism and renovate politics under more or less prestigious figureheads who
failed not least because they lacked the support of a strong enough
territorial domain of their own.

In such circumstances, the individual and collective bid by the Third
World for ascendancy faltered, not surprisingly, over relatively minor
obstacles and issues, coincidentally with the faltering of decolonization
itself. Small but determined communities of settlers in Algeria and
Southern Rhodesia deranged an apparently irresistable process of decolonization while small Portugal brought it to a temporary halt in
her African dependencies. One may condemn such last-ditch resistance
as anachronistic and belittle it as foredoomed, but its near success in
Algeria and the still undecided outcome in Southern Rhodesia (subjected to economic sanctions) and Portuguese Africa (exposed to a

guerrilla warfare so far unsuccessful in Angola and Mozambique) have had redeeming features. The resistance to indigenous supremacy by forces closely resembling the original colonizers was part and parcel of a sum of events and conditions that, beginning with the late 1950s, conspired to delimit the power and cohesion of the Third World. The Organization of African Unity failed to coordinate a common action against either the Portuguese denial of independence or the Southern Rhodesian assumption of it. Zambia, the black African neighbor of Southern Rhodesia, merely tolerated African freedom fighters, or what there was of them; and the support of guerrillas in Portuguese Angola originating in Congo-Kinshasa was not sufficient to prevent the rebellion's being rolled back for the time being. Where lacking communist organization and discipline, the traditional East was as yet no match for even the fragmented remains of the traditional West. While this was painful for leaders of the Third World to accept, it was useful for them to recognize in the longer run.

Other events stalled the surge of the Third World toward a privileged position and an unassailable status. India's invasion of the Portuguese enclave of Goa, though this occurred only after vain efforts to negotiate Portugal's surrender, cost the leader of the Third World much sympathy in the West. The Sino-Indian "war" in the Himalayas and in Assam cost India prestige in the Third World, and the Third World itself, the last semblance of solidarity. The invasion of Goa was a trifling thing compared with Indonesia's assault on Malaysia, but it revealed more sharply the double standard regarding the use of force (and the double-talk regarding colonialism and aggression) practiced by those with the highest stake in nonaggression by the powerful against manifestly weaker parties. A similarly ambiguous attitude toward the Soviet repression in Hungary only confirmed Western impressions of cynicism or myopia in the Third World. The desertion of India by the so-called Colombo powers in the face of perversely efficient Chinese forays, finally, hurt the policy of nonalignment in India—the very site of its origin.[3] Just as Japan's victory over Russia in 1905 crushed the assumption of white superiority, India's conflict with China exploded the assumption of non-white solidarity. The slightest pressure of reality brought to the surface, first, local animosities (against India) unrelieved by a shared fear (of China); and, second,

3. While the Ceylonese criticized India for accepting Western arms—as if the moral force of nonalignment could really be a substitute—it was reserved for a non-Asian nation (the U.A.R.) to urge unequivocally the withdrawal of the victorious (Chinese) troops from occupied territory, for understandable reasons of its own.

the impossibility of agreement on the wider meaning of nonalignment going beyond a general attitude toward one specific conflict, that between the superpowers. Under these conditions, only a clear and demonstrable relationship between investment and return on the part of the contesting superpowers could have established the status of the Third World. Yet by the time India was collapsing before China, U.S. influence was rising in the Middle East even while the Soviet Union was underwriting the Aswan Dam—the most spectacular and politically the most controversial project of assistance in the Third World.

With sympathy for the Third World reduced, as were its internal solidarity and the presumption of its solvency, the wave of postcolonial buoyancy was rapidly subsiding. Its ebb revealed local and internal conflicts and those disorders that could be concealed or overlooked as long as the high tide of postcolonialism commanded attention. However displeasing at the moment, this ebb prepared for a second (perhaps a real) beginning for the unavoidably protracted evolution of the Third World into an integral part of the global system, on terms all the sounder for not being either peculiar to one segment or unprecedented.

We have already pointed to the parallel of the Third World with the Holy Roman Empire—another attempted shortcut to the uniting of intrinsically diverse communities, loosely linked by a shared doctrine of salvation, but riven by contention for leadership even before being subjected to a schism concerning the implementation of doctrine. As in the earlier case, in the Third World, too, nominal unity was broken up by the self-assertion of local territorial units, opposing efforts to coordinate them in a whole and engaging in mutual conflicts, often in collusion with external powers.

As the ostensibly united global campaign against colonialism and for postcolonial ascendancy subsided, Afro-Asia split into its two main component parts, expressed by their differences in temper and concerns. Within both Asia and Africa, in uneven degrees, the last remnants of Western colonialism shared the limelight with new postcolonial imperialisms of local vintage. Latin America, on her part, though eager to find an identity differentiating her from both Europe and North America, has never developed interest in or a sense of identity with either the new Asia or the new Africa—apart from temporary exceptions, such as Cuba under Castro and Brazil.

A developing sense of realism bade fair to divide the Third World into sundry regions and subregions, and, within these, into several separate entities having more or less crystallized "national interests." In 1955 Afro-Asians might feel alike at Bandung, so long as their leaders abstained from concern with the concrete implications of independence, notably the economic. By the mid-1960s, simultaneous set-backs in high policy and mundane economics had produced a shift toward a new type of military leadership, all the way from Burma to the ex-Belgian Congo and from Pakistan to Upper Volta. This new leadership was not necessarily more competent than the postcolonial parliamentarians, labor-unionists, and ideologues; but it tended to be more positive as well as parochial, more African or Asian than Afro-Asian, and more Ghanian than pan-African.

A side effect of the progressive demythification lay in the vital area of local imperialism. The expansionist attitudes of Nassar or Sukarno were ever the less easily hidden under the loose garb of an anticolonialism qualified by a pan-Arab or a pan-Malay ideology. Both their bids hardened into specific power drives for primacy in the area comprising the Red Sea and the Persian Gulf in the one case, and in the area surrounding the Strait of Malacca in the other. The apparent aim was unilaterally to appropriate the last positions of Western imperialism, rather than to defeat that imperialism on a broad front, and to preempt alternative aspirant successors to the West (whether Soviet in the one case or Chinese in the other) while the going was or seemed to be good—in part because the United States might still be tacitly counted on to provide protection from the communist rival allies. The fact that both breeds of regional expansionists were struck down by a yet more pragmatic and better organized force (the Indonesian and Israeli armies) indicated that it was still as difficult for a leader of the Third World to drive with an awe-inspiring success toward Aden via Yemen (Nasser territory) or in the direction of Singapore via Sabah and Sarawak (Sukarno territory) as it had been for Ben Bella to strive for concerted revolutionary action in Africa by way of Havana. Nonetheless, it was regional geopolitics, rather than continental or intercontinental ideological politicking, that indicated the shape of things to come in the Third World.

If its concerns were concretized during this period, so were the concepts of the enemy or rival. Such a development could hardly proceed without a heightened incidence of interstate conflicts of the most conventional kind. The occurrence of such conflicts might depress the Third World's collective ego and blight schemes for unity; but it would do so only for a specific reason. Once again inspired by the unpracticed ideology of the West and eager to make this ideology a moral weapon against the West while elevating a necessity of the anticolonial interlude into a principle of the postcolonial era, the Third World bestowed upon itself immunity to conflict. To make a collective virtue out of individual weakness, the Afro-Asians followed the Latin Americans in the belief that military conflicts might be easily replaced by arbitration and that conflicting interests, however specific and intensively held, might be reconciled within some new principles of politics, allegedly typical of ancient Asia, or else principles of law and peaceful settlement, peculiar to contemporary Africa.

Almost any development diverging from such myths would be in some ways salutary. This occurred when concern with security (with respect to a manageable local danger) came to replace the sense of immunity or unconcern. That sense had been carried over from the era of protection by imperial powers, and it was confirmed whenever the unmanageable magnitude of the threats from a superpower militated against avowing their existence. As long as the dominant pattern was unacknowledged reliance on outside force, Asians could hope (or pretend) that some vague principles of coexistence would simultaneously take care of a global détente and also the threat from China, while Africans could hope that a temporary coincidence of policies among radical or moderate leaders would at one and the same time promote regional unity and thus peace and power, national consolidation, and personal political ambitions.

The penchant for sweeping vistas rather than local perspectives was something that postindependence Asians and Africans shared with the first generations of European empire builders and liberators of Latin America, as well as the medieval founding fathers of the European state system. This disposition was brought down to earth in two phases overlapping in time. First came rivalries over basic postcolonial strategies owing to differing estimates of what any one strategy would produce for the Third World, the individual countries or regimes, and their domestic and international advancement. In this rivalry the division lay between regimes that were relatively moderate and relatively pro-Western and regimes that were radical and in some way neutralist, between still royalist Iraq and already republican Egypt in the Middle East, Pakistan and Indonesia (before the Sino-Indian conflict and the fall of Sukarno, respectively) in Asia, and the Ivory Coast and Ghana (before the fall of Nkrumah) in Africa. The schism was aggravated by its connection with an intrinsically unrelated dominant schism between East and West. This connection at first nourished the Third World quarrels by supplying avowable stakes and physical means; then it denatured them by introducing into the Third World alien and extraneous ideologies and techniques peculiar to a different degree of development; and it ultimately saved the Third World from irreparable damage by communicating to it the tendency of mature politics to a progressive deconcentration of polar oppositions.

In any event, the schism between the moderates and the radicals had only a preliminary negative function of demonstrating what was impossible in practice. As the political significance of the schism waned with changes in Third World political leadership and the more basic changes in the East-West conflict, pettier conflicts could emerge. These conflicts were reminiscent of those during the second postempire phase of Latin American independence, following the collapse of the unifying visions of Bolivar and his peers. Warring successor states will tend to conflict over the final division of imperial spoils when attempts to set up a corporate heir have failed.

Conflicts over succession may be and were of different kinds: (1) over a territorial boundary (for example, between Argentina and Chile or Peru and Ecuador, just as more recently between India and Pakistan, Pakistan and Afghanistan, Cambodia and Thailand, or between Somalia and Ethiopia, or Morocco and Algeria); (2) over access to the sea (as Bolivia's was denied by Chile, or Mali's by Senegal, or Cambodia's by South Vietnam, or Israel's by Egypt); or (3) over regional primacy (for example, the conflict between Argentina and Brazil with regard to Paraguay and Uruguay, between Egypt and Iraq with regard to Syria, or between the U.A.R. and Saudi Arabia with regard to Yemen, between India and China with regard to Nepal or Burma, between Indonesia and the Philippines with regard to Malaysia, or between Ghana and the Ivory Coast with regard to Upper Volta). In virtually all such cases the conflicts were restrained by insufficient resources and communications; they diverted human and material resources from remedying shortcomings; and (for the most part indirectly) they helped inject into domestic politics the problem of the armed forces. On the other hand, in the case of the older Latin American countries the conflicts also helped develop a sense of sovereign statehood and—even in deprived and defeated countries like Peru and Bolivia—an incipient sense of nationhood.

These are inestimable values for inchoate entities caught between an excessive concentration of power on the exterior and a too fragmentary socioeconomic base in the interior. So far the great war of the Pacific and the lesser wars had failed to convert Latin America into either a unified continent or a coherent and autonomous system of states. In the more recent period, the Latin American countries were not aided, however, by the conflicts' becoming intrastate rather than interstate, with an ensuing polarization of the proponents and opponents of domestic social change; or by diversion of energies into internal developments, such as the construction of a new Brasilia in lieu of a greater Brazil. The growing tendency has been to disclaim any responsibility for events and to shift the blame onto exterior exploitative interests.

At the end of the 1960s, the states more recently arrived at post-colonial independence could still hope to escape either the blight of bloody interstate wars or the futility of conflicts that are unproductive in their political and institutional consequences. So far they have done quite well on the first score, reserving serious bloodshed for internal conflicts. Nothing like conclusive returns are in on the second score. In South Asia the early outburst of postcolonial violence in the politically unproductive Hindu-Moslem strife in due course took on further definition in the Indo-Pakistani conflict over Kashmir. Halfhearted attempts at negotiating a compromise on that issue paralleled the less than halfhearted support for either side by old allies (CENTO and SEATO on behalf of Pakistan) or new friends (the Soviet Union on behalf of India), until in 1964 the military phase of the conflict was set off by Pakistan, which was as frustrated by India's policy of inte-grating its part of Kashmir and refusing negotiations as India was by Portugal's analogous policy in Goa.

The short and inconclusive war gave rise to new moves toward pacification and settlement. The most conspicuous of these was asso-ciated with the Soviet-sponsored summit at Tashkent. Yet, coming after India's humiliating military encounter with China over the carto-graphic and logistical implications of China's integration of Tibet, the course of the conflict was more important than its immediate outcome. The conflict with China destroyed illusions. The later conflict helped the Indians discharge their humiliation over their defeat, and the Pakistani, their frustrations over earlier inaction. The two conflicts together involved the three regional powers (China, India, and Paki-stan) in controlled hostility and shifting alignments, while the external powers (the Soviet Union and the United States) became comple-mentary in their efforts at control and conciliation. The newly crystal-lized situation constituted a greater progress than could have been achieved by either summit conferences or other mediation. Pakistan could no longer rely plausibly on declaratory policies to gain support against India in the United States or in the Middle East; India could no longer act as if an exaggerated concern about Pakistan somehow might make her calculated policy of pretended unconcern over China more plausible; while China could not behave after 1964 as if she could or would gratuitously dispense unrestrained military support in favor of Pakistan any more than she had dispensed political self-effacement in favor of India.

In Southeast Asia, a similar case might be made for Indonesia's "confrontation" with Malaysia. There overt conflict brought into the open old resentments such as those concerning the still dependent Malaya's and Singapore's role in equipping Sumatran rebels against the central government in Java. Moreover, the confrontation (in which the Philippines were also involved) substituted direct, if initially hostile, contacts for reciprocal contempt or ignorance, and it tested and clarified Indonesia's potential as the dominant power in that region. By contrast, the partly real, partly simulated disputes of the much weaker state of Cambodia with her neighbors, South Vietnam and Thailand, only masked her greater fear of North Vietnam. These disputes were intended to foster tentative options in Cambodian foreign policy with regard to which great power would be her ultimate protector, the United States or China.

However different they were in particulars, the Asian conflicts expressed a common apprehension of dominance by an indigenous regional power, whether India, Indonesia, a unified Indochina, or China. Since external powers continued to be involved (more directly in Southeast Asia than in South Asia), this concern could be expressed within manageable limits. Thus by the late 1960s it could be hoped that—concurrently with, but also independently of, the war waged by the United States in Vietnam—the key Asian countries were evolving the rudiments of regional subsystems that might eventually lead to realistic forms of regional organization.

In the Middle East the situation was less promising, and in Africa it was apparently less advanced. The Middle East had experienced longstanding inter-Arab conflicts revolving around the issue of Greater Syria as against a "greater" Egypt comprising Syria and beyond. The second source of the area's identity as a politically significant region was an organization for unity that was initiated in the mid-1940s under the name of the Arab League. The two components—protracted conflict and up-to-date organization—had failed so far to coalesce in anything more stable or creative than a kaleidoscopic Arab "cold war" that was largely separate from (if partly exacerbated by) the evolving conflict with Israel. The key difficulty seemed to lie in one idea and one fact. The idea was that of Arab solidarity, which, not unlike the alleged solidarity of the "socialist" states, effectively forbade overt conflict without producing cooperation. This tended to repress conflict to the level of intrigue, while heating it up on the level of propaganda and a war of nerves. The fact was the apparently unmanageable, overt conflict with Israel. Of Israel's three military victories, only that of 1967 even opened up the possibility of defining the issues—or at least the alternatives—for the Middle East. The war marked one more failure of the Arab policy of neither peace nor war as a solution until the Arab states could catch up with and overtake Israel. In its origin, the war was at once unwanted by the Arabs and provoked by them;

and it resulted from inter-Arab rivalry even more than from Israeli reprisals. Its outcome generated pressures for a potentially healthy choice between a degree of peace that would end belligerency and all-out war, with guerrillas substituting for conventional armies.

Yet it appeared more likely that internal divisions and external influences would continue to paralyze a Middle East whose global significance was decreasing. The divisions were not reduced by Algeria's projection into inter-Arab politics, while the influences were not simplified by the Soviets' massive but still ambiguous role in the Arab-Israeli contest. Such a state of things could only obfuscate options, prolong the festering crisis, and bar a conclusive test of all forms of strength without facilitating any formula for an honorable peace.

The clarification of interests and concerns in the Middle East was further delayed by its opening up toward sub-Saharan Africa in the late 1950s. Notably Egypt's probing policy in this direction was expected to generate new leverage for local conflicts and fresh alternatives to intraregional achievement. This process paralleled the expansion of North Africa as an area of potential cooperation and conflict toward sub-Saharan Africa and the Middle East. If one discounts the fighting in Yemen as an ostensibly internal, revolutionary struggle, the military conflict between Morocco and Algeria over postcolonial frontiers was an exception—though only a moderate one—to the rule of formal peace among Arab states. That overt conflict represented progress over the earlier contention between Morocco and Mauritania over a much larger objective, when Rabat sought by varied means to absorb Mauritania in the Sharifian empire. It remained to be seen whether a cathartic clash of arms in North Africa could not only relieve frustrations (like that in the Indian subcontinent) for the moment but also clear the way for long-term cooperation with tangible stakes in an area lacking both a self-imposed political boundary and the sobering presence of a potentially dominant major power.

The outlook was bleakest in sub-Saharan Africa, whose relative decline in the later postcolonial phase revealed the degree to which it had been uplifted, but not self-sustained, during the "African decade."

The declared conflicts among states were relatively few in Africa, where the territorial stakes derived from tribal overlaps, such as those between Somalia, Ethiopia, and Kenya, and between Togo and Ghana. They could not be brought to anything like a conclusive test, in view of the lack of military resources and social cohesion, without mortal danger for the regimes. While the absence of hard-core strength hampered the resolution of conflicts by force, the width of the de facto frontier zones and the scarcity of frontier contacts tended to reduce the occurrence of conflicts. Sketchy economic cooperative arrangements settled or deferred some unenforceable claims, such as Tunisia's with regard to Algeria in North Africa and Somalia's with regard to Kenya in East Africa. On the whole, Africa's potential for manageable conflict was confined to intracountry struggles, such as those convulsing the Sudan and Nigeria in the wake of the fighting in the Congo. The continent's limited capacity for interstate conflict was shifting from inconclusive quarrels preceding the establishment of the OAU to an increasingly ritualistic pursuit of the unmanageable contention between the white and black African communities.

It appeared that Africa had first to define her component members before she could begin to define their interrelations and thus herself. Having faltered in her leap ahead of the anticolonial revolution, she had to take up a more modest place at the rear of the postcolonial evolutionary procession.

The African decade from the mid-1950s to the mid-1960s ended in a year of military coups. The battle for Africa was called off without its being really fought, when the United States diverted attention to a real war in Asia. While this was happening, the communist powers discovered separately that the African continent would not provide a fertile battleground for their internal contests any more than for their respective rivalries with the Western powers. And the Africans themselves had to make what in effect was a truce with the remaining outposts of Western colonialism. Following upon the virtual split between the waning Asian and the exuberant African radicalism, the disarray in the potentially most revolutionary continent (according to Chou En-lai) signaled the end of a period of great fears for some and expectations for others concerning the Third World as a whole. In retrospect, neither fears nor hopes appeared to be founded in real possibilities for good or evil. The Third World's saliency resembled in this respect other phenomena, such as the merely diplomatic ascendancy of a state or the institutional authority of an organization, which are the products of transient constellations and fixed ideas rather than of lasting and inherent capabilities.

It is important to dwell on this aspect of the past two decades, since in regard to the Third World assumptions and expectations are likely to count for more than the few demonstrable facts and achievements, and perceivable over-all trends matter more than ephemeral local events and inchoate structural elements. To reach any conclusions about the psychological environment and evolutionary trends in political behavior and structures is as important as it is to analyze the "concrete" environment formed by long-term economic potentials or short-term political alignments.

The decline of the less developed countries as the third element in the global balance after the two superpower blocs has had its peculiar aspects. But also, in a way congruent with its character, the Third World has fitted into a pattern common to all bids for preeminence. Its external signs were the great conferences under Afro-Asian or nonaligned auspices; the internal history was reflected in the characteristic tensions of these conferences. The Bandung Conference in 1955 gave rise to the "Bandung myth" of a harmonious Afro-Asia comprising China, while it pitted the nonaligned cohorts against the anticommunist allies of the West. In the Belgrade Conference of 1961, the apparently triumphant nonalignment was already engaged in an internal contest over its principal thrust and direction—whether more or less forcefully against European colonialism, more or less impartially against Cold War superpower conflict, or for economic development in a more or less "socialist" manner. All this while the mantle of leadership was slipping from Nehru without settling on either Tito or Nasser or Nkrumah. The failure to meet the sensed need for a new collective role in a world increasingly polycentric either at the first nonaligned summit meeting (at Belgrade) or at the second (in Cairo, in 1964) prepared the way for the debacle of the second Afro-Asian Conference to have been held in Algiers in 1965. The failure to hold that conference reflected the decline of good will toward Communist China in the Third World in general and in Africa in particular—a good will whose first climax in Bandung (1955) and second (1964) in many African capitals was each time heightened by the personal success of Chou En-lai and then dashed by the subsequent performance of China.

The contest over Afro-Asia shifted from an East-West to a Sino-Soviet confrontation, while the center of gravity of radicalism shifted from Afro-Asia to Castro's Cuba and Latin America. These changes occurred against the background of military coups in Africa, military conflict in Asia, and the beginnings of disengagement from or "nonalignment" in the Third World in the West. Thus the conference era began by the consolidation of the nonaligned Afro-Asian countries against the Western system of alliances. It reached its apogee when nonalignment became largely uncontested, only to encounter the dilemma of where to find a substitute unifying purpose. And it apparently ended in self-dissolution (in Algiers) in an effort to thwart extraneous forces bent upon subverting a dispirited movement. By that time the bulk of the Third World movement was growing increasingly moderate or conservative, while surrounded by a shrinking lunatic fringe of extreme antineocolonialists allied with the neocommunism of Chinese and Cuban origins. Concurrently and fittingly, the institutional center of gravity shifted from specifically Afro-Asian and nonaligned conferences to the United Nations Conference on Trade and Development (UNCTAD), which marked a tentative shift from sweeping ideology and high policy toward a not yet quite realistic but earnest economic theory and practice.

Though on the surface some of its features seemed uniquely its own, the political rise and decline of the Third World was not a unique phenomenon. It coincided in time and in its main characteristics with the emergence, the climax, and the subsidence into the long pull of the other three great events of the post-World War II era: the superpower rivalry in the Cold War; the development of nuclear weaponry and the arms race; and Europe's quest for rebirth and unity. Normally, a bid for pre-eminence subsides after the driving power has been split between fanaticism (either contained or fostered by authoritarianism) and defeatism (calling itself realism) under the stress of an increasingly unified resistance. In the case of the progressively polarized Third World, a fitful resistance merely opposed certain of its aggressive spearheads, such as Sékou-Touré of Guinea (opposed by France) or Nasser and Sukarno (opposed also by Great Britain and, even less resolutely, by the United States).

Thus the factor that critically debilitated the bid was less the growing resistance to a drive than a weakening response to a claim. When it is being thwarted, a bid for pre-eminence tends to modify its environment, which has eventually to assimilate or reintegrate the driving power. This usually happens as the driving power involuntarily diffuses some of its strength—in military power, political organization, or social cohesion—in the process of being imitated so that it might be contained. It may be that the only strength the Third World had was a certain kind of political opportunism (since spreading), which justifies itself by a low estimate of the risks and dangers flowing from crises involving other powers.

Further, a drive for pre-eminence usually changes the configuration of power that initially permitted the drive. Such a change is temporary as a rule, lasting only long enough to defeat the drive, and in part it is reversible to the extent of permitting the reintegration of the defeated power. The bid of the Third World for a central role was possible because there seemed to be a relative equilibrium between the two superpowers. The drive itself affected the relationship of those powers only marginally (1) by the ultimately undecisive strains and distractions it caused in the Western camp on such occasions as the "police actions" involving Indonesia, Suez, and Vietnam; and (2) by the opportunities or incentives for expansion it presented to the communist camp in the 1950s and for internal differentiation, even discord, in the 1960s—in Asia between the communist great powers, and in the Middle East among the communist European states. The bid failed to harden the Third World into either a coherent third force or a compact ally of a third superpower (China). It failed to shift the balance of forces toward one of the authentic superpowers which would have managed to exploit the Third World for its ends, or to convert superpower rapports into condominial control over a Third World moving toward either its own disintegration or its integration with China.

In consequence, instead of changing the configuration of power, the Third World endured three concurrent and only superficially conflicting structural trends. One trend was toward a disparity between the superpowers favoring the United States, which the latter could not so much consolidate as give practical meaning to by action in the Third World. A second trend was toward a three-power configuration of the United States, the Soviet Union, and Communist China, one which had immediate substance if China could hope to rally substantial parts of the Third World. And yet a third was toward a polycentric diffusion of power (or at least foreign policy initiative) in both the Eastern and the Western camps, one which could be pursued most flamboyantly and with the least risk on one of several possible levels of involvement with the Third World. Any of these trends tended to transform the stakes and concerns of the major powers in the Third World from being obligatory to being merely optional, by reducing competition or generating alternative allies. And in the process they all tended to reduce the cohesion and the bargaining power of the Third World in general and its more radical members in particular.

Moreover, the continuing changes in the nuclear strategic and technological field reduced the importance of the Third World as the arena of conflict, and the importance of most individual countries as suppliers of bases and controllers of communication bottlenecks. Together, the changes in the configuration of power and in its technological makeup brought things back full circle. After World War II there was a feeling that in the nuclear era the continued control of colonial holdings could not significantly alter the standing of the colonial powers relative to the superpowers. This facilitated a rapid decolonization and, consequently, the postcolonial political boom. The boom ended when the superpowers had worked their way to parallel appraisal of the Third World's utility and potential. This appraisal dampened superpower conflict over that world. In somewhat the same sense, the acceptance of a military draw in Korea in the 1950s ended the temporary economic boom in the Third World after it had helped finance the self-redeeming achievements of departing European colonialism and foster the self-deceiving assumptions of the seekers for instant independence.

A thwarted bid for pre-eminence will normally force the subdued power to re-evaluate the future utilization of its reduced resources. Ideally, this would happen in a way which would make another bid by another power impossible. One classic way is to support the reorganization of the international environment undertaken by the leader or leaders of the earlier containing effort. Responsible decision-makers in most Third World countries have apparently revised their view of what could be secured by applying to the political contests of the superpowers, for partly economic ends, the technique of exploitation which the colonial powers are accused of having practiced in the sphere of economics, for partly political ends.

The Third World has been undergoing the first pangs of conversion into industrially productive economies. On the whole, however, it did not progress far beyond being political raw material for superpower competition that appeared to be increasingly regulated, limited, and qualified. This demeaning condition was being fed by every instance of real or apparent superpower "impotence" in the face of local disorder or defiance—disorder and defiance that could only superficially be mistaken for evidence of the growing weight of the Third World in the East-West (or even the North-South) relationship.

There are doubtless members of the Third World willing to go beyond ad hoc adaptations to the new relationships of need between the industrial and nonindustrial countries and to seek a long-term purposeful role in a post-postcolonial international order. Such an order would have to emerge under the reliable auspices of the power that contributed most to containing the earlier effervescence. The Third World was largely contained by its own internal schisms and insolvencies. The indispensable external condition has been chiefly the work of the Western superpower, however. The United States has managed to contain the more ominous bid of the Soviet Union without conspicuously propitiating and courting Third World radicals—a course that would have frustrated self-containment. Consequently, the responsibility has fallen to it, along with the merit.

3. The American Revolution:
From Anticolonialism to the First "Colonial War"

The process that led the United States to examine its national purpose regarding the Third World must be reconstructed, if the component parts of the climactic Asian crisis are to be disentangled and assessed.

There was originally a positive moral purpose behind America's world role. It has been too general a purpose to serve as policy, yet too ingrained in the national character to be overruled by pragmatic politics. It spread abroad an idealized conception of self that was manifested in several situations: (1) toward China before World War II, when it helped project the United States into the war; (2) toward Israel after the war; and (3) toward Africa in particular during the Cold War. In each case the moral purpose was reinforced by an articulate group with special interests or concerns at home.

The ready way to implement the ideal has been to oppose it to an evil embodied in a concrete enemy. In the case of China that enemy was clearly Japan. In the case of Israel, British imperialism and the Arab protégés of the British were more ambiguously the enemy because other perspectives were in conflict. In the case of colonialism in general and the African sector in particular, the formerly colonial European powers were first rivaled and then replaced by their communist would-be inheritors. The ideal's negative bias was demonstrated successively in the opposition to colonialism, communism, and (less sweepingly) neutralism: for a utopian dream these were the sources of present anxiety and of fear for the future.

The utopian-cum-apocalyptic strain was slow to give rise to the formulation of a positive new objective in keeping with traditional ideals. In connection with the war in Vietnam, the intellectual void created by the growing difficulty of identifying "international communism" as a compact enemy was automatically filled by the discovery of a new enemy produced by magnifying long-standing problems: racism, pauperism, and social alienation. This substitute enemy has so far made it possible to evade the need to define and implement a positive role for the United States in creating order in the international arena.

There was yet another obstacle to a more positive and creative approach, which the negative bias helped to circumvent. It is the question: What has been the "value" of the Third World when the assets it offered were such only because if it were neglected or "lost" it would then become a liability? If the Third World has had any contribution to make to the West and the United States in particular in the area of security (bases, local defenses against attack or subversion, cooperation in peacekeeping operations) or in the economics of trade and the supply of raw materials, that contribution has to be measured not only by the cost of evolving substitutes but also by the cost of allowing oneself to be replaced by an adversary who would convert a U.S. "base" into an enemy "outpost." Similarly, Third World assets have to be reckoned not only in terms of the aid they have given in crises, but also in terms of the outlay they have saved by helping prevent such crises. In view of such complexities, it was easier to fix the value of the Third World by an extraneous factor: a conception of the American purpose or else a doctrinaire assessment of the "identifiable enemy." The evil implicit in such an enemy could be assigned steady magnitudes. By contrast, if the value of the Third World in itself could be magnified but hardly assessed, a positive purpose (in maintaining world order) seemed either to be too abstract or to entail a built-in tendency toward overextending U.S. involvement, both because of the resistance such a purpose encounters abroad and the vested interest it develops at home.

The moment for reappraising the basic negative approach by the United States came only when the supporting conditions shifted. In the Cold War phase, specific values could be and were assigned to such assets as U.N. votes or strategic materials for waging wars, and bases for preventing or conducting wars, in Korea and Vietnam, as part of the policy of containment. If initially American concern for U.N. votes placed a special premium on the Latin American countries as principal U.S. supporters and as possible "bridges" to the Afro-Asians, later a more direct policy of containment progressively shifted American attention to Asia. There as elsewhere specific contributions to American policy, it was thought, could best be secured by placing them in the context of an ideal, that of the "free world," just as the ideals of the "open door" and "free and independent" China had earlier been exalted without their being wholly reducible to specific economic interests. More recently, the specific assets have remained essential in some places, because of continued U.S. involvement in the Third World. But these assets have been decreasing in importance as the United States enhanced its economic self-sufficiency within its continental or Atlantic framework and moved to recover a fair measure of strategic self-sufficiency through small-island or seaborne facilities, while the superpowers occasionally came to prefer the real reduction of risks in the Third World to hypothetical gains in it.

Changes such as these have created the need for reversing the procedure: to evolve an ideal definition of the value of the Third World and then to match it by appropriate specific means and objectives to be pursued in it. Its value could then be expressed in terms of both the international system and the domestic political system. The first rests on the supposition that the balance of international power, even more than the stability of the balance of international payments, could not be indefinitely served by gaping structural voids in world economy and world politics. While the most developed states could further sustain the fictions of a world economy and a global international system by funding joint institutions and by substituting themselves either as friends or as foes for any failing or absentee members from the Third World, such a situation might legitimately be viewed as neither ideal nor stable nor indefinitely practicable. Moreover, on the domestic side, for a still evolving multiracial country like the United States, the ideal value of the Third World might be formulated in terms of its indirect bearing on domestic order, by postulating (1) the ultimately adverse effects of either stagnation or cataclysmic upheavals in the Third World on internal conditions in the United States and (2) the positive effects of involving the multiracial American community as a whole in the positive objective of order in a Third World also multiracial.

For such an intellectual revolution to occur, the United States had to demonstrate in the global framework at least the degree of concern it has been displaying in Latin America, that part of the Third World closest to home and oldest in association. That continent has long provided the most conclusive evidence of America's embarrassment in the face of a missing "identifiable enemy." In the name of a utopia eventually to be called Pan-America, the Monroe Doctrine had attained (in collusion with Great Britain) the negative objective of keeping in check successive European interlopers. With that negative object seemingly secured and the utopia proven irrelevant, the United States groped for a substitute purpose. Largely in function of extra-hemispheric conditions and crises, the United States vacillated between aloofness (with but sporadic interventions from Nicaragua through Mexico to Guatemala) and an active quest for a new form of cooperative security, to be obtained in the Inter-American system, and of regional welfare, most recently through the Alliance for Progress.

The Alliance initially retained too much of the negative, anti-Castro stimulus and the utopian, constitutionalist fallacy. As a result it ran into opposition from both traditional U.S. allies in Latin America that represented the old order and feared to lose too much by radical reform even while legitimizing the remainder, as well as from hoped-for new allies, the presumed architects of the new order, who feared to forfeit everything but actual socioeconomic improvement through their association with the leading exponent of reaction in the world.

In time, however, new elements were introduced into the picture. The Alliance for Progress survived the high-water mark of the threat from Castro, reached perhaps in the Cuban attempt at subversion in Venezuela in 1963 rather than the one in Bolivia in 1967. The criteria for eligibility in the Alliance were adjusted downward to include reform-minded military juntas, along with socioeconomic criteria of effectiveness in action. In the Dominican Republic support for basic reform was coupled with marginal repression. All these factors—while the Alliance was not converted into either a panacea for Latin America or a foolproof model for Afro-Asia—represented a greater political maturity on the part of the United States. They represented (at least temporarily) the use of pre-eminent power and resource on behalf of order and progress. If nonetheless antagonistic or uncongenial forces still persisted as stimuli to effort, these were essentially local in character, only loosely linked to, and not identifiable with, "world communism" or any other direct global adversary of the United States.

Compared with Latin America, Afro-Asia has so far occupied a mid-position in the spectrum. It never fell as low in U.S. priorities as did Latin America at the peak of the Third World alliances for containment. Nor has it yet qualified in any of its parts for a commitment of the kind that was inherent in or symbolized by the Alliance for Progress. The principal identifiable enemy that strengthened U.S. incentive to assume the role of a world power was "international communism." At one time or another the other enemies were colonialism and (still less single-mindedly and at a later date) a neutralism of an internationally militant, left-wing kind. Over time, the relative priorities of the three targets shifted somewhat. U.S. opposition to the colonialism of its European allies was the first to be moderated by a revived need for those same allies against the new primary enemy, communism. And neutralist resisters to the postcolonial U.S. policy of alliances became secondary enemies before they regained favor as exponents of rediscovered virtues in neutrality. They have since progressed toward becoming more or less unashamed dependents of the United States in one way or another. Despite their differences, the similarities of colonialism, communism, and neutralism fitted sufficiently into the evolution of U.S. policy for the Third World to offset any variations in the kinds of problem they presented and the methods of countering them they called for. Each identifiable enemy implied an ally or allies, and each represented a possible form of order, while the U.S. opposition to them separately and collectively produced at best only a partial or provisional order.

Anticolonialism appeared first in U.S. policy. Its doctrinaire features were derived from the infantile disarray of the United States as an emerging world power. It did not mature into a settled policy, though it conditioned one. While private Negro organizations in the United States were preparing the groundwork for an African renaissance,

Franklin D. Roosevelt's selective anticolonialism bore mainly on the Middle East, North Africa, and (in relation to Asia) India, without actually informing U.S. policy during the malleable wartime period. The President's predilections on behalf of independence for a "democratic" India fell in due course on fertile ground. Thus any additional pressure became largely redundant. By contrast, the futility of trying to reduce the decolonization process to a single, democratic or other denominator was shown when the short-lived and clandestine liaison of U.S. agents with a supposedly noncommunist, nationalist type of Vietminh revolt in Indochina produced nothing like the hoped-for consummation. Beginning with the San Francisco Conference, the presidential policy of verbal anticolonialism yielded to an institutional one favoring compromise at the cost of some incompatibilities: (1) between favoring revolutionary change and stipulating an orderly, evolutionary manner of achieving it; (2) between wanting the European powers to freely shed their colonial liabilities and the same nations' allowing themselves to be rushed into new burdens to defend their curtailed patrimony from a spreading communist threat.

Overt and decisive U.S. opposition to "colonialism" occurred only twice, first against the military action of the Dutch in Indonesia, and second against the English and the French over Suez. If this was an extreme form of anticolonialism—aimed at establishing the anticolonial record of the United States in the eyes of Third World forces while keeping them out of communist hands at a tolerable immediate cost to interests in Europe—the other extreme was represented by U.S. opposition in the Kennedy era to granting an unsafeguarded independence to communist-tinged anticolonial movements in any area adjoining the innermost sphere of U.S. security, specifically British Guiana in the West Indies. An attitude of concerned neutrality and a qualified support for decolonization occupied the large middle of the spectrum of U.S. policy. These attitudes were implemented in cases such as West New Guinea (Irian) in Asia, or Tunisia, Morocco, and Algeria in Africa, and—when North African emancipation spread southward—in sub-Saharan Africa. This policy held good as long as it was consistent with the progressively heightened anticommunist concern in the United States. By and large, U.S. opposition to colonialism as the "identifiable enemy" became supplanted by the desire to do no more than avoid conspicuous association with the European colonial allies of the United States in the Third World. This attitude affected the Middle East before (and even more so after) the Suez debacle, and Southeast Asia before and after the Korean War.

One reason why U.S. anticolonialism was neither consistent nor conclusive was the paucity of bona fide and effective allies for an anti-colonial crusade. The natural, because "noncolonial" (in the Third World sense), ally against British imperialism was the Soviet Union, whose credentials were soon damaged by its seeking in North Africa (just as the United States had secured in the Pacific for military strategic reasons) a share of the postcolonial pickings. And the Soviet Union further undermined its qualification by moving via its quasi-colonial dominance in Eastern Europe into policies repugnant to the United States on a broad front. Any idea of a solidarity of the two "new" great powers in confronting the old had to be abandoned, or at least postponed indefinitely.

There remained two other potential allies of the United States. Of these, the liberal and left-wing anticolonialists within the metropolitan areas were less compromised than compromising, as the United States moved toward conservatism in its international relations. In contrast, the newly independent, excolonial countries could render only discreet service to the United States as long as they were headed by a moderate party in India. Their chief usefulness lay in their serving as models of successful decolonization, or as states to be wooed (in what were presumed to be common Western interests) by anticolonial interventions. These countries became a nuisance when under a more extremist leadership they resorted to persistent solicitations in the United Nations for anticolonial resolutions as part of their convergence with, and pilgrimages to, unfriendly communist capitals.

It was not long before communism replaced colonialism as the main "identifiable enemy" in the Third World. It took longer for it to spawn a succession of secondary enemies. Soviet communism already had preoccupied most of U.S. foreign policy before a spreading revolutionary extremism came to be comprised, as "objective" ally, in the concept of "international communism." Hostility outside Europe flared up first over Nationalist China, and turned really violent against communized China (in Korea and indirectly in Vietnam). Much of the interval was occupied by the relatively stately contests of the Eisenhower-Khrushchev era, which focused on the Middle East geographically and on foreign aid instrumentally. While Eisenhower's name became attached to an interventionist doctrine against "international communism," Khrushchev strove to update an older Soviet doctrine of counterattack against "capitalist encirclement." Since he was trying for less and from a stronger position, the American was less conspicuous a failure than was the Soviet leader. Both set the stage on which their successors could invert the earlier roles—the Russians setting out to achieve solidly after vainly attempting to shine and seduce, and vice versa for the Americans. The Soviet Union failed to subvert any one noncommunist regime or to supplant the United States in any part of the Third World outside Cuba. But it did establish itself as an attractive (if not equivalent) alternative to the United States in the Middle East and beyond. This cardinal fact could not fail to affect techniques, prospects, and problems in the post-Khrushchev era.

Anticommunism as U.S. strategy in the Third World was sustained by the enemy's own dynamic. As time passed the communist camp diversified its techniques over a widening spectrum, became more promiscuous in its partnerships and less unifying. The techniques of the Soviet Union and its East European helpers became more conventional, emphasizing foreign aid rather than domestic propaganda and intergovernmental rather than inter-party channels. The Negus of Ethiopia and the Shah of Iran joined (or even replaced) the rabble-rousers of Guinea and Ghana as the chosen partners. The Soviet objective changed from quick absorption to long-range atmospherics. The Soviet Union was less "moving in" to make things happen and more seeking to "be around" should disruptive events occur. But military aid remained a principal feature of Soviet policy—aid for the U.A.R., and later (by way of the U.A.R. at first) for revolutionaries in Yemen; aid to Pathet Lao by way of China, as later aid to India against China. Its supplying arms helped keep the Soviet Union viable as an antagonist of the United States, even when the ever cruder embodiments of "international communism" tended to make it an ally of the United States, or at least a parallel constraint.

As the role of spearheading world communism in the Third World passed from the Soviet Union to Maoist China and on to Castro's Cuba, the cultural level of its allies in the Third World sank accordingly. In lieu of revolutionaries with epaulettes (Nasser and Kassim) and university degrees (Sukarno and Nkrumah), there were now witch doctors of tribalism and terror (the Simba rebels in the Congo and the National Liberation Front in South Yemen). The new wave was uglier than the first but also easier for the United States to handle. It took more to oppose Soviet action in the Congo and in Cuba in the very early 1960s than to snuff out Communist Chinese forays into the Congo in 1964. Fewer Soviet resources invested and more extremism and inferior local affiliations permitted the United States to modify its counteraction from Cold War militancy to applied humanitarianism in the Congo and low-scale, indirect intervention in Bolivia.

Still, the problem was far from solved. The "enemy" was far from being either defeated or dispensable. As it became harder to identify as a centrally directed threat, critics of U.S. policy began to argue that it was being invented. The difficulty derived from the immense ambiguities surrounding the Sino-Soviet split. That split decentralized the communist movement. Whereas before there had been a unified spectrum of techniques and objectives assumed (and plausibly so) to respond to the least directive pressure of Soviet policy-makers, there were now variously assorted clusters of such techniques and objectives not subject to a centralized control. The split achieved this. But it did not generate a reliable basis for a discriminating U.S. approach to its communist protagonists, one that would clearly identify both principal and secondary, more and less "revolutionary," enemies. The communist offensive had ceased to be a tactical unity. The strategic defense against it, however, tended to aim at a target no less central for all its new unsteadiness. It was possible to assign the blame for this condition to the blindness of U.S. foreign policy makers. Yet another cause was the ideological lucidity of the Soviets, hesitant to draw irreversibly the last, bitter consequence from having been outflanked on the left. As Vietnam demonstrated, the two communist antagonists, Russia and China, were still unwilling (or unwitting) allies wherever a gain for the United States would be a loss for both—and the greater loss for the more passive or compliant communist power.

Until the United States could begin to view the Soviet Union as at least an occasional ally against the Peking-type (even if not Peking-controlled) revolutionary enemy, it needed allies against the Soviet Union itself. It readily found them in a reasonable colonial power like Great Britain, less smoothly in a militant colonial power like France, and less happily in rearguard colonialists like the Netherlands and Portugal. Such allies represented the greater embarrassment for the United States, the more incompatible they were with the new allies or potential allies emerging from the decolonization process. The awkwardness was least evident in respect to India, which was not seriously hostile to Britain but was even less so toward the Soviet Union. It was greater in the case of Tunisia whose moderate, but also egotistic, leader resented being kept (out of regard for America's "oldest" ally) in the diplomatic shadow of a France resisting decolonization in Bizerta as well as in Algeria. And the awkwardness was greatest in the case of a country like Algeria itself, alienated from the United States by an apparent American affinity with the *pieds noirs* of greater Africa, from South Africa through Southern Rhodesia as far north as Israel.

Despite all such difficulties, the more or less real Soviet threat and more or less opulent U.S. economic and military assistance equipped the United States at the peak of the East-West conflict with enough declared and undeclared allies in the Third World to fight its political war at least to a stalemate with economic means. Thus the United States could long avoid putting to the test its lesser ability to cope with revolutionary violence by chiefly political means—as it was later and unsuccessfully urged to do in Vietnam.

Two developments intervened to win America's battles in time to turn the tide. One was the growing tendency for the Soviet Union's bourgeois-nationalist allies to fight communism at home while exploiting its contest with the United States in the international sphere. The other was the Moscow-Peking cleavage, which destroyed the politico-economic profitability of the Moscow-Washington confrontation. If the first development made many Third World radicals into America's tacit allies against communism, the second eventually forced many of them to assume a more modest role as moderated dependents of the United States alone or alongside the Soviet Union.

The third-party neutralists in the two-power contest quickly turned into a confused and largely passive witness of a more complicated three-power competition comprising the two giants and China. As with the colonial powers, so with the neutralists: the erstwhile target of U.S. policy became a somewhat resentful ally, having suffered a psychological defeat. This happened, not because U.S. policy was always right, but because the United States could afford to stand relatively still, while the weaker and therefore more restless participants were being proved wrong about the role they could hope for.

If the Afro-Asian neutralists were to be worth subduing as communism's allies, they had to be built up as worthy targets for the United States. This operation took place in the middle and late 1950s. Stressing their disruptive self-assertion meant substantiating the threat coming from their Soviet "ally." However, the neutralists also provided distraction for the two superscorpions facing each other in the global bottle. If neutralism as a third force largely invented itself as a power, it was quickly patented by two willing patrons who were at a loss for what to do next to avoid the worst. The fiction was too elaborate to last: before a decade had passed, neutralism ceased being "immoral" and became largely immaterial.

Before they waned in influence, the "neutrals" grew stronger and more positive. Their early leaders posited nonalignment as a moderate stance between the two camps, in response to historical experience and internal needs. New leaders gradually turned that posture into a militant strategy with an anti-Western, anti-U.S. bias. If the United States had already had mixed feelings about the neutrals' effect on war and peace in Korea, relations worsened in the mid-1950s. In 1954 Egypt refused to enter a U.S.-sponsored defense organization (MEDO), and Nasser turned to the Soviet bloc for arms after the United States denied him arms without alliance. Concurrently the nonaligned countries drifted toward Communist China at Bandung and into strident opposition to Western alliances for the Middle East and Southeast Asia. There followed a war of nerves lasting some five years between the new West and the new East.

Yet even at the peak of its effort to gain allies, U.S. opposition to neutralism was as halfhearted as neutralism was equivocal. The official American attitude was a "No, but" mirror image of the "Yes, but" attitude toward the Third World alliances which were denied implementation along NATO lines and conspicuously preferential aid. As for neutralism itself, this implied a "neutrality" toward the great powers (often with a pro-Moscow or pro-Peking bias) while domestic communism was neutralized by internal repression (Nasser) or a kind of equilibration (Sukarno). Unhappy about the "neutrality," but delighted with the "neutralization," U.S. policy then took a middle course. It came to treat Nasser and (until the very last) Sukarno, as Great Britain did Mussolini and his imperial dreams after World War I, as the last safeguards against internal chaos or communism. They were to be kept from getting too big without being driven irrevocably into the enemy camp by being denied all gains in prestige or power.

If neutralism was opportunism clothed in ideology, opposition to it was largely a matter of interest posing as principle. Opposition to the more radical neutralists came from their local rivals: Nuri, Hussein, and Saud opposing Nasser; the leaders of Thailand, the Sumatran rebels and the loyalist Indonesian army, and the Tunku of Malaysia opposing Sukarno; Houphouet-Boigny and Senghor opposing Sékou-Touré and Keita; the Nigerians and Nkrumah's own generals opposing Nkrumah.

If self-interest inclined America's Third World allies against neutralism, it hardened the reluctance of the European powers to perpetuate the traumas suffered from their former colonial experience by accepting a back-seat role as colonialism faded and communism failed to scare. Exceptions could be found mainly in the few instances in which their strategies of decolonization were at stake, pitting Great Britain against Egypt and Indonesia and France against Egypt and Guinea. Fortunately, America's need for help soon diminished as local or global developments made nonalignment largely irrelevant or self-liquidating. Nonalignment became irrelevant when its former exponents approached alignment with one or both of the superpowers (as not only India but also post-Sukarno Indonesia and latterly Nasser did) and its targets became less aligned (as did Pakistan and also Iran, not to speak of Ceylon earlier). Nonalignment was self-liquidating, when its more moderate founders defected from radicalized neutralism (as did Nehru and latterly the post-Nehru India) or actually withdrew into isolation (as Ne Win's Burma did), while isolation befell the weakening radical wing. That wing in its last phase comprised a spectrum defined by Cuba, by Mali tentatively leaning toward China while still under Keita, and by Sihanouk's Cambodia, while Algeria's Boumedienne hesitated between Moscow and Peking, and Sékou-Touré of Guinea considered retreating toward Paris, on a rebound from both Moscow and Washington.

In the late 1950s and early 1960s, U.S. policy entered on a second five-year campaign, one no longer in opposition to, but in celebration of, the policy of nonalignment and of toleration by and large for neutralism. By this time there were incipient signs of what soon matured into the trends just discussed. The United States rode high in the Third World, ceasing its earlier unpopular policies (designed to reveal incompatibilities between neutralist and communist powers) in favor of the politics of popularity. Now the United States could seemingly afford to act serenely as the secure world power while speaking of its beginning as a neutral small state. A universal pronationalism was to succeed in the 1960s to the communist-obsessed antineutralism of the later 1950s. The new U.S. posture was first tried out in the Middle East, and then was more extensively practiced in Africa. It seemed only temporarily hampered in Southeast Asia by the persistent misbehavior of the neutralist Pathet Lao and the nationalist-imperialist Sukarno. The prospects seemed promising for a new Augustan Age—one in which America's updated power of attraction could win over the neutralists and neutralize their sobered communist backers. Both now appeared too weak or sufficiently well understood to warrant harsh opposition, and in any case it seemed no longer necessary to retain them as "identifiable enemies."

The dream of serenity vanished more quickly than the preceding nightmare of suspicion. It may be argued whether the dream was based on a misapprehension of the possible or the awakening due to a later miscalculation about what was still necessary. At this point it is more appropriate to ask what other "utopian" kinds of order had been thwarted and what conditions were taking shape for a feasible order in America's postwar progression in the Third World.

Each of the three targets of U.S. policy represented a form of order for the less developed areas—order in the sense of moderately stable and increasingly equitable relations between participants having unequal resources.

An order administered by sufficiently strong but chastened colonial powers might well have been the best for some time yet. Postwar French and British colonialism in particular managed to achieve conservative values—such as combining physical security with a minimum of conflict, and administrative stability with a minimum of corruption—at the same time as it encouraged the new, progressive virtues of socioeconomic development. France and Britain were helped in enlightened colonial administration by improved terms of trade for colonial exports and by additional metropolitan subsidies. However, since nothing could really succeed for the colonial powers in the new political climate, their intensified program of economic development could be impugned as a form of stepped-up foreign colonialization (because of the influx of technicians), just as their increased investment could be branded as exploitation, despite the relatively low rate of returns.

The postcolonial system was to become largely (and often at best) a continuation of the task of colonization with increased foreign aid under partially changed auspices. It is noteworthy, therefore, that the colonial powers did not deal effectively with racial problems either through multiracial federations (Great Britain) or through cultural assimilation (France), notably wherever one of the critical races involved was that of the governing group; and also that the colonial powers fought shy of regional cooperation or coordination, except where one of them was clearly dominant, as Britain was in East Africa and the Middle East and France was in West Africa. Left to itself, postwar colonialism still might have moved toward a regional coordination that would reflect metropolitan associations in Europe. But it could hardly have combined the development of material resources, locally and regionally, with promotion of world order. Only an unlikely growth of empire-patriotism in the dependencies could have significantly helped compensate the postwar disparities between the weakened metropolitan countries and the strengthened noncolonial superpowers in the world balance of power. It is in this respect that the colonial order was most clearly outdated and potentially destabilizing. The colonies had to be freed, so that they could relate themselves to new centers of power, while the old were recovering the strength and will for a revised role, or else withdraw like hermits from the power field with but local effects, a facility that the colonial powers themselves could not match.

The practical contribution of colonialism may thus have been mixed at best, though of real value to the less developed countries themselves. Communism, on the other hand, has represented, ideally, a possibility of order in all respects—local, regional, and global. In actuality, its potential achievement has not substantially differed from that of colonialism. Both aimed at superimposing a supranational principle, together with extraneous rationality, morality, and discipline, on indigenous elements that were more self-willed than self-controlling. A basic weakness of communism in the Third World has lain in this very disparity between mold and matter, notably in Africa. Like other would-be universals (such as French culture) communism will always risk coming to grief over the strategy of assimilation, especially if it ever achieved world monopoly.

As a potential framework of order, nonalignment had the advantage of depending by definition on two poles of power and vision. The monopoly of power was neither a lure nor a threat for nonalignment, any more than it was for any particular colonial empire, even within the limited confines of the Third World. Hence, if both the superpowers abstained from excessive pressure and if the nonaligned countries displayed a pragmatic impartiality, "neutrality" might have constituted a principle for order within regions and an element in global order by virtue of organizations excluding the great powers, a voting bloc in the United Nations, ethnic pan-movements, and areas of formal neutralization. Any such realization was impeded by the absence of what both communism and colonialisms displayed in excess at one time or another: a disciplined rationality transcending personal advantage and a central directive capable of constraining local diversities and animosities. As regards internal development, any advantages from pseudo-socialist radical neutralism, even more than those from competitive foreign aid programs, proved to be imaginary when discounted by mismanagement.

Thus, none of the three targets of U.S. policy represented a fully satisfactory order for the Third World in all respects. Moreover, their respective strengths could not be combined in any presently feasible configuration of world powers.[4] By contrast, the U.S. competition for control has averted the full potential for corruption implicit in all the alternative orders, and has kept at bay the propensity of the postcolonial world for anarchy and chaos.

First, the American attitude toward colonialism has probably helped reduce the violence attending decolonization. It has enhanced pressures

---

4. The nearest thing to a synthesis would be a communist commonwealth practicing the postwar type of enlightened colonialism and anchored in a strong Third World power observing nonalignment between power blocs based on free enterprise and state-capitalism. Such a commonwealth would further have to be kept both cohesive and enlightened by its need of support to resist pressures by both blocs.

on the colonial powers to withdraw peacefully; and it has influenced the more dogmatic opponents of colonialism, both communist and neutralist, to desist from violence in seeking to accelerate its passing.

Second, U.S. moreover, anticommunism has injected elements of order into the Third World through its strategies and instruments, notably foreign aid, intervention, and alliances. Of these, intervention and alliances induced order insofar as they comprised aid, and helped in generating the military-political conditions in which aid could prosper and would be politically defensible within the United States. An early example was seen in Iran following the Zahedi coup that liquidated the Mossadeq-Tudeh disorders. By and large, U.S. allies such as Pakistan, Taiwan, in later stages South Korea, and de facto ally Israel had as good or better records of turning aid to advantage than did the neutrals in Asia. In Africa the former metropolitan states continued to carry a large share of the burden of aid. The over-all positive potential of foreign aid was in principle (though not always in practice) enhanced by both the United States and the Soviet Union piling up aid in critical Cold War countries such as India, the United Arab Republic, and Indonesia. In Latin America, the Alliance for Progress stressed showcase countries with a democratic potential—such as Chile, Colombia, Argentina, the post-Trujillo Dominican Republic—and armed services oriented to programs for civic action, disposed to shift their concept of maintaining order by repressive means to a reformist and "nation-building" concept.

The results were bound to be mixed. The competitive and matching foreign aid strategies of the two superpowers (later imitated by Communist China) did not produce the conflict and confusion initially feared. But neither was the early hope that foreign aid would induce speedy industrialization and instant democratization (or communization) realized. This fact eventually disheartened the most singleminded of the early supporters of foreign aid, who then shifted their concern to domestic programs. It also helped reorient the flagging program of foreign aid by allotting resources for agriculture, prevention of famine, and in general less for economic development and more for humanitarian purposes. This trend paralleled not only decline of the expectations attached to foreign aid, but also a debasement in the level of violence, type of disorder, and kinds of revolutionaries in countries like the Congo and Yemen. Foreign aid for development implies upheavals in the existing order. Such upheavals were to be preferred to the explosions stagnation promotes when it is resented. Similarly, at the height of the Cold War, politically biased economic and military aid was preferable to none at all. The interdependence of economic bounty and political need is demonstrated whenever the most articulate opponents of injecting a "tactical" bias into U.S. foreign aid withdraw or weaken support for any aid once communism (or at least a centrally controlled communism) is believed to be a threat to American values no longer.

Third, U.S. antineutralism had a positive effect on building the bases of order to the extent that the seekers of only moderate socioeconomic change and political influence in the Third World were reinforced by Western sanctions or discrimination inflicted upon the neutralist radicals. Thus the United States withdrew from aiding the United Arab Republic in constructing the Aswan Dam, and France withdrew from aiding Guinea at all. In the long run, however, these policies had an undeniable if immeasurable effect. Hostile pressure will aid any "revolutionary" force to reach its extreme form before it subsides—sometimes by way of a cataclysmic explosion, for which neutralism, however, lacked the wherewithal. In a uniformly permissive environment, it would take longer for a revolution to devour its children and for conservative reaction to supersede both the revolution and its begetters.

American policies of negating colonialism, communism, and neutralism would have had a more clear-cut record if they had not been qualified by secondary or parallel concerns. This might be deplored if in the absence of such modifiers the United States had had the will to impose alternative solutions. But since this was not the case in the United States of the 1950s and 1960s, the general effect of such secondary or parallel concerns was not very damaging and in some instances it was even positive by dampening fitful zeal.

The chief modifier of anticolonialism was the desire for security in the Cold War. What had a modest beginning at the end of World War II in the Joint Chiefs' opposition to U.N. trusteeship for the strategically important Pacific islands that had formerly been Japanese mushroomed into a radical change in fundamental foreign policy. Initially, the United States favored decolonization as a means of liberating the war-weary nations of Europe from the colonial incubus and of hastening their regeneration. After the communist victory in China and the military contest in Korea, the United States tended to test each individual instance of decolonization by the effect on its NATO allies and the containment of its Cold War adversaries. The shift in U.S. policy—from declaring for any simple principle of justice to mediating between various rights and interests—brought dissatisfaction to all, but also some ultimate advantage to most. Only occasionally did the idea of a postcolonial millennium reappear as an objective. In the Suez crisis an extreme sensitivity to neutralist feelings (and some hurt feelings on the part of the U.S. decision-makers) prodded the United States into a spectacular "second declaration of independence" from European imperialism, thus injuring U.S. relations with its European allies in the long run even more than in the short. In Indochina the United States first rationed its support of France to promote local nationalism and then superseded the former colonial power only to become its updated version. This illustrates the impossibility (often neglected by would-be reformers) of superseding a power administering even an imperfect order without somehow taking its place, especially if alternatives are ruled out.

U.S. concern for local nationalism came to modify also U.S. anticommunist and antineutralist strategies. Thus the United States was induced to withhold its support of Batista in Cuba—thus ensuring his overthrow by Castro—and to minimize its aid and comfort to the Dutch and to Malaysia, beset by the regional imperialism of Indonesia. The same concern precipitated U.S. recognition of the "modernist" rebels against the traditional Imam in Yemen. Xenophobic nationalism in the Third World is a dubious and uncreative force. Yet identification with it was to turn U.S. policy away from the sterility of negative strategies. The hope was that the main thrust of indigenous nationalism would be directed against "international" communism in favor of development. Persistence governed any positive long-term effects of such a pronationalist strategy. These were diminished whenever prudence forbade going too far, either by assenting to the full reach of Castro's revolution or by moving to disentangle the more active neutralists from the accumulating frustrations of their imperialist forays. Thus at the height of its pronationalist strategy in 1963, the United States was unwilling to increase its diplomatic efforts at pacifying the Yemeni conflict to the point of supervising the military disengagement of both the Egyptian and the Saudi Arabian troops.[5]

Another modifier of U.S. anticommunism and antineutralism was the preoccupation with economy. This was manifest in the allocation of funds for foreign aid and in utilizing politico-military instruments. Economy set limits on what should be done for U.S. friends and allies. Sometimes this meant invoking a theory regarding the amount of aid they could absorb economically. Economic aid and related "economism" (the belief in the benign political effect of economic change induced by means other than "tactical" Cold War instruments) introduced into

5. The avowed reason was a misplaced deference to the U.N. alternative, which was time-consuming and wasteful of opportunity. See John S. Badeau, *The American Approach to the Arab World* (New York: Harper & Row, 1968), pp. 127 and 150ff.

the debate on policy the idea of the long-term effect as qualitatively different from the sum of short-term effects. Unfortunately, the United States—unlike some of the European allies engaging in variously motivated foreign aid programs of their own—could not actually choose between short-term and long-term perspectives. But neither did it evolve a conception of their relationship in practical policy.

The U.S. failure to evolve such a conception also affected its contest with the Soviet Union. The immediate requirements of the contest were not properly dovetailed with the long-range U.S. concern for expanding the "negative" community of superpower interests in the area of nuclear weaponry so as to avoid reciprocal provocations, and at a later stage, to ensure the nonproliferation of nuclear arms. Furthermore, the failure affected U.S. antineutralism. Most U.S. alliances continued to be regarded as strategically essential or tactically desirable in the short run, while neutrality or neutralization came to be regarded as a long-term stance preferable not only over militant neutralism but also, in a growing number of cases, over militant anticommunism expressed in alliances that were politically or economically ever more costly to the United States, its small-state ally, or both. The long-term preference for a neutral stance was expressed in policies such as (1) keeping Africa out of the Cold War, (2) morally disengaging the United States from Pakistan (even before Pakistan disengaged itself diplomatically from the United States after the Indochinese and Pakistani wars), and (3) shifting to neutralization as the formula for Laos and—in due course—Vietnam.

Mixing negative strategies with secondary or parallel considerations of a different kind produced incoherences but avoided the outright collapse of either the Third World or the U.S. position in it. Such a collapse might have followed either U.S. noninvolvement or its staking everything on any one negative strategy, however enlightened, or any one utopia, however pragmatic. The main achievement was thus to keep the situation fluid and the options open; the adverse effect of the negative U.S. policies was to help generate the obverse of some of the anticipated results, and to inhibit any positive strategy as a result.

U.S. support of anticolonialism strengthened the moral and political case for it. This accelerated the spread of decolonization to countries that were either too big and disparate (Nigeria and the Congo, and possibly even India) or too small and exiguous (Sierra Leone, Dahomey, South Yemen, etc.) for a viable political economy. It further reduced the remote possibility of consolidating colonial agglomerations in racially relatively homogeneous areas of Africa, Indochina, or the West Indies by the gradual devolution of colonialist authority, so as to prevent these areas from dissolving under the impact of instant independence.

Opposition to colonialism advocated domestic self-government and international independence, producing a peaceful and stable evolution into mature and modern statehood. Populations that were largely inert all too often reaped the opposite under insufficiently prepared and responsible leaders. In the name of popular will and national independence, there evolved internally various species of pseudosocialist, cryptofascist, and conservative-military forms of autocracy and mass "mobilization," and internationally forms of exhibitionism or sybaritism. In lieu of its promoting modernization and peaceful change, decolonization freed particularisms that were ethnically, tribally, or religiously animated. These in turn encouraged separatism and its repression. The general tendency to disappoint early expectations influenced some of the new countries to apply the old remedies of expansionist imperialism, interstate war, or civil conflict. The first affected Ghana and Indonesia in particular and was designed to convert priority in decolonization into postcolonial primacy while infusing a one-man state with collective pride if not progress. The second affected Pakistan versus India, Morocco versus Algeria, and (less overtly) Somalia versus Ethiopia. Interstate war relieved their accumulated tensions and demonstrated the de facto existence of the state or regime as well as its continued right or reason to persist. The third (savage civil war in the Congo and Nigeria, and stylized in Algeria) was set off by drives to split up the few incongruously surviving colonial conglomerates (Congo, Nigeria) or inflated and centralized entities (Algeria). Not all of such conflicts were wholly unproductive, but they were almost uniformly condemned by both liberal anticolonialists and Cold-War anticommunists as exaggerations promoting either the arms race, or communist influence, or both.

The outcome of the modified anticolonial posture was likewise disappointing in relation to the former colonial powers. Anticolonialism profited from European weakness, while it was encouraged by the United States so as to enable the European powers to undertake responsible defense action in Europe. When the United States later desired the European "middle" powers to extend their responsibilities to the postcolonial arena as part of a joint Western strategy, it found that, if European weakness had been replaced by a growing economic strength, involvement in colonial decadence had been replaced by indifference to postcolonial development or by a somber delight over the familiar predicaments of the new world powers. Even where the eximperial powers (including Japan) were contributing some foreign aid, they were governed by one-sided rationales hardly appropriate to America's multipurpose strategies. These rationales were too influenced by commercial interests on the part of Great Britain, Japan, and the nonimperial European aid-giver, West Germany, or else they were political in a too specialized sense, such as France's objective of perpetuating some degree of unity for the French-speaking civilization in Africa or the Federal Republic of Germany's desire to promote unity for the German-speaking nation. What was even less satisfactory from the U.S. viewpoint was the lack of allied support for American military-political defense efforts in the wake of Suez and Dien Bien Phu.

If anticolonialism precipitated the independence of a state regardless of its readiness, anticommunism tended to elevate the importance of the less developed countries, allied or neutral, beyond their intrinsic value. Anticommunist strategy aimed at perpetuating the favorable balance of power between the communist powers and the West (prevailing while the latter still retained a hold over the former colonies) by preserving from communist control most of the independence the new countries had progressively won from the West. Anticommunist strategy sought to do this by promoting attachment to the West and its principles of government. Instead, postcolonial retrogression and U.S. anticommunism together engendered calculating allies, ill controlled in policy, uncongenial in their political practices, and often unwilling either to give support in return for protection or provide facilities for the U.S. protector in advance of an emergency. There was some (if insufficient) comfort to the West in knowing that its plight was not unique. If the West for instance had to cope with a Pakistan more preoccupied with India than with the global Cold War, the Soviet Union had to cope with a United Arab Republic more concerned with the Arab "Cold War" involving Middle Eastern radicals and conservatives than with either the East-West struggle or even the Arab-Israeli conflict.

Moreover, to the extent that anticommunism helped induce the Soviet Union to practice reason, it made the West's allies doubt the old reasons for continuing an exclusive alliance with the West. The result was not only a newly dangerous (because more decorous) Soviet Union of Tashkent fame, but also—when American anticommunism combined with insufficient antineutralism—increasingly detached allies. Thus, for example, Iran was more and more inclined to accept Soviet aid for its long-term development and Soviet support for a last-minute claim to postcolonial pickings in the Persian Gulf area (in anticipation of Britain's withdrawal and in competition with another U.S. protégé, Saudi Arabia).

Antineutralism merely rounded off the prestige buildup of the less developed countries whenever it meant contesting the pretensions of the most assertive among them. Moreover, inconsistent efforts by the United States to contain inflated ambition tended to deepen the involvement of adventurist regimes with the communist powers, without dispelling their sense of U.S.-guaranteed immunity from communist seizure. Thus the entry of the Soviet Union into Cuba, Guinea, and Yemen was aided by lukewarm U.S. attitudes toward Castro, Sékou-Touré, and Nasser, respectively. In the mid-1960s, the declining careers of radical neutralists in Africa were prolonged somewhat by an eager drive for influence by Communist China, while Sukarno almost opened the way to power to a Maoist communist party on his way out of office. Fortunately for the West, the Soviet and even more the Chinese inroads tended to produce compensating reactions by showing up the local disciples or by forcing the patron's hand in areas in which the conditions for a communist-style revolution or communist orthodoxy (Cuba) were far from excellent.[6] The more recent decline of neutralism has not so far produced a stabilizing regional organization for peaceful development, however, despite a promising trend toward newly pragmatic approaches to international relations, even with the former colonial powers. Rather, the reaction often took the form of a passive parochialism, both among most members of the Casablanca group in Africa and—to a lesser degree and less conclusively—in postconfrontation Indonesia and post-Panch-Sheel India.

Yet on the whole the outcome was less disappointing than would have seemed likely. Through its sundry strategies for the Third World, the United States hoped to foster strong, stable, and positive factors for peace and order compatible with Western ideas. What resulted instead was only a measure of tranquility owing to the internal weaknesses of regimes no longer what they had been, or countries not yet what they hoped to become. Their weakness ruled out any positive action either for or against peace, whether such action crossed political barriers and territorial frontiers more sacrosanct than materially secured, or not. The weak links in the international order have become its mainstays (next to superpower stalemate and, some would argue, incipient introversion) through the kind of political physics with enough precedents to make such an order appear tenable without its being more than precarious.

The long evolution of U.S. foreign policy was dramatically foreshortened by the Vietnam War. It has amounted to a chemical compound of the broader, negative U.S. policies in the Third World. This compound unexpectedly exploded because of the sheer accident of its

6. Contrary to Chou-en-lai's estimate of communist chances while he was visiting Africa in 1964.

assortment of elements in an environment decompressed by the apparent decline of the Sino-Soviet bloc, or else (as critics argued) because of the untoward introduction into the compound of a detonator in the form of a utopian objective: the American role as a global policeman. The course of the Vietnam War has illumined the state of the Third World in general and in particular the current balance of authority in that world. And the possible alternatives of its outcome have defined the problem of America's evolution as a world power.

In the course of the Indochinese war of the last quarter-century, U.S. anticolonialism with its changing emphases has had an unquantifiable but hardly beneficial effect on that war. The early U.S. anticolonial token support had doubtless only a marginal effect on helping the Vietminh get under way.[7] Subsequent official U.S. reserve toward a "colonial war" did nothing to aid the French crush the rebellion in its beginnings. Following upon the loss of China to the communists and the threat to South Korea, massive U.S. support of the anticommunist crusade in the Indochinese theater was sufficient only to prolong the struggle without reversing the outcome.

The very length of the travail helped permeate the anticolonial elements with communist militants. Subsequently, the protracted Geneva truce helped integrate the severed North and South in their political elements, as refugee North Vietnamese rose to leadership in the South and antiregime South Vietnamese descended South from their Northern training grounds. The two processes injected into the conflict all the appearances of a civil war and all the realities of a holy war. Things had been different in Korea. There, a prompt removal of the Japanese colonial power permitted (despite the longer tradition of Korean unity than in Vietnam) a sufficiently rapid consolidation of the noncommunist South to compel the northern communists to trample upon their civil-war argument while crossing the partition line in force and en masse.

The protracted process of decolonization created the basic conditions in Vietnam for renewed insurgency without any overt initiative by the North. But the pretext for the renewal, and its immediate precipitant, are traceable to the anticommunist plank in U.S. policy, while the subsequent difficulty in pacifying the resumed conflict was increased by the merger in that policy of anticommunism with a residual distrust of neutralism as a truly autonomous force. The anticommunist strategy contributed decisively to the hardening of the "provisional" division of Vietnam that was effected by the Geneva

7. See p. 379 for the involvement of the OSS.

Agreements of 1954 by two related acts. The almost simultaneous Manila Treaty comprised South Vietnam in the SEATO guarantee as a protected state, and the United States extended an unqualified support to the Diem regime as an instrument for implementing the condition attached by the Eisenhower administration to its halfhearted adhesion to the Geneva Agreements—that the South remain outside communist (North Vietnamese) control.

From these early U.S. commitments, the rest could only follow, short of an abrupt and damaging U.S. reversal, unless Hanoi should be cowed by these commitments into giving up its aim of a united Indochina. It was therefore somewhat academic (however passionately debated) to try to determine the precise rights and wrongs in the tangled secondary issues. Prominent among these were such questions as whether the communist-tinged rebellion in the South was precipitated by the successes or the oppressions of the Diem regime; how deeply and at what stage the North Vietnam regime became involved in the insurgency; and whether Hanoi was provoking or being provoked by the growing American involvement. The debate was academic because, once the U.S. commitment was made known, Hanoi was unmistakeably on notice that it might have to choose between exerting its influence over disaffected Southern elements by supporting them, on the one hand, and arousing a U.S. counteraction, on the other. A small power is normally expected to yield before a greater power, unless the former is prepared to fight to the death for gaining exemption from a fact of life. The history of events suggests that Hanoi understood the dilemma better than its apologists did.

To allow Hanoi to entertain a brief hope that it might escape its dilemma was the most portentous failure of U.S. policy in the long run. The successive U.S. administrations allowed a disparity to emerge between the well-known, basic U.S. commitment and the questionable degree of American readiness for actual involvement on the level necessary to implement the commitment. This uncertainty was greatest in the period between 1959 and 1962 and its residue persisted up to 1965. It confused Hanoi—somewhat as Secretary Acheson's too explicit definition of the U.S. defense perimeter in Asia is believed to have confused Moscow and led Pongyang into invading South Korea— and led it into pursuing its long-term aim with less than level-headed strategies.

American acceptance of neutralization in embattled Laos under weak international supervision encouraged the belief that the United States would not intervene directly in Vietnam. This belief seemed to warrant a forward if discreet Hanoi policy in South Vietnam during the first phase. In the later stage of the Kennedy administration, when the United States showed an inclination to repair flaws in the Laos formula in Vietnam rather than replicate there the formula, the increased if still ostensibly inactive U.S. military assistance and the ferment following the fall of Diem drove Hanoi from its discreet posture to an unabashedly radical one, while a verbally militant Communist China reverted to a hard-line support of Hanoi. Between 1963 and 1965, whether reluctantly or not, Hanoi substantiated its military presence in the South by dispatching North Vietnamese regular troops. Perhaps misled by American temporizing into burning its bridges to retreat, Hanoi escalated its efforts in response to a likewise accelerating U.S. military involvement on land and in the air in a debatable pattern of initiatives.

As the struggle began in earnest, North Vietnam exchanged its radicalist leaning toward China for a determined course aided and (presumably) restrained by the Soviet Union. The latter's own ambiguously expressed concern about the issue was in turn governed by the partly conflicting requirements of relations with the two Asian communist parties, on the one hand, and the presumed requirements of détente *and* parity with the United States, on the other.

If Hanoi was confused by the fitful increase in actual U.S. involvement, the Johnson administration was even more confounded by the problem of how to relate the ebbing anticommunist sentiment in the United States to the vindication of the U.S. deepening commitment in Asia. The anticommunist stance seemed most justified when Communist China appeared to be in remote control at the time when the U.S. involvement in Vietnam was relatively low. It seemed least warranted when the need of the communist great powers to respond to America's rising involvement publicly exposed the divergencies between them. In terms of official rationale and public relations, militant anticommunism was thus self-defeating. There remained the possible argument that U.S. intervention—if less justified as a means of thwarting aggressive "monolithic" communism—was more than ever justified by the need to demonstrate in the face of a divided communist movement (tending toward conservatism or caution in some of its parts) the falsity of the Chinese thesis that the United States was a "paper tiger" unable to affect prospects for revolution in the Third World.

In either case, the anticommunist rationale could be criticized on two divergent grounds: (1) that it caused U.S. involvement unwarranted by any U.S. interests in national security or (2) that it provided opponents with ammunition against an intervention that was fully justified in the interests of world order as a defense of U.S. access to an area threatened by North Vietnamese imperialism. In the latter view, the communist character of North Vietnam was important in determining the severity of its thrust but it was not decisive in determining the allied response to it. Moreover, the precise long-term relationship between Hanoi and Peking could be left in the realm of hypothesis, all the more speculative the more effective the American intervention.

The ambiguities generated by communism and the opposition to it were compounded by neutralism. On the "positive" side, Hanoi could be pictured as essentially unaligned in relation to the two communist superpowers, pursuing nationalist aims, and better left alone so as to come into conflict with both Communist China and the more equivocally communist and more universally neutralist National Liberation Front in South Vietnam. Such a conflict in interest (the argument ran) had a good chance of producing benefits in the long run. That argument ran counter not only to a cautious concern with the immediate consequences of U.S. inaction in Vietnam, but also to the persisting measure of distrust of neutralism. Neutralist opposition had helped prevent SEATO from acquiring enough local legitimacy to forestall efforts at forcible revision of the status quo. At a later stage, the neutralization of Laos increasingly appeared as merely a provisional arrangement that facilitated Hanoi's action in South Vietnam while the conflict lasted, though it was not destined to outlast for long the application of a like formula to South Vietnam under even worse internal conditions than prevailed in Laos. Throughout, the difficulty in identifying the NLF leadership hampered serenity about either Hanoi's self-restraint in pushing for unification or the capacity of separatist NLF elements to resist Northern dominance, especially if unification became necessary to help the NLF and its sympathizers to final success in the South.

The resulting qualms were heightened by both Hanoi's and the Front's continuing call for the removal of all U.S. military presence in South Vietnam. To an objective viewer, that presence could be justified for some time after a political settlement. It alone could safeguard the physical security of both the NLF and the Saigon components of a postwar political system. A multilateral international body along the lines of the International Control Commission in Laos could hardly do as much. And ideally the presence would last for a period long enough to (1) enable the United States to set up a compensatory structure of inducements and deterrents that would militate against the enforced absorption of the South into a unified Vietnam; and (2) permit a necessarily heterogeneous coalition government (presiding only lightly in order to preside at all) to evolve a balance of power among factions and a balance of authority between regions and the center as a means to stabilization.

So intensified, doubts about NLF neutralism and Hanoi's restraint could not but temper the growing appeal of the neutralization formula as a way to a "no victory" peace in a lengthening war producing no decisive military advantage for either side. Yet even before the outcome of the war could reveal the relative standing of the adversaries and supply hints as to their future orientation, its course disclosed much about the general environment, comprising both the candidates for authority in the Third World and its innermost components.

If the war illuminated any feature of the Third World, this was its fragmentation. South Vietnam diverged not only along lines of religion, region, and racial background, but also in conceptions of government, alliances, and warfare. Internal splits aggravated the management of the war and deepened U.S. involvement almost as much as did North Vietnamese infiltration.

By contrast the fragmentation of camps in the Third World on balance facilitated the U.S. management of the war. Whereas the less developed countries in the Korean War tended to cluster as neutrals or U.S. allies, their increased numbers and more widely differentiated postures produced no such common fronts for or against the war in Vietnam. A supporting factor, which the war highlighted, was the decline of the militant, leftist regimes. This made it easier for Third World governments to avoid taking well-defined positions on a war that would ultimately be decided by the great powers and was being fought in a country whose rival leaderships were committed to one or the other Cold War philosophy rather than to anticolonialism per se. This factor worked in favor of the United States as the forward party, as compared with the Netherlands in Indonesia, or France in Algeria. Moreover, the fact that the likely beneficiary of a U.S. defeat would be a China of the 1960s (rather than the Soviet Union or the China of the early 1950s) gave the United States more covert official support in Vietnam than it had enjoyed in Korea. This was true notably among the Asian countries, while the growing cleavage between the Asian and the African wings of the Afro-Asian movement tended to reduce the repercussions of the war outside Asia.

By and large, the salient responses evoked by the Vietnam War were governed by an essentially healthy pragmatism—or, to put it less kindly, opportunism. Particular attitudes reflected specific local and immediate concerns about the anticipated effects of alternative outcomes. The disposition was manifest in Singapore or Malaysia, muted in Burma, and most pronounced on the part of countries adjoining Vietnam. Thus Prince Sihanouk in Cambodia varied his attitude according to his estimate as to which great power (China, if the United States lost, or the United States, if it remained present) could best protect Cambodia from North Vietnam, Thailand, or South Vietnam, as well as from Cambodia's own orthodox communists. The neutralist premier of Laos veered toward overtly supporting the U.S. war effort, as the survival of the neutralist regime and of the remaining independence of Laos came increasingly to depend on an alternative to a total North Vietnamese success. And America's closest Asian ally, the Philippines, inched toward nationalism by de-emphasizing association with the United States, as Washington veered away from a military solution toward a partial disengagement in Southeast Asia. Finally, the rightist regime in Thailand continued to adhere to its alliance with the United States as long as it could suppose that a tolerable outcome in Vietnam—combined with relatively favorable local conditions against spreading insurgency—would prevent Hanoi from helping Thailand's northeast become another South Vietnam.

The fragmentation within the Third World created new challenges and opportunities for external authorities. But neither was markedly enhanced or debased by the war in Vietnam. Rather, the respective standing of the United Nations, the Soviet Union, and the United States was transmuted by the war, perhaps because of concurrent changes in the Third World and in the world at large.

The United Nations was less prominently involved in Vietnam than in the Korean War of "collective security." What the Organization as a body lost in consequence, the U.N. Secretary-General gained for its soul by repeated if futile efforts at mediation. The Vietnam problem reconfirmed the awareness that, other than belligerents, only the great powers (whether or not sitting formally in the Security Council) could really affect peace or war—especially in conflicts involving both superpowers, however unevenly. But the United Nations trend to a flexible independence appeared helpful in the long range though somewhat unproductive, even superficially humiliating, in the short term.

Meanwhile, the Soviet Union lost some authority in the Third World by its inability to prevent U.S. air attacks on a small, communist protégé in the Third World. This loss may have been recovered by its subsequent willingness to increase its defensive military aid to North Vietnam and thus retain its influence on Hanoi's offensive political aims. Soviet interests appeared to favor a peace settlement that would favor neither the United States nor Communist China. To achieve this delicate equilibrium, the Soviet Union depended on the reluctant technical cooperation of Peking, induced to tolerate the transit of Soviet material through China while protesting its allegedly pacific purpose. And it also depended on the political cooperation of the United States, willing to tolerate important Soviet military aid without retribution while waiting for its pacific purpose to reveal itself. The upshot was a high-wire balancing performance, which enhanced the remaining authority of the Soviet Union as leader in the divided communist world while further improving its appeal as a reasonable power in a postrevolutionary Third World.

The United States as the principal tragic actor ought to have been the loser if others were partial gainers. But so mechanical a relationship did not necessarily apply, in so far as the Vietnam War paralleled the transformation of the bipolar, Cold War system into a new order of political magnitudes. In this new order the United States was cast in the role of an externally embarrassed and internally troubled world power, still towering in its strength and weakness while striving for a larger order at the cost of internal and external disorders. In World War II, the United States was involved in Asia largely as a withdrawing imperial power—one that first protected and then recovered the Philippines before setting them free. It was involved there as the emerging principal Atlantic power, fighting in Asia to help keep Britain fighting in Europe. In the Korean War the United States relied on the legalistic and ideological instrumentalities of the Cold War in a first-line defense of a Europe threatened by Soviet-led communism. The two-phase U.S. involvement in Indochina seemed to show its progression toward a new posture, however—that of a salient and therefore a solitary power, asserting its right to its writ wherever it chose. The only tenable purpose of this claim has been to defend America's prerogative in shaping regional orders even more than in defeating communism as a world movement, so as to prevent any other great power (communist or not) from shaping such regional order to its will.

The transition from the U.S. posture in the Korean War to that in the Vietnamese remained unavowed and was even unnoticed in sufficient time for the nation to make psychological and organizational adjustments. This fact accounted for many of America's internal shortcomings during the Vietnam War and for some of the military shortcomings in the field. The latter shortcoming fed into the widening domestic opposition to the war in Vietnam as being not so much the wrong war as an absolute wrong. Its failings should have reduced the authority of the United States in the Third World as a power which could be relied upon to protect small countries from either superior external power or subversive internal power—and at an acceptable cost to local allies and protégés. This should also have been the consequence of such weaknesses as the U.S. failure to establish a productive relationship with the Diem regime, or with its partners in negotiations with Hanoi after the fall of Diem. Yet the changes simultaneously occurring in the Third World militated against such logical conclusions.

These changes had one key effect: they placed the United States in the position of the indispensable support. And they wrought a change in the purpose of that support—no longer one for indulging in postcolonial fantasies but for coping with post-postcolonial realities. The United States remained on probation as the world's pre-eminent power—not on account of its uneven performance in a hard and in many ways a qualifying war, but rather because of its uncertain disposition to persevere in its evolution away from its irresponsible isolationism and infantile anticolonialism toward a more enduring and mature posture.

4. Patterns of Power and Policy:
From Containment to Devolution

The elements that constitute the Third World have been contradictory in nature and incoherent in sum. Extremism has contrasted with exiguity and only gradually yielding ideological "isms" have been at odds with more pragmatic adjustments to reality. Holy wars have been conducted as tournaments or intrigues, while ruthless force has been reserved for half-hidden civil conflicts. A "new politics" of a quasi-parliamentary internationalism oriented to social welfare has contended for ascendancy with the subversive strategies of some regimes and with reciprocally exploitative practices by virtually all governments, widely different in power and in sense of responsibility. In consequence, the politics involving the lesser states and spanning at least two distinct stages of political development has been harder to manage than the bipolarity of the superpowers.

In this situation the United States has had to act in a multiple capacity: (1) as a culture that stands—and can afford to stand—outside the disarray in the Third World; (2) as a society in partly comparable turmoil; and (3) as a power constrained by its own interests to try to contain some of the general ferment. Whether that can be done has depended—apart from U.S. material and moral resources—on the distribution of power, influence, and freedom from constraint in the world at large.

As the Johnson administration was leaving the stage, it passed on to its successor a heterogeneous international arena that was also increasingly heterocentric. This meant that thought and action have had increasingly to consider any or all of four perspectives: unifocal, bipolar, tripartite, and polycentric.[8] Each entailed a different situation as regards the role of the pre-eminent world power, the two super-powers, an assertive third power, and certain middling or minor states with some independence in policy.

In the unifocal perspective the United States stands out as the one global power that could be called imperial. Without being a transcendent umpire, it constrains and limits what others can hope to achieve by disturbing the status quo. The United States has been as critical a consideration for the Soviet Union in making decisions as for the most insignificant individual or collective actor. While the U.S.S.R. rationed its aid to the U.A.R. in Yemen and presumably to North Vietnam so as to avoid a direct confrontation with the United States, much lesser parties in Vietnam or Bolivia have had to assess likely American reactions in handling local insurgency.

For most countries the possible relations with the United States have been more important than their relations with geographically closer states. Thus Cambodia or Tunisia in relation to the United States might constitute a protégé or an *enfant terrible*; Israel and South Africa might constitute an outpost or an irritating liability; Thailand and South Arabia might be an ally or a defecting neutralist; Japan or Brazil might serve as regional vice-regents or as challengers; Soviet Russia and China (or a Western European power complex) might function as a global co-manager or as rival. These options have a greater order of magnitude than do the alternatives surrounding Cambodia's relations with North Vietnam, or Tunisia's with Algeria. The same might be said of Israel's or Saudi Arabia's relations with the U.A.R. and South Africa's with Zambia; of Thailand's relations with Indonesia or even China; of Japan's relations with Soviet Russia or China or South Korea, and of Brazil's with Argentina; or even Russia's and China's relations with each other or with any third entity such as Western Europe or Japan.

The strains of so focal a position have made the United States intermittently seek a lower level of responsibility. This has naturally created uneasiness and uncertainty abroad, for it has intensified the problems of adjustment of the weaker states. The unifocal perspective

8. An earlier discussion of the levels of the contemporary international system can be found in my *Nations in Alliance: The Limits of Interdependence* (Baltimore: The Johns Hopkins Press, 1962), pp. 161–67. See also Stanley Hoffmann, *Gulliver's Troubles* (New York: McGraw-Hill, 1968), pp. 17–51; and Donald S. Zagoria, *Vietnam Triangle: Moscow, Peking, Hanoi* (New York: Pegasus, 1967).

has at times prescribed a different approach to concrete problems than the narrower local perspective would have indicated vis-à-vis a local adversary or alternative protector. Cambodia or Jordan have wanted to remain in the good graces of the United States whatever the occasional tactical disguises, but they have also been influenced by fear of local allies or adversaries of the United States (Thailand and the two Vietnams in the case of Cambodia, Israel, and the U.A.R. in the case of Jordan), as well as by expectations of protection from America's rivals, China and the Soviet Union.

Thus qualified, the unifocal perspective has not meant so great a predominance for the United States as to replace bipolarity with unipolarity, but it has modified bipolarity insofar as the latter means an actual or imminent parity between the United States and the Soviet Union. Bipolarity has been modified further in its other two key aspects: (1) the degree of antagonism between the superpowers and (2) their joint monopoly of conflict. Regarding the first, the superpowers have acted as antagonists in supplying the critical matériel for conflict to lesser antagonists such as Israel and the Arab states, India and Pakistan, South Yemen and Saudi Arabia. Insofar as such conflicts had to be contained so as to allow the superpowers full control of the escalatory ladder, however, the so-called negative community of interests with regard to nuclear weapons (and their proliferation) has been progressively extended to include a range of concordant political operations. The Cold War has thus been affected by the idea of a "Russo-American peace" as an alternative (or supplement) to an "American peace." As regards the second aspect—the superpowers' monopoly in defining a significant conflict as one involving them—decolonization and postcolonial politics have progressively reduced the political theater and actors subject to the superpowers for the definition of stakes and payoffs.

The sustained antagonisms which pitted the European powers against radical anticolonialists, or the Third World allies of the United States against assertive neutralists, have conformed more closely to the global East-West pattern of the Cold War than have the military engagements between countries of the Third World. But since the third-force neutralists have also been wooed by the superpowers, they have represented the first relatively independent entity to which the superpowers have had to adjust. By the end of the 1950s this fact had introduced a tripartite dimension into bipolarity. The lesser allies of the superpowers, too, came eventually to qualify for third-party status. Partly because of superpower involvement in the Third World, the more independent of these allies had to be taken into account by the superpowers in calculating the odds and assessing the likely gains and liabilities of alternative policies. Thus French support of the Arab states against Israel, or of Biafra against Lagos in the last two years of the de Gaulle regime, and the support shown in Rumania and other Eastern European states for Israel, weighed on superpower policies as liabilities in one degree or another. In terms of the Third World alone, the tripartite concept was at work in the Khrushchev era, when the Soviet Union displayed caution in pushing its advantages—in penetrating more deeply in Syria or Afghanistan for instance—for fear of alienating many more countries in the Third World by a flagrant take-over. And the tripartite concept was manifest when the United States hesitated to impose the strict rules of the game on the more forward leaders of the Third World, such as Nasser and Sukarno, for fear of generating short-term advantages for the Soviet Union, even though self-restraint imposed serious strains on U.S. leadership of its European allies.

While these intangibles were being sorted out, the self-assertion of a compact China gave substance to the tripartite concept. It appeared to offer the lesser (allied or neutral) states an alternative to the two superpowers. It also converted the relations between the two into a three-power configuration by generating both an alternative concern and a potential consort for either. The Laos crisis of the early 1960s following the Sino-Soviet split in the 1950s initiated in earnest a three-power global politics that continued in the Vietnamese conflict. It inclined the Soviets to promote a safe draw between the United States and China by means of controlled aid to Hanoi, and moved the United States to seek the best possible outcome by means that would not reunite the two communist powers, while China sought to defeat both superpowers in different but complementary ways.

Any two parties in a tripartite situation will be concerned about the effect of what they do on the third party. They will be concerned not to turn that party into either a laughing or a panic-stricken third. For either the United States or the Soviet Union to win in the Third World in a way that would confer an advantage on an ambitious China or another regional expansionist would be as undesirable as to propel such a third party into alignment with the other superpower. This makes for difficult calculations. They are further aggravated when the third power becomes strong enough to initiate some action vis-à-vis one of the superpowers that would place the other superpower in the position of the third party, and either benefit it or alarm it sufficiently to inspire it to an imprudently radical course (the Soviet Union) or a passive course (the United States).

In the three-power relationship of the two superpowers and one authentic middle power (having a long-term superpower potential), evolving issues and domestic policies would decide which of the three would be the centrist power, one that would be less forward than the other two, that would react rather than initiate, and would seek advantage in the mistakes of the other two rather than in any grand designs of its own. Thus China could veer toward the centrist position if it were to reduce its international activism in favor of internal development and encourage the United States toward a détente with China in preference to an entente with the Soviet Union. Or the United States might occupy the moderate center between an aggressive Soviet Union and an aggressive China, in conflict over Central Asia or over the leadership of the communist "commonwealth."

In the 1950s its reasonable Bandung posture seemed to place China in the centrist position in the Third World. In the 1960s, with increasing consistency and toughness, owing not only to the Vietnam War, the Soviet Union seemed anxious to entrench itself in that position. To gain political advantage and to minimize ideological losses, the Soviet Union sought to do as little as possible to contain China and as much as possible to aid elements in Asia which were reserved or potentially hostile vis-à-vis both China and the United States, even if this meant a temporary eclipse or worse for local communist parties. Among such elements was India after the Chinese invasion, the Indonesian Army before the attempted putsch of the Chinese-sponsored communist party, and North Vietnam after escalation had removed the war beyond the limits of China's material resources. The governing purpose of the Soviet Union was to avoid the triumph of either the United States or China as well as total rupture with either, and most of all to avoid a rapprochement between the two principal (American and Chinese) contestants over Southeast Asia in the wake of an "honorable" peace that would leave each more exasperated with the third (Soviet) party than with one another.

As one of the two main adversaries in Southeast Asia, Communist China sought to update (to her advantage) the tripartite relationship of the 1950s into one among near-equal three powers. That meant China would assume leadership of the formerly neutralist third-force elements against both superpowers by demonstrating that the two industrial giants were alien to the Third World and ineffectual in it. To this end—besides dispensing a faltering economic assistance and castigating U.S. imperialism—China sharpened its ideological differences with the Soviet Union on the unsubstantiated assumption that the Third World countries were intrinsically revolutionary, while shielding from its own Cultural Revolution her breakneck pursuit of nuclear capability, on the possible assumption that those that proved "counterrevolutionary" would bow to nuclear blackmail by a studiedly irresponsible China. Alternative courses for Chinese leadership, however, were implicit in the fact that these ideological, propagandistic, and nuclear strategies could be turned to a defensive end—that is, deflect threats from China's permanent revolution and national power substance.

The policy of the United States (the other active adversary) had been roughly to contain China by isolating it. This policy entailed inducing the Soviet Union to cooperate in containment while limiting its political penetrations that could be secured by cooperating with the American purpose or by remaining aloof. The never wholly successful isolation of China depended on trade embargoes from the Western allies, on political ostracism by Asia and Africa, and on the economic outperformance and assistance by Nationalist China. It also entailed a policy of a dual standard in both ideological and practical matters. The dual standard in ideology meant the United States permitting a détente with European communism while remaining strict with its Asian varieties. With respect to military and political assistance to America's enemies, it meant tolerating a growing Soviet military assistance to Hanoi during the Vietnam War, on the assumption that such assistance—by protecting Soviet Russia from Chinese charges of collusion with the United States—would enable her to isolate Peking from Hanoi and make Hanoi receptive to a compromise peace.

The dual standard was rooted in common superpower concern about nuclear proliferation and in China's equivocal position in that regard. But it also expressed the fact that the United States welcomed Soviet aid in containing Chinese influence in South and Southeast Asia. The less assistance the United States received from its European allies, either directly through SEATO or indirectly through NATO, the more Soviet assistance appeared to supplement the cooperation of the lesser Asian states against Chinese incontinence, should it go beyond verbal claims to Formosa and doctrinal revolutionary pronouncements matching in ambiguity Peking's historical record in this area. In so doing, the United States was apparently hoping (rather than stipulating) that Soviet manipulation of supplies of arms (in Laos and India) and its soundings for peace (in the Indo-Pakistani conflict as well as in Vietnam) would not open up the way to Soviet political hegemony in South Asia under the cover of barring China's more blatant self-assertion.

In part to safeguard such a hope, the United States did little toward penalizing the Soviets for barring U.S. efforts at a "peaceful engagement" with members of the Soviet bloc in Europe so as to match a growing Soviet engagement with U.S. allies and present or past friends in the Middle East and South Asia. That is to say, the United States did not visibly aim at a facility indispensable to the three-power game: the ability to move closer to China if and when antagonism between the United States and China should encourage the Soviet Union to move too far away from (or against) the American view of things. The possibility (in response to such things as apparent Chinese feelers late in 1968) rested on one of two presumptions about the communist great powers: (1) that they were either realistic gamblers for relative advantage, or (2) that they were more divided by heresy than hostile to the United States as a mere unbeliever.

Such an equalization of options was implied in the new slogan, "Containment without isolation," for a new American policy toward China. It was a future concern so long as the Vietnamese war continued unabated. In late 1960s, the three-power situation could still be stated in the following terms: the United States was seeking to contain China militarily and otherwise; the Soviet Union was seeking to contain China politically and ideologically. Both wanted to achieve their objectives without creating a major advantage for the other superpower. And China sought an ideological defeat of the Soviets, hoping perhaps one day to detach some Soviet territory, without giving the United States a decisive politico-military advantage.

All three powers depended first of all on a continuous calculation of the resources and responses of the other two; but all three also had to comprise in their calculations the interests and attitudes of both the European and the Afro-Asian lesser states. The United States had to avoid alienating too many; China sought to win over as many as possible, while keeping in line a small group of congenially radical Afro-Asians and keeping the lines open to an even smaller number of European powers (by continuing as a potential source of political aid to Eastern Europeans and of economic advantage for Western Europeans). Last but not least, the Soviet Union invested great effort in conciliating such widely disparate countries as France, Japan, Iran, and Pakistan, so as to avoid being some day isolated in a German-Sino-Japanese vice, under the auspices of a United States thus freed to combat Soviet prospects in the Middle East, South Asia, and Europe.

Under any conceivable three-power configuration, the number of options for other states would exceed the number of choices open in a bipolar context. The possession of options does not automatically mean either a control over the outcome or even a significant influence on events, but it does mean diplomatic independence, which may even increase as either control or influence decreases. The tolerance of the major powers would grow—and the significance of polycentrism would decline—if the three major powers came to see their internal changes and their reciprocal alignments outweigh the support of the divided lesser states. Conversely, if China or any other major third power did not attain "parity" with even the weakest superpower, the political independence of a growing number of centers elsewhere would be all the more significant—especially if the material power implied in multipolarity (as compared with polycentrism) were comparably diffused.

By the late 1960s polycentrism—energized by the "loosening" of bipolarity—seemed secured. But it did not seem any the deeper rooted in power usable for more than temporary and local dislocations. Its scope was not even visibly expanding, since even independence in policy-framing tended merely to shift from minor to middle powers. The impact of polycentrism has been limited by the rigidities of Chinese policy, by the insignificance or immobility of most of the other states that might in principle gain from the triangular contest, and by the nonproliferation of nuclear weaponry as the symbolic and defensive basis for serious diplomatic initiatives. Consequently, polycentrism has not been so far much more than a parliamentary expression of sovereignty, in the United Nations and in occasional initiatives toward causing or resolving deadlocks regionally.

As the postcolonial aggregates and transient unions split up and postcolonial economic and political regionalism failed to crystallize while the relations between the superpowers relaxed further, powers of actually or potentially middle rank emerged as the critical factors in any possible progression from polycentrism to authentic multipolarity. It came to be increasingly the turn of the middle powers (including now, next to a few of the bigger less developed countries, also the former colonial powers of Europe and Japan) to enact the continuing tension between performance and pretension, real impact and nominal influence. It was, in other words, increasingly up to India and Indonesia rather than Ceylon or Cambodia, France rather than Yugoslavia, to represent "independence" in initiative and policy— while even India was being slowly overshadowed by the power of China. The definition of middle power has not yet crystallized into anything as precise as the traditional definition of a great power, positing an independent capacity to wage war within the central balance of power. But the basic requisites for being a middle power have already emerged as comprising the capacity and disposition to support with roughly commensurate material resources an internationally useful role—or internationally disturbing ambition.

In terms of resources (the material basis of power) only Japan and China have so far clearly qualified for middle-power status in the Third World. They join France, Great Britain, and West Germany as actual or potential participants in Third World politics. Yet since all these countries also qualify (either individually or in conglomerates) as first-rate powers, other Third World countries could also be envisaged as vying for the pertinent privileges and responsibilities. Yet internal setbacks for early favorites such as Nigeria and India have shown how difficult it is to guess at the winners in this particular "race."

One reason was the lack of continuous cohesion shown when Nigeria disintegrated (at least provisionally) and India stopped short of disintegration perhaps only for the time being. Another aggravating factor was the lack of coherence in assets and liabilities (in population, size, economic and technological resources, and managerial and military organization). This lack of staying power and coherence made it difficult to assess the total capacity of populous countries such as China, India, Indonesia, Brazil, or (in African terms) Nigeria, and of territorially large countries like Argentina, the Congo, Mauritania, and Mali, not least because the population increment tends to exceed increases in productivity. Moreover, the fragile economic development of some of the most sizable or populous countries (such as Brazil, India, presecession Nigeria, or Algeria) was also unevenly distributed in ways that mortgaged the valuable core areas of such countries. Furthermore, such economic disparities tend to intensify divisions, whether ethnic or racial, tribal or religious, regional or sectional (to which most or all potentially major Third World countries are subject, India or Indonesia no less than Brazil and Nigeria). As in all other respects, Japan stood apart, increasingly untypical of a world that it has been unable to dominate and therefore is leaving behind.

Accordingly, to name a future political middle power matches in difficulty the earlier attempts to pinpoint the pilot countries most likely to qualify as models of economic development. Nigeria exemplifies the wrong assessments in these two respects. A complicating feature is the difference between a conspicuous political self-assertiveness and a steady growth—the difference between, say, the U.A.R. and South Africa, between China and Japan, or Indonesia and Thailand, or, over a much longer period already, between Argentina, Brazil, and Mexico. Since long-term potentials for development are uncertain, conspicuous comportment has carried a disproportionate weight. Neither India, nor Brazil, nor even China could hope soon to become a major industrial power and acquire a conventional military capability for both a secure and dynamic posture. China has loomed larger than the economically stronger Japan or any other Third World country only because it has been ruthless in producing and occasionally even using ostensible power, both economic and military. By contrast, an at once traumatized and shrewdly calculating Japan has clung to a modest conventional capability even after China attained nuclear capability, relying on the stronger United States and combining feelings of guilt with contempt for Chinese technology. Japan's reluctance to employ its small conventional military power has so far extended even to multilateral frameworks. Brazil, on the other hand, was prepared to act through the OAS (in the Dominican crisis) and India through the United Nations (in both the Middle East and the Congolese crises). India's distaste for the use of force was never total (witness the Goa incident), and became even less in the wake of encounters with China and Pakistan. While Japan was compensating for its invasion of China, India was smarting from being China's easy victim. Psychological complexes loomed as large in the Third World as did political and economic complexities.

Sukarno's Indonesia stood closer to China in the disposition to use its available (or not so available) power. Both combined grandiloquence with a more limited, partially disguised, but still real deployment of power beyond their national borders. The U.A.R. did resort to forceful means, but never successfully or even deliberately enough to make up for its intrinsic deficiency, thus qualifying for only a very local middle-power status. Egypt's inability to master the Yemeni guerrilla tribesmen with a large conventional force was mercifully dwarfed by the parallel with American difficulties in Vietnam—although the Egyptian deployment was proportionately bigger and her adversaries qualitatively inferior. The bigger war in 1967 that terminated the U.A.R. engagement in Yemen brought Israel a so far temporary acquisition of vast territories and a sizable subject Arab population. These acquisitions threatened to convert Israel into a regional middle power by the economic and military processes it had instituted to safeguard its existence as as small state.

Should this come to pass, Israel's acquisition of middle-power status, along with a comparable increase of strength in South Africa and Australia, could reassert the white-European characteristics of the late colonial system in a postcolonial setting—regardless of the degree to which the excolonial powers themselves re-entered the Third World in new force as middle-ranking world powers. To play a major role, the European powers would have to go beyond postcolonial rearguard actions, usually consisting in the redeployment of a token military-police power (such as those of Britain and France in Africa) and in supplies of arms and economic subsidies—all more or less in the service of waning political commitments or both old and new economic interests. A more significant reinvolvement would require their aiming a more systematic and system-wide political action, with both economic and military backing, at a concrete global and European order.

Even a strong and active state could not be a middle power unless it played a relatively independent regional or global role. Independence means at the very least the will and capacity to choose with whom to be interdependent and for what purpose. Once a power is deemed unwilling to act alone in any contingency, it decreases its capacity to act effectively even in combination with others. It can no longer significantly contribute means while co-determining the ends of action. Thus, following the failure of its unilateral action in the Middle East in 1956 and its extreme caution in the Malaysian crisis in the mid-1960s, Britain did not substantially contribute to the U.S.-led efforts in either area or even sway them, though claiming to support them. Japan weighed still less on events in Asia, even within the United Nations.

An important regional role will entail some competition with intra-regional and extraregional states over defining the conditions of local "order." Thus in the nineteenth-century struggles over regional primacy, Chile was briefly able to exclude the United States from interfering as mediator in the South American War of the Pacific. On the other hand, neither Mexico, Brazil, nor Argentina could more recently interpose effectively between the United States and the local states, either by traditional or updated means of influencing lesser countries. They had to be satisfied with only an occasional and temporary thwarting of the United States—for instance in the matter of collective sanctions against Cuba in 1962.

In Asia, neither India nor Japan was prepared to commit itself toward shaping power and order in its area. India was handicapped by economic dislocations, Japan by apprehensions that a too forward stance might jeopardize her profitable trade and propitiatory economic aid activities. Both were reluctant to exchange the continuing advantage of superpower protection for the risk of provoking either aggressive China or apprehensive Burma or South Korea, still undecided which potential regional hegemony to fear the most. Compared with the inertia of India and Japan, the regional ambition of countries like Algeria, the

U.A.R., and Indonesia was weakened by the failure of their too volatile policies to choose between prizes at hand or more distant and vaster areas of potential influence.

Except for France in French-speaking Africa, only China appeared to be pursuing a regional role sufficiently ambitious and achievable to qualify for exceptional status. China's minimum objective appeared to be a kind of neotraditional "benevolent" hegemony, aimed at "harmonizing" relations among the adjoining lesser states. These were to be subdued by their awe for China's military power, their admiration for its ancient culture and its contemporary economic achievements, and by the progressive elimination of the alliances of such states with the United States. To gain leverage for the vital objective of eliminating such alliances and to strengthen its regional pre-eminence by widening its influence, China extended its search for political and economic access to Africa and Latin America, in what could be termed a cross-regional approach to a regionally centered status as a world power.

This policy was not peculiar to China. Tito's Yugoslavia and later de Gaulle's France also added worldwide initiatives to their earlier efforts to gain a prominent role in their part of Europe, hoping to show their independence from, and their capacity to interfere with, the superpower that had denied them a more salient regional role. At one time or another, both countries were tempted to escape from the exigencies of a regional leadership to the global arena, which seemingly rewarded mere self-exhibition as a model of economic development and political independence. Thus Yugoslavia invaded the areas of Russian imperial interests in the Middle East and India, while France approached Latin America (and reapproached Southeast Asia)—each with its respective packages of ideological or cultural assistance, economic aid, and diplomatic advice. Yugoslav global strategies reached an inconclusive peak somewhere around 1960, as did the French in the later 1960s. What followed was a new emphasis on the problems nearer home in the face of compelling economic or political stresses.

The more discreet, the less ambitious, and the better funded multiregional activities of Japan, West Germany, and even Nationalist China seemed to promise sturdier and more durable results. Such measures were undertaken, in different degrees, as a means of asserting a new identity, an old unity, or both. The interregional efforts of Brazil (with respect to Portuguese-speaking Africa) and those of Great Britain (in applying most of its long-term economic aid to reinforce its waning ties with the Commonwealth and the colonial countries) appeared uncertain.

The fragility of middle-power global ambitions was owing to both the means employed and the objectives. The characteristic means was personal diplomacy coupled with permissiveness in the ideological and other spheres. The immediate result tended to be captive leadership. Thus Yugoslavia diluted her revolutionary radicalism for the sake of influence in the Third World; and France acceded to Third World radicalism (as influenced by Yugoslavia) in Algeria and elsewhere so as to retain contact and, through contact, influence.

If the lesser powers bestirring themselves round the world had a common objective, it was to revise the dominant styles and instruments of global politics away from a too strict correlation between role and power—that is, an actively employed material (most specifically military) power. Thus Great Britain aspired to perpetuate its influence, to civilize the employment of American power, and to adjust international politics in general to its means, aided by its inherited genius for compromise and temporizing. Thus France sought to revitalize the widest employment of classic statecraft and formal diplomacy while downgrading usable military power (other than nuclear), not least in regard to the Third World. Similarly, India (under Nehru) and pacifist elements in Japan aimed at guiding raw forces into safe channels while directing polemical fire at alliances, bases, and other politico-military dams built by others. The middle-power orientation was not wholly wrong or self-regarding. In most cases it was owing in part to past frustrations in the use of military power in the wars of empire or of decolonization. Those conflicts had revealed the contemporary material limitations of the middle-ranking states. But—less creditably—such an orientation also derived from the desire not to expose their weakness, in part self-imposed, by a more effective use of material (including military) strength by either the superpowers, local small states, or any aspirant state.

To conclude: Only China and France and Britain—in regard to the diminishing range of formerly dependent areas—could be regarded as middle powers by virtue of their internationally applied power and their systematic performance in foreign policy in the post-postcolonial world. Japan could claim middle-power status by virtue of its domestic economic performance. Its peaceful reintegration into the international system was in large part owing to the international context. None of the potential middle powers, not even France or Britain, could secure middle-power status either by its nuisance potential if ignored (as was increasingly possible for China) or by its utility as an auxiliary of the greater powers if co-opted (as had been true for Canada and Australia in World War II).

In the circumstances, the semblance of middle-power status might derive from one of two things: a position between two or more authentic great powers, or a position owed to the power and position of one such power—to context or to convenience. In the not so remote past in Latin America, Argentina under Perón sought to enhance its standing by exploiting the first position between the Axis and the Allies, while Brazil sought to elevate itself to the position of a middle-ranking spokesman for Latin America by alliance with the United States. More recently, India under Nehru, Yugoslavia under Tito, and France under de Gaulle exemplified an enhanced status based on the constellation of real power, in a system tending toward an inter-superpower stalemate, and on the charismatic intangibles emanating from a national hero conspicuously endowed for international leadership. All those countries enjoyed a wider range of options than is available to more intensely committed powers. And all the leaders had a certain capacity to legitimize policies and events by virtue of their moral authority, their relatively safe geographic location, and their authentic (and at times excessive) anxiety over an apparent global trend toward major conflict.

Conversely, Britain and Japan, often resentfully, enjoyed a superior status derived from a towering ally. Unlike the posture resting on constellation and charisma, their status depended on a policy of caution (both exercised and urged on the major ally) and on the charity of the major ally in concealing the ultimate bases of the middle power's status. Whereas France or India sought to multiply options, the derivative middle powers sought to develop and exploit a commitment. Their special relationship to a superpower was expected to strengthen their influence, prevent a further decline (in the case of Britain), or facilitate a rehabilitation (in the case of Japan).

The alternative sources of middle-power standing have been neither mutually exclusive nor fixed. After experimenting with the advantages of the balancing position, the U.A.R. and India have recently seemed to gravitate tentatively toward a more derivative stance: the U.A.R. has shifted toward the Soviet Union and India toward both of the superpowers. Japan, by way of an economic and political rapprochement with the Soviet Union, may have been groping toward an enhanced status by gaining access to both the superpowers. While economically vital, the American alliance has seemed to be decreasingly productive for Japan in regard to either regional rehabilitation or (with respect to Okinawa) national reconsolidation.

Whether their status was chiefly positional or derivative, the role of the parasitic middle powers has been linked with their capacity to moderate conflicts involving the authentic powers or to act as supplemental agents of order when the greater powers were unable or unwilling to act directly. The moderating role was exercised by India in Korea and was proffered inconclusively by France and Britain in Vietnam. The supplemental role was performed by India in the Middle East and the Congo and, to a degree, by Britain in the Indonesian confrontation with Malaysia, largely because of Britain's sense of residual responsibility for the defense of Malaysia.

Unless anchored in something solid or plainly evolving, such functioning by the middle powers was only little less vulnerable than when performed by wholly minor states. Moreover, the function and status of the middle powers were continually endangered. Their derivative influence was precariously dependent on the toleration of the greater power from which influence ultimately flowed, was unusable against its source, and was subject to functional atrophy and political nullity through its being unused. This was true, diplomatically, of the "independent" nuclear capability of Britain (which depended on the concurrent employment of the American deterrent) and in more substantial terms of the vanishing British conventional capability "east of Suez." The weakness of positional influence lay elsewhere. While usable if backed by a last-resort resource, such as France's nuclear capability or India's territorial vastness, it was unlikely to generate an undeniable claim to a role in the co-management of regional or world order. So much seems indicated by the French failure to secure a world-power approach to Middle-Eastern and Southeast-Asian crises in the 1960s as long as superpower preferences pointed elsewhere, and by the secondary character of its role in such an approach when these preferences converged with those of France. Nor was a mere positioning in real power constellations likely to generate cumulative political achievements in the fluid medium of the Third World, deficient in effective leverages and sanctions short of compelling force. So much was true of first India, then Yugoslavia, and most recently France in their abortive efforts to stabilize a posture of leadership in the Third World.

A major asset of the freer middle powers may be their creativity in evolving new techniques or even policies. Yet when China, for instance, preceded the Soviets into the policy of "peaceful coexistence" with Third World countries or when Yugoslavia and France evolved distinctive approaches to foreign-aid activities and to Third World sensibilities, the more endowed superpowers have tended to appropriate such promising policies and techniques. Inadequately equipped for the stabilizing influence a strong middle class can have in domestic political societies, the middle powers have had to settle for sharing the predicament of seminal small political parties in a two-party political system.

Shortcomings and frustrations may eventually converge to favor a strict definition of middle power. Such a definition would stress the economic and military resources possessed and employed for either expansion, containment, or control for order, within the limits set by the superpowers through their activities in a given region. Only when thus qualified can middle powers aspire in the long run to share meaningfully in any existing or evolving interregional management. The factors favoring a strict definition of middle power were likely to survive the employment of military power in Southeast Asia, since the outcome there was unlikely in any profound or lasting sense to change the approach to the use of force in regional and global politics by either great or small powers. The degree and kind of influence the pre-eminent world power would exercise in shaping the sluggishly evolving but fluid international system were more likely to be decisive than any single event.

Any interest on the part of the Third World countries in the development of relatively autonomous regional systems coincided with the interest of the United States in the development of a self-sustaining global system. And the American concern that this evolution should occur within tolerable limits of disruption and violence was also the interest of the Third World countries. The requirements of an evolving system of states are not necessarily the same, where violence is concerned, as are those of managing an elementary international order. But any such contrasts can be reconciled by a confident and consistent U.S. policy. Such a policy must be confident enough to allow a considerable amount of ferment, even a limited interstate conflict, for ferment fosters evolution though it disturbs order. And it must be consistent in undertaking a timely devolution of power and responsibility while retaining the capacity to intervene against gross infractions of order, regardless of the identity of the agent creating the disorder.

A measure of composure in such an undertaking may be found in the fact that many bids for power have been self-containing by virtue of the insufficient strength and the economic dependence of Third World countries. Furthermore, no major power could simply add the results of disturbances to its assets. Self-containment was most clearly at work in the collective aspiration of Third World countries in their first postcolonial elan. Nevertheless, self-containment is not assured if the disturbances are wrought by a determined individual power. Moreover, self-containment will continue to depend ultimately on the active presence of the United States and other external powers, that militates against a thrust for moral ascendancy or political domination.

Two possible changes must be taken into account in this connection.

First, the drift in Third World countries toward more pragmatic conduct may have reduced the tendency to self-containment by narrowing the disparity between a goal and the means to it. Moreover, individual bids and collective disorders on less conspicuous levels may trigger countervailing processes from within or action from without less promptly or automatically. Thus, though a pragmatic policy may have a potentially positive effect on the evolution of a political system in the long run, this effect may be offset by the premature aloofness on the part of external powers in the short run. Second, if post-postcolonial changes in the international structure away from integral bipolarity have reduced the importance of Third World stakes, thus making outside involvement more optional, they have not eliminated the Third World as a critical area for contests among major powers. Owing to the propensity to reciprocal deterrence and stalemate of nuclear weaponry in general and its manifestation in intra-European relationships in particular, the Third World became and continues to be an important indicator of role and rank for the major powers. Moreover, the rise of China as a major power capable of generating pressures which reverberate in both Europe and Afro-Asia has only strengthened the position of the Third World as an arena for applying leverages affecting also European developments.

As the pre-eminent world power, the United States can conduct itself within all three of the unifocal, bipolar, and tripartite structural perspectives and can substantiate an otherwise irresponsible polycentrism in policy-making by diffusing usable nonnuclear power. Its two critical activities are intervention wherever necessary in the short run and the progressive devolution of its role as it reduces its primary responsibility. To have a chance at succeeding in a policy avoiding both an unwise monopoly and an unseemly abdication, the United States has to combine a measure of serene detachment (due to its margin of permissible error) with an irreducible degree of involvement. Conditional detachment is facilitated by the capacity for self-containment among the lesser states; continuing fundamental involvement is made imperative by the damaging psychological consequences of a sense of drift in the Third World or beyond.

Increased power and responsibility for order in an area may go (alternatively or concurrently) to the regional middle powers, the regional associations of lesser states (variously related to local or remote greater powers), and the global organization of security. The relationship between a regional system and regional order is critical in the context of devolving power. Assertive local states can dislocate existing order while stimulating the evolution of a system, and act as local agents for order after they achieve a measure of ascendancy. Organization complicates further the problematical relationship between system and order. Organization can aggravate the inhibiting effects of excessive concern for order (defined as absence of all force) if it is equated with an apolitically construed, "positive" purpose of cooperation in development and peacemaking or with the unmanageable purpose of a joint defense against a vastly superior power. This has been the case with too many presently burgeoning regional Third World organizations and the official rationale of the U.S. support for them. In most Third World situations, local organizations are more likely to promote the evolution of regional systems benefiting regional order in the longer run if they do not seek to comprise just about everyone in their membership, but are instead prepared to test their capacity for survival against individual local states and parallel associations with a comparable potential and complementary or hegemonial aspirations.

To say so much is to indicate that small-state groupings such as the Association of South-East Asian Nations (ASEAN, relating post-Sukarno Indonesia to her smaller neighbors) can substitute only to a limited extent for the involvement of the United States or another major power in any one region. They cannot even act as reliable buffers between local and remote great powers without at the same time introducing into great-power relations new possibilities for miscalculation, new precipitants of conflict and intervention, or pretexts for excessive delay in intervention. Consequently, the relation of local middle powers to predominantly small-state associations is as decisive as is the relation of the world powers to such middle powers. A balance between cooperation and constraint is hard to achieve, but it is necessary. The United States should progressively shift some of its responsibility to local middle powers as they develop the resources and the will for a responsible role in regional order. But it ought to retain the capacity to safeguard its access to, and the integrity of, local small states against greater-power abuses or insufficiency.

The most general purpose of a systematic devolution of resource and responsibility in favor of lesser powers is to harmonize the political perspectives of states that are at different levels of development and engagement. This means, preferably, curtailing both subversive and declamatory politics in favor of conventional politics which relate usable overt resources to commensurate goals and are constrained by the nuclear setting. Such a uniformity may entail nuclear diffusion, as the less developed countries reach the appropriate levels of industrial capacity and, having formed the state, seek to safeguard the further development of society and its economy.

A devolutionary policy on the part of the United States (if achieved) undoubtedly creates new problems by encouraging rivalry along with responsibility. Even if this is acceptable as a long-range price for avoiding even less desirable alternatives (for example, an overextended United States facing decline or anarchy, with evolution of world power structure left entirely to haphazard), the process of devolution is strenuous and often unrewarding. It entails denying performance while being visibly capable of it, and making other states assume burdens for which they claim to be unprepared and which may produce adverse immediate repercussions. The paradox thus appears of a power aiming at the liquidation of its own pre-eminence by exerting an imperial control—and self-control. As with all deliberate and orderly transfers of authority, it is tempting to shirk such a task as long as possible—until it becomes imperative and as such no longer feasible.

The task is rendered more complex but in some ways also easier by the existence of the communist great powers. With respect to the Soviet Union, the second-ranking superpower, U.S. devolution aims at co-responsibility and implies the development of rules restraining the exercise of great and growing power rather than promoting the diffusion of power. As an objective of U.S. policy, Soviet co-responsibility for order expresses several conditions. Foremost is the fact that bipolarity is modified by a less than complete equality and total antagonism between the two superpowers, and a less than automatic responsiveness of other states to the superpowers' definition of what constitutes legitimate conflict. Paralleling this is the failure of the Third World countries, their claims and contests, either to shift the balance of forces in favor of one superpower or to propel both of them toward an all-out condominial posture either by intense disorder or by successful assertiveness.

Furthermore, the situation is one in which the Soviet Union has shifted in the Third World toward more "responsible" policies along the Tashkent lines after it had derived from its identification with "revolutionary" forces little more than an unsavory association with subversion in the minds of moderate Third World leaders. But the Soviet Union has also continued to strive toward parity with the United States on several planes, including its presence in contested areas of the Third World; and therefore it has remained eager to exploit specific conflicts and embarrassments of other states (including the United States) in order to aggrandize its position unilaterally and simultaneously to improve its image by apparent moderation and conciliation.

Finally, the situation is one in which at least one third power

(China) has moved sufficiently into the world picture to represent a less than wholly hypothetical alternative to, and leverage against, the Soviet Union should the latter be too long reluctant to draw the final consequences from its growing power, respectability, and its stake in stability, and accept the more onerous implications of its advance toward parity. The United States would be well-advised to condone Soviet aspiration to parity in any one region or in the global arms balance only if these were accompanied by a sharing of liabilities in the Third World and the equalizing (or better) of diplomatic options with respect to China.

Soviet co-responsibility for order would require several basic changes in the U.S. attitude. One concerns the possible responses to Soviet penetration in areas of the Third World, especially areas of traditional concern to the Russian state. Such an involvement would benefit the United States if it compromised the position of the Soviet Union in at least some directly concerned states; if it made it less easy for the Soviet Union to play the role of a disinterested and unbiased conciliator in regional controversies; if it made the Soviet Union jointly responsible for setbacks in creating order in a region, and, equally, willing to derive only accidental and mostly self-nullifying gains from disorder. In short, if its involvement would help expose the Soviet Union to the full predicament of a world power. Moreover, as long as the presence of the Soviet Union in the Third World is largely one antagonistic to the United States, it may serve as a restraint on local disorder as a comparatively rational and accountable adversary-partner, one less immune to U.S. persuasion than often are members of the Third World. In short, Soviet penetration creates hostages for U.S. power as well as headaches for American policy-makers. And it may make local disorders the more manageable, even while interfering with recent trends toward their localization—which in any event is desirable only if it affects all interested parties equally.

These are grounds for a somewhat detached serenity in viewing the extensions of Soviet presence and influence. It remains necessary, however, to combine serenity with a stern and active concern for reciprocity in some respects, and for a continued U.S. capacity to control the scope and direction of co-responsibility in all its crucial respects. To reconstruct the distribution of global power and responsibility for world order does not mean enduring one-sided and cumulative shifts of power to the inferior (Soviet) side, least of all without concurrent and irreversible changes in the goals and attitudes of that side. Coresponsibility need not and should not entail anything like complete equality in military capability or political weight, nor act as an insurmountable barrier to unilateral U.S. action in previously accessible areas. Moreover, the U.S. policy of admitting or even drawing the Soviet Union into involvement and co-responsibility in areas that have so far been closed to Soviet influence must be subject to the norm of rough symmetry in superpower behavior in comparable situations. This is especially true as regards the degrees of control to be sought in the various areas penetrated and in the modes of exerting control in areas in which the influence of one superpower became exclusive in the Cold War. Otherwise, to open up the world at large to the Soviet Union would not be compensated for by opening up Soviet-controlled areas to world currents. This would carry portentous implications for the kinds of order the Soviet Union would seek to establish in the new areas where it had succeeded in creating a predominant influence, under the cover of reason and responsibility.[9]

To require symmetrical behavior of a superpower in comparable situations is an elementary substitute for dormant rules of international law governing conduct and for an insufficient identity of interests in motivating behavior. While schematic in general statement, the requirement of symmetry will be qualified in practice by ad hoc considerations in never wholly comparable conditions in a region or a situation. The key difference between regions and situations is the presence (or absence) of a local middle or great power, capable of either propelling the superpowers into attempting to deal with it jointly, or else capable of dividing the superpowers by presenting one or both with a preferred alternative. Conversely, the absence of such a power will mean one of two things: (1) the area is under the control of one superpower, limiting the scope of co-responsibility to merely marginal concessions of "nonpolitical" access to the extraregional superpower, or (2) the area is open to the contest or the co-responsible management of the superpowers without another power's either inhibiting the contest or aiding progress toward co-responsibility. The Western Hemisphere, Eastern Europe, and to a large extent Western Europe are dominated by one superpower. Degrees of access allowed to the other superpower are contingent on reciprocity. Most of the various subregions of Asia involve a militant third power (China) and other potential third parties. The Middle East (in view of Israel) is an intermediate case, while Africa constitutes a relatively open region, in which the terms of any eventual American-Soviet co-responsibility will be shaped by the course taken by both the interested European powers and the more substantial local states.

At present the principal attraction of a U.S. policy fostering co-

9. For illustrations of the symmetry principle, see my "Patterns of Devolution: Disengagement without Desertion," *International Journal*, Spring, 1969.

responsibility for a regionally differentiated world order is the escape it offers from a sterile alternative. Such an alternative has been to pursue arms superiority and climactic summit negotiations from strength, while the reaction to Soviet penetration of the Third World is one of mingled alarm and passivity. The U.S. objective is to steer the Soviet Union toward assuming bona fide tasks in containing both China and disorders elsewhere that are lesser in scale but potentially cumulative. To this end, the United States must promote every possible leverage on Soviet behavior in the Third World, in Europe, and in China herself (mollified by successful instances of superpower "collusion" in matters of concern to her and by the continuing alienation of lesser states as devolutionary strategies equip them to participate in containing China as long as necessary).

The long-range goal of U.S. policy is a global concert of powers. Its development is contingent on intermediate achievements. One is the emergence of globally active European and Third World states of middle- or great-power status. To encourage their assumption of wider duties the United States ought to withhold status satisfactions due to global constellation no less firmly than it denies to the Soviet Union or to China free gains flowing from purely local conditions. Another intermediate objective is the initially ad hoc implementation of co-responsibility, as interchangeable, alternative pairs of powers combine against the delinquent or passive—and therefore the provisionally isolated—third power or powers. And the third achievement (partially derivative from the first two and partially instrumental to them) is the development of a genuinely global system of states. Such a system can best function if it is supported by the diverse regional systems and by the willingness of the major powers to regulate their control within particular areas toward something like symmetry by either blocking, limiting, or condoning and thus legitimizing one another's self-assertion. Thus promoted, a concert of world powers can never constitute a wholly harmonious directorate. But it could in due course coordinate a multiregional, global balance of power and organization of security, while regional greater powers or organizations would provide the underpinnings.

Selected Bibliography

Andreski, Stanislav. *Parasitism and Subversion: The Case of Latin America.* London: Weidenfeld and Nicolson, 1966.

Badeau, John S. *The American Approach to the Arab World.* New York: Harper & Row (for the Council on Foreign Relations), 1968.

Burr, Robert M. *Our Troubled Hemisphere.* Washington, D.C.: The Brookings Institution, 1967.

Crozier, Brian. *Neo-Colonialism.* London: Bodley Head, 1964.

Draper, Theodore. "The American Crisis: Vietnam, Cuba and the Dominican Republic," *Commentary,* January, 1967.

Eban, Abba. "Reality and Vision in the Middle East," *Foreign Affairs,* July, 1965.

Emerson, Rupert. *Africa and United States Policy.* Englewood Cliffs, N.J.: Prentice-Hall, 1967.

Evans, Rowland, and Robert Novak. *Lyndon B. Johnson: The Exercise of Power.* New York: New American Library, 1968.

Gann, Lewis H., and Peter Duignan. *Burden of Empire: An Appraisal of Western Colonialism in Africa South of the Sahara.* New York: Frederick Praeger, Inc., 1967.

Geiger, Theodore. *The Conflicted Relationship: The West and the Transformation of Asia, Africa and Latin America.* New York: McGraw-Hill Book Company (for the Council of Foreign Relations), 1967.

Geyelin, Philip L. *Lyndon B. Johnson and the World.* New York: Frederick A. Praeger, Inc., 1966.

Goldman, Marshall I. *Soviet Foreign Aid.* New York: Frederick A. Praeger, Inc., 1967.

Good, Robert C. "The United States and the Colonial Debate," in Arnold Wolfers (ed.), *Alliance Policy in the Cold War.* Baltimore: The Johns Hopkins Press, 1959.

Gordon, Bernard K. *The Dimensions of Conflict in Southeast Asia.* Englewood Cliffs, N.J.: Prentice-Hall, 1966.

Greene, Fred. *U.S. Policy and the Security of Asia.* New York: McGraw-Hill Book Company (for the Council on Foreign Relations), 1968.

Hilsman, Roger. *To Move a Nation: The Politics of Foreign Policy in the Administration of John F. Kennedy.* Garden City, N.Y.: Doubleday & Company, 1967.

Howe, Russell Warren. "Man and Myth in Political Africa," *Foreign Affairs,* April, 1968.

Hunter, Guy. *South-East Asia: Race, Culture, and Nation.* New York: Oxford University Press (for the Institute of Race Relations), 1966.

Hurewitz, J. C. "Regional and International Politics in the Middle East," in The American Assembly, *The United States and the Middle East.* Englewood Cliffs, N.J.: Prentice-Hall, 1964.

Iriye, Akira (ed.), *U.S. Policy Toward China.* Boston: Little, Brown and Company, 1968.

Jansen, G. H. *Afro-Asia and Non-Alignment*. London: Faber, 1966.

Kahin, George McT., and John W. Lewis, *The United States in Vietnam*. New York: Dial Press, 1967.

Kashamura, Anicet. *De Lumumba aux Colonels*. Paris: Buchet/Chastel, 1966.

Kerr, Malcolm. *The Arab Cold War 1958–1967: A Study of Ideology in Politics*. 2d ed. London: Oxford University Press, 1967.

Kraft, Joseph. *Profiles in Power: A Washington Insight*. New York: New American Library, 1966.

Lamb, Alastair. *Crisis in Kashmir 1947–1966*. London: Routledge & L. Paul, 1966.

Lefever, Ernest W. "The Limits of U.N. Intervention in the Third World," *The Review of Politics*, January, 1968.

Leifer, Michael. *Cambodia: The Search for Security*. New York: Frederick A. Praeger, Inc., 1967.

Lewis, Bernard. "The Arab-Israeli War: The Consequences of Defeat," *Foreign Affairs*, January, 1968.

Lieuwen, Edwin. *U.S. Policy in Latin America: A Short History*. New York: Frederick A. Praeger, Inc., 1965.

McKay, Vernon (ed.). *African Diplomacy: Studies in the Determinants of Foreign Policy*. New York: Frederick A. Praeger, Inc. (for the School of Advanced International Studies), 1966.

Mazrui, Ali A. *Toward a Pax Africana: A Study of Ideology and Ambition*. London: Weidenfeld and Nicholson, 1967.

Mozingo, David. "The Maoist Imprint on China's Foreign Policy," in Frank E. Armbruster, *et al.*, *China Briefings*. Chicago: The University of Chicago Center for Policy Study, 1968.

Nolte, Richard H. "United States Policy and the Middle East," in The American Assembly, *The United States and the Middle East*. Englewood Cliffs, N.J.: Prentice-Hall, 1964.

Oliver, Roland, and Anthony Atmore. *Africa Since 1800*. London: Cambridge University Press, 1967.

Pfeffer, Richard M. (ed.). *No More Vietnams? The War and the Future of American Foreign Policy*. New York: Harper & Row (for the Adlai Stevenson Institute of International Affairs), 1968.

Pincus, John A. *Trade, Aid, and Economic Development: The Rich and Poor Nations*. New York: McGraw-Hill Book Company (for the Council on Foreign Relations), 1967.

Reidy, Joseph W. *Strategy for the Americas*. New York: McGraw-Hill Book Company, 1966.

Reischauer, Edwin O. *Beyond Vietnam: The United States and Asia*. New York: Alfred A. Knopf, 1967.

Rouleau, Eric, *et al. Israël et les Arabes: Le 3e Combat.* Paris: Editions du Seuil, 1967.

Rustow, Dankwart A. *A World of Nations: Problems of Political Modernization.* Washington, D.C.: The Brookings Institution, 1967.

Schatten, Fritz. *Communism in Africa.* New York: Frederick A. Praeger, Inc., 1966.

Schlesinger, Arthur M., Jr. *A Thousand Days: John F. Kennedy in the White House.* Boston: Houghton Mifflin Co., 1965.

Stevens, Georgiana G. *The United States and the Middle East.* Englewood Cliffs, N.J.: Prentice-Hall (for The American Assembly), 1964.

The United States in World Affairs. New York: Harper & Row (for the Council on Foreign Relations), 1965–1967.

Wenner, Manfred W. *Modern Yemen 1918–1966.* Baltimore: The Johns Hopkins Press, 1967.

Whitaker, Arthur P. and David C. Jordan. *Nationalism in Contemporary Latin America.* Glencoe, Ill.: The Free Press, 1966.

Wolf, Charles Jr. *The United States and the Third World: Problems and Analysis.* Boston: Little, Brown and Company, 1967.

Yost, Charles W., "The Arab-Israeli War: How It Began," *Foreign Affairs,* January, 1968.

Zagoria, Donald S. *Vietnam Triangle: Moscow, Peking, Hanoi.* New York: Pegasus, 1967.

Zartman, I. William. *International Relations in the New Africa.* Englewood Cliffs, N.J.: Prentice-Hall, 1966.

❦ THE JOHNS HOPKINS PRESS

Designed by James C. Wageman

Composed in Caledonia with Augustea display
by Monotype Composition Company

Printed offset on 50 lb. Warren's "1854"
by Universal Lithographers, Inc.

Bound in Columbia Riverside Linen
by L. H. Jenkins, Inc.